Routledge Questions & Answers Series

Land Law
2013–2014

Routledge Q&A series

Each Routledge Q&A contains approximately 50 questions on topics commonly found on exam papers, with comprehensive suggested answers. The titles are written by lecturers who are also examiners, so the student gains an important insight into exactly what examiners are looking for in an answer. This makes them excellent revision and practice guides. With over 500,000 copies of the Routledge Q&As sold to date, accept no other substitute.

New editions publishing in 2013:

Civil Liberties & Human Rights
Company Law
Commercial Law
Constitutional & Administrative Law
Contract Law
Criminal Law
Employment Law
English Legal System
Equity & Trusts
European Union Law

Evidence
Family Law
Jurisprudence
Land Law
Medical Law
Torts

Published in 2012:

Business Law 2012–2013
Intellectual Property Law 2012–2013

For a full listing, visit http://cw.routledge.com/textbooks/revision

Routledge Questions & Answers Series

Land Law

2013–2014

Martin J Dixon

Reader in the Law of Real Property, Cambridge University and a Fellow of Queens' College, Cambridge. He is visiting Professor of Law at City University, London.

Gerwyn LL H Griffiths

Professor of Law, Cardiff University

and

Emma Lees

Researcher in the Department of Land Economy at Cambridge University

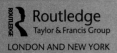
Routledge
Taylor & Francis Group

LONDON AND NEW YORK

Eighth edition published 2013
by Routledge
2 Park Square, Milton Park, Abingdon, Oxon OX14 4RN

Simultaneously published in the USA and Canada
by Routledge
711 Third Avenue, New York, NY 10017

Routledge is an imprint of the Taylor & Francis Group, an informa business

© 2013 Routledge

First edition published by Cavendish Publishing 1993
Seventh edition published by Routledge 2011

British Library Cataloguing in Publication Data
A catalogue record for this book is available from the British Library

Library of Congress Cataloging in Publication Data
Dixon, Martin, MA.
  Q&A land law : 2013–2014 / Martin J Dixon, Gerwyn Griffiths.—8th ed.
    p. cm.—(Routledge questions & answers series)
  ISBN 978-0-415-50598-7 (pbk)—ISBN 978-0-203-08380-2 (ebk)
  KD833.D593 2013
  346.4204'3—dc23

                                                                        2012026327

ISBN: 978-0-415-50598-7
ISBN: 978-0-203-08380-2

Typeset in TheSans
by RefineCatch Limited, Bungay, Suffolk

Printed and bound in Great Britain by the MPG Books Group

Contents

Table of Cases

Table of Legislation

STATUTES

SECONDARY LEGISLATION

Guide to the Companion Website

http://cw.routledge.com/textbooks/revision

Visit the Routledge Q&A website to discover even more study tips and advice on getting those top marks.

On the Routledge revision website you will find the following resources designed to enhance your revision on all areas of undergraduate law.

The Good, The Fair, & The Ugly

Good essays are the gateway to top marks. This interactive tutorial provides sample essays together with voice-over commentary and tips for successful exam essays, written by our Q&A authors themselves.

Multiple Choice Questions

Knowledge is the foundation of every good essay. Focusing on key examination themes, these MCQs have been written to test your knowledge and understanding of each subject in the book.

Bonus Q&As

Having studied our exam advice, put your revision into practice and test your essay writing skills with our additional online questions and answers.

Don't forget to check out even more revision guides and exam tools from Routledge!

Lawcards

Lawcards are your complete, pocket-sized guides to key examinable areas of the undergraduate law.

Routledge Student Statutes

Comprehensive selections; clear, easy-to-use layout; alphabetical, chronological, and thematic indexes; and a competitive price make *Routledge Student Statutes* the statute book of choice for the serious law student.

Introduction

Land law holds a certain fascination for the student: usually one of dread. We do not deny that it can be a difficult subject, and students face conceptual and practical problems of a kind not always found in other branches of the law. The fact that the subject is often composed of statutory provisions overlaying ancient principles of common law and uses a vocabulary that can be, to say the least, unusual does not make things easier. However, with the correct approach – both as to how the subject is studied and revised and how questions are tackled in examination – many of the perceived problems and pitfalls can be identified and avoided. The new edition of this book is designed to help you to find and develop that approach with consequent success in your examinations.

At the outset, you need to be aware that an examination in land law cannot be treated as a series of separate questions, nicely compartmentalised. Anyone who attempts to understand land law in this manner is in for a rude awakening, as the subject can be viewed only as an integrated whole. What the student learns in their first week of study may well be relevant in a question set on work they cover in their last week. This is not a subject in which topics can be picked from a menu and eaten piecemeal in the examination. Land law has a clear structure. If you can understand the principles of land law and how they relate to each other, most students will see the picture fall into place and be able to answer the practical problems raised by land law in an examination setting. For that reason, the questions in this edition are presented in a logical order – an order that gives the student a slowly developing but clear picture of the subject as a whole. Of course, the answers can be taken on their own for what they are: an aid to revision and examination performance. However, this book can also be used as a teaching aid.

There are a number of new questions in this edition, and every one has been updated to reflect legislative changes and the addition of new and recent case law. In particular, there are now a number of cases interpreting and applying the Land Registration Act 2002 and the importance of these, and this statute, cannot be overestimated. Likewise, the Supreme Court has been active in matters of property law, with significant cases in co-ownership and leases, and there have been very many cases on a range of topics decided in the Court of Appeal.

ESSAYS, PROBLEMS AND EXAMINATIONS

Although a feature of many land law courses over recent years has been the introduction of a variety of assessment strategies, in the vast majority of cases it is your performance in written examinations that counts most. Consequently, it is most important that you develop a proper approach to legal writing. Not only is it one of the skills expected of a practising lawyer but, more immediately, it is the foundation for your examination success. Many students fail to do themselves justice in the examinations through lack of a technique that they could and should have learned in their written work during the year.

The essay is used in most disciplines for general exposition and analysis of a topic, looking down and over it from a vantage point. In land law, you may be asked to explain, illustrate or discuss a particular doctrine or institution (proprietary estoppel, or the impact of the **Land Registration Act 2002**), or to analyse recent developments or proposed reforms in a particular area (e.g. human rights and property, easements or Law Commission Reports), or to comment critically on a quotation (e.g. 'Interests which override are in no more a satisfactory state now than they were prior to the 2002 legislation. Discuss'). Where imaginary facts are given and your advice is sought, this is called a problem question. In what follows, guidance is offered first on essay-writing and then on tackling problems, although answers to both types of question require similar skills of analysis and discussion.

ESSAYS

In answering essay questions, it is vital to read and consider carefully the question before plunging into your actual writing. Whatever you do, do not waste time writing out the quotation or whatever else comprises the question. You should start with an idea of the general area in which the question falls – and this is especially important where the question is in the form of a quotation – but you should not simply repeat your lecture notes or study notes. The question almost certainly will require an answer different from the general exposition given in a lecture and simply repeating lecture notes tells an examiner that you do not really understand the question. So think what further depth or breadth is required (more detail? more history? more comparison? more criticism?) and let your own opinion develop, as to both the treatment of the topic and its content, and then concentrate on these aspects. Otherwise you may well find you have not answered the actual question but have written a 'tell me all you know about' response. You should always be prepared to come to some sort of conclusion: something, however tentative, should follow logically from your discussion of the topic. If the question was in the form of a quotation, look back at it and say how valid it was. Remember that attributed quotations are often selected for discussion because they are thought to be provocative and not necessarily sound, whilst unattributed quotations are often concocted by the question-setter. It is perfectly acceptable to agree with the quotation, provided that you have given reasons. As always, you must support what you say by reference to, and discussion of cases, statutes and, where appropriate, academic or judicial opinion. In land law, you hardly ever will need to repeat the facts of a case. Cases stand for points of law and a good technique will give a case – just the name, not the facts – for every point of law made. Absence of cases, even in an essay answers, inevitably means a weak mark.

PROBLEMS

The purpose of problem questions is to see how you are able to apply legal rules and principles to a given set of facts. These rules and principles are derived from cases and from statutory provisions. Rules derived from cases necessarily may be dependent on the facts of the particular case but very often in land law they stand for important general statements of principle: e.g. 'that proprietary estoppel is established by assurance, reliance and detriment in circumstances of unconscionability' (*Thorner v Majors* (2009)). Nevertheless, one set of facts in Case A may be very like the facts in Case B – so much so that the judges' decision in Case A will be applied by the judges to the facts in Case B in order to reach a decision. Thus, when you are presented with a problem question, you are being asked to apply rulings from previous cases and pieces of statute law to the facts before you in order to decide what the solution to the legal problem is.

It is important to remember that the first step is to analyse the problem in order to determine the particular legal issues involved. One possible approach is as follows:

❖ consider what legal issues are posed by the factual circumstances presented in the problem;
❖ locate and discuss the law relevant to such issues (i.e. case law, statutes);
❖ suggest an appropriate answer based on your application of relevant legal principles to the facts you have before you;
❖ if you are asked to give advice, do so. Remember, however, it is not your job to tell your client that everything is well. The advice must be accurate, even if the advice is not what your client would like to hear;
❖ remember that the answer must be supported by cases and statutes wherever possible.

It must be emphasised that there is not really any such thing as a 'model answer'. Rarely is it possible to provide an answer that is the only acceptable or authoritative one. As suggested above, what is important is that law students should develop an ability to highlight the main legal issues to which a particular set of facts gives rise and then arrive at a conclusion that is accurate, comprehensive and justifiable in the light of those facts.

EXAMINATIONS

Much 'advice' on examination technique is, in fact, little more than common sense and the following points are obvious, but easily forgotten.

❖ Make sure you have the correct date, time and place for the examination. It may not be the same venue as your last examination.
❖ Do you have all you need, e.g. pens, statutes, watch etc? If you are permitted to take in materials – e.g. a statute book – make sure that you do. Materials are not

permitted just for fun. The examiner will deduct marks if you fail to follow a statute correctly when you are meant to have a statute book in front of you.

❖ Read the paper thoroughly: how many questions need you answer? Decide on your choice of questions and quickly plan your answer; divide your time. You *must* answer the correct number of questions.

❖ You will NOT get any generosity for answering three questions really well if you should have answered four. Examiners will be fair to all candidates and that means applying the rules equally.

❖ Do not be 'smart'. Little 'notes' to the examiner about your personal circumstances at best are ignored and at worst irritate the examiner.

❖ Do NOT expect to know the answer to every question. You get no extra marks by being able to answer all questions. You get marks for producing good answers to the required number of questions.

Dr Martin J Dixon
Emma Lees
June 2012.

Common Pitfalls

The most common mistake made when using Questions & Answers books for revision is to memorise the model answers provided and try to reproduce them in exams. This approach is a sure-fire pitfall, likely to result in a poor overall mark because your answer will not be specific enough to the particular question on your exam paper, and there is also a danger that reproducing an answer in this way would be treated as plagiarism. You must instead be sure to read the question carefully, to identify the issues and problems it is asking you to address and to answer it directly in your exam. If you take our examiners' advice and use your Q&A to focus on your question-answering skills and understanding of the law applied, you will be ready for whatever your exam paper has to offer!

Registered Land

INTRODUCTION

Land lawyers in England and Wales fall into two broad groups. First, there are those who believe that the 1925 property legislation and, specifically the 1925 and 2002 Land Registration Acts (LRA), established new machinery for controlling the creation and transfer of land and interests in land, but did not radically alter the nature of property law. Thus, some textbooks will explain in detail the nature of, say, easements or mortgages, and add a section at the end of each chapter on the implications of 'registered land'. Others take the view that the system of registered conveyancing has produced fundamental changes in the nature of the rights and interests falling within the concept of 'land law'. Thus, on this view, a detailed understanding of the *mechanics* of registered land is necessary *before* a student can fully appreciate substantive property concepts such as easements or mortgages. There is, of course, merit in both views, but even without the powerful theoretical arguments that could be used, there are practical advantages for the student in following the second approach and this is the course adopted in this edition of Questions & Answers.

Since 1 December 1990, all of England and Wales has been designated as an area of compulsory registration of title and it is now estimated that over 80 per cent of all potentially registrable titles are in fact registered. In the fullness of time, therefore, unregistered conveyancing will all but disappear from the legal landscape and this process has accelerated since the entry into force of the LRA 2002 on 13 October 2003. In fact, the LRA 2002 operates on the fundamental assumption that registered land is intrinsically different from land of unregistered title. Moreover, and more importantly for students, examiners set problem questions that require students to explain how easements or mortgages, or whatever, operate in registered land and no amount of pre-1925 property law will solve these puzzles. There is, for example, no point in discussing the 'doctrine of notice' in registered land when it is entirely irrelevant and an answer that includes such a discussion might lead an examiner to conclude that the student fundamentally misunderstands the nature of modern land law.

If a plot of land is described as 'registered', this means that 'title' to it (that is, an estate of freehold, or leasehold of over seven years) is recorded and guaranteed by the Land Registry. In contrast, 'unregistered land' is land to which title is not registered but is established by the title deeds of the particular property. Whether title is registered or unregistered depends simply on whether there have been any dealings with the land such as to give rise to an obligation to register (compulsory registration), or whether the 'owner' has applied for voluntary first registration of title. As such, there is no magic about land being 'registered': it is simply a way of saying that the title is recorded and guaranteed and that dealings with the land fall within the procedures established by the LRA 2002 and the Land Registration Rules 2003 (as amended in 2008 and 2011). When answering problem questions in an examination, one of the first things to establish is whether the land is registered, and normally you will be told. For example, there may be references to the 'registered proprietor' or the land's 'title number'. If you are not told, it cannot be important for your answer as there is no way that you can deduce whether title is registered. After all, whether there has been registration of title does not depend on the quality of the land or the interests in it, but whether an event has occurred that has triggered registration of title.

> **Aim Higher**   ★
>
> The system of registered land falls into four parts and a sound knowledge of these distinctions will enhance answers to examination questions.

Registered titles: these are the freehold or legal leasehold over seven years and they are substantively registered in their own right with a title number. Most questions in land law examinations require no more than a basic knowledge of the mechanics of registering or transferring titles and of the different qualities of title with which a person may be registered. A wider knowledge enhances the answer. Of more complexity are the rules relating to the transfer and creation of interests in the land such as easements, mortgages, covenants and shorter-term leases (that is, those that cannot be registered as titles, being currently leases for seven years or less).

Unregistered interests which override (also known as overriding interests): these are interests in the land that will have automatic priority over a registered proprietor (such as a new purchaser of the land). They do not have to be registered anywhere to take effect against the registered proprietor. They are defined in Sched 1 to the 2002 Act in relation to first registered proprietors and in Sched 3 in relation to purchasers of an existing registered title (although the Schedules are broadly very similar). In substance, most of these unregistered interests which override are inherently proprietary (i.e. capable of binding third parties), although some are legal and some are equitable. No student should attempt a land law paper without a thorough understanding of overriding interests and an ability to use the statutory Schedules. Being aware of the small differences between the Schedules, and why they exist, will improve an essay question on the 2002 Act in general and overriding interests in particular.

Registered protected interests: these are those interests enjoyed by third parties (i.e. not the registered proprietor) that are entered on the register of title against the burdened land and thus are protected in the event of a transfer of that registered title. If they are not registered, generally they do not have priority over a purchaser, unless the right falls (fortuitously) into the category of overriding interest. The 'doctrine of notice' is entirely irrelevant in this regard and talking about it in a registered land question will create a poor impression. In essence, under the LRA 2002, this class of interest is meant to comprise the great majority of third-party rights in land, the point being that as much as possible about the registered title should be clear from the register of title itself. Examples include easements, covenants, options to purchase and shorter leases.

Registrable charges: these are essentially mortgages. They, too, must be registered to take effect as legal mortgages (otherwise they may be equitable) and are considered in more detail in the chapter on mortgages. Sometimes an Examiner will leave doubt about whether the mortgage is legal or equitable as this may affect remedies and so understanding this distinction can add marks.

QUESTION 1

'The primary reasons for the introduction of a land registration system in England and Wales were realised by the Land Registration Act 1925. That system was not perfect, but it has been enhanced by the entry into force of the Land Registration Act 2002.'

▶ Discuss.

How to Answer this Question

- ❖ Pre-1925 problems – briefly.
- ❖ The mechanics and principles of land registration, including the priority rules (s 28 and s 29 LRA 2002).
- ❖ Titles and the mirror principle.
- ❖ Trusts and the curtain principle.
- ❖ The insurance principle.
- ❖ The role of unregistered interests which override.
- ❖ The role of registered protected interests.
- ❖ Some problems and solutions: undiscoverable but binding interests and the changes made by LRA 2002; protecting the purchaser or the occupier?; the need for clarity under the LRA 2002 because of the drive to electronic conveyancing.

Applying the Law

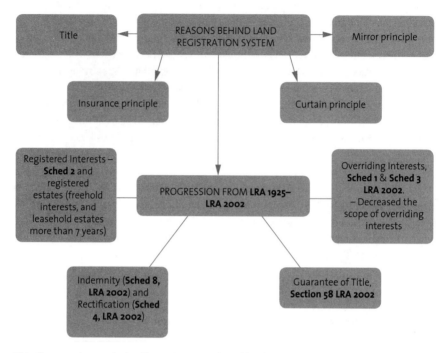

This diagram demonstrates the main principles of land registration and the progression from the **Land Registration Act 1925** to the **Land Registration Act 2002.**

ANSWER

The 1925 property legislation, and the Land Registration Act 1925 inaugurated a fundamental change in the structure of land law in England and Wales. Before then, the mechanics of conveyancing were hindered by formalism and beset with danger for all but the most conscientious purchaser. Likewise, the operation of the doctrine of notice meant not only that holders of equitable rights could have their rights destroyed through chance or caprice, but also that purchasers of property might find their land burdened by legal rights of which they had no knowledge and which they may not have discovered when making enquiries of the seller. Similarly, the reliance on title deeds to prove ownership of land was both cumbersome and, for the purchaser, an expensive way to prove title. The net result was a choking of the property market at a time when the free movement of capital was essential for economic development. In conjunction with the Law of Property Act 1925 and the Settled Land Act 1925, the LRA 1925 sought to simplify and codify. It aimed to bring certainty where there was obscurity and to bring equity where there was often inequality. The Land Registration Act 2002, which has replaced the Land Registration Act

1925 in its entirety, seeks to reinforce these goals and make the system fit for the twenty-first century and the electronic age.[1]

The basic principle of the LRA 1925, and now the LRA 2002, is that title to land should be recorded in a register and guaranteed by the state. Registration of title replaces deeds of title. The original 1925 timetable called for full registration of all titles by 31 December 1955, and it is a matter of some regret that only on 1 December 1990 did all of England and Wales become subject to compulsory registration of title. It will be a while longer before near-universal registration of title is achieved, but currently over 80 per cent of all potentially registrable titles are in fact registered and the LRA 2002 does much to encourage voluntary first registration by owners of unregistered land (for example, by local authorities). However, in addition to establishing a mechanism for registering ownership, the Land Registration Act 1925 also established three other mechanisms for protecting other people's rights in that land and this has been continued under the LRA 2002. If correctly used, these procedures will ensure that rights in land are not destroyed by a transfer of a registered title to a new owner. First, there are registrable charges (mortgages), which must be registered before they can be regarded as legal mortgages – ss 25, 27 of and Sched 2 to the LRA 2002. Once registered, these bind subsequent transferees of the mortgaged land unless, of course, the mortgage is paid off (as most will be) by the proceeds of that sale. If not registered, such mortgages take effect as equitable interests only and will not have priority over a purchaser of the registered title unless protected by the land registration system in some other way (which will be unlikely given the initial failure to register).

Second, there are unregistered interests which override ('overriding interests'). These are interests, once defined in s 70(1) of the LRA 1925 and now found in Scheds 1 and 3 to the LRA 2002, that take effect automatically against a first registered proprietor (Schedule 1 rights) or a transferee of an existing registered title (Schedule 3 rights).[2] That is, they require no registration and the old pre-1925 doctrine of notice is entirely irrelevant – ss 11, 12, 29 and 30 of the LRA 2002. It is immaterial whether such interests are legal or equitable, so long as they fall within one of the classes defined in the appropriate Schedule to the 2002 Act. The logic behind the automatic effect of such interests is that they comprise such rights as *should* be obvious to a purchaser on physical inspection of the property or are such that they benefit the community as a whole without seriously restricting a purchaser's enjoyment of the land.

---

1   This essay is asking for an assessment of the progress towards meeting the principles of land registration from the position pre-1925 to the current day, and this introduction does a good job of setting this out clearly.
2   The examiner here will be looking not only for a description of the rules contained in the 1925 and 2002 legislation, but will also be looking for you to draw parallels between the provisions.

Third, there are registered protected interests, once called 'minor interests' under the LRA 1925, but *not* so-called under the LRA 2002. This category essentially comprises all other interests that may subsist in or over land. In order to have priority over a first-registered proprietor or a purchaser of a registered title, such interests, whether legal or equitable, must be protected by entry on the register, either by way of a unilateral or agreed notice. Actual 'notice' of the right (or lack of it) is irrelevant – ss 11, 12, 29, 30 of the LRA 2002. Under the LRA 2002, this class is meant to comprise the vast majority of third-party rights in land, the point being that the goal is to ensure that as many third-party rights as possible are entered on the register of title of the land affected. Failure to make such an entry means that the right loses its priority over a purchaser of the registered title unless the right fortuitously falls within the category of overriding interests. Note, however, that such rights, whether registered or not, will have priority over a transferee of a registered title who is not a purchaser, such as when there has been a gift or an inheritance (s 28 of the LRA 2002).

This classification of property rights within the land registration system obviously places much more emphasis on statutory definition than it does on the legal or equitable quality of a right. Likewise, in registered land, it is clear that the pre-1925 doctrine of notice is irrelevant. Such a radical shift in 1925 was designed to relieve the post-war conveyancing log-jam, as well as to bring certainty and stability for persons with interests in land. In this connection, land registration is said to operate on three principles: the mirror principle; the curtain principle; and the insurance principle. The mirror principle suggests that the register should be a mirror of all the proprietary rights that exist in any given piece of land. Thus, the register should amount to a comprehensive picture of the land for any prospective purchaser. Obviously, however, this was not the case with the 1925 Act and the situation has been only partially altered by the 2002 Act. The inclusion of overriding interests necessarily compromises the mirror principle. But, in itself, this is not a cause of serious criticism.[3] Overriding interests were not an accident in the 1925 legislation, and although redefined and narrowed in the 2002 Act, they remain crucial to the proper functioning of the system. They were deliberately created by the legislature and exist precisely because such rights should be obvious to any prospective purchaser or because their enforcement is too important to depend on registration. The problem is, however, that social and judicial developments have enlarged the opportunity for the existence of overriding interests with the result that it is conceivable that a purchaser might not be able to determine whether such interests exist by inspection of the land. The most obvious example is the right of equitable co-ownership, originally stemming from *Pettitt v Pettitt* (1970), the effect of which under the old s 70(1)(g) of the LRA 1925 on an unwary purchaser was first fully appreciated in *Williams and Glyn's Bank v Boland* (1981). Another example is *Ferrishurst Ltd v Wallcite Ltd* (1999), in which the plaintiff's overriding interest in respect of the property was undiscoverable because his

---

3   This section is good in that it goes beyond simply assessing whether the mirror principle is complied with and considers whether full compliance with this principle is in fact desirable.

'actual occupation' (under the then s 70(1)(g) of the LRA 1925) extended only to part of that property. However, this difficulty has been largely overcome by Sched 3 to the LRA 2002. Under Sched 3, actual occupation gives rise to an overriding interest *only* where the occupation is discoverable by a purchaser (or the purchaser already knows about the right) and then only achieves priority to the extent of the land actually occupied (thus reversing *Ferrishurst*). This should do much to alleviate the problem of undiscoverable adverse rights.

The curtain principle was, perhaps, the most ambitious goal of the original 1925 Act and it remains a key principle under the 2002 Act. The aim is to keep *certain* types of equitable interest off the register completely. Such equitable rights, being those taking effect behind a trust of land (see e.g. *Jones v Kernott* (2011)), will not bind a purchaser on sale of the land because of overreaching. In essence, a purchaser will not be concerned with such equitable rights – they are behind the curtain of a trust – so long as the purchase money is paid to two trustees of land: s 2 of the LPA 1925.[4] The equitable interests then take effect in that purchase money, so that, instead of having a right (or share) in land, the equitable owner has a share in money. Such a system works well when the statutory requirement of two trustees exists. However, the direct result of *Pettitt, Stack v Dowden* (2007) and *Jones v Kernott* (2011) is that, on some occasions, there will be just one trustee of land and so overreaching will not be possible. In such circumstances, a purchaser must 'look behind the curtain' to determine whether any equitable interests exist and then must negotiate with the equitable owners as required. As *Boland* shows, if the purchaser does not raise the curtain, the purchaser can easily be bound by such equitable interests. This problem clearly involves striking a balance between protection of the purchaser and protection for the occupier of land and it arose largely due to social and judicial changes (viz, the rise of the equitable co-owner through the *Pettitt* line of cases). Cases such as *Abbey National Building Society v Cann* (1991), *Mortgage Business plc v Cook* (2012), *Equity & Homes Loans v Prestridge* (1992) and *Birmingham Midshires Mortgage Services Ltd v Sabherwal (Sudesh)* (2000) illustrate that the results of this balancing act are complex.

Finally, there is the insurance principle or, rather, the idea that, once title is registered, the state guarantees the authenticity and effectiveness of that title against the world: s 58 of the LRA 2002. Obviously, such a system cannot be absolute and there are provisions for alteration of the register in cases in which registration has produced hardship or inequity: s 65 and Sched 4 of the LRA 2002. The potential wide-ranging discretion to alter the register is clearly a cause for concern – contrast *Derbyshire County Council v Fallon* (2008), *Baxter v Mannion* (2010) and *Walker v Burton* (2012) – and the interaction of s 58 and s 65 still needs to be clarified. A second limb of the 'insurance principle' is to be found in Sched 8 to the LRA 2002, which stipulates the circumstances in which a person suffering loss by reason of the operation of the registration system can receive an indemnity (money compensation).

....

4   It is important always to be as specific as possible in the use of statutory provisions – cite **section 2** here, rather than just the **1925 Act** etc.

Although it is not always the case that compensation will reflect the real loss to the person injured, these provisions support strongly the effectiveness of the land registration system.

On a general level then, the current land registration system now found in the 2002 Act is a success. The success was built on the 1925 Act and has been enhanced by the 2002 Act. The introduction of a system of land registration brought certainty, fairness and relative simplicity to a pre-1925 system of conveyancing that was completely unsuited to the modern age. Of course, there were and still are problems of detail: for example, the question of the interpretation of Sched 3 to the 2002 Act may cause problems in the future. However, the overhaul of the law by the LRA 2002 has been beneficial. Indeed, the LRA 2002 goes further than a mere tinkering with the system and brings the system up to date, although whether its system of 'electronic conveyancing' becomes a reality in the near future is less certain. Currently, there is a tension between the purchaser of land and the occupier of it, but generally speaking the provisions on overreaching can deal with this if the statutory mechanisms are observed. It is no fault of the LRA 1925 or the LRA 2002 that the incidence of single trustee co-ownership (*Pettitt*) has increased, and may continue to do so after *Stack v Dowden* (2007) and *Jones v Kernott* (2012). This does produce problems, but the way to tackle this is to establish clear rules on *when* joint ownership of property can arise rather than to alter the machinery that merely regulates it.

DON'T BE TEMPTED TO

The temptation with such a routine question is simply to repeat the sections of the LRA 2002. However, it is important to use case law to illustrate points and in essays academic comment.

Try to avoid discussing only the mirror, insurance and curtain principles: every student will know this basic information and you need to be more critical.

QUESTION 2

In 2012, Karen sold her large farm, title to which is registered, to Bonny. At the time of the purchase, Bonny's solicitor made an official search of the register and obtained a clear result. Unfortunately, the search was carried out by an inexperienced clerk and failed to reveal a restrictive covenant correctly registered against the land for the benefit of the adjoining farm owned by Richard. The covenant stipulated that no trade or business other than farming may be carried out on the land. When walking over the farm on the day after she had been registered with title, Bonny discovered that Zeus, a new-age squatter, had established a home in a derelict farm cottage. Next door, Bonny found Lulu who claimed to have been paying rent to Karen for the last two years under an agreement that she could live in the cottage for six years. Lulu produced a written record of the agreement typed on a plain piece of white paper.

▶ Bonny comes to you for advice as she wants to build an out-of-town supermarket on part of the site and, in any event, wants possession of the cottages.

How to Answer this Question

❖ the effect of registration as owner – s 29 of the LRA 2002 and the special priority rule;
❖ whether there are any overriding interests under Sched 3 to the LRA 2002;
❖ the role and effect of registered protected interests;
❖ the primacy of the register over search certificate;
❖ the possibility of alteration, rectification and indemnity.

Applying the Law

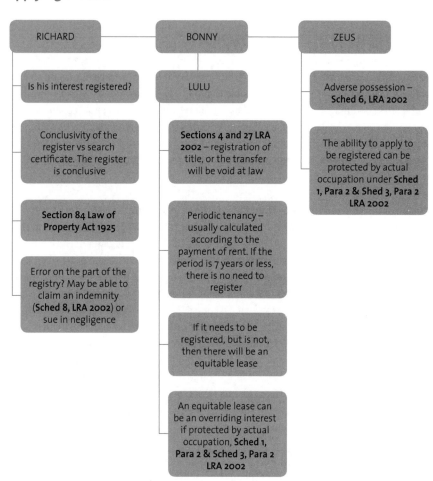

This diagram shows how to apply the rules of registered land to the situation involving Bonny.

ANSWER

When Bonny is registered as proprietor of the farm, the estate in the land is transferred to her statutorily and conclusively under s 58 of the LRA 2002. However, under s 29 of the LRA 2002, a new registered proprietor who gives value (i.e. a purchaser) takes the land subject to any interests appearing on the register and any unregistered interests which override under the provisions of Sched 3 to the LRA 2002. It is necessary, therefore, to establish whether Bonny's registered title is subject to any third-party interests that may prohibit her proposed development. Second, if Bonny's title is affected by a third-party interest, the next question is whether she can ask for alteration of the register or claim an indemnity.

(A) THE RESTRICTIVE COVENANT[5]

Bonny will be unable to build the proposed supermarket if she is bound by the restrictive covenant because the person entitled to the benefit of it (i.e. to enforce it) may be able to obtain an injunction, although it is possible that damages be awarded instead. Assuming that all the conditions for its enforceability required by the law of freehold covenants are established (see – s 78 LPA 1925 and *Tulk v Moxhay* (1848)), the issue turns on whether the restrictive covenant has been properly protected within the system of registered land – in other words, whether it has been protected by means of a unilateral or agreed notice: ss 29 and 32 of the LRA 2002.

When Bonny requested a search from the Land Registry (through her solicitor), she received a clear search certificate. However, it is clear from s 32 of the LRA 2002 (and see the earlier case of *Parkash v Irani Finance Ltd* (1970)) that it is the register itself that is conclusive, irrespective of any statements made on an official certificate or by an officer of the Registry. In our case, therefore, Bonny is bound by the restrictive covenant because it has been properly registered by means of a notice, and this is so even though she is entirely blameless in failing to discover it. Of course, Bonny can make an application to the Lands Tribunal under s 84 of the Law of Property Act 1925 to have the restrictive covenant modified or discharged if she wishes to proceed with her proposed development, but as a matter of property law it is binding on her. It is possible that Bonny will be eligible for a statutory indemnity under Sched 8 to the 2002 Act, para 1(1)(c) if she can show that she has suffered loss by reason of a mistake in an official search. Failing this, she should be advised to sue the Land Registry in negligence (*Minister of Housing and Local Government v Sharp* (1970)).

(B) THE SQUATTER

Zeus appears to be in the process of trying to establish a right to the land under the law of adverse possession – see *Pye v Graham* (2002). Again, whether Bonny is bound depends

---

5   The use of sub-headings here makes the answer easier for the examiner to follow and also assists in time management.

on the application of the relevant provisions of the **LRA 2002**. In the case of adverse possessors, it is clear that they may have an overriding interest against a new proprietor under **Sched 3, para 2** to the **LRA 2002**. This is because even a person in the process of adverse possession has a property right in the land, albeit one that is weak and liable to be defeated. Thus, so long as Zeus was in the process of acquiring his rights on the day when Bonny was registered with the title to the farm (*Abbey National BS v Cann* (1991); *Mortgage Business plc v Cook*), and was in discoverable actual occupation (or Bonny knew of his right when he was in occupation), he has an overriding interest under **Sched 3, para 2** to the **LRA 2002** that has priority to the limited extent that any adverse possession is effective under the **LRA 2002**.[6] However, this overriding interest merely protects the period for which he has been in possession and he will not actually acquire title unless he applies for registration as proprietor under **Sched 6** to the Act. If he does so apply, assuming none of the exceptions are relevant (estoppel, boundary disputes, other entitlements – **Sched 6 LRA 2002**), and they appear not to be), Bonny will be able to object and she will have a further two years to evict him. If she fails to object, or after objecting does not evict within two years, Zeus will acquire title. However, given the circumstances of this problem, it is more likely that Bonny will proceed to evict if Zeus applies for title. If he does not even apply, she may evict him in the normal way.

(C) THE LEASE

Lulu is in occupation of the second farm cottage under some form of lease given to her by Karen. Is this lease binding on Bonny? Clearly, the lease claimed by Lulu is of less than seven years' duration (in fact, it is six), so it need not have been substantively registered in its own right – it is not currently within **ss 4** or **27** of the **LRA 2002**. So, the lease can only be binding on Bonny if it is a registered protected interest or an overriding interest.

If this is a legal lease, then it constitutes an overriding interest under **Sched 3, para 1** to the **LRA 2002**. However, the lease is not made by deed – it is *written*, but not in a deed – so the only circumstance in which it could be a legal lease is if it amounts to a legal periodic tenancy under which the period is three years or less – see **ss 52(1)** and **54(2)** of the **Law of Property Act 1925** (and Chapter 5). The question makes no reference to the period for which Lulu pays rent; we are told only that she has been in occupation for two years and expects to be free to occupy for another four. In such circumstances, the implication is against a legal periodic tenancy. It is worth noting, however, that, even if this were a legal periodic tenancy, binding as an overriding interest under **Sched 3**, there would be nothing to prevent Bonny from terminating it according to its own terms – that is, the giving of notice to quit of one period.

....

6   Although this problem is concerned largely with the operation of the registration requirements, it is important to be aware of the strength of the rights thus protected and the consequences of that right for the purchaser.

It is more likely that the lease is equitable. There is written evidence of it and it is probably capable of specific performance (see s 2 of the Law of Property (Miscellaneous Provisions) Act 1989 and _Walsh v Lonsdale_ (1882)). Equitable leases can be protected by an entry on the register by way of a notice, but Lulu has not done this. However, this lease – assuming it is equitable – is still binding on Bonny for its intended duration (six years from grant by Karen) because Lulu falls within Sched 3, para 2 to the LRA 2002 being a person with a proprietary interest (the lease) in discoverable actual occupation at the time the property was transferred:[7] s 29 of the LRA 2002 and see _Thompson v Foy_ (2009) and _Link Lending v Bustard_ (2010) for the general principle.

To conclude, then, there is every possibility that Bonny must allow Lulu to occupy one cottage until her lease expires, assuming, of course, that, in the meantime, Lulu does not breach the terms of the lease and continues to pay rent to her new landlord. Although Zeus's rights as an adverse possessor are binding on Bonny, she can resist any application he may make for the title and can evict him. She is bound by the restrictive covenant even though it was not disclosed on the search certificate because it is registered. Bonny's real hope for substantive remedies because she has innocently purchased a property bound by an adverse right (the covenant) lies in negligence against her solicitor and possibly in contract against Lulu.[8]

DON'T BE TEMPTED TO
Avoid skipping over the substantive law behind this problem. For example, the Examiner will not assume that you know the law concerning restrictive covenants if you do not make reference to it, even briefly.

In the absence of information about how a property right comes into existence, do not assume that formalities exist. For example, do not assume that Lulu's lease is 'by deed' and note the difference between a lease by deed and a lease 'in writing'.

QUESTION 3
In 2012, Oswald owns a large detached house, divided into two self-contained flats, title to which is registered in his sole name. In anticipation of an overseas posting, Oswald had advertised for a tenant for the upper flat and entered into negotiations with Bluebell. Unfortunately, they could not agree terms but, on payment of a deposit, Bluebell was allowed to occupy the flat while their solicitors negotiated an acceptable lease. Meanwhile, Oswald agreed in writing to sell the bottom flat to his daughter Nigella should he be posted abroad. Hearing of Oswald's possible departure, Eric, his neighbour,

---

7   A common mistake is to assume that actual occupation itself is a right which registration will protect. This is wrong. The right protected by the actual occupation must itself be a recognised property right – here, a lease.

8   This is a creative alternative solution to the problem and one worth mentioning like this in a conclusion.

asks whether he can use Oswald's drive for easier access to his large double garage. Oswald readily agrees, provided that Eric pays for resurfacing of the drive. Eric employs contractors and the drive is completely resurfaced. On hearing of his overseas posting, Oswald realises that he needs to raise some capital. Hera, his mistress, is willing to buy the property at much more than his daughter could ever afford. Realising that Nigella has not registered her interest, he sells the entire property to Hera by registered disposition. Hera wishes to re-convert the house and asks Bluebell to leave. She also erects a fence preventing Eric from using her drive. Nigella hears of the sale and seeks to enforce her right to buy the bottom flat against Hera.

▶ Advise the parties.

How to Answer this Question

❖ the effect of registration as owner – ss 58 and 29 of the LRA 2002;
❖ the extent and effect of any overriding interests;
❖ the existence of any registered protected interests;
❖ the formality rules for the creation of leases;
❖ the conditions for proprietary estoppel and s 116 of the LRA 2002
❖ *Midland Bank Trust Co v Green* (1981).

Applying the Law

This diagram demonstrates which interests are binding on a purchaser under the **Land Registration Act 2002.**

ANSWER

As the new registered proprietor of the land, Hera will be bound only by those overriding interests subsisting at the date of registration of her new title (that is, those in **Sched 3** to the **LRA 2002**; *Abbey National BS v Cann* (1991), *Mortgage Business plc v Cook* (2012)), as well as any registered protected interests – see **s 29** of the **LRA 2002**). In addition, there is the possibility that she could be bound by proprietary interests that are not protected in the proper fashion if there has been some fraud or bad faith associated with her purchase (see, for example, *Lyus v Prowsa Developments* (1982), but note *Lloyd v Dugdale* (2002) and *Chaudhary v Yavuz* (2012)).

(A) BLUEBELL

The question here is whether Bluebell has any estate or interest in the land and, if so, whether it has been protected against a third-party purchaser under the appropriate mechanism of the **LRA 2002**. In order for a right to have priority over a purchaser, it must be *capable* of being binding – that is, it must be proprietary. In this case, there is the possibility that Bluebell has a lease and, of course, this is a proprietary interest. For example, Bluebell has paid some money and she appears to have gone into occupation in pursuance of it. Indeed, her lease in these circumstances could be a legal periodic tenancy of three years or less and having priority (until terminated by appropriate notice) as an overriding interest under **Sched 3, para 1** to the **LRA 2002**. (There is no possibility of an equitable tenancy because there is no written document within the formality requirements of **s 2** of the **Law of Property (Miscellaneous Provisions) Act 1989**.) However, there is also the possibility that Bluebell does not have a lease at all. She has, in fact, gone into occupation pending the negotiation of a lease in the knowledge that no agreement has been concluded with the landlord. Following *Javad v Aqil* (1991), there will be no lease if there was no intention to create legal relations, as seems likely while negotiations are still proceeding. Bluebell will, therefore, be a 'tenant at will', which (contrary to its name[9]) confers no estate or interest in the land, being a mere licence. If this is the case, there is no proprietary right capable of being a registered protected interest or an overriding interest and so Bluebell must vacate the flat (see *Ashburn Anstalt v Arnold* (1989) and *Lloyd v Dugdale*.)

(B) ERIC

In the case of Eric, the position is not so clear. From his point of view, he will be claiming, first, that the right to use the drive amounted to an easement (right of way), and, second, that this easement is binding on Hera. First, does the easement exist? It is axiomatic that a right of way can amount to an easement but, in this case, there is the question of whether it has been properly created. Clearly, there is no deed nor even a written record

---

9   Short 'asides' such as this are a good way to introduce some analysis without detracting from main point being made.

of the agreement between Oswald and Eric: thus the easement is not legal and cannot be equitable within *Walsh v Lonsdale* (1882). However, it may be that Eric can claim the creation of an easement in his favour under the law of proprietary estoppel, as explained generally in *Taylor Fashions Ltd v Liverpool Victoria Trustees* (1982) and *Thorner Majors* (2009) and, in respect of easements in particular, in *Ives v High* (1967). In our case, there appears to have been an assurance – by Oswald to Eric that he could use the drive – which was relied upon by Eric to his detriment. How else is it possible to explain Eric's expenditure on the driveway: see *Greasely v Cooke* (1980)? This may well mean that Eric has the benefit of an easement, albeit an easement that must be equitable because of the informal manner in which it was created. If this is true, Eric has a right that is capable of binding Hera and will do so if it is registered by means of a notice against the title or can amount to an overriding interest (s 29 of the LRA 2002 and see the analysis in *Chaudhary v Yavuz* (2012)). Clearly, there is no registration in this case. Moreover, under the LRA 2002, equitable easements are not capable of amounting to overriding interests, for the Act deliberately reverses *Celsteel v Alton* (1985) and *Thatcher v Douglas* (1995) and equitable easements do not fall within para 3 of Sched 3 (which applies only to legal easements).[10] Likewise, use of the easement on the servient land does not amount to 'actual occupation' of it so as to generate an overriding under para 2 of Sched 3 (*Chaudhary v Yavuz* (2012)). Consequently, it looks as if the easement, if it exists, will not have priority over the purchaser of the registered title.

(C) NIGELLA

By his written agreement with his daughter, Oswald has granted Nigella some right in connection with the flat. What is the nature of that right?[11] At first sight, it appears that Nigella's right could be a 'right of pre-emption' – a right of first refusal to the land should the owner decide to sell. If this were the case, it would amount to a proprietary right (s 115 of the LRA 2002; see also *Dear v Reeves* (2000)), but it would be effective against the purchaser *only* if Nigella were in discoverable actual occupation of the flat to which it relates (or the purchaser knew of the right and she was in occupation) under Sched 3, para 2 to the LRA 2002 (overriding interest) or if she has registered it by means of a notice.

However, the better view is that Oswald has granted Nigella an option to purchase the flat. The essence of an option is that the grantee (Nigella) has an enforceable right to purchase the property at a moment of their choosing, provided that any conditions in the option are fulfilled (see, for example, *Ferrishurst Ltd v Wallcite Ltd*

---

10 Referring to the motivation behind the particular rule in the LRA here brings an extra dimension to this section.

11 It is always best to outline the precise right it is suggested that someone in a problem has, even if this ultimately does not affect the conclusion reached.

(1999)). Here, the fact that the option is conditional upon the overseas posting does not alter its character because, if Oswald is posted, Nigella has an enforceable right to buy at her choosing. Oswald has no choice if the condition is fulfilled (if he is posted) and he has no control over whether the condition will be fulfilled (see *Haslemere Estates Ltd v Baker* (1982) in support of this view). Assuming this to be an option, it is clear that it is a proprietary right, capable of binding third parties. Yet, once again, in order to take priority over a new purchaser/owner, the proprietary right must be protected in the proper manner under the **LRA 2002**. There is no prospect of the option being an overriding interest as it does not fall within any of the statutory definitions of **Sched 3, LRA 2002** (e.g. Nigella is not in actual occupation under **para 2**). Moreover, in this case, the option has not been protected by entry on the register, and therefore has no priority against a purchaser. It cannot be enforced against Hera: **s 29** of the **LRA 2002**.

In such circumstances, the only slender hope – and it is very slender – is for Nigella to establish that her unregistered interest has been defeated by fraud and for this reason should remain valid. However, even if Hera knows that Oswald is selling the property partly to defeat his daughter's claim, the better view is that this is not fraud – see, for example, *Midland Bank Trust Co v Green* (1981) in a similar context in unregistered land. In this respect, *Peffer v Rigg* (1977), which seemed to require the purchaser to act 'in good faith' if they were to be free of unregistered interests (where 'good faith' is defined almost synonymously with notice), was probably bad law and in any event such a concept is irrelevant under the **LRA 2002** (see also *HSBC v Dyche* (2010) and *Chaudhary v Yavuz* (2012)). Only if Hera had promised Nigella and/or Oswald that she would honour the option despite the lack of registration (and had, thereby, obtained the property more cheaply) could the purchaser be said to have committed fraud – see *Lyus v Prowsa Developments* (1982), although this is very difficult to establish and *Chaudhary*[12] regards *Lyus* as a very special case. If that were the position – and there is no evidence to support it – Hera would be a constructive trustee of the option for Nigella and necessarily bound by it.

In conclusion, then, Hera is not bound by the easement as it does not qualify as an overriding interest and is not registered. She is not bound by the option to allow Nigella to purchase the ground-floor flat and may ask Bluebell to leave as she has no estate in the land capable of being binding on Hera.[13]

---

12 *Chaudhary* is relied on a lot in this answer – this demonstrates good knowledge of very recent case law and will be given much credit by the examiner.

13 It is always good to have a short conclusion like this in problem questions to summarise the application of the law to the facts.

DON'T BE TEMPTED TO

Do not assume that the purchaser *must* be bound by the claimant's rights. It may be that the purchaser takes the land free of the claim, even if this looks 'unfair' in some general sense. Land registration is about certainty.

Avoid importing unregistered land concepts into land registration questions: it is not about what the purchaser 'knows' but about the rules of the LRA 2002.

QUESTION 4

The Law Commission proposed fundamental changes to the system of registered land and these have now taken shape in the form of the LRA 2002 The LRA 2002is a considerable improvement on the 1925 Act although some uncertainties in its operation have come to light.

▶ Discuss.

How to Answer this Question

❖ the general thrust of Law Commission Report No 271;
❖ the potential problems with overriding interests identified by the Law Commission – nature, extent, and undiscoverability;
❖ potential problems with other interests – simplifying the methods of protection;
❖ adverse possession of registered land and its relation to the 2002 Actsystem of registration;
❖ the future – formalities for the creation of interests in land, rectification of the register and electronic conveyancing.

Applying the Law

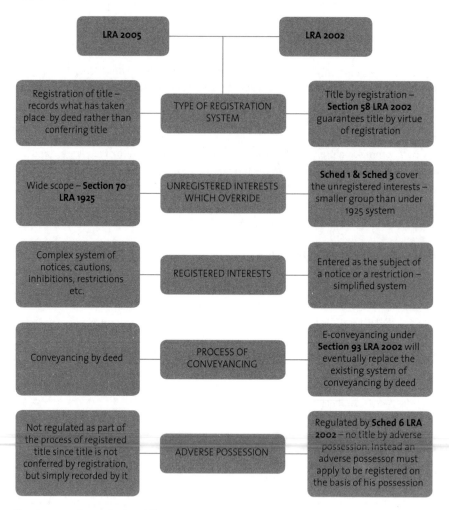

LRA 2005		LRA 2002
Registration of title – records what has taken place by deed rather than conferring title	TYPE OF REGISTRATION SYSTEM	Title by registration – **Section 58 LRA 2002** guarantees title by virtue of registration
Wide scope – **Section 70 LRA 1925**	UNREGISTERED INTERESTS WHICH OVERRIDE	**Sched 1 & Sched 3** cover the unregistered interests – smaller group than under 1925 system
Complex system of notices, cautions, inhibitions, restrictions etc.	REGISTERED INTERESTS	Entered as the subject of a notice or a restriction – simplified system
Conveyancing by deed	PROCESS OF CONVEYANCING	E-conveyancing under **Section 93 LRA 2002** will eventually replace the existing system of conveyancing by deed
Not regulated as part of the process of registered title since title is not conferred by registration, but simply recorded by it	ADVERSE POSSESSION	Regulated by **Sched 6 LRA 2002** – no title by adverse possession. Instead an adverse possessor must apply to be registered on the basis of his possession

This diagram shows the key differences between the **Land Registration Act 1925** and the **Land Registration Act 2002.**

ANSWER

The land registration system inaugurated by the **LRA 1925** had been in operation in England and Wales for over 75 years before it was reformed by the **LRA 2002.** Throughout this period, the role of 'land' within the economy and the practical realities of property ownership had changed, as had the methods by which legal transactions could be undertaken, and it was perfectly accurate for the Law Commission to conclude that the system of land registration needed modernising and adjustment to reflect the realities of the twenty-first century. We should not forget that the **LRA 1925** was itself an experiment in title registration and no one would argue that it was flawless. Time has revealed, however, that it was not fatally flawed.

The underlying rationale of the **LRA 1925** was relatively straightforward: title to land was to be recorded and guaranteed by the state through title registration and interests in land were either obvious on physical inspection of the land itself or noted in a clear and unambiguous fashion on the register of title. The advantages were also obvious: purchasers could buy in the certainty that they were purchasing land suitable for their requirements because the existence of 'hidden' burdens was minimised, and owners of interests in land, such as easements and covenants, had a relatively easy and inexpensive method (inspecting the register) of ensuring that their rights survived a conveyance of the land to a third party. These remain fundamental objectives of the land registration system. However, we now live in a different age, in which both technological advances and the need to iron out deficiencies in the original 1925 system required that title registration should be overhauled. The Law Commission had been working on this task for some time, but the publication of Law Commission Report No 271 (*Land Registration for the Twenty-First Century: A Conveyancing Revolution*) including a draft Bill, brought the process to fruition. The Land Registration Bill 2001 became the **LRA 2002** and this far-reaching statute came into force on 13 October 2002, with full implementation of e-conveyancing to come later. The **LRA 2002** has then completely replaced the **LRA 1925** and the new statute, supplemented by the **Land Registration Rules 2003**, now governs all matters concerning registered title.

The 2002 legislation therefore represents a complete overhaul of the system. Many of its provisions deal with technical matters that, while important, establish no new principle. These are the 'tidying up' aspects of the legislation. However, there is a portion of the **2002 Act** that is groundbreaking and truly significant, not least the claim that the **2002 Act** replaces 'registration of title' with 'title by registration'. In essence, this means that no longer is it the case that a person acquires a title that is then registered; rather, under the **LRA 2002**, the act of registration itself, and only that act, comprises the grant of title. Registration as proprietor is conclusive: **s 58, LRA 2002** – see *Burton v Walker* (2012). This means, of course, that a person dealing with the registered proprietor can deal with them in complete confidence (see **s 23, LRA 2002**) without fear that they are not really the owner, even if it should later emerge that there was some 'flaw' in the proprietor's title (e.g. even that they never should have owned it – *Burton v Walker*).

Another major issue addressed by the Law Commission is that of overriding interests (now called 'unregistered interests which override'): being those rights that bind a purchaser of the land without entry on the register and irrespective of whether the purchaser has any knowledge or notice of them. Indeed, under the **LRA 1925**, they bound the purchaser even if they could never have discovered such rights (i.e. they were undiscoverable, as opposed to undiscovered, as in *Chhokar v Chhokar* (1984)).[14] Of course, the great majority of overriding interests under the LRA 1925 were in fact discoverable from a reasonable inspection of the property and it is a common error to believe that the 1925 system intended to do away with inspection of land by potential purchasers. Nevertheless, it is true that the mere existence of a category of 'overriding interests' compromises the integrity of the register and raises the possibility that people could be bound by an adverse right irrespective of the circumstances in which they have purchased the land. Consequently, the 2002 legislation attempts to reduce the effect of overriding interests, both by eliminating certain categories of overriding interest and by inaugurating a change in the way that we think about these important rights. Thus, the rights that once fell within s 70(1) of the LRA 1925 were reclassified. Under the 2002 Act, there are some rights – the larger category – that override a first registration of title – that is, they override the estate of the person who first registers when the land ceases to be unregistered land (see ss 11 and 12 of, and Sched 1 to, the LRA 2002). These rights include the major categories of legal leases of seven years or less, interests of persons in actual occupation of the relevant part of the land (reversing *Ferrishurst v Wallcite* (1999) and excluding the person in receipt of rents and profits who once qualified under s 70(1) of the LRA 1925), and legal easements and profits. Other lesser rights, such as feudal franchises, manorial rights and the like override a first registration for ten years from the date of entry into force of the Act (13 October 2003), after which they must be entered on the register if they are to endure. Second, there is a narrower category of rights that override a disposition of registered land – that is, a transfer of the land after it has been registered (see s 29 of, and Sched 3 to, the LRA 2002). These include the above categories narrowed down to reflect the fact that some rights that override a first registration should have been entered on the register after first registration if they are to continue to be binding. Thus, any lease that is required to be registered as a title is excluded (at first, this will be those over seven years – reduced from 21 years under the old law); a right of a person in actual occupation is excluded if, either, the occupation is not patent (that is, if it is not discoverable) or the right is not known of by the purchaser (para 2) and see *Thompson v Foy* (2009), *Link Lending v Bustard* (2010) and *Thomas v Clydesdale Bank* (2010);[15] expressly granted easements are excluded (because they will not exist at all unless entered on the register (para 3)), equitable easements, and certain types of legal easement not falling within para 3. Significantly, in no category are the rights of squatters per se protected, although most squatters will be protected (in so far as that is possible under the LRA 2002) under the 'actual occupation' category. Obviously, there is a general emphasis on discoverable overriding interests (with undiscoverable ones generally not having priority over a purchaser) and there is a connection with the way in which rights in land are to be created.

....

14 This essay is asking not only for an outline of the changes brought about by the 2002 Act, but of an assessment of the seriousness of the problems that existed in the earlier legislation.

15 Listing cases in this way is a good technique for showing off knowledge without taking up too much time in the exam.

A second area of reform was the way in which so-called 'minor interests' were to be protected. Under the **1925 Act**, the provisions concerning the various forms of protection for a minor interest (notice, caution, restriction, inhibition) were complicated and unsystematic and, as we know, from *Clarke v Chief Land Registrar* (1994), the caution offered only procedural protection. The **LRA 2002** has only two means of protecting 'minor interests' and, in fact, they are no longer even called minor interests! A new form of restriction performs the functions of the old restriction and inhibition, and a new form of the notice combines the functions of the old notice and the caution. The new notice may be either 'agreed' (for rights acknowledged by the registered proprietor or by the court) or 'unilateral' (for rights not acknowledged by the registered proprietor). Unilateral notices can be cancelled, but will confer priority and protection until they are cancelled (if ever), so offering a protection that the old caution could not. Similarly, despite criticism of the rule concerning the priority between minor interests under the **LRA 1925** (that is that, inter se, the first in time prevails, irrespective of whether either are registered: *Barclays Bank v Taylor* (1973)), the **2002 Act** provides that the rule concerning priority of competing registered interests should remain essentially unchanged because electronic conveyancing will ensure that creation and registration occur at the same time. Likewise, although there seems to be no definition of a 'purchaser' for the purposes of the **2002 Act**, there is equally no reference to 'good faith', so it seems that (fortunately) *Peffer v Rigg* (1977) will not be reappearing (although note its apparent use in *HSBC v Dyche* (2010)).

Third, the **2002 Act** envisages a new method of creating and transferring rights in land – electronic conveyancing. The details of this system are not yet clear (although a 'pilot' with mixed results has taken place) and it may be that, at first, it will be possible to create an enforceable contract or a 'deed' in electronic form so as to satisfy the formality requirements that currently exist for the creation of rights and interests in land. Currently, the project is 'on hold' pending resolution of technical difficulties and a more favourable economic climate.[16] However, it is clear that the ultimate aim is to ensure that many (indeed most) property rights concerning registered land will not exist at all unless they are entered on the register of title. Given that such entry also ultimately will be electronic, it seems that much of the old law about how rights in land can be created will be swept away. The act of creation will be the act of registration and this will be electronic. Eventually, this will apply to all registrable estates (freeholds and leases over seven years) and to many other rights such as mortgages and expressly created easements. Clearly, this will revolutionise the way we think about rights in land and it is probably just as well that the Act also confirms that rights arising under proprietary estoppel are to be regarded as rights in land along with mere equities (see **s 116** of the **LRA 2002** and *Lloyd v Dugdale* (2002)). Even more importantly, the fact that creation and registration will be achieved by the same act of electronic registration means that it is

....

16   This shows awareness of the practical circumstances in which these rules must operate.

certain that the 'registration gap' will disappear. This will mean that transfers of land can be effected electronically in safety. Thus, despite the delay in bringing the system 'on-line', e-conveyancing has much to offer. In the next few years, Network Access Agreements will be needed to regulate who may use the electronic system, security issues will need to be addressed, training provided and fears overcome. Judgement as to its success will have to wait.

The 2002 Act also reforms completely the law of adverse possession as it relates to registered title. In effect, there is no longer a limitation period – that is, no time after which the registered owner loses their title. Instead, an adverse possessor has the ability to apply for registration as owner after ten years of adverse possession. If this occurs, the Registrar will then notify the 'true owner' (the current registered proprietor) who, if he objects, will be given a further two years to evict the adverse possessor unless certain exceptional situations exist. Failure to evict within these two years will result in the adverse possessor being registered as owner. There is no obligation on the adverse possessor to apply for registration after ten years, so if he waits for 30 years before applying for title, the registered owner still has a further two years in which to take action. Obviously this will mean – and is intended to mean – the end of adverse possession in the great majority of cases in registered land. The paper owner will be notified and will usually object and evict within two years. Moreover, given that the 'old' law of adverse possession will remain for unregistered land, this new system provides a powerful incentive for owners to register their land voluntarily.

These are far-reaching reforms of the 2002 Act. Other reforms include the ability of the Crown to register its land for the first time and that legal leases are registrable if granted for more than seven years (rather than the previous 21), thus bringing many more titles on to the register, and this 'trigger period' may well be reduced further in years to come. Again, the registered charge is now the only way of mortgaging registered land (no more mortgages by the long-lease method), charge certificates are abolished and land certificates will disappear. A new office of adjudicator has been established to resolve land registration disputes and the new system is being administered with efficiency and skill.

Of course, the general success of the 2002 Act should not blind us to the fact that there have been some difficulties. The delay in introducing electronic conveyancing is a serious setback, as it was one of the main motivations for the reform. Likewise, uncertainty about the extent of the power to rectify the register (*Baxter v Mannion* and *Burton v Walker*) raises issues about the integrity of title guarantee under s 58 and there may well be further difficulties in defining overriding interests within Schedule 3, especially the meaning of 'actual occupation'. The consequences of the changes to the law on adverse possession are also still being worked out – see e.g. *IAM Group v Chowdrey* (2012). Nevertheless, taken as a whole, the 2002 Act remains a remarkable achievement given that, relatively speaking, there has been so little difficulty in the application of its provisions since 2003.[17]

DON'T BE TEMPTED TO

Do not frame the answer in terms of 'mirror', 'insurance' and 'curtain' principles. The question asks about the 2002 Act, not general theories about land registration.

Avoid generalities, and consider specific provisions of the Act, especially ss 23, 28, 29 and 58.

Do not forget case law. There are now a number of decisions on the 2002 Act and these will enhance an answer.

17 This balanced conclusion demonstrates that the writer is aware of the practical difficulties in implementing the entirety of the 2002 Act and the consequences this must have for our assessment of the Act's success.

Unregistered Land

INTRODUCTION

On 1 December 1990, all land in England and Wales became subject to compulsory first registration of title. In effect, this means that on the first conveyance of a title to an estate in unregistered land (or one of various other dealings with it: s 4 of the **Land Registration Act (LRA) 2002**), the title must be registered and thereafter, ceases to be governed by unregistered land rules. It is most unlikely, therefore, that a question in an examination will turn entirely on the conveyance of an unregistered title unless it is made clear that all of the relevant transactions are completed before 1990. It is much more likely that a question will focus on the transfer of an unregistered estate that triggers compulsory first registration of title under the 2002 Act. That does not mean, however, that the rules concerning unregistered land are no longer important. There are many situations in which questions concerning the enforceability of interests in unregistered land are relevant, especially as a vehicle for assessing a student's understanding of other areas of law, such as the creation and enforceability of freehold covenants or easements.

Aim Higher ★

When land is described as unregistered, this means that title is to be found in title deeds rather than on any register. The law of unregistered conveyancing is, therefore, related to the rules of property law as they stood prior to the 1925 property legislation. However, it would be a mistake to think that the law of unregistered land was unaffected by the 1925 reforms. The **Law of Property Act (LPA) 1925** applies in full to unregistered land in the same manner as registered land. What is different is that the enforceability of rights and interests in unregistered land – being those rights and interests capable of existing under the provisions of the **LPA 1925** – is governed by its own set of rules and procedures separate from the law of the **Land Registration Acts**.

Remember the four principal rules of unregistered conveyancing

❖ Legal estates, both freehold and leasehold, are generally to be found in title deeds, not on a register.

❖ In unregistered conveyancing, it is still true that 'legal rights bind the whole world'. Once it is established that a right is 'legal' that estate or interest is binding on whomsoever comes into possession of the land. There is, by definition, no question of registration and no relevance for 'the doctrine of notice' in relation to legal estates and interests. The sole exception to this is the 'puisne mortgage', a legal mortgage for which the documents of title have not been deposited with the lender as security. Such a mortgage, despite being a legal interest, is registrable as a 'land charge' under the Land Charges Act (LCA) 1972 as discussed immediately below.

❖ With certain well-defined and very limited exceptions, the 'doctrine of notice' plays no part in unregistered land. It is a common mistake to believe that it does. By statute, unregistered land has its own system of registration of equitable interests. This was the LCA 1925, and is now the LCA 1972. One of the most frequent errors is to forget that in unregistered land there is also a requirement of registration for certain – indeed most – equitable interests. These 'registrable' equitable interests (called 'land charges') are binding if registered correctly under the LCA 1972 but void against a purchaser if not, irrespective of whether the purchaser has notice. This registration system has *nothing to do* with registered land.

❖ There are a small number of equitable rights that, either deliberately or by subsequent judicial development, are excluded from the operation of the LCA 1972. In other words, they are 'non-registrable' as *land charges*. For these rights, their enforceability against a purchaser still does depend on the doctrine of the 'bona fide purchaser of a legal estate for value without notice' (sometimes known as *equity's darling*). This is the *only* circumstance in which notice should form part of the answer to an examination question in land law today.

QUESTION 5

Analyse the way in which third-party property rights are protected in unregistered conveyancing. Was the Land Charges Act 1972 successful in protecting these interests in the event that the land over which they existed was transferred?

How to Answer this Question

❖ The crucial distinction between legal and equitable rights in unregistered land.
❖ Briefly, the problems prior to 1926, especially in protecting equitable interests.
❖ The general scheme of the Land Charges Act 1972.
❖ Identification of problems with a name-based system.
❖ Identification of problems with 'root of title' and compensation rules.
❖ There is no protection for occupiers per se.
❖ Analysis of rights that are not land charges and the continuing relevance of the doctrine of notice.

Applying the Law

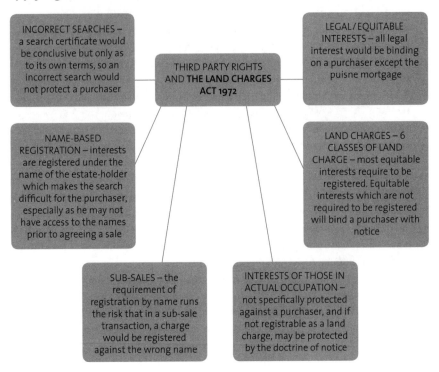

INCORRECT SEARCHES – a search certificate would be conclusive but only as to its own terms, so an incorrect search would not protect a purchaser

LEGAL/EQUITABLE INTERESTS – all legal interest would be binding on a purchaser except the puisne mortgage

THIRD PARTY RIGHTS AND **THE LAND CHARGES ACT 1972**

NAME-BASED REGISTRATION – interests are registered under the name of the estate-holder which makes the search difficult for the purchaser, especially as he may not have access to the names prior to agreeing a sale

LAND CHARGES – 6 CLASSES OF LAND CHARGE – most equitable interests require to be registered. Equitable interests which are not required to be registered will bind a purchaser with notice

SUB-SALES – the requirement of registration by name runs the risk that in a sub-sale transaction, a charge would be registered against the wrong name

INTERESTS OF THOSE IN ACTUAL OCCUPATION – not specifically protected against a purchaser, and if not registrable as a land charge, may be protected by the doctrine of notice

This diagram shows the position of third party rights in relation to the **Land Charges Act 1972**.

ANSWER

Prior to 1 January 1926, the conveyancing system in England and Wales was under considerable strain. On the one hand, purchasers of land were faced with many difficulties when trying to establish whether any other person had rights or interests in that land and, on the other, an owner of an equitable interest in that land might find that the interest was destroyed by a simple sale to a purchaser who was unaware of its existence. To meet both of those problems, it was decided to move towards full title registration wherein all titles and many interests in land would be recorded and guaranteed by the state. It was recognised, however, that this mammoth task had to proceed in stages and that a set of transitional provisions was needed. The result was the Land Charges Act 1925 (now the Land Charges Act 1972), which was intended to operate for only some 30 years. Unfortunately, it was not until 1 December 1990 that all land in England and Wales became subject to compulsory first registration and the fact that full title registration is still a little way off means that a certain amount of unregistered conveyancing will remain with us for a while yet.[1]

The LCA 1972 is something of a hybrid. On the one hand, it adopts some of the rules of the old common law: thus, it is still true with unregistered conveyancing that (with one exception) legal estates or interests 'bind the whole world'. However, many equitable rights would not be apparent to a purchaser on physical inspection of the property and their simple informality made them vulnerable in the event of a transfer of the land. To deal with this, the LCA 1972 substantially replaced the common law doctrine of the bona fide purchaser of a legal estate for value without notice. In its place, the LCA 1972 established a system of registration of its own.

The scheme of the LCA 1972 is relatively straightforward. Equitable interests are divided into various categories known as land charges. These classes – Classes A–F – are statutorily defined and were intended to cover most of the equitable interests that could exist or could be created in land on or after 1 January 1926. Bearing in mind that these equitable interests affect the title of land belonging to another person, s 3 of the LCA[2] provides that a land charge should be registered in its appropriate class against the name of the estate owner whose land is to be bound by the charge. Under s 4 of the 1972 Act, if the owner of an equitable interest has not registered their interest as a land charge, it will be void against a purchaser of the land (*Petrou v Petrou* (1998); *Midland Bank Trust Co v Green* (1981)), provided that the transferee is a true purchaser who actually provides consideration (*Merer v Fisher* (2003)[3]). To be more precise, an equitable interest that should have been registered as a Class C(iv) or Class D land charge will be void against a purchaser of a legal estate in the land for money or money's worth, and an equitable interest that should have been registered in any one of the other classes will be void against a purchaser of any estate in the land for valuable consideration. The corollary of this is that, if an equitable interest is correctly registered, it will be binding on any purchaser of the land as stipulated in s 198 of the Law of Property Act (LPA) 1925. It should be noted at this point that even an unregistered equitable interest is binding against someone who is *not* a purchaser, such as an adverse possessor, or a person who in fact provides no purchase money at all despite being called a 'purchaser' (*Merer*). In principle, therefore, the position is relatively straightforward.

Unfortunately, this simple picture masks serious difficulties that have emerged in the application of the LCA in practice.[4] These problems are both inherent in the machinery as

---

1   The background and intended role of the LCA is an important aspect of this essay and the introduction helps to put the rest of the analysis into its context.
2   It is always better to give a precise statutory citation where possible.
3   Cases or statutes should be used to back up every principle stated – this is the best way to ensure really good marks in both essay and problem questions.
4   A difference between the theory behind the rules and their operation in practice is always a useful angle of analysis.

it was established, and have emerged because of changes made in the substance of property law since 1926. One of the most serious criticisms of the land charges is its reliance on a name-based system of registration. Thus, an owner of an equitable interest has to register it as a land charge against the *name* of the estate owner and all depends on both the owner of the equitable interest and any prospective purchaser knowing the correct name of the current estate owner. This has caused problems in three respects. First,[5] there are some circumstances in which a prospective purchaser has no way of ascertaining the name of the estate owner of the land he is purchasing and so no knowledge of whom to search against. So, for example, under the rule in *Patman v Harland* (1881) an intending purchaser of a lease has no automatic right to examine the title of the freeholder and so has no way of obtaining the names of previous owners of the land against whom he should make a land charges search, unless this is volunteered or specified in a pre-lease contract. He is, nevertheless, bound by land charges registered against former estate owners because s 198 of the LPA 1925 takes priority over the purchaser's apparent protection found in s 44(5) of the LPA (*White v Bijou Mansions* (1937)). Likewise, now that 'root of title' in unregistered land is only 15 years (s 23 of the LPA 1969), the purchaser may well have no way of ascertaining the names of persons who held the land previously: these names can be behind the root of title, if contained in a conveyance executed more than 15 years before the date of the impending sale. However, any charges registered against these names are binding on the purchaser (s 198 LPA 1925) irrespective of the fact that the purchaser could not have discovered those names. Although a partial remedy is provided by s 25 of the LPA 1969 (compensation), this is a problem that will only get worse the longer it takes to complete full registration of title.

Second, there is the problem of incorrect searches. It is axiomatic that a name-based system will work only if all parties both register and search under the correct names. This is by no means a foregone conclusion. In *Diligent Finance Co Ltd v Alleyene* (1972) for example, a wife had registered a Class F land charge against her husband, but not against his full name as shown on the title deeds. When the purchaser then searched against the correct name, they received a clear search certificate (which is conclusive: s 10 of the LCA) and the wife's rights lost their priority. An even more complicated set of circumstances arises when there is both a defective search and a defective registration. Thus, in *Oak Cooperative Building Society v Blackburn* (1968) both the registration and the search were made in different, but incorrect, versions of the estate owner's name. In the event, the registration was deemed less defective than the search, but this was simply a pragmatic solution made necessary by the deficiencies of the system. It is also true that registration of a land charge against the *correct* name will be effective, even if the land to which it relates is incorrectly described, provided that the description is a reasonable version of the land described in the conveyance (*Horrill v Cooper* (2000)).

---

5   The use of the list of problems here is a good way to make the structure easy to follow.

Third, there is a problem with sub-sales. The LCA requires interests – such as a contract to buy the land – to be registered against the actual estate owner at the time the charge is created: s 3. If, therefore, a person is buying land at the end of a chain and their seller has not yet completed his own purchase, the sub-sale should be registered against the head vendor – that is, the estate owner at the time the sub-sale was agreed. Obviously, this can happen only if the end-purchaser is aware of the existence of the chain and, if not, they are likely to register their charge against the wrong person, as in *Barrett v Hilton Developments Ltd* (1975). It will then be void if the property is sold elsewhere (albeit in breach of contract). Apart from problems arising out of the use of a name-based registration system, there are other difficulties too. Thus, when a purchaser has exchanged contracts with the vendor, only then will he be in a position to search the Land Charges Register, for that is when previous owners are revealed in the title documents. Of course, by that time he is bound to complete the contract and also bound by any registered land charges. Again, it is only because of later statutory amendment, in the form of s 24 of the LPA 1969, that a remedy has been found that enables a purchaser to pull out of the contract if he had no actual knowledge of the charge that he subsequently finds.

Further, in unregistered land there is no equivalent of para 2 of Scheds 1 and 3 to the LRA 2002. So, even those owners of equitable interests who are in actual occupation of property at the time of a sale to a purchaser are not protected. As *Hollington Brothers v Rhodes* (1951) shows, these interests must be positively protected through land charge registration (or the doctrine of notice if that is applicable – see below). Whether or not this was deliberate – and there is some doubt that it was – clearly, it is a significant weakness in the system. Finally, there is one problem that is not so much inherent in the system as originally devised but which has emerged due to legal, social and economic changes in the use of land. As noted above, it is essential to the success of this legislation that virtually all equitable interests fall within its ambit. Unfortunately, that is not the case. There are a number of equitable interests that case law and, indeed, the LCA 1972 itself, establishes are not registrable as land charges. These unregistrable interests are still capable of binding a purchaser, but their effect depends entirely on the capricious doctrine of notice. In this respect, one of the most important aims of the LCA 1972 – namely the virtual abolition of the doctrine of notice – has not been achieved. The equitable rights included in this residual category are diverse. On the one hand, there are estoppel easements (*Ives v High* (1967)) and, on the other, such matters as the right of re-entry in an equitable lease (*Shiloh Spinners v Harding* (1973)) and the right of a tenant to recover fixtures at the end of an equitable lease (*Poster v Slough Estates* (1968)). However, the most important is the right of equitable ownership behind a trust of land. Such rights are specifically excluded from the category of land charges by s 2(4) of the LCA 1972, mainly because they are overreachable (on a sale by two trustees and so take effect in purchase money). As we now know, however, not all cases of a trust of land will have two trustees (*Pettitt v Pettitt* (1970); *Stack v Dowden* (2007); *Geary v Rankine* (2012)) and, in such cases, the doctrine of notice plays a vital part in assessing whether the purchaser of the co-owned land is bound (*Kingsnorth Finance v Tizard* (1986)).

The simple fact that there is an entire class of equitable rights that cannot be 'land charges' and the viability of which still depends on the doctrine of notice is a serious criticism of the LCA 1972. This criticism would have been tolerable had the LCA 1972 really been the temporary measure that it was intended to be. That, however, is not the case, although we may at least be seeing the demise of unregistered conveyancing. Of course, if one has registered an equitable interest properly and against the correct name, the system of land charge registration is much more reliable than the doctrine of notice. That, however, is not saying a great deal and it will be something of a relief to conveyancers, purchasers and owners of equitable interests when the system of unregistered conveyancing is fully replaced by that of the LRA 2002.

Don't be Tempted To

This is not a question about the LRA 2002 and it is easy to misread the question, it cannot be answered simply by reciting the provisions of the Land Charges Act. You need to be clear that the cases you rely on – and you must use them – are actually cases about unregistered land. Many land law courses no longer study this topic precisely because unregistered conveyancing is being replaced by registered conveyancing.

Do not confuse land charges, which fall within the LCA 1972, with 'charges by way of mortgage'. A *land charge* is a third party equitable right in unregistered conveyancing and is a generic term that could mean any type of third party right (e.g. option, certain leases, equitable mortgages, covenant, equitable easement). A 'charge by way of mortgage' is a legal mortgage and specifically security for a debt.

QUESTION 6

In 1970, when he retired, Alfonso sold his large farm to Benedict and produced a conveyance from his (Alfonso's) father dated 1935 as proof of title. Benedict, through his solicitors, made an official search of the Land Charges Register against the name of Alfonso and Alfonso's father. The certificate revealed a restrictive covenant, registered against Alfonso's father in 1934, preventing the building of more than one domestic residence on the farm. In 1970, Alfonso wished to live in peace and quiet (in the house he had built on the edge of the farm on land that he now retained), and so a restrictive covenant was inserted in the sale to Benedict preventing any trade or business on the farm except agricultural works. This was correctly registered against Benedict. In 1982, Benedict granted his daughter (Vanessa), for £100, 'the right to buy my farm when I retire from farming at half its current market value'. By 1984, Benedict had fallen in love with a younger woman and wished to start a new life in Australia. Realising that his farm had quadrupled in value since 1982, he decided to sell the land to Desmond, his friend who was also a property developer. Desmond thought he might turn the farm into an industrial estate. Desmond paid three-quarters of the market value in order to get a quick sale. The farm was not then in an area of compulsory first registration of title. Desmond searched against the name of 'Benny' (always having known his friend by this name) and Alfonso. He received a clear certificate.

Vanessa has just heard of the sale and wishes to buy the farm at the cheaper price. Desmond has just received a letter telling him that he cannot build the industrial estate. Desmond wonders whether this is true and asks whether, in any event, he can build a housing estate instead.

▶ Advise the parties.

How to Answer this Question

❖ the period necessary to obtain good root of title;
❖ the possibility of registered, but hidden, land charges;
❖ whether compensation for hidden land charges may be obtained under the LPA 1969;
❖ the various classes of land charge under the LCA 1972;
❖ the effect of land charge registration under the LCA 1972;
❖ the possibility of fraud and its effect.

Answer Structure

This diagram shows how to apply the rules relating to purchasers of unregistered land to Vanessa.

ANSWER

As indicated in the facts of this problem, all the relevant transactions and events are completed *before* registration of title became compulsory in England and Wales and there is nothing to suggest that the land is of registered title or that it needed to be registered. Thus, this problem falls to be decided under the rules of unregistered conveyancing. These rules, it might be noted, are a mixture of common law and statute, the most important being the Land Charges Act (LCA) 1972 (a replacement for the LCA 1925).[6]

(A) VANESSA'S CLAIM TO PURCHASE THE PROPERTY

Whether Vanessa can claim a right against Desmond to purchase the property depends on whether her father, Benedict, granted her a proprietary right over the land and, second, whether this right is enforceable against Desmond. First, there may well be some dispute about the nature of the right granted to Vanessa, for it may be that it cannot be regarded as proprietary in nature. On the one hand, the right may be a right of pre-emption – that is, a right of first refusal in the event that the grantor (Benedict) wishes to sell the property. If this is the case, despite the wording of s 2 of the LCA 1972, *Pritchard v Briggs* (1980) and *University of East London v LB Barking & Dagenham* (2004) suggest that a right of pre-emption cannot be regarded as proprietary until it is exercised (thus, registration would be effective from this later date only). (Note however, if the title had been registered, the right of pre-emption would be proprietary from the moment of its creation: s 115(1) of the LRA 2002)[7] Nevertheless, in any event, the better view is that the right in this case is an option to purchase. An option to purchase is clearly an interest in land from the moment of its creation, whether conditional or not (*London and South Western Railway v Gomm* (1882); *Ferrishurst Ltd v Wallcite Ltd* (1999)).[8] Moreover, it is clear than an option to purchase is an 'estate contract' within s 2 of the LCA 1972 (*Armstrong v Jones* (1869)) and, therefore, it must be registered against the name of the estate owner who created it (that is, Benedict) if it is to bind a subsequent purchaser of a legal estate for money or money's worth: ss 3 and 4(6) of the LCA 1972 In our case, there is no evidence to suggest that Vanessa has registered her option as a land charge and, presumptively, it is void against Desmond – clearly, he is a purchaser of a legal estate for money's worth.

There is, however, one small hope for Vanessa. She may be able to claim that she was fraudulently deprived of her right because of dishonest collusion between Benedict – the creator of the right – and Desmond, the purchaser who obviously benefits from the fact that it is not binding on him. As the problem tells us, Benedict wished to sell to Desmond

---

6   The dates of a problem are always crucial.

7   This aside shows awareness and understanding of the rules of registered conveyancing without suggesting they are applicable here and this is a good technique to show off extra knowledge.

8   Where possible, two cases will be better than one!

in order to obtain a higher price and he must have known that he would thereby defeat his daughter's claim. However, there is no suggestion that the sale was solely in order to defeat the daughter's claim or that Desmond ever knew that she had an option to purchase. Indeed, even if this was the case, the House of Lords'[9] decision in *Midland Bank Trust Co v Green* (1981) makes it clear that mere knowledge by the purchaser of the existence of a third party's right in or over the land would not be enough to enable the right to be enforced. To recognise the validity of the sale to Desmond, even though it destroys Vanessa's right, is to uphold the policy of the LCA, not to subvert it.

(B) THE RESTRICTIVE COVENANTS

(I) THE COVENANT AGAINST INDUSTRY

If Desmond wishes to build an industrial estate, he must establish that the covenant against non-agricultural trade is not binding on him. This will be difficult. Desmond has obtained a clear search certificate and we know that under s 10(4) of the LCA 1972, an official search is conclusive. However, it is conclusive only 'according to its tenor' and, therefore, is conclusive only in respect of the names actually searched. Here, Desmond searched against 'Benny'. 'Benny' is not the estate owner and so the clear certificate is of no avail. In fact, Desmond will be bound by the correctly entered covenant under s 198(1) of the LPA 1925. In consequence, he cannot use the land for industrial purposes unless he can persuade the person entitled to enforce the covenant (Alfonso) to waive it, possibly in return for a sum of money.

(II) THE RESTRICTION ON BUILDING DWELLING HOUSES

In the original conveyance from Alfonso's father to Alfonso in 1935, there was a restrictive covenant against building more than one dwelling house. This had been registered against Alfonso's father and clearly was binding on Alfonso. The question arises whether it is also binding on Desmond, the successor in title to the burdened land.

Assuming that there was originally some land that could benefit from this covenant and that the benefit of it has passed in orthodox fashion to the person now seeking to enforce the covenant (that is, the rules in *Tulk v Moxhay* (1848) and s 78 LPA 1925), the question here involves consideration of the particular problems caused by the Land Charges Register being a name-based register. When Desmond buys the land, he must investigate root of title. Under s 23 of the LPA 1969, root of title is 15 years, and so Desmond can rely for good title on the conveyance by Alfonso to Benedict (his vendor) in 1970. This was the first conveyance, which was at least 15 years old. Seeing this document, Desmond will realise that he must search against Benedict and Alfonso – both are revealed in the root of title. Of course, he would not have discovered the restrictive covenant because it was registered against Alfonso's father, of whom Desmond knew nothing and, indeed, about

---

9   Not only does this show that the writer knew that the case was decided in the House of Lords, it also demonstrates the strength of the authority being relied on.

whom he could not have known. The covenant is hidden behind the root of title and was in effect 'undiscoverable'. However, because of s 198(1) of the LPA 1925, Desmond is deemed to have notice of all covenants correctly registered 'for all purposes' and it is binding on him. It may be enforced by the person entitled to the benefit of the covenant.

However, even though Desmond is bound by a registered, but essentially undiscoverable,[10] land charge, he may be entitled to compensation under s 25(1) of the LPA 1969 if he can fulfill the three conditions stipulated therein. First, it is clear that the transaction that caused him loss has occurred after the commencement of the Act (that is, after 1 January 1970). Second, we can infer that Desmond has no actual (that is, real) knowledge of the charge, as he would not otherwise have purchased the property and, third, the name of the estate owner against whom the charge was registered (Alfonso's father) was not comprised in any title document that Desmond would have seen when purchasing the property. He would be aware of Alfonso and Benedict only. Although, then, he cannot build if the person entitled decides to enforce the covenant, he can claim compensation.

Don't be tempted to

Do not ignore entirely matters of substantive law. For example, restrictive covenants are only enforceable if the relevant conditions of *Tulk v Moxhay* (1848) have been met and covenants may be discharged by application to the Lands Tribunal under s 84, LPA 1925. These may be discussed briefly BUT the main thrust of the question is about the mechanics of unregistered conveyancing.

Do not confuse a purchaser with a person who receives the unregistered title 'not for value'. Examples of non-purchasers include people who inherit under a will and who receive a gift. Non-purchasers and purchasers are treated differently in unregistered conveyancing.

Do not use the 'doctrine of notice' when talking about a land charge. The issue is one of registration, not whether the purchaser 'knows' of the right. Talk of 'equity's darling', even in unregistered conveyancing can be confusing.

QUESTION 7

Emily is the freeholder of a large house, title to which is unregistered. In 1988, Emily contracted to sell the land to Cedric. Even though Cedric did not register his rights, Cedric agreed in writing to sell the land to Nigel. Nigel has registered his rights against Cedric. However, none of these sales have taken place. Emily also agreed to allow her son, Joe, to occupy the basement while he was working as her cook. Joe, being a clever law student, has registered his right against his mother's name. Emily's neighbour, Mathew, has just

---

10 In problem questions as well as in essays you want to analyse the law, and where the rule causes significant difficulties in practice, comment on this can be woven into the answer.

bought three horses and asks whether he can make a path for walking access across Emily's back garden to reach his (Mathew's) field. Emily agrees, but only after they have agreed by deed that Mathew should pay £1,000 for this right. The next day, Mathew asks whether he can build a wider drive over part of Emily's garden in order to take his horse-trailer to the field. Emily agrees. Emily also grants a restrictive covenant in favour of Mathew saying she will not build in her garden. Mathew's solicitor registers this covenant against 'Mo'. In 1989, Emily sells the house to Peter who, using the same solicitors as Mathew, searches against 'Milly'. At all relevant times, all parcels of land were outside an area of compulsory first registration.

Peter wants to build in his garden and to stop Mathew's access. He asks Joe to leave and is faced with a claim by Nigel to purchase the land.

▶ **Discuss.**

How to Answer this Question

❖ the protection of legal interests in unregistered conveyancing;
❖ the various classes of land charge under the LCA and the effect of their registration and non-registration against transferees – *Midland Bank v Green* (1981);
❖ the limited residual role of the doctrine of notice;
❖ the circumstances in which a name-based system of registration of land charges causes problems.

Applying the Law

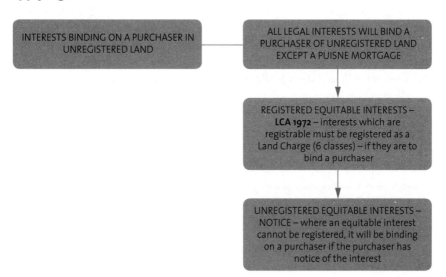

This diagram shows which interests are binding on a purchaser in unregistered land.

ANSWER --

This problem concerns the sale of unregistered land and the consequences for a purchaser of the existence of other people's rights over that land. In the normal course of events, the position is simple: Peter the purchaser will be bound by any legal rights over the land as 'legal rights bind the whole world' (save only the puisne mortgage) and also will be bound by equitable rights if they have been correctly registered under the LCA 1972. He must also be aware that certain equitable rights may bind him apart from registration if they fall into the category of unregistrable equitable rights the binding effect of which depends on the doctrine of notice.

(A) THE CONTRACTS OF SALE ENTERED INTO WITH CEDRIC, AND THE SUB-SALE TO NIGEL"

Clearly, both these contracts of sale (Emily/Cedric and Cedric/Nigel) amount to 'estate contracts' within s 2 of the LCA 1972. They are Class C(iv) land charges, each being 'a contract by an estate owner or by a person entitled at the date of the contract to have a legal estate conveyed to him to convey or create a legal estate'.[12] As such, they must be correctly registered against the name of the estate owner if they are to bind a subsequent purchaser of a legal estate for money or money's worth – s 4(6) of the LCA 1972. On these facts, there is no doubt that Cedric's contract with Emily is not binding on Peter. Peter is a purchaser of a legal estate for money and the charge is not registered. It is void: s 4(6) of the LCA 1972. However, what of Nigel's estate contract, for he has registered his rights? Unfortunately for Nigel, he is a victim of one of the flaws in the system of unregistered conveyancing and the registration of interests under the LCA 1972. Despite being registered, Nigel's estate contract is also *not* binding on Peter because, under s 3 of the LCA 1972, a land charge must be registered against 'the name of the estate owner whose estate is to be affected'. When Nigel entered into his contract for sale, he registered the land charge against Cedric, but Cedric was not then (nor has he ever been) the 'estate owner' whose estate is to be affected. That was, and still is, Emily. So, as in *Barrett v Hilton Developments* (1975), a sub-purchaser under an initial contract for sale that is not completed at the time of the sub-sale, loses their rights against a subsequent purchaser of the land (that is, someone to whom the land was sold in breach of the initial contract for sale) if they have registered the estate contract against their vendor instead of the estate owner. Of course, Nigel may have a remedy for breach of contract against Cedric, but even then, his remedy lies only in damages because Cedric does not have title to the land and so the contract cannot be specifically enforced.

....

11   The complicated facts of this problem are much more easily handled if the problem is split into sections.

12   As most universities allow statutory material in the exam, you will always be able to cite the exact wording of the statute where that will back-up your argument – but don't do it too often, or you will simply end up wasting time copying out material that the examiner knows you have in front of you.

(B) JOE

As we are told, Joe has registered his right to occupy his mother's flat and we know that correct registration of an equitable interest will bind a subsequent purchaser: s 198 of the **Law of Property Act 1925**. However, it is axiomatic that only those rights *capable* of binding third parties (that is, proprietary rights) can, if registered, bind third parties. Registration can never make binding something that is inherently incapable of being binding (unless specifically provided for by statute). On this ground, Peter may be able to require Joe to leave, as it appears that Joe has only a licence to occupy the basement. We are told that the occupation of the flat is granted while Joe acts as his mother's cook. The strong presumption on these facts is that this is a service occupancy, under which the occupation is for the better performance of the duties of the employee, as in *Norris v Checksfield* (1991), or maybe occupation born of family generosity or friendship (see *Gray v Taylor* (1998)). If either is true, the arrangement between Joe and his mother amounts to a licence and a licence is not an interest in land: *Ashburn Anstalt v Arnold* (1989); *Lloyd v Dugdale* (2002). It cannot, therefore, be binding on anybody, whether 'registered' or not. Of course, if it transpires that Joe has a lease, the registration is effective to bind Peter to the terms of that lease.

(C) MATHEW AND THE PATH

From the facts of the problem, we know that Emily allows Mathew access by foot over her garden. This might be a right of way – an easement – that is perfectly capable of binding subsequent purchasers of the land. We are told, further, that the right is created by deed. In such circumstances, it is reasonably clear that Emily has granted Mathew a legal easement to use the garden path (*Re Ellenborough Park* (1956)). In such circumstances, there is no doubt that Mathew may continue to use the path because, as is the rule in unregistered land, 'legal rights bind the whole world'. Peter is bound by the terms of the deed to allow Mathew access on foot.

(D) MATHEW AND THE DRIVEWAY

To some extent, this issue may be resolved as a matter of construction. If the right to use the path (above) encompassed the right to drive to the field, then the matter is as (c) above. However, this is unlikely, not only because the issue of the driveway arises after the easement over the path is created, but also because of the general rule in the law of easements that a specifically granted right of way does *not* include a more general right: *London and Suburban Land and Building Co v Carey* (1991). On this ground, Mathew has no claim on Peter. He had no easement against Emily, so nothing can be binding on Peter. There is, however, one possibility. It may be that Emily has generated an easement in respect of the driveway in Mathew's favour under the rules of proprietary estoppel. As we know, an assurance relied upon to detriment can give rise to a proprietary right by reason of estoppel (*Thorner v Majors* (2009)).[13] In fact, in *Ives v High* (1967), an equitable

---

13 Although many cases could be used as authority for this point, **Thorner** being both recent and of high
    authority is a good one to choose.

easement was created by just such a process. Here, it is arguable that Emily has encouraged Mathew to believe that he may use the driveway and also that Mathew had relied on that assurance to his detriment, viz, the construction costs. If this is an equitable easement by estoppel, does it bind Peter? In this respect, the general rule is that equitable interests must be registered as land charges to be binding in unregistered land: ss 3 and 4 of the LCA 1972. This is not registered. However, certain equitable rights – outside the statutory definition of land charges – are binding in unregistered land under the old doctrine of notice. According to Lord Denning in *Ives*, the equitable estoppel easement is just such a right. Although it is true that Class D(iii) land charges include 'equitable easements', Lord Denning suggests that this category refers to easements that would have been legal before 1925 but which because of the changes then made in the way rights could be created, can now be equitable only. Estoppel easements, by contrast, can never be legal, and so are outside Class D(iii). The consequence is that their validity is determined by the doctrine of notice and whether 'notice' exists is a question of fact. If, for example, the drive is under construction when Peter inspects the land, or the existence of the easement is obvious, or if Peter does not inspect at all but would have had notice had he done so, Peter will be bound, because he will have 'notice' of the equitable easement (*Hunt v Luck* (1902)).

(E) MATHEW AND THE RESTRICTIVE COVENANT

This particular aspect of the problem shows how difficult the system of land charge registration can be in practice given that it depends on name registration.[14] Clearly, Mathew has registered his charge against the wrong name and it would not, therefore, be binding against a purchaser who made a correct search (*Diligent Finance Ltd v Alleyene* (1972)). Likewise, Peter has searched against the wrong name and it is clear that he would have been bound had the charge been registered correctly: s 198 of the LPA 1925. In this case, therefore, we have two errors – a defective registration and a defective search. This was exactly the situation in *Oak Cooperative Building Society v Blackburn* (1968) and the solution must be a pragmatic one. According to that case, it seems that precedence will be given to either the registration or search according to which is in the most sensible version of the estate owner's correct name. In our case, this *might* be the registration (Mo instead of Emily). If that is the position, then Mathew's covenant is binding on Peter. If, however, we were to take the view that 'Milly' was a more sensible version of the true name, the search certificate would take priority and, having been clear, it would absolve Peter under s 10(4) of the LCA.

---

14 Where the facts of a problem question demonstrate a practical problem in the law this can be used as an easy way to introduce analysis into your answer.

Don't be tempted to

Do not ignore substantive questions of law. It is critical to identify the right claimed in order to see if it is legal or equitable and a land charge or not.

Do not apply the LCA 1972 until you have identified the claimant's right and have told the Examiner about any uncertainties in this regard: e.g. what are the consequences of having a lease or licence?

Do not forget s 25 of the LPA 1969 and the issue of hidden charges and compensation.

Do not confuse a purchaser of a legal estate for money or money's worth (for Class C(iv) or D land charges) with a purchaser of *any* estate for valuable consideration (for the other Classes).

QUESTION 8

The protection of equitable interests in unregistered land is far weaker than the protection given to equitable interests in registered title.

▶ Do you agree?

How to Answer this Question

❖ A brief outline of the systems of the LCA 1972 and the LRA 2002 for the protection of equitable interests.

❖ The differences in the registration procedures between the systems.

❖ The role of the search certificate and different priority periods.

❖ The protection for the rights of persons in actual occupation under the LRA 2002 in contrast with the LCA 1972.

❖ Loopholes in unregistered land – the continuing relevance of the doctrine of notice and questions of 'knowledge' in registered title.

Applying the Law

This diagram shows the rules that apply to equitable interests and their effect on purchasers in registered and unregistered land.

ANSWER

The machinery instituted by the LCA 1972 and the LRA 2002 was intended to achieve the same objective, albeit that the latter is far more wide-ranging than the former and has been developed even further since the original LRA 1925.[15] In essence, both of these systems are intended to bring stability to the system of conveyancing in England and Wales by protecting purchasers of land and owners of rights over that land. In addition, the LRA 2002 is designed to facilitate the introduction of e-conveyancing and to that end makes further modifications to the original LRA 1925 scheme for the protection of equitable interests.

The LRA 2002 achieves these objectives by ensuring that title to land and many interests over land are recorded or otherwise statutorily protected. In respect of equitable interests, the protection is twofold. First, equitable interests can be protected by substantive registration against the title register (by an Agreed or Unilateral Notice) or, second, they

---

15 Acknowledging from the outset that the aim of the two systems is largely the same is an interesting perspective from which to begin comparing them.

may qualify in limited circumstances as unregistered interests which override under one of the categories defined in Sched 1 (first registration) and Sched 3 (registered dispositions) to the LRA 2002. Indeed, it is the ability of an equitable interest to qualify as an 'overriding interest' that gives registered land its advantages over unregistered land. Thus, under para 2 of each of the Schedules (which are broadly similar in scope), an owner of such a right is protected so long as they are in occupation of the land to which the right relates (and are 'discoverable' in that occupation or the right is known about if Sched 3 applies) whether or not the claimant knew they had a right (as may be the case with many claims of estoppel under *Thorner v Majors* (2009)) or whether they knew that it should be registered. This is particularly useful if the equitable rights are acquired informally, as with estoppel or common intention constructive trusts (*Stack v Dowden* (2007); *Geary v Rankine* (2012)[16]).

Of course, problems with registered land do exist. The fact that an owner of certain equitable rights need not actually register their right in order to achieve priority poses something of a problem to a prospective purchaser. It undercuts somewhat the policy of land registration that all rights should be registered. However, the range of binding, but unregistered, rights has been reduced by the LRA 2002 and we must remember that the Schedules (particularly Sched 3, which applies when there is a material change in ownership of the land), seek to ensure that interests override only when they are (or should be) obvious to a purchaser conducting a reasonable inspection of the land. In other words, even with overriding interests, a sensible purchaser should not be unaware of binding overriding interests.

The protection of equitable interests in registered land also has problems in other respects, although these are relatively trivial after the changes made by the LRA 2002. Thus, the provisions dealing with the choice of method of protection can be complicated. For example, it is important to appreciate that in certain circumstances an Agreed Notice must be used, but that in others a Unilateral Notice is an option (s 34 of the LRA 2002). Both forms of notice give substantive protection to the interest, but an Agreed Notice may contain details which the right-holder would choose to keep private and so would have preferred a Unilateral Notice. Again, an Agreed Notice cannot be challenged after entry by the landowner who is bound by it, but there is a process by which a Unilateral Notice may be challenged (ss 35, 36 of the LRA 2002). Indeed, in some circumstances, a Notice (of either type) cannot be used at all (s 33 of the LRA 2002) and so the right-holder must utilise other provisions of the legislation (for example, enter a restriction, s 40 of the LRA 2002) or rely on Scheds 1 and 3 for protection as an overriding interest.[17]

....

16 There is an enormous range of cases that could be used here, but *Geary* in particular is a good choice because it shows an awareness of recent case law.

17 This section shows very good knowledge of the detail of the statutory provisions.

Of course, the LRA 2002 makes it clear that an equitable interest that does not qualify as an overriding interest or is not protected by an entry on the register loses its priority against a correctly registered purchaser of the title (s 29 of the LRA 2002). It is not yet clear what 'loss of priority' means, for while it certainly means that the right is unenforceable against the immediate purchaser, it is not clear whether the unprotected equitable interest is rendered unenforceable against only the particular purchaser or is 'void' for all purposes – see *Halifax v Popeck* (2009).[18] Be that as it may, it is clear that the purpose of the LRA 2002 is to ensure that as many interests as possible are registered – and therefore protected – and, as a corollary, that failure to protect through registration will cause loss of the right unless the limited provisions concerning overriding interests come into play. One such overriding interest – the right of a person in actual occupation – is a sensible and appropriate way to protect the valuable social and economic rights of people who have not (or cannot) register and the LRA 2002 does achieve a balance between these interests and that of a purchaser.

Perhaps, however, these are but small issues compared to those found when considering the protection of equitable interests in unregistered conveyancing. It is true that unregistered land also has a system of registration of equitable interests that is intended to give those interests the same degree of protection as would be available in registered land, but it is equally obvious that the LCA 1972 falls considerably short of this goal. In unregistered land, equitable interests can be divided into three broad categories. First, there are those equitable interests that are registrable as land charges. Land charges fall into six distinct categories: Classes A–F, the most important of which are Class C and Class D. These registrable land charges must be protected by entry on the Land Charges Register in order to bind a purchaser of the land they burden: s 4 of the LCA 1972. In the case of Classes A, B, C (except C(iv)) and F, an unregistered charge will be void against the purchaser for valuable consideration of any interest in the land, while Classes C(iv) and D will be void against the purchaser of a legal estate for money or money's worth. In short, as with registered land, registration means validity and non-registration means invalidity (*Midland Bank v Green* (1981)).

However, the system of land charges does suffer from one considerable defect: its lack of protection for persons with equitable interests who occupy land. In unregistered land, the fact of actual occupation of property does not, of itself, protect the equitable interest of the occupier. There is no equivalent of para 2 of Scheds 1 and 3 to the LRA 2002 as amply illustrated by *Hollington Brothers v Rhodes* (1951), in which an equitable lease was void against a purchaser for lack of registration as a Class C(iv) charge despite the occupation of the tenants. If this had been registered land, the purchaser would have been bound. It

---

18 The meaning of loss of priority is a highly complex question and there would not be time to go into it in detail in the exam in this question, but it is worth showing that you aware of the difficulty nonetheless even if there is no scope within the answer for resolving the difficulty.

is regrettable that equitable interests in unregistered land are not protected in this way (see Harpum [1990] CLJ 277 for further discussion).[19]

The second category of equitable interests in unregistered land is the 'family' interests which are overreachable as existing behind a trust of land. As with registered land, if there are two trustees of land or a trust corporation, there is nothing the equitable owners can do to prevent sale or to remain in occupation of the property against a purchaser (*City of London BS v Flegg* (1988); *Birmingham Midshires BS v Sabherwal* (2000)). However, if there is only one trustee, in registered land, the equitable interest may be overriding (*Boland* (1981)), whereas, in unregistered land, these equitable interests are not registrable (protectable) as land charges (s 2 of the LCA 1972) but can bind a purchaser only under the old doctrine of notice (*Kingsnorth v Tizard* (1986)). Although it will be rare that a purchaser does not have notice (for example, occupation will equal constructive notice of the equitable interest), it is undesirable that the inherently uncertain concept of notice should play a part in such a vital area as co-ownership of domestic property.

Indeed, it is not only with these equitable interests that notice is still relevant, for there is a third category of equitable interest within the scheme of unregistered land. These are equitable interests that either by design or by accident are outside the operation of LCA 1972. These are unregistrable (as land charges) equitable interests the validity of which against a purchaser rests on the doctrine of notice. They have no equivalent in registered land as the categories of overriding and registered protected interests are all-embracing (although the Schedules do mention the concept of the purchaser's 'knowledge'). Of course, some rights, such as leasehold covenants, cause few problems (although see *Dartstone v Cleveland* (1969)) and this is why they were deliberately omitted from the scheme of the LCA 1972. Indeed, equitable co-ownership would not have been a problem had the 'two-trustee' trust of land been the norm. However, such matters as estoppel easements (*Ives v High* (1967)), equitable rights of re-entry (*Shiloh Spinners v Harding* (1973)) and a tenant's right to remove fixtures at the end of an equitable lease (*Poster v Slough Estates* (1968)), which have emerged as unregistrable interests since 1925, can cause difficulties, as these cases show. The existence of these rights means that a purchaser cannot rely with total security on a search of the land charges register. There is always the possibility that an unregistrable but potentially binding equitable interest will exist that will affect the purchaser's title through the medium of notice. Such matters would not have been so important in practice had the LCA been replaced swiftly by full title registration, but only now is that coming to fruition.

Finally, there are some other differences in the application of the LRA 2002 and the LCA 1972 that can cause practical difficulties. An obvious one is the fact that the

---

19 Credit will always be given where an answer shows awareness of academic commentary.

LCA 1972 depends on a system of name registration. The problems that this gives rise to are well known, as in *Barrett v Hilton* (1975) (sub-sales), *Oak v Blackburn* (1968) (defective registration and defective searches) and *White v Bijou Mansions* (1937) (hidden charges). These are difficulties that do not arise under the LRA 2002 because the system is based on titles rather than names. Likewise, it should be noted that the priority periods conferred on a person are different under the Land Charges Acts and the Land Registration Acts (15 business days and 30 business days, respectively) and that, in unregistered land, it is the official search that is conclusive – s 10(4) of the LCA (even if a charge is actually registered) – whereas, in registered land, it is the register that is conclusive – *Parkash v Irani Finance* (1970) (even if the official search is clear).

The LCA and the LRA 2002 have both done much to introduce certainty into the whole area of the purchaser and the third party's equitable interest. There is no doubt, however, that, as far as protecting equitable interests is concerned, the LRA 2002 offers considerably more comfort than the LCA. Above all, the safety net provided by the concept of actual occupation under Scheds 1 and 3 to the LRA 2002 provides a considerable advantage over the unregistered land system, even after the reforms of the LRA 2002. Indeed, even for the purchaser, the registered land system has its attractions. Although the existence of overriding interests may compromise a title, most of these interests are reasonably ascertainable on inspection of the property. In any event, by introducing the concept of 'discoverable' actual occupation in Sched 3, the chances of a purchaser being bound by an interest of which they were not aware, or of which they should have been aware, are reduced considerably. If the right is not protected through 'discoverable' actual occupation, or is not known about (assuming actual occupation), it will not usually override in the first place. (There may, of course, be problems in defining when a purchaser 'knows' of a right.) Furthermore, at least the purchaser in registered land has the benefit of indemnity provisions in cases in which defective title registration causes loss. There is no such safety net in unregistered land. Moreover, the purchaser in unregistered land must always fear the existence of an unregistrable equitable interest that will be binding on him through the mechanism of constructive notice. These problems and the name-based registration system made the introduction of countrywide compulsory registration of title on 1 December 1990 very welcome. The widening of compulsory triggers under the LRA 2002, and the incentives for voluntary first registration found in the Act and Rules, necessarily provided further impetus.

Don't be tempted to

This is a question which requires you to contrast registered and unregistered conveyancing. Do not describe one in detail and add a few sentences about the other. You need some detail about each.

Do not think that everything in registered land is wonderful! There are difficulties, but the issue is whether registered title is an improvement on unregistered title.

Do not merely describe how the legislation works. You must reach a conclusion about its effectiveness in the light of the question actually asked.

Co-ownership

INTRODUCTION

The law relating to concurrent interests in property (co-ownership) has changed considerably in recent years. This is a result both of changes in the legislative framework surrounding co-ownership (that is, the **Trusts of Land and Appointment of Trustees Act (TOLATA) 1996**) and because the increased incidence of co-ownership has revealed many practical problems for which the 1925 legislation did not clearly provide. Many difficulties have been caused by social and economic changes in the pattern of property ownership, particularly of residential or domestic houses. The emergence of the *Pettitt v Pettitt* (1970), *Lloyds Bank v Rosset* (1989) and *Stack v Dowden* (2007) line of authority, whereby a partner or spouse can acquire an interest in a house that formally belongs to someone else, has done much to channel the law of co-ownership in new directions. Co-ownership is no longer confined to commercial or business situations but is virtually an expected attribute of domestic life. The **Law of Property Act (LPA) 1925**, which established the original scheme of co-ownership, was ill-equipped to deal with this shift of emphasis and the changes made by the **TOLATA** (which came into force on 1 January 1997) have done much to remedy deficiencies in the law, although many would argue that much remedial work had been done already by sensible judicial application of existing statute. As we shall see, where land (for example, a house) is deliberately co-owned, in the sense of having been conveyed originally to two or more people (for example, husband and wife, or an unmarried couple), few serious problems exist about who owns it, although there may be issues about the size of each owner's share. However, where co-ownership arises informally – usually in respect of land that was conveyed originally to only one person (for example, the man alone) – considerable practical problems can arise, and not even the new legislation has dealt with all of these. Importantly, the issues remain the same even if the co-owners are not in an intimate relationship. Thus, a number of recent cases concern parents and children and some arise in non-family relationships, such as the infirm and their live-in carers.

Checklist ✔

In this chapter, the various issues relating to co-ownership will be considered in turn and the student needs to have an understanding of the following issues. First, there is the question of the statutory machinery and the reasons for the 1925 reforms. This must be addressed in the light of the legislative changes made by the **TOLATA 1996** and the reasons for them. Without this background understanding, much of the law of co-ownership will make no sense. Second, there is the question of the actual share that each co-owner really has in co-owned land: problems of severance and the like. Third, there are important issues as to how implied co-ownership can arise or, in other words, when does single ownership turn into co-ownership without any formal documentation? This is the law of resulting and constructive trusts based on House of Lords' decisions in *Pettitt v Pettitt* (1970), *Lloyds Bank v Rosset* (1989) and, most importantly, *Stack v Dowden* (2007) and *Jones v Kernott* (2011). Fourth, there are issues about the consequences for purchasers when buying land subject to co-ownership, especially if that co-ownership has been informally created. In this context, 'purchasers' means mortgagees (banks, building societies, etc) who lend money and so 'purchase' an interest in the co-owned land as security. In an examination, it is quite common for at least two questions on co-ownership to appear on the examination paper and it is quite possible for one question (usually a problem question) to raise all four matters.

QUESTION 9

Analyse the reforms introduced by the **Trusts of Land and Appointment of Trustees Act 1996**. Does the 'trust of land' differ significantly from the 'trust for sale of land'?

How to Answer this Question

- ❖ Definition of 'co-owned land' and brief discussion of the types of co-ownership: joint tenancies and tenancies in common.
- ❖ Legal and equitable ownership distinguished.
- ❖ Analyse the statutory scheme prior to the **TOLATA 1996**: the trust for sale of land.
- ❖ Note the judicial application of the pre-**TOLATA** scheme and mitigation of some of its problems.
- ❖ Analyse the effect of the **TOLATA 1996**: the trust of land.

Applying the Law

This diagram shows the main differences between the trust for sale and the trust of land.

ANSWER

Concurrent ownership of land describes the situation in which two or more persons are entitled to the simultaneous enjoyment of property, whether that land is to be used for commercial or residential purposes. Prior to 1925, there were several forms of co-ownership: in other words, the legal relationship between the individual co-owners could take various forms. However, this caused numerous problems and one of the most important reforms of the **Law of Property Act 1925** was to limit the types of co-ownership that could be created thereafter. From 1926, land may be co-owned only under a joint tenancy or, alternatively, under a tenancy in common. In a joint tenancy, as far as the rest of the world is concerned, the individual persons are as one owner (although, of course, as between themselves they do have separate rights). So, there is but one title to the land and the individuals own that title jointly. Under a tenancy in common, although each tenant in common is in physical possession of the whole of the property in common with the others (that is, there is no partition), nevertheless they are regarded as having a distinct share in the land (for example, one third). Consequently, a tenancy in common is sometimes known as 'an undivided share in land'.

This simple picture is complicated by further reforms introduced by the **LPA 1925** that made crucial changes in the legal scheme for holding co-owned land.[1] Under the **1925 Act**, a legal tenancy in common cannot exist – **s1(6)** – thereby eliminating the prospect of multiple legal titles for co-owned land. So, after 1925, all legal titles to co-owned land must take the form of a joint tenancy even if the document of conveyance purports to create a tenancy in common. This means that, whenever land is conveyed to two or more persons for concurrent ownership, it is statutorily deemed to be conveyed to them as joint tenants of the legal title (**ss 34** and **36** of the **LPA**). Originally, this was a special form of joint tenancy because, under the **LPA 1925**, the statutory joint tenants were trustees for sale of the legal title. So, these joint tenant legal owners held the land on such trusts for the equitable owners (who may be themselves!) and, in equity, the co-ownership could take the form of either a joint tenancy or tenancy in common according to the circumstances existing when the land was conveyed. The mandatory imposition of a trust was, therefore, a device to ensure that all legal title to co-owned land is held as a joint tenancy whilst also ensuring that in equity (where, after all, the real interest lies) the co-owners can be either joint tenants or tenants in common as before. Frequently, the 'trustees' will be the same people as the 'beneficiaries', and there is no real change in their rights to use and enjoy the land.[2]

The overriding aim of the use of the trust was to make co-owned land more saleable while at the same time giving some degree of protection to the rights of all the co-owners, especially those not on the legal title. To this end, as noted, the original statutory trust was a trust for sale, meaning that the trustees were under a duty to sell the property unless they all agreed to postpone sale.[3] Of course, in the normal course of events, at least with residential property, the two trustees (for example, husband and wife) would obviously agree to postpone sale because they had purchased the property to live in it. Yet, if such agreement to postpone sale could not be maintained and the legal owners disagreed, an application could be made to the court under what was then s 30 of the **LPA 1925** for an order for sale. Such an order would be granted – because of the duty to sell – unless there were pressing contrary reasons relating to the purpose for which the land was originally acquired (*Jones v Challenger* (1961); *Banker's Trust v Namdar* (1997)). Moreover, when a sale did take place, the statutory mechanism revealed its considerable advantages. First, because the legal title must be held by way of joint tenancy, the purchaser need investigate only one title, irrespective of the number or type of co-owners

1   This is a good transition from the general introductory remarks about co-ownership into the more specific and complex issues that arise in relation to the **1925 Act**.

2   This paragraph explains the context of the trust of land and how it fits into the general co-ownership picture.

3   Tying the shape of the provisions to their original purpose is a good starting-off point for analysis.

that exist in equity. Second, s 34(2) of the LPA 1925 limited the number of potential legal co-owners (that is, trustees) to four – being the first four persons named in a conveyance. Thus, the purchaser only ever had a maximum of four people to deal with and, in most domestic situations, it will only be two. Third, because there must be a joint tenancy of the legal title, the right of survivorship applies. So, if one legal owner dies, no formal documents are needed to transfer title to the remaining legal owners. Fourth, if there are two or more legal owners (trustees), any purchaser automatically will receive the land free of the rights of all the equitable owners, be they equitable joint tenants or equitable tenants in common, because, by statute, a payment to two or more trustees overreaches the equitable interests existing behind the trust (ss 2 and 27 of the LPA 1925; City of London BS v Flegg (1988); State Bank of India v Sood (1997)). Of course, the equitable owners' rights are not destroyed; rather, they take effect in the purchase money paid by the purchaser, which is then held on trust by the trustees in the same way that they held the legal title to the property.

It should be apparent from this that the changes made by the 1925 Act greatly assisted the easy transfer of co-owned land, both by simplifying the conveyancing machinery and by protecting the purchaser through the device of overreaching. However, this original scheme was not without its problems. First, the equitable owners may have their rights transformed from rights over land to rights in money by action of the legal owners conducting an overreaching transaction. Second, as noted, the duty to sell, under the then trust for sale, meant that disputes between trustees (that is, legal owners) very often resulted in a court-ordered sale, even if one party wished to remain in the property. Third, in theory, the equitable owners' rights were regarded as interests in money, not land (because of the doctrine of conversion), and this could affect the rights of the equitable owners to require the legal owners to allow them into possession. This was mitigated somewhat by Bull v Bull (1955), but there were further problems in ordering a co-owner in possession to pay rent to the other if the latter were excluded, although, again, Re Petrou (1998) alleviated this (the court 'found' a general equitable power to order such a payment).[4]

To meet these difficulties, and generally to re-cast the scheme of co-ownership for the modern era, the Trusts of Land and Appointment of Trustees Act (TOLATA) 1996 was enacted based on Law Commission Report No 181. This came into force on 1 January 1997 and applies to virtually all co-ownership trusts. Its effect is, broadly, to ensure that the legal scheme of co-ownership accords with how co-owned land is owned in practice. However, many of the changes simply put into statutory form the pre-existing judicial gloss that had been placed on the original 1925 scheme.

First, and most importantly, existing trusts for sale of land become simple *trusts of land* and all future co-ownership trusts must operate under the trust of land scheme found in the

---

4   Showing the problems with the trust for sale gives a good background and direction to the discussion about the changes made by **TOLATA**.

TOLATA. The land remains held by trustees (still a maximum of four) on trust for the equitable owners, but the nature of the trust has changed. There is no longer a duty to sell the land so, in cases of dispute, it may well prove to be the case that courts do not feel such a compulsion to order a sale (see *Mortgage Corp v Shaire* (2001) but note the contrary in *Bank of Ireland Home Mortgages v Bell* (2001)).[5] This was undoubtedly a sensible reform and accords with the expectations of most co-owners, who would have been astonished (pre-TOLATA) to find that they had a duty to sell immediately they had purchased the land. Second, the doctrine of conversion is abolished, effective for all new and nearly all existing trusts of land (s3 of the TOLATA). So, no longer are the interests of the equitable owners regarded as interests in money rather than land. Although, de facto, this had been the position under the old trust for sale and so may not have great practical import (see, for example, *Williams and Glyn's Bank v Boland* (1981)), it is a welcome recognition of reality. Third, as under the original scheme, the trustees have all the powers of an absolute owner, but their ability to delegate such powers to an equitable owner is made explicit and the only non-delegable power is the trustees' role in overreaching (ss6–9 of the TOLATA). This may be useful in cases in which the equitable owner is not also a trustee but where the trustees are content to leave the everyday management of the land to the person in possession of it – the equitable owner. Fourth, the trustees of land must consult with the equitable owners, and give effect to their wishes in so far as is consistent with the purposes of the trust of land (s11 of the TOLATA) but, as under the old system, failure to consult (or to agree after consultation) does not appear to invalidate any dealings with the land by the trustees (see *Birmingham Midshires BS v Sabherwal* (2000)). More significantly, under the TOLATA 1996, the ability to make any of the trustees' powers subject to the consent of the beneficiaries is explicit. Granted, this occurs only if such a 'consent requirement' is found in the instrument creating the trust (s10 of the TOLATA) or if imposed by the court under an application under s14 of the TOLATA, but this may be a mechanism by which trustees may be controlled: for example, by placing a restriction on the registered title saying that the co-owned land cannot be dealt with by the trustees unless the consent of the equitable co-owners is obtained. Fifth, the TOLATA now formally recognises that the equitable owners have a right to occupy the property (s12), which can be modified subject to safeguards, including being made subject to an obligation to pay compensation to a non-possessing co-owner (s13). Again, this is formal confirmation of judicial developments prior to the TOLATA. Finally, again in similar fashion to the position under the original scheme, any person with an interest in the land can make an application to the court under s14 of the TOLATA for a variety or orders (replacing s30 of the LPA 1925) – for example, sale, no sale, override consent requirement, impose consent requirements. As before, there are special criteria specified for cases of bankruptcy (s15 of the TOLATA; s335A of the Insolvency Act 1986) and these largely mirror the position under the old scheme.

---

5   This quick reference to arguably conflicting case law shows that you are aware of the potential for the shift in attitude from trust for sale to trust of land to be less significant than the language of the statutes might suggest.

Clearly then, the fundamentals of the statutory co-ownership scheme under the **TOLATA 1996** are the same or similar as under the original **LPA** scheme.[6] There may be only joint tenancies of the legal estate, the legal owners are trustees and overreaching applies. In matters of detail, however, changes have been made. Some of these introduce new law (for example, no longer a duty to sell, no doctrine of conversion), while others give statutory recognition to principles previously validated by judicial decision alone (for example, a right to possession). All in all, the **TOLATA 1996** is a success.

Common Pitfalls X

This is not an essay asking you to repeat the provisions of **TOLATA 1996** – which, after all, is likely to be part of the material available to you in the examination. You must contrast the old law with the new, and so do not attempt such a question unless you are aware of the nature of the now defunct 'trust for sale' of land. Case law is vital as it illustrates both the problems pre-**TOLATA** and how judges interpreted away some of those difficulties.

QUESTION 10

In 2008, Tim and Tina decided to live together as an experiment before getting married. They purchased a semi-detached house, of registered land, in the centre of town with the aid of a 90 per cent mortgage from the Steady Building Society. The rest of the purchase price was provided by Tim out of his savings. The house was conveyed to Tim alone, as Tina does not have a full-time job. Tim had an excellent job in the construction industry and Tina had no need to work. She stayed at home from where she did occasional work as a dressmaker, the money from which she used to pay for holidays. In 2009, with the construction industry in decline, Tina's income was useful to help pay the mortgage and Tim often said that he did not know how they would meet their commitments if Tina gave up dressmaking. Later that year, however, Tim inherited enough money from his uncle to pay off the mortgage and the couple decided to get married, as Tina was now pregnant. They had a tropical wedding costing several thousand pounds but, on their return, they found that Tim's employer had gone into liquidation and he was unemployed. Despite the birth of their child, Tina took on more dressmaking to meet the mounting bills. Unfortunately, Tim's attempt to start his own business has failed and he owes the bank several thousand pounds. He is now bankrupt and his trustee in bankruptcy is pressing for the house to be sold.

▶ Advise Tina.

How to Answer this Question

❖   A résumé of the statutory machinery of co-ownership; in particular the trust of land under **TOLATA 1996** – ss 34 and 36 of the **Law of Property Act 1925**, as amended, and ss 4 and 5 of the **TOLATA 1996**.

---

6   The provisions may be the same, but the philosophy behind them is different. Has this difference been overplayed, underplayed etc in the case law?

- ❖ Analysis of the acquisition of beneficial ownership – *Stack v Dowden* (2007); *Abbott v Abbott* (2007); *Fowler v Barron* (2008); *Jones v Kernott* (2011).
- ❖ The sale of co-owned property – s 14 of the **TOLATA**.
- ❖ **Insolvency Act 1986**, as amended by the **TOLATA**.

Applying the Law

This diagram demonstrates how to find an implied trust in a domestic homes context.

ANSWER

Much depends in this case on whether Tina owns a share of the house or, in other words, whether she has any equitable interest in it. If Tina can establish that she has an 'ownership interest' in the property, she may (although it is not by any means certain) be able to resist the application of her husband's trustee in bankruptcy for sale of the property. If Tina has no interest in the property, her only hope would be to show that she had taken advantage of s 30 of the **Family Law Act 1996**. This gives non-owning spouses a right of occupation against their partner, which, if registered, can bind subsequent purchasers of the property. Although Tina clearly has such a right, there is no evidence that she has entered it (by way of an agreed notice) on the registered title. In any event, if such a right is registered, a trustee in bankruptcy can apply for an order for sale to defeat such right under s 336(2) of the **Insolvency Act 1986** and the position would be very similar to that discussed below in respect of sale if she does have an equitable interest.

Does Tina have an interest in the property? When the property is purchased, it is conveyed into the sole name of Tim. The purchase is by mortgage and by cash deposit. Tim pays the entire cash deposit and, because he is to be the sole legal owner of the property, the mortgage is made with him. Title is registered in his name alone and there is no express declaration of trust in writing in favour of Tina.[7] Clearly, therefore, at the time of purchase, Tim is owner of the property both at law and in equity. There is no co-ownership – express or implied – and there is no trust of land. In such circumstances, if Tina is to establish any interest at all, she must fall back on a line of authority stemming from the House of Lords' landmark decision in *Pettitt v Pettitt* (1970) and now remodeled by *Stack v Dowden* (2007) and the recent decision in the Supreme Court in *Jones v Kernott* (2011).

The *Pettitt* case, and a whole range of decisions following it (for example, *Lloyds Bank v Rosset* (1989), *Stack*, *Abbott v Abbott* (2007), *Kernott* (2011)), have established that it is possible for a non-legal owner of property (that is, Tina) to claim an equitable ownership interest in someone else's property. The principles are not limited to situations in which a couple is married and, indeed, there need be no personal relationship between the parties. These rules are the application of traditional property law concepts to new situations. The basic principle flowing from *Pettitt* and a similar House of Lords' decision in *Gissing v Gissing* (1971) is that a person may claim an equitable interest in property belonging to another if they can establish a common intention that this was to be the case. This may either be by way of resulting trust – based on contributions to the purchase price at the time of purchase, as in *Curley v Parkes* (2004) and *Laskar v Laskar* (2008) – or by constructive trust – based upon inequitable conduct and detrimental reliance, as in *Grant v Edwards* (1986) and *Abbott v Abbott*.

---

7   If there were such a trust, there would be no room for an implied trust, *Goodman v Gallant* and *Roy v Roy*.

The ability of a non-legal owner to claim of another person's land has always been controversial and the law has ebbed and flowed in the way it views such claims. The House of Lords' decision in *Lloyds Bank v Rosset* placed the law on a firm, but relatively narrow, footing whereby a person could establish an interest in the property by one of two routes. This has now been supplemented by a third route, expounded in *Stack v Dowden* and confirmed in *Kernott*.[8] First, the claimant could show that the legal owner had made an express promise to her that she should have an interest and that she has relied on that promise to her detriment, as in *Eves* (1975), *Grant v Edwards* and *Babic v Thompson* (1998).[9] Such an interest arises under a constructive trust, but it seems that, on the facts, Tina cannot establish such a claim. It is doubtful whether Tim's words of gratitude about the value of her dressmaking count for this purpose. There is no oral promise that she should have an interest. Second, the claimant may establish an interest if she contributes directly to the purchase price of the house. If Tina contributed at the time of purchase, the size of her interest will be in proportion to her payments (probably a resulting trust see *Curley v Parkes*, but note that *Kernott* suggests that resulting trusts are inappropriate in the domestic homes context) or, if contributions were later, the share can be equivalent to the share she agreed with Tim that she should get as a result of making the payments, or even that which is fair in the circumstances (*Crossley v Crossley* (2005); *Oxley v Hiscock* (2004)). Does she have an interest by this 'payment' route?

Lord Bridge[10] in *Rosset* accepts that such an interest can arise through mortgage repayments (being a referable contribution to the purchase price) and we are told that Tina does make these payments. Tina's payments towards holidays would not count for this purpose, although that is immaterial in view of her other financial contributions. As noted, the court now appears to be able to quantify this 'payment interest' by either the traditional route of awarding a proportional share in the property (see, for example, the discussion in *Drake v Whipp* (1995)) or, on the basis that the parties had a shared intention as to the size of the claimant's interest (or what is fair absent that intention), the payments being the trigger for it (*Cooke* (1980); *Oxley*). In order to quantify Tina's share (which may well be important if the property is sold), we would need to know whether she and Tim had ever discussed the question of share of ownership. If they have not, the court will follow *Jones v Kernott* and take a holistic approach to quantification which takes account of all the dealings with the property and which can rely on an imputed, as well as an implied, intention. This would be by reason of a constructive trust (based on common intention) because the payments were made after initial acquisition of the property.

---

8 Highlighting the history of a set of case law principles helps to put them into context.

9 In this context, it is tempting to rely on the main cases but putting in some of the less well-known or older cases will show a breadth of knowledge.

10 Mentioning the name of the judge gives off a good impression.

However, even if Tina is unsuccessful by either of these two 'traditional' routes, she may well be able to rely on *Stack v Dowden* and *Jones v Kernott*, which together have expanded the law away from the relatively narrow approach of *Rosset*. According to the Supreme Court in *Jones v Kernott*, a person may establish a common intention, sufficient to justify an interest by means of a constructive trust, on the basis of the parties' entire course of dealings with each other, in relation to the property. In other words, even if there is no express promise (route 1), and no payment towards the purchase price (route 2),[11] a constructive trust can arise if the parties entire relationship to each other and the way they regard the property indicates a common intention as to ownership. This is now the third route to an interest under a constructive trust. It is important to remember however that although imputation is permitted at the quantification stage of the process, it is not permitted at this, the 'acquisition' stage. The parties must show a genuine, if implied, intention that their equitable interests would not be the same as the legal interest. This, clearly, is a more flexible approach. Of course, there must still be detrimental reliance, but this too can be raised from the facts of the parties' relationship. Once again, the size of the share can then be quantified by taking the holistic approach, relying on an imputed intention if necessary.

If Tina can establish her interest in the above fashion, it is clear that the property is now co-owned. According to *Bull v Bull* (1955) and s1 of the **TOLATA 1996**, this means that an implied statutory trust of land comes into existence: Tim, the legal owner, holds the property on trust for himself and Tina as tenants in common in the shares determined and subject to the statutory machinery of the **TOLATA 1996**. This gives Tina some measure of protection. There is, of course, only one trustee of land and, therefore, no possibility of overreaching (*Williams and Glyn's Bank v Boland* (1981)). Any purchaser may well be bound by Tina's interest under the normal rules of registered conveyancing – s29 of the **LRA 2002**. If Tina is in discoverable actual occupation of the property at the time of any sale to the purchaser (*Abbey National BS v Cann* (1991)), or being in occupation the purchaser knows of her interest, she will have an overriding interest under **para 2** of **Sched 3** to the **LRA 2002** in similar fashion to *Williams and Glyn's Bank v Boland*.

However, that is not the end of Tina's difficulties. When Tim becomes bankrupt, the trustee in bankruptcy becomes vested with all his property, including the legal title to the house. As we have just established, the trustee cannot sell the property immediately, as Tina's interest would be binding on a purchaser. In such circumstances, the trustee will apply to the court for an order for sale under s14 of the **TOLATA 1996**. Under this section, 'any person who . . . has an interest in property subject to a trust of land' (which includes a trustee in bankruptcy) may apply for an order for sale. If such an application is made, the court will have to balance the claims of the creditors against the claims of Tina (assuming

---

11   Labelling the routes in this way avoids spending too much time explaining the same factual situation multiple times.

she resists the sale) and s 335A of the Insolvency Act 1986 (inserted in that Act by Sched 3 to the TOLATA) provides a list of the criteria that the court should consider (as required by s 15(4) of the TOLATA). These include her interests and any children, but, in any event, the court will permit a postponement of sale for only one year unless there are 'exceptional circumstances' (s 335A(3) of the Insolvency Act 1986 and see *Nicholls v Lan* (2006)). In our case, much might turn on the size of Tina's interest. If it is small (perhaps based directly on the proportion of the purchase price she paid through mortgage instalments[12]), the court might refuse to postpone sale at all. If postponement is ordered – perhaps to give Tina a chance to find another home irrespective of the size of her share – one year is the maximum she can hope for. There are no exceptional circumstances here (see, for example, a refusal to postpone in *Re Harrington* (2001) and note *Barca v Mears* (2004) on how the court is to approach exceptional circumstances in a way that is compatible with human rights). In short, then, Tina will have an interest, but a court is likely to order sale in due course. Of course, Tina's interest will not be subject to that of Tim's creditors and will be satisfied out of the proceeds of sale before those proceeds are distributed. As above, the precise amount will depend on how the court quantifies her share.

QUESTION 11

Carrie, a rich widow, is the registered proprietor of a large house in London. Recently, at a friend's party, she met Simon, an 18-year-old student, and, after a passionate affair of a few weeks, she invited him to live with her. Simon accepted. Being a proud man, Simon insisted that he share the expenses of running the house and, over the next few months, he paid the occasional bill and even paid for the cost of having the house redecorated both inside and out. Simon was a little concerned that, because of the difference in age, Carrie would soon tire of his charms and he repeatedly asked her about the future. Last year, after one particularly splendid dinner together, Carrie told Simon: 'What's mine is yours!' Next day, thinking that his future was secure, Simon spent his life savings on a sports car. Unfortunately, unknown to Simon, Carrie was paying school fees for her five children and, two months ago, she had to take out a mortgage with the Harrow Building Society to cover next year's fees. The building society visited the property when Simon was on a field trip abroad and Carrie executed the mortgage that day. The building society registered its charge at the Land Registry the day after he returned.

Carrie has now met someone more her own age and has emigrated to Australia. The building society is seeking possession of the property in order to realise its security.

▶ Advise Simon.

How would your answer differ if title to the property had been unregistered?

12 In a question which does not give precise figures on financial contributions it will often by very difficult, if not impossible, to estimate the size of an individual's share. The examiners are likely to be reasonably happy with any sensible suggestions, as long as you explain where the estimate has come from.

How to Answer this Question

❖ Acquisition of beneficial interests under resulting and constructive trusts.

❖ The implied trust of land: *Bull v Bull* (1955).

❖ Analysis of the overreaching machinery: ss 2 and 27 of the **Law of Property Act 1925**.

❖ Registered land: one trustee; overriding interests; meaning of discoverable actual occupation; time of occupation.

❖ Unregistered land: one trustee and the doctrine of notice.

Applying the Law

This diagram shows how the rules relating to implied trusts operate in relation to third parties.

ANSWER

This question concerns the acquisition of beneficial interests in property belonging to another and the effects of such ownership, if any, on a third-party purchaser – here, a mortgagee. In concrete terms, this problems revolves around a contest between the building society, who have an interest in the property and a power of sale under s 101 of the LPA 1925 by virtue of their duly registered mortgage, and Simon who must claim, if he is to have any prospect of remaining in the property, an equitable right of ownership to it. The crucial questions are, therefore, whether Simon has such an interest and, if so, whether the building society is bound by that interest. If the building society is bound, there is no prospect of a sale of the property with vacant possession unless an application is made to the court under s 14 of the TOLATA 1996 (see *Bank of Baroda v Dhillon* (1998); *Bank of Ireland v Bell* (2001)) and, in any event, Simon would be entitled to the monetary equivalent of his interest before the building society could be paid.

If Simon is to have an interest in the property, it is clear that this must be established under the principles elaborated in *Pettitt v Pettitt* (1970) and codified by the House of Lords in *Lloyds Bank v Rosset* (1989) and *Stack v Dowden* (2007) and by the Supreme Court in *Jones v Kernott* (2011). In our case, there is no express conveyance to Simon as owner and no express written declaration of trust by Carrie in his favour.[13] His only hope is the law of constructive or resulting trusts. In this respect, *Stack* and *Kernott* make it clear that a person claiming an equitable interest in property, legal title to which is vested in another, must be able to show either some contribution to the purchase price of the property at the time of purchase – so as to raise a resulting trust in their favour (see *Laskar v Laskar* (2008) – although *Stack* and *Kernott* cast doubt on the appropriateness of using resulting trusts in the domestic homes context[14]) – or must prove some express oral assurance that they were to have an interest in the property, or a common intention implied from later contributions to the cost of acquisition, or a common intention derived from the parties' whole course of dealings with each other, provided in each case that there is detrimental reliance. On the facts as stated, it seems clear that when Simon met Carrie, Carrie was sole legal owner of the property and that it was not subject to any charge by way of 'purchase mortgage'. In other words, the property was hers, paid for and complete. It follows that Simon cannot pursue the resulting trust path to an equitable interest – there is no purchase price to which he can make a contribution, not even monthly mortgage payments. Moreover, even if there were an outstanding 'purchase mortgage', Simon's contributions to the cost of running the house cannot be considered, for they are part of the costs of sharing property, not of acquiring it – *per* Lord Bridge in *Rosset* and Court of Appeal in *Burns v Burns* (1984). The payment of the decoration expenses might have been relevant if the couple had been married: there is every chance that Simon could have relied on s 37 of the Matrimonial Proceedings and Property Act 1970 to establish a beneficial interest by way of improvement expenditure. However, this is not the case, and it is doubtful whether contributing to the costs of improving a house that is already purchased can, without any agreement, give rise to an equitable interest (*Bank of India v Mody* (1998)).

---

13   Where time permits, explain why the existence of an express trust means that there is 'no room' for an implied trust – *Goodman v Gallant* (1986).

14   Why might the resulting trust not be appropriate here?

It would seem, then, that Simon should rely on the doctrine of constructive trusts: he must plead an express promise plus detrimental reliance or rely on the parties' whole course of dealings with each other. Once again, are the costs of decorating the house relevant here? If Simon can show that he spent his money on improvements because there was a promise or agreement that he should part-own the property, then a case is clearly made out. Once again, however, there is no evidence to support this and such statements that Carrie does make are made *after* Simon spends money. Such expenditure could not have been made as a result of those particular statements. There is no reliance.

Eventually, Carrie does make a promise of sorts to Simon and it is a matter of construction whether this is sufficient for the *Stack* and *Kernott* principles. First, a problem exists with intention: does Carrie, after a romantic dinner, intend by her words 'what's mine is yours' that Simon should have an interest in the property? Although it is not entirely clear, dicta in *Gissing v Gissing* (1971) suggest that the oral promise (the 'common intention') must be real rather than imagined, and it is questionable whether Carrie's statement meets this criterion. On the other hand, no case has denied that, if a reasonable person would have believed that the property owner was making a statement about ownership of the property, the particular promisee is entitled to rely on it even if this was not the actual intention of the property owner (see, for example, *Eves v Eves* (1975)). In our case, we do not know what Carrie actually meant, but a reasonable person in Simon's position might well conclude that this was an assurance about the ownership of the shared home. This would also fit in with the underlying reasoning in *Stack* approved in *Kernott*, which suggests that a court should not be too formulaic in seeking to find a common intention. On this ground, Simon has a case that the relevant promise was made and it seems clear from the facts that he relied on that promise when he spent his life savings on the sports car. There is here, however, a further problem. Certain cases, such as *Gissing* and *Christian v Christian* (1981) suggest that the detriment suffered as a result of the promise must be related to the property in question; for example, spending money on improvements. However, another view is that, so long as the detriment was referable to the promise – that is, was caused by it – it does not matter that the actual detriment suffered was not property-related. If the reason why an interest arises under a constructive trust is that a promise has been made and relied on (not that the property has been paid for), it should make no difference what form that detriment takes: whether it is property-related or not, the promisee has still spent money that they would not otherwise have done – a view again supported by *Stack*. On this view, Simon has an equitable interest in the property if he can show that his lavish expenditure was a direct result of Carrie's promise. The size of his interest seems to lie in the discretion of the court (*Oxley v Hiscock* (2004)) unless there is express agreement as to share (*Crossley v Crossley* (2005)), but it may well be substantial, given the content of the promise made to him and the level of his detriment. Indeed, as the Supreme Court has made clear in *Kernott* the court is entitled to impute an intention (where it is not possible to imply one) with regard to quantification of the relevant share, and this may well take account of Carrie's leaving the property (as was relevant in *Kernott* itself).

Assuming, then, that Simon does have an interest, what is his position vis-à-vis the purchaser-mortgagee? Clearly, when Harrow advanced the money, it did not pay it to two trustees of land: Carrie is the single trustee and, therefore, there can be no overreaching.[15] The statutory conditions of s 2 of the LPA are not met. This makes the building society potentially subject to Simon's interest under s 29 of the LRA 2002 if he can establish an interest which overrides under Sched 3, para 2 to that Act.[16] First, Simon must have an interest in land and this we have just established. Second, he must be in discoverable actual occupation or, if not in occupation, his interest must be known to the purchaser. Absence from the land does not destroy actual occupation (*Chhokkar v Chhokkar* (1984)), but it is a moot point where this occupation is 'discoverable' – although if 'discoverable', he does do not actually have to be 'discovered' (*Thompson v Foy* (2009)). On the facts, given that the house is his regular home, we might expect there to be some evidence of his existence that would mean his occupation would have been discoverable to a reasonably prudent purchaser making the usual enquiries – see a similar view taken in *Link Lending v Bustard* (2010) in respect of a person who was temporarily absent. However, we cannot be sure, and if his occupation is deemed undiscoverable, he would not qualify for an overriding interest under Sched 3 to the 2002 Act – a change from the position under the LRA 1925. (Note, there is no evidence that the building society knew of his interest within Sched 3, para 2.) Third, Simon must be in actual occupation at the relevant time and, following *Abbey National BS v Cann* (1991), it is likely that the crucial time under the LRA 2002 is the moment of creation of the mortgage or time of purchase (confirmed in *Barclays Bank v Zaroovabli* (1997)).[17] Thus, in our case, it is irrelevant that Simon returns before the charge is registered; we must determine whether he was in discoverable actual occupation at the time the charge was created. On the above facts, this seems to be established.

To conclude, then, Simon has an interest under a constructive trust (possibly of one half, as this is what he seems to have been promised) and he was in discoverable actual occupation of the property at the time the mortgage was made. Thus, under Sched 3, para 2 to the LRA 2002, he has an overriding interest against the building society and takes priority over it: s 29 of the LRA 2002. It cannot obtain vacant possession under its normal powers as mortgagee and must apply to the court under s 14 of the TOLATA for an order for sale. Even if this is granted, it is unlikely to recover its money in full as Simon's interest takes priority and he must first be paid out of any proceeds of sale. The building society might pursue Carrie personally for the mortgage debt and make her

---

15 Remember in problem questions like this your answer should not end with establishing that Simon has an interest in the house – you must demonstrate the consequences of this conclusion for the parties.

16 A lot of students struggle with the interaction between overreaching and overriding but it is a fundamental issue and you will want to demonstrate that you have clearly understood it.

17 The timing of actual occupation has been the subject of much discussion, both judicial and academic, and so you can bring in much analysis when discussing this issue.

bankrupt (*Alliance & Leicester v Slayford* (2001)). This could trigger a sale by the trustee in bankruptcy, but at least Simon would be paid his share before any settlement for the creditors.

Finally, if the land had been unregistered, Simon would still have acquired an equitable interest as the principles are identical, but whether that interest would have bound the building society would have depended on whether it had had notice of it at the time the mortgage was created. In unregistered land, these types of equitable interest cannot be registered as land charges (s 2 of the **LCA 1972**) and, thus, their enforceability depends on the doctrine of notice. Following *Kingsnorth v Tizard* (1986), it is highly likely that Simon's occupation of the property (that is, his presence in a general sense even though he was temporarily absent) would have given the building society notice of his interest and, therefore, it would be bound accordingly.

Aim Higher ★

The nature of discoverable actual occupation has been discussed at length in *Thompson v Foy* (2009) and *Link Lending v Bustard* (2010) and is the first consideration of the **2002 Act**. The very best answers would deal in more detail with this and also an issue raised in *Thompson* – the time at which a person must be in actual occupation. Contrary to the prevailing view, Lewison J in *Thompson* suggests (obiter) that a person might have to be in actual occupation at the time of registration of the purchaser's title as well as the earlier time when the sale was completed. This issue will, however, disappear under e-conveyancing.

QUESTION 12

'Far from clarifying the position of co-habiting couples and their proprietary interests, the decisions in *Stack v Dowden* (2007) and *Jones v Kernott* (2011) have served only to introduce more discretion and increase uncertainty.'

▶ Discuss.

How to Answer this Question

❖   The background to the decisions in *Stack* and *Kernott*.
❖   *Lloyds Bank v Rossett* – restrictive approach.
❖   Sole names and joint names cases.
❖   Role of imputation.
❖   Quantification and variation over time.

Applying the Law

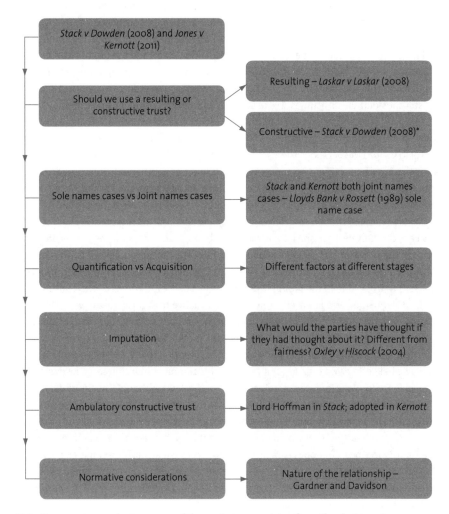

This diagram demonstrates many of the main issues arising from the decisions in Stack v Dowden *and* Jones v Kernott.

ANSWER

The House of Lords and then the Supreme Court have recently taken two opportunities to analyse the law relating to co-ownership in the context of co-habiting but unmarried couples. The decisions have proved not only controversial, but also in a sense revolutionary. Crucially also the decision in *Stack v Dowden* prompted the Law Commission to consider the matter. The legislative proposals have not thus far been taken forward, but it is important not only to consider *Jones v Kernott* in the context of

Stack v Dowden, but also in the light of the concerns of the Law Commission and the many academics who have commented on *Stack* and *Kernott*. In order to look at the levels of uncertainty that persist after *Kernott*, it is necessary to look a certain key areas of the decisions – the importance of joint versus sole names distinction; the role of imputation; and the correct approach to be taken at the acquisition stage and the quantification stage. The cases without doubt do provide some certainty with regard to the preferred approach to this question that the highest court wishes lower courts to take, but there are still considerable difficulties. There is much, in short that remains uncertain.

Before looking into these clarifications and remaining uncertainties however, it is perhaps useful to go into the decisions themselves in more detail.[18] In *Stack v Dowden*, the parties were an unmarried co-habiting couple who had children together but who through the entirety of their relationship had kept their finances largely separate. The legal title to the property was registered in their joint names, but there was no express declaration of trust. Ms Dowden argued that on sale of the property she was entitled to a greater share of the proceeds of that sale since she had provided the bulk of the money for the house, both in terms of the provision of the deposit, and in terms of the mortgage payments. The court considered that in order to demonstrate this, Ms Dowden, unable to rely on the principles of resulting trusts due to their inappropriateness in a domestic homes context (although see Lord Neuberger), would have to rely on a constructive trust arising in response to a common intention. The first step in so-doing, in the language of the court, is to establish that the 'presumption that equity follows the law' is rebutted. In this a joint names case this meant establishing that there was a common intention that the equitable interests would be held otherwise than as joint tenants. This common intention could be express or implied (or potentially imputed, as will be discussed below). Although the Court did not give comprehensive guidance as to when such an intention could be implied, it seems that in this case the separate finances of the parties was sufficient evidence to constitute the 'unusual circumstances' that would demonstrate the existence of such a common intention. Once the intention is established at the so-called acquisition stage, the next step was to quantify the parties' shares. Lady Hale suggested that a court should take a holistic approach when quantifying the share and should take account of all the parties' dealings with the property, as well as the nature of their relationship. In *Stack* this calculation resulting in Ms Dowden being awarded an equitable share of 65% – the same result in fact as if a resulting trust analysis had been adopted.

Jones v Kernott was also a joint names case. Here the parties had also lived together as an unmarried couple but had separated some time before Ms Jones sought a declaration as to the size of her share under **Section 14 TOLATA 1996**. Ms Jones, like Ms Dowden, was claiming that she was entitled to more than the 50% of the proceeds of sale that the joint

---

18 This approach of 'before *x*' is a good way to situate your discussion of the background context to your analysis into the overall structure of the essay.

names would suggest she would receive. Mr Kernott had left the house some 12 years previously and in that time Ms Jones had paid for the mortgage, bills and general upkeep of the house. The court was thus grappling with the question as to whether this change in the parties' circumstances from the time of purchase should be taken into consideration when assessing the parties' shares, and in what way. They were also asked to clarify the ruling in *Stack v Dowden* in the face of much criticism of their earlier decision, and to provide information in particular in the role of imputation in this area. The court, far from moving away from their earlier decision, expressly supported the approach in *Stack* although acknowledged that some areas of the judgment could have been clearer. In terms of the result, the court concluded that the conduct of the parties after the split was sufficient to 'rebut the presumption' such that Ms Jones could acquire a larger share in the property than 50%. This was based on an implied common intention. From here the court would quantify the parties' shares, taking a holistic approach bearing in mind all their dealings with the property. This process led them to conclude that Ms Jones was entitled to a 90% share of the proceeds of sale.

The decisions then have certainly moved away from the restrictive approach seen in *Lloyds Bank v Rossett* (1990) and have clarified that resulting trusts are no longer to be relied on in this area (see *Laskar v Laskar* (2008)). There are still some areas of potential uncertainty however. The difference of approach (if any) that ought to be taken in sole names cases versus joint names cases is not clear; the role of imputation is left in some doubt; and we finally are left wondering about the difference in treatment between the acquisition and the quantification stage and the rationale and application of this. There is no doubt that in terms of certainty and clarify we are further on after *Kernott* than we were in the immediate aftermath of *Stack*, but there are still some areas where further clarity could be provided.[19]

The primary area of uncertainty remaining is the position in sole names cases although some assistance on this matter can now be derived from the Court of Appeal decision in *Geary v Rankine* (2012) (but see *Garwood v Ambrose* (2012)). Both *Stack* and *Kernott* were joint names cases, and no consistent approach emerged from these cases as to how we are to treat sole names cases. Certainly there are suggestions that although the starting point in sole names cases would inevitably be different, that the overall approach should be the same. We are still to presume that the party who is not registered title holder is not entitled to an equitable share in the property unless there is a common intention to that effect. The difficultly is that the starting point is not just different, it is quite radically different, since the acquisition stage has much more important consequences for both parties than it does in joint names cases, and it is not clear whether, for example, a more

. . . .

19 It is important to take a balanced approach in questions like this because it is very difficult to argue that any case could leave all matters completed settled or totally in doubt and a one-sided argument is unlikely to be convincing.

stringent test will be applied, and indeed whether only the methods outlined in *Rossett* will be available to those who are attempting to argue that they have any interests in the property at all, not simply that they are entitled to more.

Furthermore, the role of imputation after *Stack* was in considerable doubt, and due to the disagreements between the judges[20] in *Kernott* we cannot say that we are necessarily much further on. In *Stack* Lady Hale suggested that the common intention could be express, implied or imputed, but it seems now that she was referring only to the quantification stage, and not the acquisition stage. In *Kernott* the majority suggested that indeed although imputation could be used when assessing the parties' difference proportions, it could not be used to assign to the parties an intention that their equitable title would be different from the legal title in the absence of a genuine intention. The difficulty with this is that the line between imputation and implication is a very fine one, and in reality more guidance will be required from the higher courts before we are confident where this boundary lies. More than this though there is an inherent and unavoidable uncertainty in the holistic approach to quantifying the share and imputation generally which lies in the unpredictability of the result. We may well be certain that the Court will impute an intention where there is no express or implied intention as to share, but we cannot know beyond that what the court is likely to feel is an appropriate allocation of the equitable title since we cannot know what makes up the policies behind the 'holistic approach' without more.

Not only is there uncertainty about the meaning and role of imputation within the holistic approach, it is also unclear as to how this concept can be reconciled with the previous case law, *Gissing v Gissing* (1971) and *Pettitt v Pettitt* (1970) in particular. These House of Lords decisions were not expressly overruled in *Stack* or *Kernott* but they explicitly prohibited imputation of intentions. Thus when imputation and fairness began to be used in the Court of Appeal (*Oxley v Hiscock* (2004)), there was an expectation that the House of Lords would use the opportunity presented by *Stack* to re-assert the orthodox position, relying, where appropriate on resulting trusts based on financial contribution to purchase, and to expressed common intentions in line with *Rossett*. This did not happen however and there is disquiet as to the interventionist stance taken by the judiciary. The decisions may well solve the problem of co-habiting couples failing to discuss their proprietary entitlements, a problem which the Law Commission recognises does indeed require a solution, but whether it is right for the higher courts to intervene in this way is another question altogether. This disquiet cannot help but add to the uncertainty surrounding these cases.

We must ask also whether we are more certain as to the distinction between the quantification and acquisition stages in general. We know two things for sure: firstly,

---

20 Not only does the highlighting of the disagreement in the court bolster the argument as to certainty here, it also demonstrates that you have read the case and are aware of the judgments themselves, rather than simply a summary of the main points.

the intention at the acquisition may be implied but it cannot be imputed; and secondly, we know that fewer aspects of the parties' dealings with the property can be taken into account at the acquisition stage. Beyond this we do not know what information is relevant to the quantification stage only, and more importantly, why. For example, the separateness of the parties' finances appears to have been taken into account at both stages in *Stack*, but the financial responsibility for the children was only relevant at the quantification stage. Why? This is a serious uncertainty, as not only does it feed into the unpredictability of the result, but it also leaves us with a deeper and more enduring uncertainty as to the normative drivers behind the court's approach.

Finally, there is uncertainty in the notion of the ambulatory constructive trust, first advanced by Lord Hoffman in *Stack* and given much support in *Kernott*. The general idea is that the parties' shares in the property can vary over time in accordance with the different circumstances and intentions of the parties at the relevant time. This again can be seen as an example of the double-uncertainty. We do not know what will transform a normal constructive trust into an ambulatory constructive trust and when this will happen. Are all constructive trusts 'ambulatory' in this sense, or do they change in response to a particular factor? If so, what is this factor? The further uncertainty comes from how the courts apply this jurisdiction to vary the trust over time without just resorting to what seems fair at any particular moment. In addition to this it is important to note that the interaction between an ambulatory constructive trust and third parties may also prove to be a highly complex one, especially where there is a charge over one party's share. These are all issues which will require guidance, and which too show that we have not clearly articulated the normative basis for this jurisdiction.[21]

Perhaps this normative background can be derived from the cases. Certainly Gardner and Davidson suggest that where the parties are in a 'sharing relationship', the Court tends to reflect this in their view of the co-ownership issues. Where, by contrast, the parties do not have such a relationship, the court will allocate the equitable title in accordance with the parties' individual financial contributions to the house and to the relationship.[22] So, in *Stack* where the parties did not share, a result akin to a resulting trust seems appropriate. Whether this is the background thinking or not, it would at least be helpful to have more information from the courts on this.

And so there is much we know now following *Kernott*. We know that *Stack* is here to stay; we know that the approaches at the acquisition and quantification stages are different;

---

21   These issues form the basis of an essay in themselves and so it is important to judge the depth of detail you go into in each section so as to leave the overall structure balanced and even.

22   Knowing in outline what academics have argued about a particular case will give you a useful bank of arguments to draw on in the exam.

and we know that imputation is permitted at the latter stage only. We do not however know how the court will treat sole names cases; the precise role of imputation; and the difference from the quantification stage. These problems can be resolved however in later decisions, but the uncertainty that comes from the open-texture of the discretion in these cases cannot be solved by more cases – instead we need to work out why the courts have quantified a share in a particular way.[23] There has already been much discussion of the principles in these cases in *CPS v Piper* (2011), *Chapman v Jaune* (2012), *Geary v Rankine* (2012), *Garwood v Ambrose* (2012) and *Gallarotti v Sebastianelli* (2012). No doubt there will be more litigation to follow.

QUESTION 13

Wendy and Wally, brother and sister, have recently discovered that their 17-year-old nephew Barry has been orphaned in a road accident and that they are his legal guardians. In anticipation of Barry coming to live with them, they decide to buy a bigger house with their savings and with some of the money left to Barry by his parents over which they have lawful control until Barry is aged 18. The new house, title to which is unregistered at all material times, is expressly conveyed into their joint names as legal and equitable joint tenants. There is no mention of the fact that Barry's money was also used. Barry arrives and Wendy and Wally employ a live-in personal tutor, Maureen. Maureen lives in a self-contained part of the house for which she pays Wendy and Wally £70 a week. Unknown to Maureen and Barry, Wendy and Wally sell the property to Peter. Peter is told, and believes, that Barry and Maureen are the vendors' children.

▶ Advise Barry (who is now aged 18) and Maureen as to their right to stay in the property. Is the law in this area satisfactory?

How to Answer this Question

❖ Co-ownership and expressly declared trusts.

❖ The acquisition of beneficial interests: implied and resulting trusts – *Stack v Dowden* (2007); *Jones v Kernott* (2011).

❖ The issue of overreaching when there are two trustees of land: *City of London BS v Flegg* (1988).

❖ Purchasers and existing tenants in unregistered land: s 4 of the **Land Charges Act 1972**.

❖ Law Commission Report No 188 and the **TOLATA 1996**.

---

23 Recognising that 'uncertainty' can mean more than one sort of problem gives your engagement with the specific question more depth.

Answer Structure

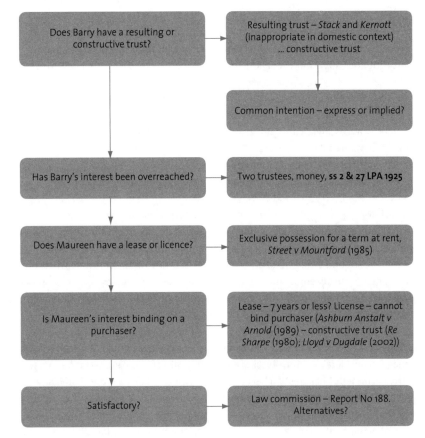

This diagram shows how to apply the rules relating to implied trusts, leases and registered land to the problem involving Barry and Maureen.

ANSWER

In this problem, we are faced with the difficulties that can arise from the operation of the trust of land and the overreaching provisions of the Law of Property Act (LPA) 1925 as the mechanism for regulating concurrent co-ownership. Under the LPA 1925 and the TOLATA 1996, when land is conveyed to two or more persons, they take that property as legal joint tenants upon the statutory trusts of land: ss 34 and 36 of the LPA and s 1 of the TOLATA 1996. In our case, therefore, when the new house is conveyed to Wendy and Wally, it becomes subject to the rules governing these statutory trusts. Wendy and Wally become the joint tenant trustees of the land, with all of the powers of an absolute owner, subject to the provisions of s 6 of the TOLATA 1996. Moreover, as the conveyance is expressly conveyed to them as joint tenants in equity, they hold the legal title on trust for themselves as equitable joint tenants (*Goodman v Gallant* (1986)).

However, what of Barry, for it appears that some of his money has been used to purchase the property? It is axiomatic that, when a person contributes to the purchase price of property but does not acquire legal title to that property, a resulting trust will arise in their favour (*Dyer v Dyer* (1788) and see *Laskar v Laskar* (2008)), unless the contribution was by way of loan or gift (*Bradbury v Hoolin* (1998)). There is no evidence of a gift or loan here and it may be that Barry's money was used without his knowledge or consent. In such circumstances, it is clear that a resulting trust is raised in his favour and this seems one of those cases that should be still be regarded as a resulting trust (rather than a constructive trust) despite the comments in *Stack v Dowden* (2007) and *Jones v Kernott* (2011).[24] The express declaration of the equitable ownership that is found in the conveyance (that is, to Wally and Wendy) does not prevent Barry claiming an interest by way of resulting trust, for in *Goodman*, it was made clear that an express declaration of beneficial interests only precludes a claim of resulting or constructive trust for the parties to that declaration.[25] Barry was not a party to it and is not bound by it. In the end, therefore, Wendy and Wally are trustees of the legal estate on the statutory trusts of land holding on trust in equity for themselves as joint tenants in the portion purchased by their own money and for Barry as a tenant in common of the share purchased with his money.

The property is now sold to Peter. This would seem to place Barry and Maureen (the other occupier) in considerable difficulty, as it is obvious that Peter will not wish to share the property with them. The question becomes, then, whether Barry's interest, and any interest that Maureen may have, can bind Peter.

First, what is the position of Barry? As seen above, Barry has an equitable interest in the property when Peter purchases the unregistered title. Normally, in unregistered land, equitable interests have to be registered as land charges to be binding against purchasers. However, under s 2 of the **LCA 1972**, these equitable ownership rights cannot be registered. They are, in fact, unregistrable and their binding effect continues in principle to be governed by the doctrine of notice. In our case, however, there is another important factor. Peter has purchased the property from two trustees of land – in other words, he has complied with the statutory requirements of s 2 of the **LPA 1925** for overreaching. As in *City of London BS v Flegg* (1987), a sale by two trustees for sale overreaches all 'family-style' equitable interests (that is, Barry's equitable ownership), so that the purchaser cannot be bound. It does not matter that Barry knew nothing of the sale or that Peter knew nothing (or everything!) of Barry: the statutory magic operates in

---

24 Once again, here the author has brought in their own view into the problem question answer, showing good analysis of the legal rules.

25 This is a point about *Goodman* that many people overlook.

favour of the purchaser and protects him. The only possible exception is if Barry's consent to the sale has been made a condition of a sale under the original trust (that is, the conveyance to Wendy and Wally) or if such a requirement has been imposed by the court consequent upon Barry's application to it under s 14 of the TOLATA. Again, there is no evidence of this and, in any event, Peter would not be affected by the violation of any consent requirement unless he had 'actual notice' of the violation (s 16 of the TOLATA). Of course, Barry's equitable interest is reflected in the purchase money and he is entitled to a share of the proceeds of sale in proportion to his share of the property – if he can locate the trustees. It is likely, however, that he has no claim against Peter and must surrender possession.

Maureen's position is less clear. On one view, the arrangement she made with Wendy and Wally amounted to nothing more than that of lodger and landlord. If this is the case, she would have a mere licence, which is not an interest in land and which cannot, therefore, bind any purchaser irrespective of all questions of notice or registration – *Ashburn Anstalt v Alfonso* (1989); *Lloyd v Dugdale* (2002). She would have to leave. Indeed, this may well be the case, especially if Wendy or Wally provided 'board and services' within the definition of a 'lodger' in *Street v Mountford* (1985). Likewise, if Maureen was given accommodation 'for the better performance of her duties' as a tutor, she would have only a licence, as in *Norris v Checksfield* (1991). Then, she would be a service occupant under a licence and could not stay on against Peter. In fact, Maureen's only hope is to claim that she has a tenancy – for this is capable of binding Peter in the right circumstances and, of course, such 'commercial' rights are not overreachable. In this case, there is evidence of 'rent' and it is payable weekly. This could mean that Maureen has a legal periodic tenancy and, as such, it would be binding on Peter under the normal rules of unregistered land: viz, legal rights bind the whole world (*Hunt v Luck* (1902)). Of course, even if there is a legal periodic tenancy binding on Peter, Peter could terminate the tenancy according to its terms, which, in the case of periodic tenancies, is usually on giving one period's notice (subject to a statutory minimum four weeks under the Protection from Eviction Act 1977[26]). Finally, Maureen might consider claiming an equitable tenancy under *Walsh v Lonsdale* (1882), but only if there is a written record of the original tenancy agreement (s 2 of the Law of Property (Miscellaneous Provisions) Act 1989). In any event, however, to bind Peter in unregistered conveyancing such an equitable tenancy would need to have been registered as a Class C(iv) land charge (*Hollington Brothers v Rhodes* (1951)). There is no evidence of this. In the end, it looks as if Maureen also has to leave and the best she can hope for is for one further period under the legal periodic tenancy until it is terminated.

This question clearly identifies one of the most striking problems of the use of the trust of land as a co-ownership device. Barry, the equitable owner, was deprived of his own

---

26 Bringing in information like this shows that you are aware of the practical options open to the parties.

property while he was in occupation of it because of the magic of overreaching. It is not enough to say that his interest is now in money form because a share of the proceeds of a house sale by no means guarantees that other accommodation can be purchased, even if the trustees do distribute the money properly. To meet these problems and to safeguard the position of the equitable owner in Barry's position, the Law Commission (in Report No 188[27]) once flirted with three alternative solutions.

(a) That, if the equitable owner registers their interest, they could not be overreached. Unfortunately, this solution would only help those equitable owners who both knew of the requirement of registration and, more fundamentally, knew that they actually had an interest; Barry did not.

(b) That, in order for overreaching to take place, one of the trustees should be a solicitor or licensed conveyancer. This presupposes that such professional persons would not consent to a sale that destroyed an equitable owner's property rights without proper consideration of all material circumstances. This might or might not be true, but it would be expensive, as well as introducing strangers into family affairs. In practice, the protection would have been negligible and formal.

(c) That no beneficiary, of full age and in occupation, could be overreached without their consent. This undoubtedly would have worked. It would have prevented sales of co-owned property such as the Fleggs suffered in the *City of London* case and Barry in this problem. Under the **TOLATA 1996**, this idea has been given partial effect, even though the Act was not specifically designed to implement Law Commission Report No 188. It is now possible for a 'consent requirement' to be imposed either in the conveyance establishing the trust or by order of the court under s14 of the **TOLATA**. This would require the trustees of land to obtain the consent of any equitable owners before dealing with the legal title. In unregistered land, however, a purchaser's title would not be invalidated merely because the land was transferred by the legal owners in breach of the requirement. This would be the result only if the purchaser had 'actual knowledge' of the violation (s16 of the **TOLATA**). In registered land, the consent requirement would be entered on the title as a restriction, so effectively blocking any dealing until the requisite consents had been obtained. This looks impressive, in the sense that equitable owners can be protected even when there are two trustees of the land. Yet, such protection as exists depends crucially on the existence of a consent requirement and such a requirement is not imposed by the Act as a matter of course. It is unlikely that a consent requirement will be built into the trust of land of domestic property at its inception, and only marginally less likely that an equitable owner will seek the imposition of such a requirement by application to the court.

Finally, we can also note that Maureen's position, if she had a tenancy, is not satisfactory. In registered land, her tenancy whether legal or equitable would have been an overriding

---

27 Highlighting the detailed recommendations of the Law Commission shows that you are aware of the proposals for reform.

interest (under Sched 3, para 1 to the LRA 2002) and would have automatically bound Peter. In unregistered land, however, there is no protection for occupiers of property under an equitable tenancy unless they positively register (see *Hollington Brothers v Rhodes*). This is an unfortunate disparity between the two systems of conveyancing.[28]

Common Pitfalls

This is a somewhat unusual question but we include it here because it illustrates the point that examiners sometimes create artificial scenarios in order to test areas of law. It is most unlikely that this situation would exist today over *unregistered land*. In reality, the land would most likely have been first registered when it was purchased by Wendy and Wally. However, the question is explicit that at all times the land remained unregistered. The examiner therefore clearly wants the issues tested as they apply to unregistered title. It would be wrong, in such a case, to determine that the sale triggered compulsory first registration – the question is clear. In addition, the question asks a potential reforms of the law – again unusual in a problem question but nevertheless the issue still needs to be addressed. The examiner here is not allowing candidates to pick different 'styles' of question – this has elements of both a 'problem' and an 'essay'-style question.

QUESTION 14

Alfonso, Bertie, Clive, Denny and Ernie are all trainee solicitors in London and they decide to buy a house together. All contribute equally to the purchase price and the house is conveyed to 'Alfonso and Bertie as joint tenants in law and in equity'. Several months later, Bertie is made redundant and forges Alfonso's signature to a mortgage made with the Easy Loan Bank. At the same time, Alfonso agrees in writing to sell his interest in the property to Ernie and the agreement is executed. Meanwhile, Clive has plans to marry and asks Denny whether he will buy his share in the house. Denny is very keen but disputes the price. Before they can come to an agreement, Clive is killed in a road accident, leaving all his property to his fiancée, Wilma. Very soon after, Ernie becomes entangled in a City deal that goes badly wrong and, owing many millions, is made bankrupt. Before Ernie is formally adjudged bankrupt, Denny commits suicide, leaving all his property to the Battersea Dogs' Home.

Ernie's trustee in bankruptcy, Wilma, the Dogs' Home, Bertie and Denny's next of kin all claim an interest in the property.

---

28 Tying the result you have reached into the wider debate as to the merits of the rules brings extra analysis into a problem question.

▶ What is your advice? Would it make any difference if, before his death, Denny had written to Ernie informing him that he wished to leave the house as soon as possible?

How to Answer this Question

❖ Construction of the conveyance and the nature of the parties' interests.
❖ The purpose of the law of severance.
❖ *Williams v Hensman* (1861):
  ❖ an act operating on one's own share
  ❖ mutual agreement
  ❖ possible course of dealing.
❖ The nature and effect of the right of survivorship.
❖ The effect of bankruptcy of co-owner.
❖ **Section 36(2)** of the **Law of Property Act 1925**: *Kinch v Bullard* (1999).

Applying the Law

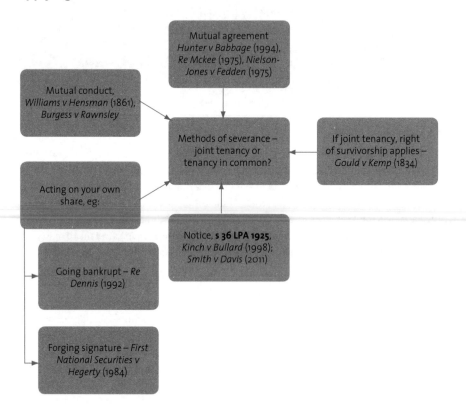

Mutual agreement
Hunter v Babbage (1994),
Re Mckee (1975), *Nielson-Jones v Fedden* (1975)

Mutual conduct,
Williams v Hensman (1861),
Burgess v Rawnsley

Methods of severance –
joint tenancy or
tenancy in common?

If joint tenancy, right
of survivorship applies –
Gould v Kemp (1834)

Acting on your own
share, eg:

Notice, **s 36 LPA 1925,**
Kinch v Bullard (1998);
Smith v Davis (2011)

Going bankrupt – *Re
Dennis* (1992)

Forging signature – *First
National Securities v
Hegerty* (1984)

This diagram shows the different methods of severance.

ANSWER

This question concerns the law of severance. Severance is the process by which an equitable joint tenancy can be converted into an equitable tenancy in common. There may be many reasons why a joint tenant should wish to sever their interest in this way, but, very often, the motivation is to avoid the operation of the right of survivorship. In a joint tenancy, when one joint tenant dies, their interest automatically accrues to the other joint tenants, irrespective of any disposition made in a will. If, therefore, a co-owner is a joint tenant but wishes to deal with their interest separately, severance of that tenancy is crucial. Before we consider the problem in detail, however, one point must be borne in mind. Under the LPA 1925, the only form of co-ownership that can exist at law is the joint tenancy. This legal joint tenancy is unseverable – s 36(2) of the LPA – because, if it were otherwise, a legal tenancy in common would result and, under the LPA, that is not possible – s 1(6). In other words, when we talk of severing the joint tenancy, we are talking about severing the joint tenancy in equity. As is made clear in the LPA, the equitable co-ownership that exists behind the joint tenancy at law can take either form and so the equitable joint tenancy can be transformed into a tenancy in common under the law of severance.

The law relating to severance is to be found both in statute and at common law. Under s 36(2) of the LPA 1925, any equitable joint tenant may give notice in writing to the other joint tenants of their intention to sever (unless it seems they have promised not to: *White v White* (2000)) and this actually results in a severance in equity – see, for example, *Burgess v Rawnsley* (1975) and *Kinch v Bullard* (1999). Similarly, at common law, *Williams v Hensman* (1861) establishes that severance may occur by three methods: first, where one joint tenant does 'an act operating on their own share' (such as a sale of his interest); second, where joint tenants agree to sever by 'mutual agreement' (this acts to sever the shares of all those agreeing, even if the agreement is never carried out or is actually unenforceable – *Burgess*); third, by 'mutual conduct' (where the party's conduct is of a kind sufficient to evince an intention no longer to be part of a joint tenancy).

In our problem, some or all of these principles may be relevant, but, first, it is necessary to identify the nature of the co-ownership between the parties.[29] Clearly, Alfonso and Bertie are the legal owners and are, by statute (s 35 of the LPA), the joint tenant trustees of the legal estate holding for the equitable owners on a trust of land under the TOLATA 1996. Who are the equitable owners, and are they joint tenants or tenants in common? Although the conveyance expressly declares that Alfonso and Bertie are joint tenants, this conveyance can be conclusive only between the parties to it: *Goodman v Gallant* (1986). Therefore, the doctrine of resulting and constructive trusts is not excluded for Clive, Denny and Ernie. Following *Dyer v Dyer* (1788), *Pettitt v Pettitt* (1970) and *Curley v Parkes* (2004), there is no doubt that Clive, Denny and Ernie will be able to claim a share of the

---

29 It is good to highlight the approach you are taking to the question in order to make your structure easier to follow.

equitable ownership by virtue of their contribution to the purchase price of the property at the time of acquisition. In fact, because all five people contributed to the purchase price equally, they are, in equity, joint tenants. So, the picture of the ownership of the house is as follows: Alfonso and Bertie hold the property as trustees of land for Alfonso, Bertie, Clive, Denny, and Ernie as joint tenants in equity.

As the problem makes clear, there are now several claimants to the property and if, as seems likely, it is sold, there will be confusion as to how the proceeds of sale should be distributed. Of course, if there have been no acts of severance, the surviving joint tenants will be entitled to the property or its proceeds by virtue of the right of survivorship. In addition, it is quite possible that only one or some of the original joint tenants have severed their interest so that survivorship might operate between only some of the surviving parties.

(A) BERTIE'S ATTEMPTED MORTGAGE TO THE EASY LOAN BANK

Bertie is a trustee of the legal title, but jointly with Alfonso. Thus, no action on his part alone can deal with the legal title and, without Alfonso's agreement, there can be no mortgage to the bank. In other words, both legal owners must genuinely agree to any conveyance of the legal title – this is at the very heart of the legal joint tenant trusteeship. So, forging the signature of the other legal owner is not sufficient to create a mortgage of the legal title – *First National Securities v Heggarty* (1984). However, following *Ahmed v Kendrick* (1987), *Banker's Trust v Namdar* (1997), *First National Bank v Achampong* (2003) and s 63 of the LPA 1925, the attempted mortgage by Bertie will be sufficient to mortgage to the bank such interest as Bertie does control – in other words, his equitable interest. Without doubt, this mortgage of his equitable interest is 'an act operating on his own share' within *Hensman* and means that Bertie severs his share of the equitable interest. He is now a tenant in common of one fifth, albeit mortgaged to the bank. The other owners are still within a joint tenancy of the remaining four-fifths. Legal title remains in Alfonso and Bertie as before.[30]

(B) THE TRANSFER BY ALFONSO

When Alfonso agrees in writing to sell his interest in the property to Ernie, this is an enforceable agreement to sell his equitable interest (see s 2 of the **Law of Property (Miscellaneous Provisions) Act 1989**). This is not an agreement to sell the legal title as Bertie would have had to concur. As above, this is an act operating on his own share within *Hensman* and will sever Alfonso's interest from the joint tenancy. Thus, when the agreement is executed, Alfonso's equitable share passes to Ernie. The overall position is now that Alfonso and Bertie hold on trust for Ernie as tenant in common of one fifth,

---

30 Severance questions are often factually complex, and it is useful to summarise where you have got to at the end of each section like this.

Bertie as tenant in common of one fifth (but mortgaged) and Clive, Denny and Ernie as joint tenants of the remainder.[31]

(C) MUTUAL AGREEMENT OR MUTUAL CONDUCT

It is unclear whether Clive's discussions with Denny lead to any severance of the joint tenancy between them. It seems that there is no 'mutual agreement' within *Hensman* as, although Denny is keen to buy, no price has been agreed. This probably prevents severance by mutual agreement. It should be noted, however, that, if an agreement can be inferred from the circumstances, the fact that this agreement would be unenforceable (because it is not in writing) does not prevent severance occurring (*Burgess*). Under an unenforceable 'mutual agreement', the transfer would not take place, but severance would occur for both parties. However, assuming that mutual agreement is inapplicable here, can the discussions between Clive and Denny amount to severance by 'mutual conduct', being a course of dealing between the parties that show an intention to hold as tenants in common? This is unclear, because, as a matter of principle, it is difficult to see why a failed attempt to agree (as here) should be treated as effective to sever even though there is no agreement to sever. If that were possible, the difference between mutual agreement and mutual conduct would become virtually non-existent. However, if one reads Lord Denning's judgment in *Burgess*, it is clear that he does suggest that negotiations between joint tenants can give rise to severance. Essentially, the answer will depend on the facts of each case and whether the court is prepared, as a matter of policy, to extend the circumstances in which severance is possible. The degree of hardship caused by the operation of the right of survivorship might well be relevant in that calculation.[32] In our case, the tentative conclusion is that severance has not occurred because of the potential overlap with mutual agreement. Thus, the position remains as at (b) above.

(D) THE RIGHT OF SURVIVORSHIP

When Clive dies, he dies as a joint tenant of three-fifths of the property with Denny and Ernie. He has not severed his interest and, thus, it accrues to Denny and Ernie under the right of survivorship. The fact that he left his property by will to Wilma is irrelevant as survivorship takes precedence over testamentary dispositions (*Gould v Kemp* (1834)).[33] Thus, Alfonso and Bertie hold on trust for Ernie as tenant in common of one fifth, Bertie as tenant in common of one fifth (but mortgaged) and Denny and Ernie as joint tenants of the remainder.

---

31 Remember that it is possible to have a 'mix and match' of joint tenancy and tenancy in common.
32 Acknowledging that such policy considerations may well weigh in the court's decision adds another dimension to your answer.
33 This is a crucial point in many severance questions and it is important to make it clear.

(E) ERNIE'S BANKRUPTCY AND THE SUICIDE

Under the **Insolvency Act** (as applied in very similar circumstances to these in *Re Dennis* (1992)), it is clear that a bankrupt's property does not become vested in the trustee in bankruptcy until he or she is formally adjudicated bankrupt. At that moment, of course, there is alienation (that is, transfer) of the bankrupt's property such as to cause a severance of any joint tenancy of which he may be part – it is really an act operating on his own share, albeit an involuntary one. In our case, however, when Denny dies and leaves his property to the Dogs' Home, Ernie has not been adjudicated bankrupt and so there has been no severance between the remaining two joint tenants. Unfortunately, therefore, Denny's interest passes to Ernie under the right of survivorship. In other words, when Ernie is adjudicated bankrupt, he is, in fact, the sole surviving joint tenant and all the property subject to that joint tenancy accrued to him and will fall to the trustee in bankruptcy to pay the creditors.

The final position is, therefore, that Alfonso and Bertie are legal owners of the property holding as joint tenant trustees in equity in the following way:

❖   for Ernie as tenant in common of one fifth, which will pass to the trustee in bankruptcy;

❖   for Bertie as tenant in common of one fifth, but as mortgaged to the bank;

❖   for Ernie as owner of the remainder, having succeeded to the shares of Clive and Denny under the right of survivorship. This also passes to the trustee in bankruptcy for distribution among his creditors.

(F) WOULD IT HAVE MADE ANY DIFFERENCE IF DENNY HAD WRITTEN TO ERNIE BEFORE HIS DEATH INFORMING HIM THAT HE WISHED TO LEAVE THE PROPERTY?

The only possible difference this could make is if this written communication can be regarded as written notice of severance under s 36(2) of the **LPA 1925**. Under that section, written notice to the other joint tenants (here, Ernie), may sever a joint tenancy provided that it is a communication of an intention to sever and there has been no estoppel not to sever: *White v White*. This will be a matter of construction but, following the liberal construction used in *Re Draper's Conveyance* (1969) (in which a court summons seeking sale of the property was held to sever under the section), this letter probably suffices: after all, an intention to leave the property almost certainly implies dealing separately with one's own share. Indeed, according to *Kinch v Bullard*, a notice to sever is effective even if never actually read by the other joint tenant(s), provided that it is effectively delivered to them. However, there is one small problem in that the words of s 36(2) say that this form of severance is available where 'a legal estate is vested in joint tenants beneficially' – that is, where the legal and equitable owners are the same people. That is not the case here – because only Alfonso and Bertie are legal owners. However, this restrictive construction is generally regarded as being incorrect and the better view is that severance by written notice is available for all joint tenants in equity, whether or not they are legal owners as well. Thus, if Denny had severed by this method before his death, he could successfully leave his one-fifth share to the Dogs' Home in his will.

Common Pitfalls

Many students make two common mistakes with this type of problem. First, as it is about the law of severance, at the outset of the problem, the parties MUST be joint-tenants. If they are not, they would already be tenants in common and severance would be irrelevant. Do not assume this – make it explicit and be clear that they are not tenants in common. In this case, the joint tenancy is expressly created by the words of the conveyance. Second, make sure you 'sum up' the position after each act of severance. This provides focus for you and for the examiner.

Successive Interests in Land

INTRODUCTION

Although it is now less frequent, it was once quite common for property to be left to one person for their life, then to another, then to another and so on. These are *successive* interests in land and they arise when one person is entitled to the possession of land in succession to another, a typical example being where land is left to A for life, with remainder to B for life, remainder to C in fee simple. In such a case, A has a life interest in possession (and is known somewhat confusingly as the 'life tenant'), B has a life interest in remainder (and will be the life tenant when A dies) and C has a fee simple in remainder (and will become the absolute owner on the death of A and B).

The reasons for creating successive interests can, of course, be many and varied, although one very common reason was so that land could be 'kept in the family' by limiting its ownership to successive heirs. Nowadays, this is less of a motivating factor, although successive interests may still be created in family or commercial relationships where the settlor (the person who makes the settlement in the first place) desires to make provision for several persons out of his land. Today, the law concerning successive interests is to be found in two distinct sets of statutory provisions. First, for 'settlements' in existence prior to 1 January 1997, the operating statute is the **Settled Land Act (SLA) 1925**. This is a complicated piece of legislation and the machinery it establishes is rightly regarded as unwieldy. Land subject to this statute (that is, land subject to successive interests created before 1 January 1997, even if 'resettled' after this date) is known as 'settled land'. Second, life interests created on or after 1 January 1997 are subject to the provisions of the **Trusts of Land and Appointment of Trustees Act (TOLATA) 1996**. Such interests are held under a 'trust of land' and are excluded from the operation of the **Settled Land Act**. To put it another way, on 1 January 1997, it became impossible to create any new 'settlements' under the **Settled Land Act** and any attempt to create a successive interest in land after this date will, by statute, create a trust of land under s 2 of the **TOLATA 1996**. This move to abolish the strict settlement for all future successive interests reflects both the changing social uses to which land subject to successive interests is put and the fact that the **Settled Land Act 1925** had become outdated, cumbersome and expensive to operate.

There is no doubt that the law of successive interests is complicated, especially when there is an 'old-style' settlement and the **Settled Land Act** is in play. Unfortunately, we cannot yet abandon the strict settlement to the legal graveyard as many existing settlements have time to run and, indeed, because any resettlement of existing settled land will be governed by the Settled Land Act, even if such resettlement takes place on or after 1 January 1997 (s 2 of the TOLATA 1996). An old-style settlement will cease to exist only when there is no land or heirlooms subject to the settlement (s 2(5) of the TOLATA 1996). The relatively new-style trust for successive interests – the trust of land under the TOLATA – is simpler and, therefore, less expensive to establish. The mandatory use of the trust of land for all new successive interests has already simplified this area of land law. One side effect is that the law of concurrent co-ownership (Chapter 3) and successive co-ownership are now governed by the same statutory provisions of the TOLATA 1996.

Checklist ✔

It is important to have a working knowledge of the Settled Land Act 1925, of the scope of the powers of the 'tenant for life' under it, of the controls placed on the tenant for life, and of the differences between the settlement and the trust of land as a means of regulating successive ownership. An awareness of the history of settled land is also helpful. In addition, for new successive interest trusts, it is imperative to have a clear understanding of the provisions of the TOLATA 1996 and much of what has been said in the previous chapter (concurrent co-ownership) is also relevant here. Particular attention should be given to the ability of the trustees under a trust of land to delegate powers to any beneficiary – such as the holder of a life interest. This will preserve the advantage enjoyed under strict settlements that the person most interested in the land has power to deal with it in specified circumstances.

QUESTION 15

Compare the mechanisms of the Settled Land Act 1925 and the Trusts of Land and Appointment of Trustees Act 1996 as a means of regulating successive co-ownership of land.

How to Answer this Question

- ❖ Identify the nature of successive interests in land.
- ❖ Analyse the effect of the TOLATA 1996 on successive interests in general.
- ❖ Discuss the salient features of the SLA 1925 and its defects.
- ❖ Identify and assess the reasons for reform.
- ❖ Draw a comparison between the SLA 1925 and the TOLATA 1996.

Applying the Law

This diagram shows the difference between the operation of the **Settled Land Act 1925** and the **Trusts of Land and Appointment of Trustees Act 1996** to successive interests in land.

ANSWER

Land can be said to be held in successive ownership when two or more persons are entitled to enjoyment of that land (or the income from it) in succession to each other. This is distinct from concurrent co-ownership, being cases in which two or more persons are entitled to the simultaneous enjoyment of land. An example of successive co-ownership is where land is left to A for life, then to B for life, then to C absolutely. Originally, the purpose of such arrangements was to ensure that land remained in the family (as where A is the grandfather, B the father and C the son), although it is perfectly possible for successive co-ownership to be used in a commercial context. Before 1926, the two methods of creating successive ownership – the settlement and the trust for sale

– were subject to the same statutory controls (**Settled Land Acts 1882** and **1884**) although, for various reasons, this was not satisfactory. After 1925, two mutually exclusive statutory regimes are in operation. First, for land subject to a 'settlement' (sometimes called a 'strict settlement') that was created before 1 January 1997, the **Settled Land Act (SLA) 1925** is the governing statute. This is 'settled land': see **ss 1** and **2** of the **SLA 1925** and *Re Austen* (1929). Second, however, all attempts to create successive interests in land on or after 1 January 1997 (save for a 'resettlement' of existing settled land) must take effect as a *trust of land* under the **Trusts of Land and Appointment of Trustees Act 1996** (**s 2** of the **TOLATA**, which came into force on 1 January 1997). Clearly, this is a major reshaping of the law of successive interests, designed to lead to the eventual disappearance of settled land governed by the **SLA**. For the present, however, the two statutes operate in parallel, each defined by reference to the time of creation of the successive interest.

The principal attributes of settled land (under the **SLA**) can be analysed quite briefly.[1] Settled land is land held on trust. Consequently, there will be 'trustees of the settlement' and beneficiaries under the settlement. These beneficiaries will be the person having a life interest (the life tenant, A above) and those persons entitled in remainder – that is, after the life tenant has died (B and C).[2] The settlement will have been created by the 'settlor', by deeds, and these deeds will usually identify the trustees and deal with the detail of the settlement. Under the **SLA**, various persons are given statutory powers to deal with settled land and it is important to remember that the major purpose behind the grant of these powers is to ensure that the land itself can be freely dealt with. As with concurrent co-ownership, if the land is sold, the rights and interests of the beneficiaries will be transferred to the purchase money via the mechanism of overreaching.

The first point of particular interest in respect of settled land is that, under the **SLA**, the tenant for life has significant powers to deal with the land. The tenant for life is the holder of the legal estate in the land and they hold that legal estate on trust for the beneficiaries under the settlement: **ss 4** and **107** of the **SLA**. Further, as just noted, in the great majority of cases, this tenant for life is also the person entitled to the equitable life interest in the property and so they will have two roles: holder of the legal estate in the land and owner of an equitable, but limited ownership. It is no accident that the person in possession of the land should also have the legal title and powers to deal with the land because, being the person in immediate possession, they are likely to be the best judge of how to deal with it.

....

1   When an essay asks for a comparison, try not to spend too much time describing each regime in isolation so that you can intergrate more analysis into your response.
2   Letters can be used to good effect in questions like this to simplify explanations of complex factual explanations.

Second, and following on from the above point, the tenant for life also exercises most of the important statutory powers to deal with the settled land. These are found in **Pt II** of the **SLA 1925** and effectively place the tenant for life in control of the land. They have the power to manage it for the best interests of all the beneficiaries. Consequently, the role of the 'trustees of the settlement' is limited. In general, they exercise supervisory functions in respect of the settlement: *Wheelwright v Walker* (1883). It is their responsibility to ensure that the rights and interests of *all* the beneficiaries under the settlement are protected, especially if the tenant for life misuses their statutory powers. The identity of the trustees is determined according to s 30 of the **SLA**, although they will usually be named as such in the trust deeds.

Third, under the **SLA**, if the person with the statutory powers chooses to sell the settled land (that is, usually the tenant for life), the interests of the beneficiaries are overreached *if* the purchase money is paid to the trustees of the settlement (who must be two in number or a trust corporation) or into court. If overreaching occurs, the purchaser need not concern themselves with the equitable interests because these take effect in the purchase money: this is the 'curtain principle'. The purchaser obtains a clean and unencumbered title to the land. If overreaching does not occur, the tenant for life cannot grant a good title to the purchaser and the purchaser may be bound by the equitable interests as specified under the provisions of the **SLA**.

Finally, brief mention also should be made of the process by which such settlements were once created (that is, before 1 January 1997). Under the **SLA**, all strict settlements had to be created by two deeds – a 'trust instrument' and a 'principal vesting deed': ss 4 and 5 of the **SLA**. The trust instrument declared the details of the settlement, appointed the trustees of it and set out any powers conferred by the settlement that were in addition to those provided automatically by the Act. The principal vesting deed was less comprehensive and described the settled land itself, named the trustees, stated the nature of any additional powers and, most importantly of all, declared that the settled land was vested in the person to whom the land was conveyed (the tenant for life) on the trusts of the settlement. The principal vesting deed was, in one sense, the indicia of ownership of the settled land. It is with this that any purchaser of existing settled land will be concerned as the equitable interests detailed in the trust instrument will be swept off the land by overreaching.

By way of contrast, 'new-style' successive interest trusts of land operating under the **TOLATA** follow a different statutory regime. This new regime represents a revamping of the old 'trust for sale' (which, prior to 1 January 1997, was the alternative to 'settled land') and is designed principally to avoid the complicated machinery of the **SLA**. As noted above, it is compulsory for all new successive interests in land.

A 'trust of land' is of course a trust, having trustees and beneficiaries. The trustees will be named in the instrument and the beneficiaries will be those entitled to a life interest and interests in remainder. Most importantly, however, under the trust of land, legal title to the land and primary control over it lies with the trustees. The trustees have legal title and have all the powers in respect of the land of an absolute owner (s 6 of the TOLATA). The exception is where the trustees' powers are limited by the TOLATA itself, or for a trust that is expressly created, by any provision in the instrument creating the trust (s 8 of the TOLATA 1996). Primarily, therefore, it is the trustees of land who control it or its capital value and they who decide whether the land should be sold or retained. This is very different from the location of power and control under a settlement in which all lies with the tenant for life.[3]

Second, while the tenant for life under a settlement is subject to some controls on the exercise of their powers (*Wheelwright v Walker*) under a trust of land, the trustees are largely unfettered. They are subject to the provisions of the TOLATA and a person with an interest in a trust of land may make an application to the court under s 14. Yet, these are not powerful fetters. Indeed, the trustees of land under the TOLATA can exercise those powers in respect of the land that the tenant for life under the Settled Land Act may not exercise unless the consent of the trustees of the settlement is obtained. It is true that, under s 10 of the TOLATA, the powers of the trustees of land can be made subject to the consent of another person, for example, the life interest holder. It is possible – perhaps probable – that settlors who deliberately create a successive interest trust of land will use s 10 to limit the role of the trustees, say in favour of the life tenant, but this will need careful drafting. In registered land, such a consent requirement will be entered on the register of title by means of a restriction, although, in unregistered land, a purchaser may deal with the trustees of land safely, even in violation of a consent requirement, unless the purchaser had actual notice of it (s 16 of the TOLATA 1996). Finally, like all trustees, the trustees of land under the TOLATA and the trustees of the settlement under the SLA 1925 are subject to the normal rules controlling persons in a fiduciary position: for example, they are personally liable in an action for breach of trust.

Third, because of the complicated workings of the SLA, on the death of the tenant for life, the legal estate can be transferred to a new tenant for life only by 'vesting deeds', a relatively expensive process. However, in a trust of land under the TOLATA, the trustees must have the legal title and must be joint tenants of it (ss 34 and 36 of the Law of Property Act (LPA) 1925), irrespective of the complicated nature of the beneficiaries' interests or the circumstances surrounding the establishment of the trust. Thus, on the death of a trustee of land, legal title accrues automatically to the remaining trustees under the right of survivorship without the need for any documentation.[4]

---

3   It is good to highlight the comparison you are drawing throughout.
4   The expense of the conveyancing requirements of the **SLA 1925** is worth highlighting. The changes under the new law are not just legal, but also very practical.

Fourth, while, under the **SLA**, the tenant for life has the statutory powers to deal with the land, we have seen that, under the **TOLATA**, the trustees have the powers of an absolute owner. However, in order to ensure that the person most interested in the land has an active part in its management, the trustees of land under the **TOLATA** may delegate to a beneficiary (for example, the life interest holder) 'any of their functions' that relate to the land (s 9 of the **TOLATA 1996**). This gives trustees of land the option of keeping the powers for themselves if, say, the beneficiary is not trustworthy, but to delegate them if this is in the best interest of the trust.

Finally, if it should happen that a strict settlement under the **SLA 1925** has arisen informally (as in *Ungarian v Lesnoff* (1990), where the plaintiff acquired a life interest by means of a constructive trust), the informal equitable right created in the claimant's favour is precarious. On a sale by a single legal owner (that is, where there is no overreaching), the equitable life interest cannot amount to an interest which overrides under the **Land Registration Act (LRA) 2002** (see Scheds 1 and 3) and cannot be protected by the entry of a notice on the register (s 33 of the **LRA 2002**). A restriction is the only possible means of controlling the trustees in order to safeguard the interest under the settlement and this is, of course, unlikely when the interest arises informally. By contrast, in an informally created trust of land, a beneficiary's interest can be one that overrides (by virtue of discoverable actual occupation within Scheds 1 and 3 to the **LRA 2002**)) and so they will almost certainly be protected should the single trustee sell or mortgage the land.

To sum up then, after 31 December 1996, it is no longer possible to create successive interests in land under the **SLA**, save for resettlements of existing settled land. All new successive interests will be trusts of land. The former are governed by the complicated provisions of the **SLA 1925**, the latter by the **TOLATA 1996**.[5] Under a settlement, the legal title and powers to deal with the land are vested in the tenant for life, who also holds an equitable interest. Under a trust of land, title and power are in the hands of the trustees, although they may delegate to a beneficiary. Again, in settled land, the tenant for life is subject to control by the trustees of the settlement; in a trust of land, the trustees are not subject to such control unless express provision is made in the trust instrument or after an application to the court. The duty of the trustees of land to consult the beneficiaries does not encompass an obligation to do as they wish. Finally, transfer of title on the death of a tenant for life under the **SLA** is expensive and complicated, but no such problems arise should a trustee of land die. Similarly, there are differences in the way the two regimes protect a purchaser of the land and how the equitable interests are protected should that sale not be an overreaching transaction.

....

5   This summarises the key difference between the regimes and allows the conclusion to draw the threads of the discussion together.

Aim Higher ★

It would be easy to expand this answer, time permitting. More consideration could be given to the case law on TOLATA, particularly discussion of whether the trustees are limited in any way – see for example *HSBC v Dyche* (2009). The impact of informally created interests is particularly interesting given that these are (relatively) easily protected under a trust of land, but very difficult to protect under a strict settlement.

QUESTION 16

'The Settled Land Act 1925 makes it clear that the tenant for life is in effective control of land subject to a strict settlement. This works well when he is a prudent manager of the estate, with a care for the interests of the other beneficiaries. However, if the tenant for life is uninterested, unskilled or downright selfish, there is little that can be done to control him in the exercise of his powers.'

▌ Do you agree?

How to Answer this Question

❖ Briefly, the nature of a strict settlement under the SLA 1925.

❖ Analyse the position of the tenant for life in relation to the trustees and other beneficiaries under the settlement.

❖ Describe the powers of the tenant for life.

❖ Analyse the controls available to the trustees and the court.

Applying the Law

Restrictions on the tenant for life under the **Settled Land Act 1925**

Powers exercisable without consent of the trustees

- Sale
- Exchange
- Lease
- Mortgage
- Options

Must give notice to the trustees

Powers requiring consent

- Dispose main house
- Cut and sell timber
- Chattles
- Compromise claims

Equitable controls

Attempts to restrict tenant for life's powers

Breach of trust, **s 107 SLA 1925**

Void, **s 106 SLA 1925**

*This diagram shows the restrictions on the powers of the life tenant under the **Settled Land Act 1925**.*

ANSWER

It is in the nature of a settlement under the SLA 1925 that there may be many occasions for conflict among the persons intended to be benefited by the settlor. A settlement necessarily gives one person a life interest in the property (the tenant for life) and another (or others) interests in the land after that life estate has ended. In this sense, therefore, two often contradictory interests need to be reconciled: the interest of the life tenant in actual possession of the property who wishes to enjoy the land (or the income it generates) during their life, and the interest of the persons entitled in remainder in keeping as much value locked into the settlement until their own interest 'falls in' on the life tenant's death. Prior to 1926, it was the persons entitled in remainder who held the upper hand as it was relatively easy to restrict the life tenant's ability to deal with the land and their ability to diminish its value. Unfortunately, this meant that much settled land stagnated because the tenant for life had no means of raising the money necessary to use the land profitably. Indeed, given that the tenant for life's rights over the land were so limited, there was little incentive for them to manage the land effectively. Under the SLA 1925, the position changed, as it is a fundamental feature of the Act that the tenant for life shall have both the legal estate in the land and extensive powers to deal with it, even to the point of selling it and converting all the beneficiaries' interests into money.

In the normal course of events, when a settlement is created, the settlor will appoint trustees of the settlement and, in some exceptional circumstances, they will have legal title and the powers conferred by the Act. In the normal case, however, these powers and the title will rest with the tenant for life. Of course, being trustees, the persons appointed as such will have fiduciary responsibilities to all the beneficiaries, especially those entitled in remainder and, as *Wheelwright v Walker* (1883) illustrates, the trustees have a general supervisory function in relation to the settlement. This can result in an application to the court to control the tenant for life. However, the SLA makes it clear in no uncertain terms that the policy behind the Act (encouraging the proper use of settled land) will be best served by giving considerable control to the tenant for life via the legal title and statutory powers.[6]

The scheme of the SLA is to give the tenant for life a wide range of powers and then subject them to varying degrees of control by the trustees. Thus, a life tenant has a power of sale over the land (which will overreach the beneficial interests), although he is obliged to obtain the best price that can reasonably be made (*Wheelwright v Walker (No 2)* (1883)). There is also the power to exchange the land, to grant and accept leases, to mortgage the land in order to raise funds for its benefit and to grant options over the land. All of these powers may be exercised without the consent of the trustees, provided that the tenant gives written notice to the trustees and their solicitor, although it is clear from *Wheelwright* that, if there are no trustees, these powers cannot be exercised. However, even if the trustees have been given notice in the appropriate manner, they are under no obligation to interfere (*England v Public Trustee* (1968)) and they may accept less than the required one month's notice or waive it in writing altogether. Indeed, except for the power of mortgaging, the tenant for life may give general notice that he intends to exercise his powers at some point and this will suffice.[7] In any event, under s 110 of the

---

6   The tension between the formal content of rules and their hoped-for application is always a source of fruitful analysis.

7   It is good to highlight exceptions to general statements like this because it gives the examiner confidence that you have detailed knowledge of the relevant rules.

SLA, a purchaser from the tenant for life is protected against non-compliance by the life tenant. These are, then, fairly limited and relaxed controls and it is unlikely that they give great comfort to the other beneficiaries under the settlement. In respect of other powers – such as the power to dispose of the main house, to cut and sell timber, to sell chattels and to compromise claims – there is more control and the exercise of these depend variously on obtaining the consent of the trustees or of the court. As such, this is not surprising, as these powers relate to those matters of a more personal nature (that is, as opposed to the land itself) in which the other beneficiaries may well have a legitimate interest. Even so, the fact that the tenant for life can sell the land with only minimal intervention by the trustees speaks volumes for the policy operating behind this statute.

Indeed, the matter is even clearer when we realise that it is virtually impossible to restrict the tenant for life in the exercise of their powers. Thus, under s106 of the SLA, any provision in the settlement itself (i.e. the original trust deed establishing the settlement) that attempts or purports to forbid the exercise of a statutory power by the tenant for life or which attempts, tends or is intended to induce the tenant for life not to exercise a power is void. Thus, in *Re Patten* (1929), certain gifts of property that would have had the effect of inducing the tenant for life not to sell the land were void. Likewise, in *Re Orelebar* (1936), a provision that forfeited the life tenant's interest if they quit the land was held void if their leaving was due to an exercise of a statutory power, although it would be upheld if the tenant for life were to leave for any other reason. Some limitation on this very wide protection for the life tenant was provided by *Re Aberconway* (1953), which decided that, if what might be lost to the life tenant by virtue of an exercise of a power was not a benefit or ancillary to their enjoyment of the land, s106 would not operate to invalidate that stipulation. In a similar vein, the tenant for life cannot give up their powers, even if parting with all their interest (*Re Mundy* (1899)), although a surrender to the person next entitled (s105 of the SLA), order of the court (s24 of the SLA) and cases of lunacy can lead to those powers being exercised by other persons.[8]

Perhaps, indeed, the only real control over the tenant for life arises under the general equitable jurisdiction to restrain breach of trust and supervise the actions of persons in a fiduciary position. By virtue of s107 of the SLA, the tenant for life is deemed to be trustee for the beneficiaries of both the legal estate and the statutory powers. This means, in effect, that they must have regard to the interests of others when exercising their powers. On sale, therefore, the life tenant must sell as fairly as any trustee would sell, for the best price and recognising the interest of those entitled after his death: *Wheelwright v Walker* (1883). Likewise, the tenant cannot accept payment in order to exercise his powers (*Chandler v Bradley* (1897); *Bray v Ford* (1896)) as he is under a trustee's duty not to profit from his trust. The tenant of course must not commit a fraud in exercising his powers (*Middlemas v Stevens* (1901)), but the transaction effected by the tenant for life

---

8   This is a good example of how to use the facts of cases in an essay question.

will not be invalidated simply because he had an uncharitable motive, such as lack of interest in the land or dislike for those entitled after him (*Cardigan v Curzon-Howe* (1885)). Of course, the extent of this general equitable jurisdiction is flexible, but it is supported by statute, particularly s 24 of the SLA, which allows the trustees to make an application to the court where a tenant for life has definitely refused (although not merely neglected) to exercise his powers under the Act (*Re 90 Thornhill Road* (1970)).

Finally, we must note that s 18 of the SLA gives a measure of protection to the other beneficiaries by providing that any transaction not authorised by the Act shall be invalidated (*Weston v Henshaw* (1950)), although it is not clear how this gels with the strong protection given to a purchaser who deals in good faith with the tenant for life under s 110 (*Re Morgan's Lease* (1972)).[9]

All in all then, the tenant for life has a very wide measure of control over settled land and the trustees of the settlement can do little to restrain them save in clear cases of abuse. This is entirely consistent with the purposes behind the SLA:[10] that use of land takes precedence over the motives of the settlor in trying to tie up land for their family. Such a strong position can work to the benefit of all persons interested in the settlement – e.g. by selling the land for a profit and successfully reinvesting the proceeds – but clearly there is room for an unscrupulous or incompetent tenant to exercise his powers largely without control and to the overall detriment of all the beneficiaries.

Aim Higher ★

The very best candidates will consider the complicated arguments about how *Weston v Henshaw* (1950) and *Re Morgan's Lease* (1972) can be reconciled. There is considerable uncertainty as to whether (or when) a purchaser is protected if a tenant for life should carry out a transaction not authorised by the Act, even if in purported exercise of his wide powers.

---

9 When under time constraints it is sometimes good to flag up problems or uncertainty even where there is no time to fully deal with the issue, as it shows that you are aware of it. Just make sure to make clear that you know there is more to be said on the matter!

10 A good technique in the conclusion is to draw a clear argument as to the relationship between the rules and their aims as it helps summarise from an analytical rather than a descriptive perspective.

Leaves

INTRODUCTION

Leasehold interests are one of the two estates (along with freeholds) that are capable of existing at law or in equity (s1of the Law of Property Act 1925). In fact, the leasehold estate, whether it be equitable or legal, is one of the most versatile concepts found in the whole of the law of real property. Even the terminology of leases reflects the many purposes to which they may be put. The 'term of years', 'tenancies', 'sub-leases', and 'leasehold estate' are all synonymous and in terms of the legal rules governing their creation and operation the principles are the same, although one particular description may be more appropriate than another depending on the situation. So, for example, the term 'lease' is most often used for commercial or long-term lettings whereas the term 'tenancy' is used for 'domestic' or shorter-term lettings.

One of the most important features of leaseholds is that they allow two or more estate owners to enjoy the benefits of the same piece of land at the same time: for example, the freeholder will receive the rent and profits and the leaseholder will enjoy physical possession and occupation of the property. Indeed, if a 'sub-tenancy' is involved, one lease will be carved out of another as where a freeholder, L, grants land to A for 30 years, who sub-lets to B for 25 years, who sub-lets to C for ten years, and so on. It is this ability of the leasehold estate to facilitate multiple enjoyment of land that gives it its special character. In addition, it is inherent in a lease that the rights and obligations undertaken by the original landlord and tenant concerning the land can be transmitted to persons who later step into the shoes of the original parties, as where a landlord assigns (transfers) the reversion or the tenant assigns the lease. The ability to make rights and obligations 'run' with the land is a special feature of the landlord and tenant relationship and legislation (Landlord and Tenant (Covenants) Act 1995) has enhanced this feature of the leasehold estate, at least for leases granted on or after 1 January 1996, the date on which the 1995 Act came into force.

> ## Aim Higher ★
> Be clear about the methods of creation of leasehold interests and the differences between creating equitable and legal leases.

Use case law to explain the difference between a 'lease' and a 'licence'; just repeating the textbook will not earn many marks

Understand how leases fit into the system of registered land: some are registrable titles, some are overriding interests and some might require protection through the use of a notice against the superior title.

Always check whether the lease was created before 1 January 1996 as this will determine which principles apply to the enforcement of leasehold covenants: the pre-1996 rules or the **Landlord and Tenant (Covenants) Act (LTCA) 1995**.

Forfeiture is a very popular topic with examiners

QUESTION 17

'There cannot be a tenancy if the grantor has no power to create a tenancy. Further, in order to have a leasehold estate there must be an intention to create legal relations, exclusive possession and a term. Identifying when these features exist will not always be straightforward. There are also some situations in which these 'indicia' or 'hallmarks' of a tenancy do exist and yet there is still no tenancy.'

(Bright, *Landlord and Tenant Law in Context* (2007)
Oxford: Hart Publishing, p. 68)

▶ Discuss.

How to Answer this Question

❖ Essentially, this question is asking, what is a lease?

❖ Definition of a lease – *Street v Mountford* (1985); *Bruton v London and Quadrant Housing Trust* (2000); *Clear Channel UK v Manchester City Council* (2005).

❖ Time certain – *Lace v Chandler* (1944); *Prudential Assurance v London Residuary Body* (1992); *Berrisford v Mexfield Housing Association* (2011).

❖ Exclusive possession.

❖ Rent.

❖ Formalities: **ss 52** and **54** of the **Law of Property Act 1925**; **s 2** of the **Law of Property (Miscellaneous Provisions) Act 1989**; periodic tenancies; *Walsh v Lonsdale* (1882).

Applying the Law

This diagram shows the fundamental features of leases.

ANSWER

By virtue of s 1 of the **Law of Property Act 1925**, a term of years absolute in possession is one of the two estates in land that may exist either at law or in equity. The term of years (or lease) is, consequently, one of the major forms of land ownership in England and Wales. It is, in addition, a concept of considerable versatility that can provide both occupation in a domestic context and premises for a commercial enterprise, as well as income for the freeholder and even the leaseholder if the premises are sub-let. It is a peculiar feature of the leasehold estate that it can give several different estate owners the use or enjoyment of the land or its profits at the same time.

According to *Street v Mountford* (1985), a lease can be defined as exclusive possession of property, for a term, at a rent. These three conditions are commonly regarded as the indicia of a leasehold, irrespective of the purpose for which the estate is created. It is clear, however, from *Ashburn Anstalt v Arnold* (1989) (relying on **s 205** of the **LPA 1925**), that rent is not essential to the existence of a lease, although it will be a rare situation indeed in which the parties to a transaction have intended to be legally bound by the relationship of landlord and tenant but have not specified the payment of rent. With this in mind, rent will be discussed below as if it were synonymous with the existence of a tenancy.[1]

In addition to the principles established by *Street*, which are, in fact, conditions required by the common law, the nature of leases is also governed by various statutory provisions. These provisions are largely to be found in the **LPA 1925** and determine whether any particular lease is legal or equitable. Briefly, the position is that any lease for a period of more than three years must be by deed if it is to take effect as a legal estate (**s 52** of the **LPA**). Leases for three years or less that give the tenant an immediate right to occupy without the payment of an initial premium (that is, a capital sum) may also be legal (**s 54** of the **LPA**) and into this category come many short-term periodic tenancies, mainly governing domestic occupancy. Equitable leases, on the other hand, usually result from a binding contract (or written agreement that can be treated as such a contract) between landlord and tenant that has not been put into effect by deed. If this contract is in writing (**s 2** of the **Law of Property (Miscellaneous Provisions) Act 1989**) and is specifically enforceable, equity will regard the relationship between the parties as one governed by an equitable lease (*Walsh v Lonsdale* (1882)). The exception to this is an equitable lease arising out of proprietary estoppel. These can be completely oral and arise out of the inequitable conduct of the landlord (see *Taylor Fashions v Liverpool Victoria Trustees* (1982); *Thorner v Major* (2009)).

Turning, then, to the position at common law. The *Street* requirements define the inherent nature of a lease and set the parameters outside of which a lease simply cannot exist, irrespective of the intention of the parties or whether the above statutory formalities are complied with. The first is the requirement of 'time certain' or, in other words, the requirement that the lease must exist for a clearly defined period of time. This means not only that the lease must start at a clearly defined moment, but also that the term granted must be certain. The lease must be of certain maximum duration at the commencement of the lease. Any lease, or rather any intended lease, that fails to satisfy this condition is necessarily void because it does not amount to a 'term'. In *Lace v Chandler* (1994), for example, a lease for the duration of the Second World War was held void as being of uncertain maximum duration. In recent years, the principle of time certain has been under attack and an important development occurred in *Berrisford v Mexfield Housing Association* (2012). In that case, the Supreme Court[2] confirmed that leases had to be of a certain duration (i.e. upholding *Prudential*). However, the Court went

---

1   This shows that you are aware of the extent to which rent is required, whilst acknowledging the centrality of rent to the reality of the landlord and tenant relationship.

2   It is always good, where possible, to include information as to which court the case you are describing was decided in since it shows the strength of the authority on which you are relying.

on to point out that, potentially uncertain leases given to *individuals* (but not companies) could be rendered certain by operation of law. This was because first, a lease to an individual for an uncertain period could be interpreted at common law as a lease for their life (*Doe on the demise of Crake v Brown 172 E.R. 992*) and then, secondly, that leases for life are, by statute (s. **section 149(6)** of the **LPA 1925**), converted to leases for 90 years, terminable by death. So, by a double step of reasoning, these uncertain leases to individuals are converted to maximum 90 year terms – they are 'certain' within the *Prudential* rule. Clearly, this will now 'save' many previously uncertain arrangements, but significantly not where the potential tenant is a company (as indeed many are). Note also, that provided that the overall duration of the term is certain, it need not be a single continuous term. So, in *Cottage Holiday Associates Ltd v Customs and Excise Commissioners* (1983), agreements under a timeshare scheme giving the right to occupy the cottages one week each year for 80 years were certain.[3] Finally, one further point needs to be borne in mind when talking about time certain. It often happens that a tenant may occupy premises and pay a regular sum to the landlord in respect of that occupation. There may well be no written record of this arrangement. In these circumstances, a tenancy of a certain duration will be presumed from the facts. Thus, if money is paid weekly in respect of a week's occupation, a periodic tenancy of one week will be presumed and, likewise, if payment is made monthly or quarterly. Obviously, if a further week's, month's or quarterly payment is made, the lease will continue and can in this sense continue indefinitely so long as the payment is made. However, although such a situation appears to be a lease for an uncertain period, in fact, it is a succession of periodic tenancies – that is, one week after one week or one month after one month and so on. These relatively short-term periodic tenancies are common in residential lettings and should not be thought to contradict the principle of time certain.

The other common law conditions for the existence of a lease are not so controversial, although they may be just as difficult to identify in practice. The concept of exclusive possession is notoriously elusive, as can be seen in the confused and confusing debate over the distinction between a lease and a licence. In essence, the existence of exclusive possession is a matter for the construction of the agreement between the parties in the light of their conduct in relation to the property (*Antoniades v Villiers* (1990); *AG Securities v Vaughan* (1990)). Thus, if the occupier has been granted the exclusive right to use the property, even to the exclusion of the landlord, then there is a strong presumption that the agreement amounts to a lease. The only exceptions to this are those cases identified by Lord Templeman in *Street*, in which, because of some special circumstances, exclusive possession may exist but a tenancy does not. An example is the service occupancy of *Norris v Checksfield* (1991), in which the right to occupy was given to an employee for the better performance of his duties, and cases in which the occupation is given as an act of generosity, friendship or charity, as in *Gray v Taylor* (1998), in which occupation of an almshouse did not indicate the existence of a lease.

---

3   This sort of detailed additional information is the kind of information that makes answers stand out.

Finally, we come to rent, the receipt of which is usually the main reason why the landlord has granted the tenancy in the first place. As noted above, under s 205 of the LPA, it is clear that rent is not an essential requirement of a lease, although certain types of tenancy such as those within the Rent Acts must be supported by rent to qualify for statutory protection. Indeed, that is why, in *Street*, Lord Templeman refers to rent, that being a case concerning the application of the Rent Acts. In fact, the existence of rent as an adjunct to a lease is so likely that, in the absence of an express promise by the tenant, a covenant to pay rent can easily be implied from the words of a deed. Likewise, the absence of a rent obligation may mean that the parties have not intended to create any type of obligation at all (see *Javad v Aqil* (1991)). It is, however, a common misconception that rent has to be in monetary form. It can be in goods, services, or payable in kind.[4] The only clear requirement is that the amount of rent must be capable of being rendered certain. Thus, in *Bostock v Bryant* (1990), the obligation to pay fluctuating utility bills could not be regarded as rent, being an uncertain sum.

The defining features of the leasehold estate have been described above and reference to its versatility has been made. This versatility is reflected in the terminology of leasehold estates where 'term of years', 'lease', 'tenancy', 'periodic tenancy' and 'sub-lease' all describe situations within which the relationship of landlord and tenant can exist. That relationship has many advantages, both for the landlord and the tenant (for example, simultaneous enjoyment of property, leasehold covenants, occupation or income generation) and that is why it has survived the many statutory reforms of the law of real property in the twentieth century. Finally, mention must be made of the House of Lords' decision in *Bruton v London and Quadrant Housing Trust* (2000). In that case, it was suggested that 'a lease' could exist in favour of an occupier even though the 'landlord' did not actually have an estate in the land himself out of which to grant a lease (the landlord had a licence). This controversial view requires acceptance of the idea that not all 'leases' are really estates in the land after all, but may be personal to the original parties (a so-called 'non-proprietary lease'). Suffice it to say that this view has not been universally welcomed and remains suspect. Moreover, even if (as in *Bruton* itself) it is accepted that the 'tenancy' is perfectly valid as between the parties to it, it can still be defeated in an action brought by the true owner of the land (*London Borough of Islington v Green* (2005); *Kay v London Borough of Lambeth* (2004) and most recently, *London Development Agency v Nidai and Others* (2009).[5]

Don't be tempted to

Do not rely simply on *Street v Mountford* and textbook knowledge. Case law is everything in this area. Most students can write a basic answer to this question and if you want to stand out, case law can help you do this.

....

4   This answer provides a nuanced account of the relevance and nature of rent in this area.

5   This conclusion highlights an additional issue in relation to the nature of leases, i.e. whether they must consist of an estate in land, but mentions the issue in such a way as to ensure that the focus of the essay is still very much on the 'hallmarks' of leases outlined in the question.

QUESTION 18

Are there any significant differences between the creation and the operation of legal, as opposed to equitable, leases and what are the effects of any such differences?

How to Answer this Question

❖ Sections 52 and 54 of the Law of Property Act 1925 and periodic tenancies.

❖ Formalities for equitable leases: 2 of the Law of Property (Miscellaneous Provisions) Act 1989 and *Walsh v Lonsdale* (1882).

❖ Legal and equitable leases in registered and unregistered land – different approaches.

❖ Leasehold covenants in pre-1996 leases – different rules for equitable leases

❖ Creating easements – s 62 of the LPA 1925.

Applying the Law

This diagram shows the difference between legal and equitable leases.

ANSWER

Under s 52 of the Law of Property Act 1925, all legal leases except those that are exempt under s 52(2) must be created by deed. This is the basic principle in respect of the creation of legal leases. The exception granted by statute is for those leases that take effect in possession for not more than three years without a fine. This is merely a complicated way of saying that leases for three years or less, which entitle the tenant to go into immediate possession and which require only the payment of rent and not an initial lump sum, are legal leases without the need for a deed. Thus, the periodic tenancy, whereby an occupier goes into occupation and pays a defined sum for a period usually of one week, one month or one quarter, will amount to a legal tenancy because the rent will be paid in respect of periods of less than three years. It matters not that, in fact, the periodic tenant may occupy for many years because, in theory, this is just a succession of periodic tenancies. Of course, this means that the tenancy can be determined by the giving of one period's notice (subject to a statutory minimum of four weeks' notice: s 2 of the **Protection from Eviction Act 1977**), but, while it continues, it is legal in character. In fact, the provisions of ss 52 and 54 are relatively simple, but they tell us only how legal leases can be created. What of leases that take effect in equity only?

The practical reality is that many leases are created in the absence of a deed (despite the fact that the **Law of Property (Miscellaneous Provisions) Act 1989** simplified the requirements for their execution), but the majority of these are for three years or less and qualify as legal interests, as discussed above. So, it is unusual for a lease of over three years' duration to be created without the use of a deed – primarily because the parties routinely use lawyers who proceed to execute the lease by deed. However, circumstances do arise where the parties do not proceed by deed, perhaps because property professionals are not involved and the need for a deed is not known, or even because the parties are content to rely on a written (but non-deed) record of their agreement. In such cases – that is, a lease of over three years not executed by deed – if there is a written contract (or a written record of an agreement that can be treated as if it were a contract), the parties may be taken to have created an equitable lease. In simple terms, an equitable lease arises from an enforceable contract between landlord and tenant to grant a legal lease, but where no grant of a legal lease has in fact occurred. There are a number of distinct steps in this process. First, the contract between prospective landlord and tenant must be enforceable: viz, the contract must in writing containing all the terms and signed by both parties: s 2 of the **Law of Property (Miscellaneous Provisions) Act 1989**, replacing s 40 of the LPA 1925 (which allowed oral contracts if supported by acts of part-performance). In this connection, 'written contract' means either a written document clearly expressed to be a contract or a written record of agreement that the law is prepared to treat as contract. A good example of the latter is where A and B set down in writing the terms on which A will let her house to B. A and B may not intend to take any further steps to create the lease, perhaps believing they have done all that is necessary, but their written agreement will be treated as a 'written contract to grant a lease'. We should also note that, in future, it will be possible to execute a 'written' contract electronically.[6]

---

6   Although the question here asks about the difference in operation between legal and equitable leases, it is important to outline when the two arise and for what reason since this will allow for more sophisticated analysis of the significance of the differences.

Second, this properly created contract must be specifically enforceable, for it is the specific enforceability of the contract that allows it to be regarded as an equitable lease. If the contract is specifically enforceable, this means that it would be executed by order of a court and, because equity regards as done what ought to be done, the unexecuted but enforceable contract will be regarded as an equitable lease (*Walsh v Lonsdale* (1882)). Of course, if the contract is in fact carried out, a legal lease by deed will be the result, but, usually, a dispute arises between the parties precisely because there is no deed. A contract will be specifically enforceable if valuable consideration has been paid by the tenant, if damages for breach of contract would be an inadequate remedy and if the person seeking to enforce the contract has not behaved inequitably. Usually these three conditions are easily satisfied (the first two almost by definition) and, in most cases, an equitable tenancy can be established. Furthermore, Walsh makes it clear that, if in the circumstances there is a choice between a legal periodic tenancy (because the tenant is in occupation and paying rent) and an equitable tenancy on the same terms as the proposed but defunct lease by deed, the equitable tenancy will take priority as this gives efficacy to the parties' agreement. So, for example, any intended covenants in the failed legal lease will take effect in the equitable lease.

It is plain to see, then, that the requirements for an equitable lease have changed somewhat since 1989, primarily because of the requirement of writing. There is, however, one small exception to this. It may still be possible to create a lease longer than three years entirely out of oral agreements provided that those oral agreements amount to a proprietary estoppel within the rules of *Taylor Fashions v Liverpool Victoria Trustees* (1982). So, if a landlord assures an occupier that they have a tenancy and the occupier relies on that to their detriment, an estoppel tenancy may well result (cf *Orgee v Orgee* (1997)).[7] This will be equitable and, even if over three years without writing, will be enforceable against the landlord.

Despite the apparent ease with which an equitable lease can be created, it is clear that the parties to a legal lease do enjoy significant advantages, not least because a purchaser of the landlord's right (his 'reversion') will almost certainly be aware of the existence of any legal tenancy. So, for example, in registered land, currently a legal lease for a period of seven years or more will be registered with its own title number. Even if it is not (say because someone has forgotten to register, as in *Barclays Bank v Zaroovabli* (1997)), the otherwise legal lease will (with only limited special exceptions) be an interest which overrides – whether the situation involves first registration or the disposition of already registered land – under Scheds 1 and 3 to the Land Registration Act (LRA) 2002 because the tenant is likely to be a person in 'actual occupation' of the land. Likewise, even in the absence of such occupation, short-term legal leases – that is, those for seven years or less – will similarly be protected under para 1 of both Schedules. This means that a purchaser of registered land is

---

7   It is important when discussing estoppel to acknowledge that the remedy given by the court in response to the estoppel may not amount to what was promised since they will only do the minimum necessary to satisfy the equity in the instant case.

going to be bound by the legal lease in all but the strangest circumstances. Similarly, in unregistered land, the deed (or fact of occupation under a legal periodic tenancy) will be obvious and, after all, in unregistered land legal rights 'bind the whole world'. As much cannot be said, however, for equitable leases, particularly in unregistered land.

Equitable leases can sometimes be difficult for a purchaser of the reversion to discover (although the requirement of writing in the 1989 Act may relieve this somewhat). Moreover, like all equitable interests, equitable leases are prima facie vulnerable to purchasers – that is, to purchasers of the freehold land over which the lease exists. In unregistered land, for example, the equitable tenant is required to register their interest as a Class C(iv) land charge under the Land Charges Act (1972). Should they fail to do so, the equitable tenancy is not binding on any purchaser of the reversion of a legal estate for money or money's worth (s 4 of the Land Charges Act). This was just the position in *Hollington Brothers v Rhodes* (1951) and no amount of occupation, obvious or otherwise, can help.[8] Moreover, if the equitable lease has resulted from proprietary estoppel, it is probably unregistrable as a land charge (cf *Ives v High* (1967)). In that case, the old doctrine of notice comes into play and this is unsatisfactory for both the purchaser and the equitable tenant. In registered land, however, the position is more satisfactory, at least for the tenant. Whereas the equitable tenant may protect their interest by way of notice (usually agreed but sometimes unilateral) as a protected interest, they may rely on the alternative on Scheds 1 and 3 to the LRA 2002 to gain an interest which overrides as a person in actual occupation of the premises. Of course, this is all very well for the equitable tenant, but it does mean that the purchaser of the reversion of a registered title may well become bound by an interest that was informally created. Of course, in many situations, the fact of occupation (and, hence, the equitable lease) may well be obvious and the purchaser will be warned of the overriding interest. This situation is certainly aided by the two Schedules to the LRA 2002 which remove the risk of apparently innocuous occupation of a small area protecting the entire plot and thus reverse the decision in *Ferrishurst Ltd v Wallcite Ltd* (1999), but this is not always going to be true especially with estoppel leases that can still be entirely oral (for example, see *Malory Enterprises Ltd v Cheshire Homes (UK) Ltd* (2002)).

Further difficulties with equitable leases also arise in the context of leasehold covenants, although these have been eliminated for leases granted on or after 1 January 1996 by the Landlord and Tenant (Covenants) Act (LTCA) 1995. So, for pre-1996 equitable leases, the general position is that although covenants in the lease will be enforceable between the original landlord and the original equitable tenant (because of privity of contract), they may well be unenforceable between successors in title to those persons. Being a pre-1996 equitable lease (and despite contrary dicta in *Boyer v Warbey* (1953)), the

---

8   A very common mistake is to assume that obvious actual occupation will always result in an interest binding a purchaser whatever the nature of that interest and whether or not the land is registered. It is important to be clear as to the relevance of actual occupation.

traditional view is that there is no 'privity of estate' between a successor to the landlord and an assignee of the tenant. In fact, it is the landlord that suffers most in this situation because the burden of covenants entered into by the original tenant (that is, the obligation to perform them) may well not be passed to an assignee of an equitable lease, unless they can be enforced as restrictive covenants under *Tulk v Moxhay* (1848). Indeed, it is worse than this because the new equitable reversioner (the new landlord) is under the burdens of the equitable lease as these are statutorily transmitted on a sale of the reversion by s142 of the LPA. Thus, the new landlord can be sued on the original covenants of an equitable lease, but unless Tulk applies, they cannot sue the new tenant. Fortunately, for equitable leases granted on or after 1 January 1996, the LTCA 1995 ensures that both the benefits and burdens of leasehold covenants pass to both an assignee of the landlord and an assignee of the tenant.[9]

Finally, there are some provisions of the Law of Property Act relating to conveyances of land that apply only to conveyances of a legal estate.[10] The most important of these in practice is s62 of the LPA, which can be used to imply easements into a tenancy in favour of the tenant; for example, an easement of way. Unfortunately, s62 is restricted to transfer of a legal estate and cannot be relied upon by an equitable tenant.

Ultimately, then, it is better for all parties if a legal lease is established. Not only is the very existence of the equitable lease dependent on the availability of specific performance, but its informal nature also poses problems for purchaser and tenant alike.

Don't be tempted to

There is more to this question that simply describing statutory formalities for the creation legal or equitable leases, although that is a good place to start. Do not ignore the land registration issues as this is an important reason why legal and equitable leases have become almost identical effect in registered land.

QUESTION 19

'*Street v Mountford* creates a rule that the acid test for the existence of a tenancy is the presence of a grant of exclusive possession for a definite period of time, possibly but not necessarily involving rent.'

(Sparkes, *A New Landlord and Tenant* (2nd edn, 2001)
Oxford: Hart Publishing, p. 150)

▶ Discuss.

---

9   It is good to show that you are aware of the pre-1996 position in relation to leasehold covenants.

10 This is the sort of information that a lot of people might miss since it relates to the creation of legal interests generally, rather than to legal leases in particular, but is nonetheless highly relevant to the question under consideration here.

How to Answer this Question

- ❖ The existence of rights versus the contractual intention of the parties.
- ❖ Lodgers and tenants.
- ❖ Cases where exclusive possession can exist without a tenancy: *Facchini v Bryson* (1952).
- ❖ Refining *Street v Mountford*: *Antoniades v Villiers* (1990); *Westminster CC v Clarke* (1992); *Bruton v London and Quadrant Housing Trust* (2000); *Kay v London Borough of Lambeth* (2004).

Applying the Law

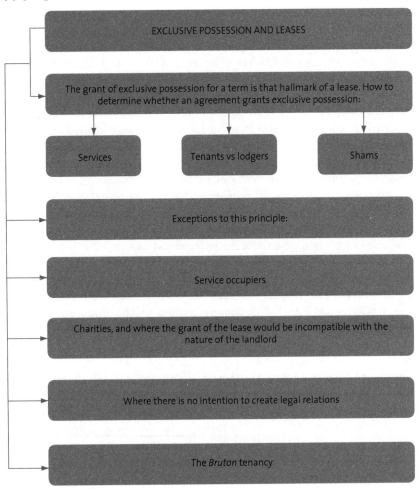

EXCLUSIVE POSSESSION AND LEASES

The grant of exclusive possession for a term is that hallmark of a lease. How to determine whether an agreement grants exclusive possession:

Services

Tenants vs lodgers

Shams

Exceptions to this principle:

Service occupiers

Charities, and where the grant of the lease would be incompatible with the nature of the landlord

Where there is no intention to create legal relations

The *Bruton* tenancy

This diagram demonstrates the importance of exclusive possession to leases.

ANSWER

A lease is properly regarded as a proprietary right, an interest in land capable of binding third parties (despite the unorthodox decision in *Bruton v London and Quadrant Housing Trust* (2000)). Moreover, despite some suggestions to the contrary (for example, *Errington v Errington and Woods* (1952)), a licence is a personal right, usually arising out of contract, which as a matter of principle is not capable of binding third parties under property law principles (*Ashburn Anstalt v Arnold* (1989), confirmed in *Lloyd v Dugdale* (2002)). It is from this basic distinction that so many practical consequences flow. Indeed, the great majority of cases on the lease/licence distinction have been the result of occupiers trying to claim the protection of the **Rent Act 1977** or later Housing Acts, because the protection they offer is available to a tenant, not always to a licensee. Of course, the ability of landlords to grant non-protected tenancies under the **Housing Act 1996** may affect the volume of litigation before the courts on this subject, but the distinction between a lease and a licence forms the boundary between property and contract and will always be contentious.[11]

Lord Templeman's judgment in *Street v Mountford* (1985) (overruling the intention-based approach of *Somma v Hazlehurst* (1978)) caused something of a stir. Not only did he propound an abstract test for distinguishing between a lease and a licence ('exclusive possession for a term at a rent'), but he told us how to apply it. First, there are certain exceptional situations in which the occupier may (or may not) have exclusive possession of the property but, for special reasons, no tenancy will result. One example is where a mortgagee goes into possession under the terms of their mortgage and another where the occupation is based on charity or friendship, as in *Gray v Taylor* (1998), or where there is no intention to create legal relations between the owner and the occupier (cf *Javad v Aqil* (1991)). These exempted categories were explained at length in *Facchini v Bryson* (1952) and that they are alive and well is demonstrated by *Norris v Checksfield* (1991). In that case, the occupier of a cottage was held to be a 'service occupant' and hence a licensee, although the Court of Appeal did warn that this was an exceptional situation justified only because the occupation of the cottage was for the better performance of the employee's duties.

Second, apart from the exceptional situations, according to Lord Templeman, an occupier must either be a lodger (a licensee) or a tenant. This practical distinction between a lodger and a tenant is crucial. A lodger is someone who receives attendance and services from the landlord, such as room cleaning or meals. Such a person will be a licensee, although, as *Markou v Da Silvaesa* (1986) illustrates, a mere promise to provide such services is not sufficient. They must actually be provided. However, if it is true that an occupier is either a lodger or a tenant, this means that no other kind of 'occupation licence' can exist. If someone is not a lodger, they are a tenant. There is no intermediate

---

11   The introduction of this answer already shows the different approach that this essay will take when compared with question 17 which on its face is concerned with similar issues. There is cross-over, but the emphasis in the two answers is different.

category of licensee who, while not a lodger, is still not a tenant. Obviously, this has far-reaching consequences, for it restricts the options open to a landlord when seeking to make use of their property. It is the triumph of property law over freedom of contract and it is precisely this that subsequent cases have found difficult to accept. Indeed, many of the apparently inconsistent decisions of the Court of Appeal have resulted from attempts to identify some middle way, some form of occupation that can still give rise to a licence, but in which the occupier is not a lodger. *Hadjiloucas v Crean* (1998) and *Brooker Estates v Ayer* (1987), both decisions of the Court of Appeal quite soon after *Street*, are of this type.

Nevertheless, under the influence of Lord Templeman in the House of Lords (for example, *Antoniades v Villiers* (1990); *Westminster CC v Clarke* (1992)) and Lord Donaldson in the Court of Appeal (for example, *Aslan v Murphy* (1990)), a degree of certainty has emerged. First, cases of multiple occupancy may give rise to licences in favour of the occupiers because of the absence of the four unities necessary to support a joint tenancy of the whole premises. This is the result of *AG Securities v Vaughan* (1990). So, if four people occupy a four-bedroom house, but each sign different agreements, on different days and for a different rent, there can be no exclusive possession/joint tenancy because there is no unity of interest, title, or time. The house, as a whole, cannot be held on a tenancy. Each occupier may have a tenancy of their own rooms, with a licence over the common parts, but there is no single tenancy of the property as a whole.

Second, there are certain types of public sector landlord who may be able to grant licences in circumstances in which a private landlord could not. Examples are *Westminster CC v Basson* (1991), *Ogwr BC v Dykes* (1989) and the House of Lords' decision in *Westminster CC v Clarke* (1992). In these cases, the licence is allowed not because of the intention of the landlord – for that would be to return to *Somma v Hazlehurst* – but because of a policy decision: namely, that public sector landlords must not be hindered in the exercise of their statutory housing duties. It is clear, of course, that public sector landlords and similar bodies will be held to have granted tenancy if this is justified on the facts (see *Family Housing Association v Jones* (1990)) and, it seems, will even be held to have given a lease if they themselves had no estate in the land (*Bruton v London and Quadrant Housing Trust*). Indeed, in *Bruton*, Lord Hoffmann was doubtful whether the identity of the landlord as such really could make a difference to the grant of a lease or licence as suggested by the earlier cases. *Bruton* is discussed more fully below.

Third, Lord Oliver in *Antoniades* suggests that there may be circumstances in which landlords can genuinely reserve to themselves the right to make use of the premises and, if such use is made, no exclusive possession is given. In effect, this is no more than a restatement of the distinction between exclusive possession and exclusive occupation: the former establishing the legal relationship of landlord and tenant; the latter describing a factual situation devoid of proprietary effect. An example might be where an academic lets his house to students but reserves the right to enter the house and use his library. This is, of course, open to abuse and, in the light of his speech in *Antoniades*, it is doubtful whether Lord Templeman would agree that it is even a possibility.[12] However, the door has been left open by Lord Oliver for future development in genuine cases, and it is implicit in the decision in *Royal Bank of Scotland v Mehta* (1999) in which, despite apparent exclusive possession, the occupier of a hotel room was said to have a licence, presumably because it is never intended to create a lease of such a property.

Fourth, in *Bruton v London and Quadrant Housing Trust*, a quasi-public sector manager of land (the Trust) was held by the House of Lords to have granted the plaintiff a valid lease to occupy, even though the Trust had no estate in the land. This is unusual as normally the absence of an estate in the landlord means, by definition, that the occupier cannot have an estate (a lease) but must have a licence. As noted, the Trust itself held only a licence to manage the land (granted to it by the local authority landowner) and argued that because it held no proprietary right, it could never have granted the plaintiff a tenancy. In its view, the plaintiff must have a licence, carved out of the Trust's own licence. In rejecting this argument, the House of Lords said that a 'lease' was not always an estate in the land, but could be a merely personal arrangement between 'landlord' and 'tenant'. Apparently, this non-proprietary lease was justified by the exclusive possession of the 'tenant', even though the landlord could not grant the kind of exclusive possession (that is, of an estate in the land) that was so crucial in *Street v Mountford*. This decision and its reasoning has attracted some sharp criticism and it is not clear why this 'non-proprietary lease' is not properly identified as a licence! It means, however, that leases can exist even if the grantor has no estate in the land. Moreover, in the case of such a 'tenancy' although as between the original 'landlord' and 'tenant' it is binding, it will not be so on the original owner of the land (*Kay v London Borough of Lambeth* (2004); *London Borough of Islington v Green* (2005)).[13]

Finally, all of the above is subject to the doctrine of pretences. Any clause, in any agreement, will not be given legal effect if it is not intended to be relied on by either party to the agreement, but is merely inserted in it to avoid the grant of the tenancy that would otherwise arise. Thus, in *Antoniades* itself, an agreement providing for the separate occupancy of an unmarried couple in what was to be their home was held to be a tenancy because the separate agreements were clearly a pretence. It should be noted in this regard, that the doctrine of 'pretences' has replaced that of shams: a 'sham' transaction is one in which only one party does not intend a clause in a lease to have legal effect and, of course, a landlord always intends in these cases to deny, by means of a clause like that used as in *Antoniades*, the creation of a lease.[14]

---

12 Discussing a potential conflict in the approach of different judges in the same case is a very good way of showing, firstly, that you have good knowledge of the case in question, and secondly of highlighting an area of controversy.

13 The discussion of *Bruton* shows why this is such a divisive decision whilst still focusing on the question set rather than discussing the merits or otherwise of *Bruton* itself.

14 The clarification of the language used here is useful as it shows that the writer is aware of the way this issue has previously been discussed.

To conclude then, the case law after *Street* has finally taken a decidedly practical path[15] whereby the emphasis is on identifying those factual situations that can give rise to a licence and those that can give rise to a tenancy. This may not be the most intellectually satisfying approach – after all, we have not defined 'exclusive possession' – but it is the most realistic. The most serious reservation is the uncertainty caused by the House of Lords' decision in *Bruton v London and Quadrant*.

Don't be tempted

Do not answer this question unless you have a reservoir of case law. It – or something like it – is a very common question on land law examinations and the best answers use a range of case law.

QUESTION 20

Rackman is the registered proprietor of freehold land comprising a large Victorian property in the centre of town. The house has four storeys, including a basement. Rackman has just inherited a small bungalow in the country and has decided to move out. He wishes to let the property, but is determined not to have long-term tenants just in case he wants to return to the city. He divides the house into two self-contained, one-bedroomed apartments on the first and second floors, and one self-contained two-bedroomed flat on the ground floor/basement. He agrees in writing with Harold and Matilda, a young unmarried couple, that they can occupy the two-bedroomed flat and produces two documents that state in each that 'this agreement does not intend to create a term of years'; he gets them to sign separately and on different days for a 'fee' of £90 per week each. He lets the first-floor flat to William, an apprentice carpenter, who is to carry out repairs to the premises. William pays no money, but each week £60 is deducted from his wages. Rackman keeps a key to William's flat, primarily to inspect the building works at the weekend when William is away. The top-floor flat is given to Rackman's daughter, Margaret, a university drop-out with nowhere else to go. Margaret is not the most reliable individual, so William is asked to keep an eye on her and to make sure that she gets regular meals.

Rackman has now decided to move to the country permanently and sells the entire premises to Edward, a property developer. Edward wishes to evict all the occupants and redevelop the site. Advise him.

How to Answer this Question

The question involves the application of the lease/licence distinction and the effect on a purchaser of the reversion.

---

15 This conclusion in describing the route after *Street* as 'practical' not only summarises the law described, but also analyses it, assessing its merits.

❖ *Antoniades v Villiers* (1990)
❖ *Street v Mountford* (1985)
❖ *Mikeover v Brady* (1989) or *Aslan v Murphy* (1990)
❖ Scheds 1 and 3 to the Land Registration Act 2002.

Answer Structure

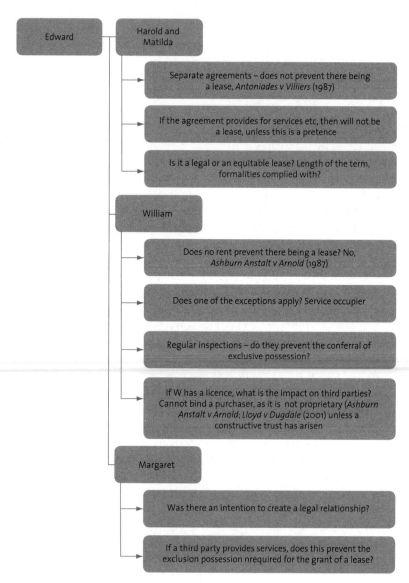

This diagram shows how to apply the lease/ licence distinction to the situation involving Edward.

ANSWER

This problem concerns the distinction between a lease and a licence. A lease is traditionally a proprietary right, whereas a licence is a mere personal arrangement between two parties (*Ashburn Anstalt v Arnold* (1989)). The practical difference this makes in this problem is clear. If the arrangements entered into by Rackman with his respective occupiers amount to leases, then they have the ability to bind Edward the purchaser when he acquires the freehold title. If, however, the arrangements are properly to be regarded as licences, then, in principle, they cannot bind Edward and the occupiers will have to vacate the premises.

In general terms, the distinction between a lease and a licence was summarised by Lord Templeman in *Street v Mountford* (1985). A lease exists where an occupier has been granted exclusive possession of the property, for a term, at a rent. The answer is not to be found in the label attached to the agreement by the parties but in the nature of the agreement created by the parties. Not surprisingly, this formula is subject to some exceptions – notably, those known as the *Facchini v Bryson* (1952) categories, which relate to special, limited, factual situations in which for some reason, external to the parties, no tenancy will exist even though exclusive possession may have been granted. The main practical distinction resulting from Lord Templeman's formula is that an occupier must be either a tenant or a lodger, the latter being someone in receipt of attendance and services from the landlord and so without exclusive possession (*Markou v Da Silvaesa* (1986)). Finally, we must also be aware of the doctrine of pretences (see, for example, *Antoniades v Villiers* (1990)), whereby the court will examine an agreement between the parties to discover whether its terms genuinely reflect the actual relationship between the parties. Only if the agreement is 'genuine' in this sense will any clauses in the agreement affecting 'exclusive possession' be given legal effect.[16]

(A) HAROLD AND MATILDA[17]

Clearly, the agreement between Rackman, on the one hand, and Harold and Matilda, on the other, is designed to allow them to occupy the premises and, from Rackman's point of view, to prevent the grant of a tenancy: this much is expressly stated in the documents which both Harold and Matilda sign. At one time, such an express statement of the parties' 'intention' (query whether Harold and Matilda can really be said to share this intention) would have been enough to prevent a lease being granted (*Somma v Hazlehurst* (1978)). Now, after *Street*, it is clear that it is the nature of the relationship that is important, not what the parties decide to call that relationship. Thus, if this

---

16 It is useful in a question like this to give an outline of the structure of the rules you are applying in the introduction.

17 Sub-headings are good in a problem question to help give clarity to an answer. It also helps to keep the answer on track in the exam.

agreement amounts to a lease under the Street formula, it will be a lease irrespective of the label attached to it.

Rackman has had some well-informed legal advice, for he has made every attempt to prevent the couple enjoying exclusive possession. He has, in fact, attempted to deny them a tenancy by seeking to grant each of them a separate licence whereby neither of them has exclusive possession of the whole but each occupies in common with the other, as in *Mikeover v Brady* (1989). The only way that Harold and Matilda can refute this is to establish that they have been granted exclusive possession jointly: in other words that they are joint tenants of a leasehold interest. As was made clear in *AG Securities v Vaughan* (1990), for a joint tenancy of a leasehold estate to exist, the 'four unities' must be present: there must be unity of interest, title, possession and time, and this is what Rackman has tried to prevent. In this case, as in *Vaughan* itself, the landlord has persuaded the parties to sign different documents on different days. It looks as if there is no unity of time or of title. In *Vaughan*, these facts, plus the different rents paid by the occupiers, clearly meant that no leasehold joint tenancy of the whole property could exist. The parties were occupying separately, not jointly. Moreover, even if *Vaughan* is not quite in point, because, in that case, the property was always intended to be for independent, ever-changing, occupants, Rackman can clearly rely on the decision in *Mikeover v Brady*. In that case, a flat was let to two people by two separate agreements, each responsible for one half of the total 'fee'. Despite the fact that the occupiers wished to co-habit jointly (that is, as a couple), the agreements were held to confer separate licences only. The facts of our case are very similar indeed, but we should note that a different result was reached in *Aslan v Murphy* (1990).

Perhaps, however, there is one further possibility. In *Antoniades v Villiers*, the appellants were a young couple, living together as if married in a joint home. This fact was known to the landlord. In the House of Lords, this arrangement was held to create a joint tenancy of the leasehold estate, despite the fact of separate 'licence' agreements similar to those signed by Harold and Matilda. According to Lord Templeman, the landlord's attempt to deny the couple exclusive possession jointly was a pretence designed entirely to avoid the imposition of a lease. As such, it would be ignored and the 'true' nature of the parties' bargain respected. If we follow *Antoniades*, then, and assuming Rackman knew that Harold and Matilda wished to live together, this agreement may still amount to a lease. Despite the fact that separate agreements were signed, and on different days, there will be a joint tenancy of the leasehold estate because this was the true nature of the bargain.[18]

If the couple do have a lease, then it would appear to be equitable. The agreement is in writing (not by deed and not legal) and probably amounts to a specifically enforceable

---

18   This analysis shows the difficulty of applying the case law in this area to a factual scenario, but uses the cases well to justify the conclusion reached.

contract. Assuming this, equity will regard this as an equitable lease under *Walsh v Lonsdale* (1882). When the property is sold to Edward, presumably the couple are in actual occupation and would, therefore, have an overriding interest under **Scheds 1** or **3, para 2** to the **Land Registration Act 2002**. If the lease is not equitable, the arrangement may well amount to a legal periodic tenancy because of rent paid and accepted for the weekly term. If that were true, it would be overriding under **para 1** of the same two **Schedules** to the **LRA 2002** (*Barclays Bank v Zaroovabli* (1997), and contrast *Mortgage Business plc v Cook* (2012)). Of course, the lease is binding on Edward only according to its terms. He may terminate it on giving the appropriate notice unless it is protected by the Rent Acts or Housing Acts.

(B) WILLIAM

William is in occupation of the first-floor flat and, again, the nature of his occupancy is crucial in determining whether Edward can acquire immediate possession. Whether or not William has a tenancy may well depend on whether William's occupancy falls within one of the exceptional categories identified by Lord Templeman in *Street* as being occasions on which, even though exclusive possession may have been granted, no tenancy results. As a preliminary point, it might be thought that the apparent lack of rent destroys any chance of a tenancy. However, as confirmed in *Ashburn*, relying on **s 205** of the **Law of Property Act 1925**, the payment of rent is not essential for the existence of a tenancy. Lord Templeman's comments in *Street* should be read in context: viz, that the case was concerned with the Rent Acts, under which tenancies do need to be supported by rent to qualify for statutory protection. In any event, we can argue forcefully that the weekly deduction from William's wages does amount to rent. There is no rule that 'rent' must be described as such, so long as the payment made is in respect of the right to occupy the demised premises.

William's problem is, however, that his occupation seems to be a 'service occupancy'. He appears to be in occupation of the premises for 'the better performance of his duties' as Rackman's employee/builder. A bona fide service occupancy clearly creates a licence and was one of the original *Facchini* exceptions. That it still can occur has been confirmed in the recent case of *Norris v Checksfield* (1991). Subject to the warning in that case that the court must be astute to detect 'pretences', as where the occupant is given minimal employment duties to make it appear as if there is a service occupancy, our case seems to fall into this category. If anything, William is more like a caretaker than a tenant. Assuming, then, that William has a licence by way of service occupancy Edward cannot be bound by the agreement. A mere licence is binding only on the parties and William will have to quit (*Ashburn Anstalt v Arnold; Lloyd v Dugdale* (2002)).[19]

---

19 It is important to follow through the consequences of your conclusion – it is not enough here to establish that there is a licence and leave the matter there.

(C) MARGARET

As far as Rackman's daughter, Margaret, is concerned, the circumstances also seem to give rise to a licence. There is every indication that Margaret's occupation of the top-floor flat can be put down to normal family considerations rather than the creation of a tenancy. As in *Heslop v Burns* (1974), this is not a situation in which the parties had an intention to enter into legal relations at all. This is within one of the *Facchini*-excepted categories: viz, occupation based on friendship, generosity or family arrangement (see also *Gray v Taylor* (1998)). Moreover, if this were not enough, Rackman could even argue that Margaret was a lodger and by definition not a tenant (*Street*). The facts suggest that Margaret is in receipt of attendance and services as provided by William, who may be regarded as Rackman's agent for these purposes. On this interpretation of the facts, Margaret could be within *Markou v Da Silvaesa* and a licensee by virtue of a genuine lodger relationship. Once again, as this is a licence there is no possibility of Edward being bound.

So, to conclude, with the possible exception of the arrangement agreed with Harold and Matilda, Rackman has successfully avoided granting any leases over his property. Edward can obtain vacant possession. Finally, we can note that Rackman would have been well advised to have granted short-term assured tenancies under the **Housing Act 1996**. These fall outside the Rent Acts and possession can be recovered easily. This would have avoided all the difficulties Rackman experienced.

Don't be tempted to

As with the previous question, this is all about case law.

In problem questions like this, it is important to allocate enough time to deal with all of the parties. Notice how the problem can be broken down into segments rather than being one long answer. This helps explanation and the Examiner!

QUESTION 21

'The [**Landlord and Tenant (Covenants) Act 1995**] introduced a new code relating to the enforceability of covenants by landlords and tenants.'

(*Oceanic Village Ltd v United Attractions Ltd* (2000) per Neuberger J)

Were the defects in the law relating to the enforceability of leasehold covenants so serious as to justify the scheme introduced by the Act for leases granted after 31 December 1995?

How to Answer this Question

Consider the law before and after the **1995 Act** and assess whether the Act was needed and how successful has it been.

- ❖ Outline of rules applicable to pre-1996 leases and defects.
- ❖ Purpose of the **LTCA 1995**.

❖ Provisions of the **LTCA 1995** carrying these purposes into effect.

❖ Overall effect and assessment of the **LTCA 1995**

Applying the Law

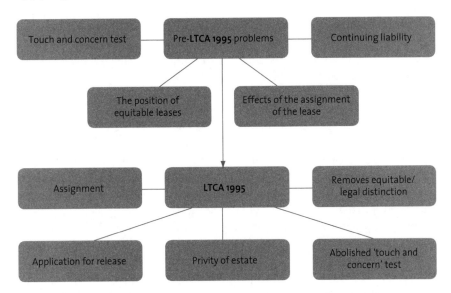

This diagram shows the problems of the pre- *Landlord and Tenant (Covenants) Act 1995* law and the solutions provided by that Act.

ANSWER

The **Landlord and Tenant (Covenants) Act 1995** sought to address the two perceived fundamental problems of principle of continuing liability throughout the entire term of the lease for the original landlord and tenant and the notoriously elusive concept of covenants that 'touch and concern'.[20] The **LTCA 1995** governs the enforceability of leasehold covenants in leases granted after 31 December 1995, whether the lease be legal or equitable. However, for leases granted prior to this, the 'old' rules apply. Consequently, there are currently two sets of distinct legal principles governing the enforceability of leasehold covenants and by comparing them, we can discover whether the radical reforms of the **LTCA 1995** were really necessary.

For leases granted before 1 January 1996 (non-**LTCA** leases), the enforceability of leasehold covenants revolves around privity of contract, privity of estate and statutory magic. The original parties to a lease will be bound throughout the entirety of the term to perform

---

20 The introduction here shows the approach that the answer will take to analysing the changes to the law by quickly outlining the main issues focused on.

the covenants they have agreed to, whether those covenants be personal or not. Thus, both the original landlord (*Stuart v Joy* (1904)) and the original tenant (*Arlesford Trading Co v Servansingh* (1971)) can be sued for failure to perform the leasehold covenants by the person who enjoys the benefit of those covenants, irrespective of the time the breach was committed or by whom. This is the principle of continuing liability and it flows from the very nature of a lease as a contract. The continuing liability of the landlord and tenant under a pre-1996 lease is a primary one, so that they may be sued on the covenants even though the plaintiff has an obvious remedy against the person actually committing the breach, such as an assignee.

The second[21] major area of difficulty was the requirement for pre-1996 leases that a covenant must 'touch and concern the land' (*Spencer's Case* (1583)) (and the equivalent under statute that it must have 'reference to the subject matter of the lease': **ss 141** and **142** of the **Law of Property Act 1925**), before it can bind successors in title. So, for pre-1996 leases, if privity of estate exists between plaintiff and defendant (that is, they are current landlord and tenant under a legal lease), the assignee of a tenant will acquire the benefit and burden of all those covenants that touch and concern the land (*Spencer's Case*). Likewise, the benefit and the burden of all of the original landlord's covenants will be passed to an assignee of the reversion if they have reference to the subject matter of the lease (**ss 141** and **142** of the **LPA**). Obviously, such a central concept for pre-1996 leases needs to be applied consistently and, if possible, have a core meaning. The Law Commission was of the view that, despite the guidance provided by the House of Lords in *Swift Investments v Combined English Stores* (1989), this was not the case.

Third, there are a number of other matters that attracted criticism and which still operate for pre-1996 leases. So, it is uncertain whether an assignee of the reversion is liable for breaches of covenants committed by the original landlord before assignment. As a matter of principle, it would seem that he should not be, but dicta in *Celsteel v Alton* (1985) suggest otherwise. Again, there is a certain inequality in the fact that landlords lose the right to sue on the covenants when they assign their reversion (*Re King* (1963)), but, according to *City and Metropolitan Properties v Greycroft* (1987), a tenant retains the right to sue the landlord after assigning the lease, at least in respect of breaches of covenant committed while they (the tenant) were in possession. All of this, however, pales into insignificance in the light of the problems that arise when the pre-1996 lease is merely equitable or where a legal lease has been assigned only in equity (that is, not by deed: *Julian v Crago* (1992)). In such cases, although the original parties are bound to each other in contract, there can be no privity of estate between successors in title to those parties. This can cause serious difficulties, especially for a landlord. Thus, whereas **ss 141** and **142** of the **LPA 1925** operate to transfer the benefit of covenants and the burden of covenants respectively to the equitable assignee of the reversion (as they do with pre-1996 legal

---

21   Clearly outlining the major problems with the old law will make it easier for the examiner to follow your analysis of the success of the solutions in the new law.

leases), the assignee of the equitable tenant does not come under the burden of the covenants due to lack of privity of estate. This is even more disadvantageous to the landlord when we appreciate that the benefit of an original equitable tenant's covenants can be transmitted to an assignee by a simple contractual assignment on the basis that benefits of a contract can be assigned. Thus, we reach the position under a pre-1996 equitable lease that an assignee of the tenant can sue an assignee of the landlord, but not vice versa.[22] Of course, there is some relief for the landlord by virtue of the fact that restrictive covenants may bind under the rule in *Tulk v Moxhay* (1848) and also that the landlord may have the remedy of forfeiture. However, forfeiture is a drastic remedy as it brings to an end the lease (and the income generated by it) and *Tulk* does not help with important positive covenants such as covenants to repair. One solution would be to regard the parties to a pre-1996 lease as being in privity of estate if they were parties to either a legal or an equitable lease, and indeed such a solution was proposed by Lord Denning in *Boyer v Warbey* (1953). Yet, it has not found favour and there remains an unfortunate distinction in pre-1996 leases between the running of covenants in legal leases and the running of covenants in their equitable counterparts.

The principal provisions of the Act – and, therefore, the new scheme for regulating the enforcement of leasehold covenants – are as follows.[23] First, the Act is applicable to legal and equitable tenancies granted on or after 1 January 1996 and the troublesome distinctions between such leases are abolished (**s 28(1)** of the **LTCA 1995**). Second, the tenant (whether original or an assignee) is released automatically from the burden of leasehold covenants when they assign the tenancy (**s 5**), subject only to the possibility that they might be required to guarantee performance of the leasehold covenants by the next (but only the next) immediate assignee under an authorised guarantee agreement (AGA) (**s 16**). The exception is for assignments made in breach of covenant or by operation law when the assigning tenant remains liable (**s 11(2)**). Third, the landlord is not released automatically from the burdens of leasehold covenants, but may serve a notice on the tenant applying for release from covenants that have passed to an assignee (**s 6**; *BHP Petroleum v Chesterfield Properties* (2002)), which release will be effective if the notice is not answered within a specified time or on the landlord's application to the county court (**s 8**). A landlord assigning in breach of covenant or by operation of law cannot serve such a notice (**s 11(3)**). However, we should note that, depending on the terms of the lease, a landlord may not be required to serve a notice at all, having limited by contract his liability on the covenants to the period only in which he is in possession of the reversion – *London Diocesan Fund v Avonridge* (2005). Fourth, the rule that covenants must 'touch and concern' the land or 'have reference to the subject matter of the lease' before the benefits and burdens can be passed to assignees of the lease or the reversion is abolished (**ss 2 and 3**). Fifth, and in consequence, the benefit and burden of all

----

22 It is worth summing up the point briefly, as in this sentence, since it gives it more impact.

23 A summary of the main provisions introduced as a result of legislative reforms allows focus on the most important changes whilst also showing that you are aware of the more minor changes without taking up too much time.

leasehold covenants pass automatically to assignees of the lease and the reversion, so that an assignee may enforce, and will be subject to, any covenant contained in the lease (s3). There is no need to show 'privity of estate' and ss141 and 142 are no longer applicable. There is automatic annexation of all leasehold covenants to the premises comprised in all leases and reversions. Only those covenants that are positively expressed to be personal will not pass to assignees, but this may include covenants that in substance would have been proprietary under the old law. Sixth, as a counterbalance to the change in the original tenant's liability, the Act permits the landlord to *require* an assigning tenant to enter into an Authorised Guarantee Agreement (AGA) to guarantee performance of the covenants by the person to whom he assigns – s 16 LTCA 1995 and *K/S Victoria Street v House of Fraser (Stores Management) Ltd.* (2011). Seventh, an attempt to enforce liability for a 'fixed charge' (for example, rent or a service charge) against a person not in possession (for example, an assigning tenant under an AGA, or the original tenant for pre-1996 leases to which this provision applies retrospectively) must comply with a 'problem notice' procedure. This requires the landlord to serve a notice on the person liable within six months of the charge becoming due. Following payment, this person may go back into the property as tenant under an 'overriding lease' and so attempt to recoup the payment by making use of the land or taking action against the actually defaulting tenant. Failure to serve such a notice within the proper time makes the charge unenforceable. Also, as indicated, this is a provision of the LTCA that applies to both pre-1996 and LTCA leases, being an attempt to control original tenant liability even under the former regime.

Clearly, the LTCA rules establish an entirely new system for the enforcement of leasehold covenants. One major feature is that the rights and liabilities of landlord and tenant should be coterminous with possession of the land (hence, no continuing liability for original tenant, but why not also automatically for the landlord?) and that the benefit and burden of all covenants should pass automatically. This also means that the right to sue runs with possession. This removes many of the anomalies under the 'old' rules. Likewise, the removal of the distinction between legal and equitable leases is greatly to be welcomed. Additionally, the landlord's position is preserved by the ability to require the assigning tenant to enter into an AGA guaranteeing the next immediate assignee's liability under the covenants. This is permissible only as a guarantee of the next immediate assignee (*Good Harvest Partnership LLP v Centaur Services Ltd.* (2010)), but, of course, if the obligation to enter an AGA is itself made a covenant of the lease, it will flow to all assigning tenants.

To conclude, then, there is no doubt that the LTCA has remedied the most serious deficiencies of the old law and it is a matter of regret that no way could be found to make every provision applicable to all leases whenever granted, although that would have been very difficult. Overall, however, there are still doubts about some aspects of the new system.[24] So, the removal of the distinction between 'proprietary' covenants (those that touch and concern)

....

24 This admission that the LTCA did not solve all the difficulties in the previous law brings balance and sophisticated analysis into the answer.

and personal covenants is thought by some to be unnecessary (but see *BHP Petroleum*). After *Swift*, is it really true that the distinction is hard to draw and if (as the Law Commission argues) few personal covenants creep into leases, why bother at all? Also, even though landlords are not entitled to automatic release from covenants on assignment, two points should be noted. First, it will be rare for tenants to oppose such requests and probably rarer for a court to uphold any objection. Secondly, the decision in *Avonridge* – whereby a landlord who in the original lease has contractually limited its obligations to the period of his possession of the reversion does *not* actually have to serve a notice to be released because it is a matter of contract – seriously undercuts the idea behind the **LTCA 1995** that tenants should have greater protection. Finally, and most importantly, the AGA concept means the landlord retains another person to sue: the assigning tenant. In residential leases, the landlord cannot refuse to agree to an assignment to a new tenant on the grounds that the existing tenant will not enter an AGA on the landlord's terms unless this would be reasonable in all the circumstances. In commercial leases, however, the long-established obligation that consent to assignment cannot be withheld unreasonably has been abolished, as this was the price extracted by landlords' interest groups for not obstructing the Bill entirely in Parliament. It is a heavy price, for it gives commercial landlords full control over the land by allowing them to deny consent to assignment unless the tenant complies with onerous (and unreasonable) obligations.

Don't be tempted to

This question calls for a comparison between pre-1996 rules and the **LTCA 1995**. It is focused more on the **LTCA 1995**, but do not forget to discuss the deficiencies in the law that it was meant to remedy.

An answer should not be merely descriptive. This is a large topic and should not be attempted unless you have a thorough knowledge of the area and the ability to put it down on paper quickly.

QUESTION 22

(a) Harry is the registered proprietor of a large industrial site on the edge of Shortbridge. In 1992, he lets Unit 1 to Julian on a 21-year lease by deed containing covenants that Julian shall not use the premises for the purpose of the manufacture of household appliances, shall not assign or sub-let the property without Harry's consent, and shall carry out all reasonable external and internal repairs to the property. Seven years later, Julian assigns his interest, with Harry's consent, to Larry, a sporting equipment manufacturer. Larry's business suffers in the recession and he sub-lets to Keith, a manufacturer of portable air-conditioning units, without Harry's knowledge.

(b) Unit 2, title to which is unregistered, is let to Esmeralda on a ten-year lease by deed in 1995 for the purpose of establishing a restaurant on the site to service the estate during working hours. Esmeralda covenants not to open after 8 pm and to sell only beers manufactured by Harry in his brewery. In return, Harry covenants not to carry on any catering business elsewhere on the site. Unfortunately, Esmeralda develops a major alcohol problem and must leave the premises for the sake of her health. She assigns her lease in writing to Nathan, who finds that the only way to make a profit is to open until 11 pm and sell a wider range of beers. Meanwhile, Harry has sold the entire site to Peter, who starts to manufacture chocolate in Unit 3. Peter finds he can make quite a profit selling chocolate cakes to the site workers at lunchtime.

Peter has discovered about Keith and the roof of Unit 1 is leaking. The police are concerned about drunkenness on the estate at night and Nathan is about to sue for breach of covenant.

▶ **Advise the parties as to the enforceability of the covenants.**

How to Answer this Question

❖ This is a pre-1996 lease – **LTCA** does not apply.
❖ Meaning of 'privity of estate' and the requirement of 'touching and concerning' – *Swift Investments v Combined English Stores* (1989).
❖ **Sections 141** and **142** of the **LPA 1925**.
❖ *Spencer's Case* (1583) and *Re King* (1963).
❖ *Tulk v Moxhay* (1848).

Applying the Law

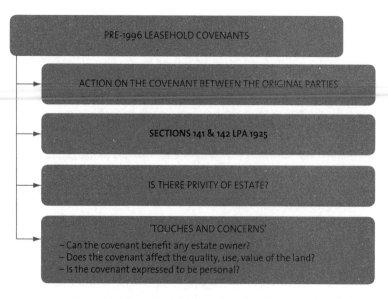

PRE-1996 LEASEHOLD COVENANTS

ACTION ON THE COVENANT BETWEEN THE ORIGINAL PARTIES

SECTIONS 141 & 142 LPA 1925

IS THERE PRIVITY OF ESTATE?

'TOUCHES AND CONCERNS'
– Can the covenant benefit any estate owner?
– Does the covenant affect the quality, use, value of the land?
– Is the covenant expressed to be personal?

This diagram shows the rules relating to the transmissibility of pre-1996 leasehold covenants.

ANSWER

This question concerns the operation of the rules relating to the enforceability of leasehold covenants, both between the original parties to the lease and their respective successors in title. Importantly, because both leases in this problem were granted before 1 January 1996, the applicable law is the 'old' mix of common law and statute.[25] The **Landlord and Tenant (Covenants) Act 1995 (LTCA)** has no application to the facts of this problem, except in so far as liability for a 'fixed' charge is sought to be enforced against the original tenant, in which case, the provisions of **s 17** of the **LTCA** apply and the 'problem notice' procedure must be observed.

On the facts, both the original landlord, Harry, and the original tenants, Julian and Esmeralda, have assigned their leasehold estates. Clearly, the original parties are bound to each other in contract to perform the covenants contained in their lease. Thus, in this problem, Harry can sue Julian, Harry can sue Larry and Larry can sue Harry in contract on all the covenants, whether or not they concern the land. This liability continues throughout the life of the contract, that being the term of the lease, although due to the wording of **s 141** of the **LPA 1925**, a landlord will not be able to sue the original tenant after he has parted with the land as that right is statutorily transferred to the new landlord (*Arlesford Trading Co v Servansingh* (1971)).

Of course, for practical purposes, the present landlord, Peter, will wish to enforce the leasehold covenants against the present tenants (and vice versa) and, in this respect, the issue turns on whether the benefit of the covenant (the right to sue on it) has passed to the plaintiff and the burden of the covenant (the obligation to perform it) has passed to the defendant. In simple terms, under pre-1996 law, both burden and benefit will have passed to successors in title of the original landlord and tenant so as to enable an action on the covenant if: (i) there is privity of estate between the parties; and (ii) the covenant touches and concerns the land. In the case of the landlord, these common law conditions are now replicated in slightly modified form in **ss 141** and **142** of the **LPA 1925**.

Before we consider the particular facts in detail, it is wise to determine, as a matter of principle, whether these covenants 'touch and concern' the land – in other words, whether they are so intimately connected with the land that they are not personal to the particular covenanting parties. Only if they do 'touch and concern' can the covenants be enforceable between successors to pre-1996 leases. The requirements for determining whether a covenant does 'touch and concern' have been re-stated by the House of Lords in *Swift Investments v Combined English Stores* (1989), viz: whether the covenant could benefit any estate owner as opposed to the particular original covenantee; whether the

---

25 Dates in problem questions are very important – make sure you check them carefully before answering.

covenant affected the nature, quality, mode of use or value of the land; and whether the covenant was expressed to be personal.

In our problem, there are six covenants in all.[26]

(i)   The covenant by Julian that the premises shall not be used for the manufacture of household appliances. This is a covenant restrictive of the user of premises and prima facie touches and concerns the land. It seems to fall within the *Swift* formula: see, for example, *Williams v Earle* (1868), in which the property was restricted to domestic use only.

(ii) The covenant by Julian not to assign or sub-let without consent – clearly acceptable, as in *Goldstein v Sanders* (1915).

(iii) The covenant by Julian to undertake all reasonable repairs – clearly acceptable, as in *Martyn v Clue* (1852).

(iv) The covenant by Esmeralda not to open after 8 pm. Although, at first sight, this may seem to be a merely personal covenant, it is clear that it is intended for the benefit of other units on the site. It is not for Harry's personal benefit and does affect the mode of use of the land within the *Swift* formula. It seems to touch and concern.

(v)   The covenant by Esmeralda to buy beer only from Harry – this also touches and concerns the land and is identical to the covenant in *Clegg v Hands* (1890).

(vi) The covenant by Harry not to open a catering business. Once again, this covenant affects the mode of use of land retained by Harry and is intended to benefit land granted by him. It is an anti-competition covenant and is also a 'touching and concerning' covenant.[27]

In result, then, all these covenants touch and concern the land and are capable of passing benefit and burden, as appropriate, to successors in title.

(A) UNIT 1

It is necessary, in respect of Unit 1, to determine a number of issues. First, which parties are within 'privity of estate', for it is only between these parties that 'touching' covenants can run under the pre-1996 leasehold rules? 'Privity of estate' exists where there is a relationship of landlord and tenant under a legal lease or, in other words, where the particular plaintiff and particular defendant are now landlord and tenant of the same legal estate. In our case, Peter is in privity of estate with Larry. There is no privity of estate

---

26 This is a good way to structure questions like this where you need to look at similar law in relation to a variety of fact circumstances.

27 In these circumstances the majority are determined according to existing case law. This shows the importance of being aware of a range of case law examples.

between Peter and Keith because Keith is a sub-tenant. (In fact, Keith is Larry's tenant and in privity of estate with him.) So, presumptively, Peter can sue Larry.

Second, does Peter have the right to sue on the covenants made by Julian to Harry after he (Peter) purchases the reversion: has the benefit run to him? The answer to this is clear. Under s 141 of the LPA 1925, the benefit of every covenant 'having reference to the subject matter' of the lease is attached to the reversion and passes with it. The requirement of 'having reference to the subject matter' is taken to be synonymous with 'touching and concerning' (see, for example, *Caerns Motor Services v Texaco* (1994)). So, Peter has the right to sue any person with whom he is in privity of estate (Larry) and who is subject to the burden of the covenant. Third, to whom has the burden run? The position here is again clear, following Spencer's case, that 'touching' covenants are binding on a successor in title to the original tenant in favour of anyone with whom they are in privity of estate. Again, this is Larry.

So, as far as Unit 1 is concerned, Peter can sue Larry on all three covenants if they have been breached. That, of course, is a matter of construction, although it is reasonably clear that Larry has broken the covenant against sub-letting and the covenant to effect reasonable repairs. If portable air-conditioning units are 'household appliances', then the third covenant is also broken. We should note here that Larry is liable for breaking the covenant against the manufacture of household appliances, even though the actual actions in breach are committed by Keith. Larry is liable throughout his term, and it is immaterial that the breach was actually committed by his own tenant. Peter will have various remedies to choose from, including an injunction to restrain production of air conditioning units, money damages and perhaps even forfeiture of the lease if there is a right of re-entry.

Finally, we should also note that, even though Keith and Peter do not share privity of estate, Peter may well be able to enforce any restrictive covenants against Keith under the rule in *Tulk v Moxhay* (1848) that normally operates in disputes between freeholders (who also are not in privity of estate with each other). Under *Tulk*, restrictive covenants can be enforced against any occupier provided that the person (here, the sub-tenant) has notice of the covenants (unregistered land) or is within s 23(1)(a) of the Land Registration Act 2002 (registered land), which appears to make such covenants automatically binding on a sub-tenant. Also, if Peter is able to utilise the remedy of forfeiture and thereby terminate Larry's lease because of his breaches, the sub-tenancy will also be terminated (*Shiloh Spinners v Harding* (1973)), subject to any claim for relief from forfeiture by Keith.

(B) UNIT 2

As above, there is no doubt that Peter, as purchaser, has the benefit of the covenants made to Harry: this is the effect of s 141(1) of the Law of Property Act 1925. Correspondingly, however, Peter also has the burden of any covenants made by Harry, such as the covenant not to carry on any catering business on the site. This is the effect of **s 142(1)** of the **LPA**, operating for the burden in the same way as **s 141** does for the benefit. Thus, Peter can sue Esmeralda on the covenants not to open after 8 pm and not to sell beer other than the landlord's and Esmeralda's liability continues for the term of the lease even though in fact the breach is committed by Nathan. If Peter does sue Esmeralda, this will not trigger the problem notice procedure under **s 17** of the **LTCA 1995** because the claim is not for a fixed charge but (presumably) for unliquidated damages for breach. Likewise, Esmeralda can sue Peter on the covenant to prevent breach of the covenant against catering (although, possibly, only if the breach was committed before Esmeralda assigned to Nathan (*Greycroft* (1987)) if as a matter of construction it has been breached. Of course, however, if possible, both the new landlord and the new tenant will wish to secure a direct remedy against the person actually acting in breach.

In this respect, there are some difficulties. For Peter to sue Nathan, the burdens of the covenant must have passed to Nathan. However, even though the original lease is by deed (and, hence, legal), the assignment is only in writing. It is not, therefore, correctly assigned (**s 52(1)** of the **LPA**) and cannot take effect as a legal assignment. Following *Purchase v Lichfield Brewery* (1915), this equitable assignment of a legal lease cannot pass the burdens to Nathan and Nathan is not liable under pre-1996 leasehold covenant rules. In essence, there is no privity of the legal estate. Of course, it is possible for Peter to seek an injunction against Nathan preventing the breach of any restrictive covenants under the *Tulk* rule, provided that the equitable assignee has notice of them (in unregistered land). Both of the covenants affecting Nathan's land are indeed restrictive and, given that Nathan should have seen the original lease before taking an assignment of it, he will have notice of the covenants contained therein. Fortunately, then, despite the fact that these covenants cannot be enforced under the 'leasehold rules', they will be binding under *Tulk*.

The position in respect of Nathan's attempt to sue Peter is not so complicated. We have seen above that Peter is affected by the burden of the covenant made by Harry and there is good reason to suppose that Nathan may well be entitled to the benefit of it. Although the right to sue cannot exist because of lack of privity of estate, it is possible that, as a matter of contract, the benefit of the covenant will have been assigned to Nathan when he purchased the lease. This is a matter of construction of the assignment from Esmeralda, but it is a distinct possibility that the benefit of any covenants would have been assigned to Nathan personally under normal contractual principles. If that were the case, Nathan could sue Peter on this covenant.

Don't be tempted to

Do not write one long answer. The question has to be divided into smaller parts so as to make the answer clearer.

Do not import **LTCA** rules into a pre-1996 problem question.

QUESTION 23 `---------------------------------------------`

Assess critically the remedies available to landlords for breach of covenant by their tenants. What factors may influence a landlord when deciding which remedy to pursue?

How to Answer this Question

- ❖ Explain and analyse the various remedies
- ❖ Law Commission proposals for forfeiture and distress
- ❖ Forfeiture – s 146 of the LPA 1925
- ❖ Injunction
- ❖ Distress
- ❖ Action for arrears of rent;
- ❖ Action for damages.

Applying the Law

This diagram shows the landlord's remedies for breach of a leasehold covenant.

ANSWER

One of the great advantages of the leasehold estate is that it allows two or more persons to use and enjoy property at the same time. In the typical case, the tenant will enjoy occupation and physical use of the property even to the exclusion of the landlord, but the landlord will reap the benefits of allowing that exclusive occupation in the form of rent and profits. It is, of course, essential if this duality is to function that both parties are able to preserve the value of their respective interests in the property. This is the function of covenants in leases, which may take many forms depending on the needs and priorities of the particular landlord and tenant.

From the landlord's point of view, they will wish to ensure that the value of the property and its marketability as an income-generating asset is preserved.[28] Thus, there may be covenants restricting the uses of the premises by the tenant, obliging the tenant to keep the premises in repair, requiring the landlord's consent before any assignment or sub-lease is undertaken and, of course, obliging the tenant to pay rent. Obviously, these covenants are designed to secure different objectives and it should come as no surprise that the landlord's remedy for breach of covenant by the tenant may well depend on the particular type of covenant that has in fact been broken. In many cases, for example, the landlord will be content to secure performance of the covenant, as with repairing covenants, or simply the payment of outstanding rent. In others, the covenant broken may be so fundamental, or the breach so serious, as to suggest to the landlord that he should end the lease, thereby ridding themselves of an unreliable tenant. Indeed, the law itself recognises that certain remedies are more appropriate to achieve certain ends and there are a whole range of statutory provisions that supplement or restrict the landlord in both the choice of remedy and the manner in which he may pursue it.

By far the most powerful weapon in the armoury of the landlord in the event of a breach of covenant is the remedy of forfeiture. A successful forfeiture of the lease effectively brings the lease to an end. It is, in other words, a remedy that can result in the tenant's estate in the land being terminated and, as such, it is not surprising that the right of the landlord to forfeit the lease is strictly controlled by statute. Furthermore, it has been the subject of significant attention by the Law Commission (most recently in 2004, see Consultation Paper No 174 (2004)) and other changes in procedure have occurred as a result of the entry into force of the **Commonhold and Leasehold Reform Act 2002 (CLRA)**.

In general terms, in order for forfeiture to be available the lease must contain a right of re-entry. This is a stipulation that the landlord is entitled to re-enter the premises should the tenant fail to observe their covenants. All professionally drafted leases will contain such a right and one will be implied in all equitable leases (*Shiloh Spinners v Harding*

---

28 It is a good approach to tie your analysis of the shape of the legal rules to their commercial or practical purpose.

(1973)). Subject to what will be said below, the existence of a right of re-entry gives the landlord two potential paths to a successful forfeiture. First, the landlord may physically re-enter the property by obtaining actual possession of it, a typical example being the changing of locks. Second, and more frequently, a landlord may seek to exercise his right of re-entry through an action for possession in the courts. At one time, a landlord had a free choice about which path to take, but this is now modified by statute, mainly to protect the tenant from an overzealous landlord using unrestricted force. Thus, a right of re-entry under a residential lease 'while any person is lawfully residing in the premises' must take place through court action (s 2 of the **Protection from Eviction Act 1977**). Any attempt to physically re-enter will result in criminal liability. Likewise, even if the lease is non-residential (or otherwise outside the scope of s 2), it is only peaceful physical re-entry that is permitted and the landlord must avoid committing offences under the **Criminal Law Act 1977**. In short, this means that physical re-entry is possible only when the premises are held under a business lease and are unoccupied.

That, however, is not the end of the statutory code relating to forfeiture. In all cases in which the landlord is seeking to forfeit because of a breach of a covenant, other than a breach of a covenant to pay rent, the procedure specified in s 146 of the **Law of Property Act 1925** must be strictly followed, together with, in the case of long leases of dwellings, additional procedural safeguards introduced by s 168 of the **CLRA 2002**. (Forfeiture because of breach of a covenant to pay rent is dealt with under separate rules.) **Section 146** requires a landlord to serve a notice on the tenant specifying the breach of covenant of which complaint is made, requesting compensation, if desired, advising the tenant of their rights under the **Leasehold Property (Repairs) Act 1938**, if appropriate, and requesting that the covenant is remedied, if that is possible. If the covenant is capable of remedy, and this depends upon the test laid down in *Expert Clothing v Hillgate House* (1986), the landlord must give the tenant a reasonable time to make amends before proceeding to forfeit by re-entry or court action. Only if the covenant cannot be remedied (is 'irremediable'), such as where the tenant has committed a once-and-for-all breach of a negative covenant (*Scala House v Forbes* (1974); *Cooper v Henderson* (1982)), can the landlord proceed to forfeit with reasonable speed. Even then, however, the landlord's remedy is controlled. If the landlord decides to proceed by way of court action, it is clear that the tenant has a right to relief from forfeiture under s 146(2) of the **LPA**. This will be granted if the tenant has performed the covenants or the court considers that it would be just and reasonable to allow the lease to survive despite the breaches of covenant (see *Shiloh Spinners v Harding*). Likewise, it is now clear after the House of Lords' decision in *Billson v Residential Apartments* (1992) that, even if the landlord proceeds to forfeit by physical re-entry, such as changing the locks as in that case, the tenant can still apply to the court for relief under s 146(2). This 're-interpretation'[29] of s 146 emphasises once again that forfeiture is a drastic remedy, almost a remedy of last resort.

---

29 This description of what has taken place with regards to the interpretation of **Section 146** not only shows that you are aware of a developing case law but also analyses that case law and its importance.

Forfeiture for breach of the covenant to pay rent is also controlled, although the procedure varies slightly according to whether action is taken in the county court or the High Court (usually the county court) and whether the inherent jurisdiction of the court (High Court), or statute (county court), is the source of a tenant's right to relief. In essence, the landlord must make a formal demand for rent, unless this is excluded by the express terms of the lease or by statute, as where more than six months is in arrears and 'distress' (see below) would be inadequate (**s 210** of the **Common Law Procedure Act 1852**). Additionally, in the case of certain 'long' leases – that is, over 21 years – of a dwelling, certain additional safeguards exist for tenants (**ss 166** and **167** of the **CLRA**). After this, in both county court and High Court, the tenant has a statutory right to have proceedings stayed by payment of rent interests and costs up to a specified time before the hearing date, although, in the High Court, this right arises only if six months' rent is in arrears. However, the High Court has an inherent jurisdiction to grant relief for forfeiture if less than six months is owing and payment is rendered before trial, and may grant relief subsequent to a possession order (or physical re-entry: *Howard v Fanshawe* (1895)), if the tenant pays within six months and probably longer in exceptional cases (*Di Palma v Victoria Square Property* (1984)). In the county court, there is a statutory right to relief if payment is made within four weeks of a possession order and the court has a discretion to grant relief up to six months after possession is obtained (**s 138(3), (9A)** of the **County Courts Act 1984** – see, for example, *Maryland Estates v Joseph* (1998)). The rationale behind these generous provisions is, of course, that the landlord has let the premises in order to generate income and should not be entitled to bring that arrangement to an end when that income is paid.[30]

Indeed, taking all cases of forfeiture together, it is clear that the remedy may well be the most powerful in result, but it is also the one that the courts control most closely. It will be the remedy that the landlord resorts to in cases of serious and sustained breach of covenant, but in other circumstances an attempt to forfeit is likely to be met with a successful claim for relief. The Law Commission has accordingly proposed a reform of the law of forfeiture that would essentially rationalise and assimilate the procedures for forfeiture for rent and non-rent covenants and seriously restrict further forfeiture by way of physical re-entry.[31]

The Law Commission has also proposed reform, or rather abolition, of another of the remedies available to a landlord for breach of covenant. The remedy of distress allows a landlord to seize certain of the tenant's goods present on the property and sell them for the purpose of realising the arrears of rent. It is a remedy for non-payment of rent pure and simple and cannot be used in respect of breaches of any other covenant. With the exception

....

30 This analysis continues the approach earlier of looking at the rules in the light of their commercial reality.
31 It is always useful to be aware not only of the existence of reform proposals, but also of some of the specific changes being suggested.

of tenancies controlled under the Rent Acts and similar legislation, distress is a remedy by way of self-help requiring no court process. It is, however, bounded by traditional and often confusing common law conditions. There are, for example, many classes of privileged goods that cannot be seized (for example, tools of the trade, goods in actual use) and there are common law conditions dictating when distress may be levied (for example, not on a Sunday, only between dawn and dusk). The Law Commission's solution to these problems, and the problem of abuse, was enacted in **Part 3** of the **Tribunals, Courts and Enforcement Act 2007**, although this is not yet in force. Under this reform, the remedy of distress would be abolished but, in respect of leases of commercial premises only, the **2007 Act** would introduce a statutory scheme for recovering rent arrears without resort to the courts. This will be the CRAR scheme. As noted, it will apply only to leases of commercial premises (and never to oral leases of any type of premises) and is, in effect, distress in all but name. If this does come into force, the abolition of the remedy would not cause significant hardship to landlords and would remove one more right of self-help and the attendant dangers of abuse. The CRAR scheme would protect landlords of commercial premises. At the moment, while distress is still possible, the most important consequence is that distress and forfeiture are mutually exclusive. Of course, should the landlord simply be concerned with rent and not wish to go to the trouble of distress or use the threat of forfeiture (which, of course, may often produce the rent), he may bring a simple action for arrears of rent up to the maximum of six years in arrears allowed under the **Limitation Act 1980**.

Finally, for covenants other than the covenant to pay rent, there remain two other possible remedies. First, the landlord may sue for damages for breach of covenant, which in general terms will follow the normal contractual rules and will place the landlord in the position in which he would have been had the breach not been committed. The exception is damages for breach of a covenant to repair, which are limited by **s 18** of the **Landlord and Tenant Act 1927** to damages no greater than the loss of value in the reversion. Second, it may be possible for a landlord to obtain an injunction to prevent continued breach of a restrictive covenant under the rules of *Tulk v Moxhay* (1848). In reality, this is just an example of the general rule that equity may intervene to restrain conduct that is contrary to explicitly undertaken obligations. Furthermore, until recently, it was thought that the landlord could not obtain the remedy of specific performance to compel the tenant to perform a covenant to repair. This was thought to be established in *Hill v Barclay* (1810), despite dicta to the contrary in *SEDAC v Tanner* (1982). However, in *Rainbow Estates v Tokenhold* (1999), the judge held that specific performance of a tenant's covenant could be ordered in special circumstances, particularly where the court could supervise the order. This remains a controversial decision and it is unclear what 'special circumstances' justify this unusual step. Nevertheless, it may mark a change in the attitude of the courts when faced with persistent breaches of covenant by a tenant well capable of performing their obligations.

It is indeed true, then, that there is a range of remedies available to the landlord in the event of breach of covenant by the tenant and that the choice of these remedies will depend ultimately on the type of covenant that has been breached and the purpose of the landlord in seeking to enforce it. If the landlord merely wishes to recover rent, there is a range of actions. If, however, the aim is to terminate the tenancy and recover possession, the remedy of forfeiture is available albeit subject to many restrictions. In essence, it will only be available to a landlord when the tenant has behaved in such disregard of the leasehold covenants that they have effectively taken themselves outside the landlord and tenant relationship.

Don't be tempted to

Do not ignore proposals for reform. These highlight problems with the current law and are a great springboard for the answer.

QUESTION 24

Arnold is the freehold owner of a large warehouse and a block of offices on the harbour in Cityport in an area of unregistered land. In 1990, he leases the warehouse to Tim, an electrical goods importer, by deed for 20 years. Tim covenants to keep the premises in good repair, not to use the premises for residential occupancy, not to employ Orlando (Arnold's deadly rival) in any capacity and to provide Arnold with a new television set every three years. The lease contains a right of re-entry. In 1997, Tim goes out of business and is forced to assign the lease to Bert, a property developer by deed. Unknown to Arnold, Bert begins to convert the warehouse into modern flats and employs Orlando as his architect. Meanwhile, Arnold has let the offices to Diana for use as company headquarters on the same terms as the lease to Tim plus covenants by Diana not to assign or sub-let without Arnold's consent and not to carry on the trade of insurance brokerage, Arnold's own profession. Diana discovers that she could have obtained a better deal in the centre of town and sub-lets to Evelyn, a financial consultant. Unfortunately, Evelyn is implicated in a City fraud and fails to pay rent to Diana, who in turn cannot pay Arnold. Discovering this, Arnold changes all the locks on the office block late one night and refuses to let either Diana or Evelyn gain entry.

Arnold now comes to you for advice, having just learnt of the proposed residential development. He is outraged that Orlando is on his property. He would also like a new television.

How to Answer this Question

- ❖ Enforceability of leasehold covenants in pre-1996 leases.
- ❖ Touching and concerning.
- ❖ Ss 141 and 142 of the LPA.
- ❖ Forfeiture – s 146 of the LPA; *Billson v Residential Apartments* (1992).
- ❖ Other remedies in brief.

Applying the Law

This diagram represents the rules relating to the enforceability of leasehold covenants.

ANSWER

This question revolves around two central issues: first, the enforceability of the covenants contained in the leases made by Arnold and subsequently assigned or sub-let by the original tenants; and second, the remedies available to a landlord in the event of breach of covenant, particularly that of forfeiture.[32] As the leases are granted before 1 January 1996, the Landlord and Tenant (Covenants) Act 1995 (LTCA) does not apply, save to the extent that a remedy is sought against an original tenant no longer in possession, in which case the 'problem notice' procedure of s 17 of the LTCA applies to attempts to recover a fixed charge (rent, service charge, liquidated damages).

(A) THE WAREHOUSE

The first point is something that Arnold should bear in mind should all other remedies prove to be unavailable. Tim, the original tenant, will be liable throughout the term of the lease as a matter of contract. Thus, if all else fails, Tim can be sued for the breaches of the covenants, even though the acts in breach were those of Bert. The only substantive restriction on this is where the original contract (that is, the lease) limited Tim's liability expressly to the period of his possession of the demised premises; there is no evidence of this in our case. Of course, if Arnold wishes to recover unpaid rent from Tim (as original

---

32 This is a good way to flag up to the examiner the overall structure of your answer from the outset.

tenant), a 'problem notice' must be served on Tim within six months of the liability arising (s17 of the **LTCA 1995**) and Tim would have the option of taking an overriding lease under **s19** of the **LTCA**. Again, there is no evidence that Arnold proposes to sue anyone for unpaid rent.

It is clear, however, that Arnold may be able to enforce the covenants against the persons more directly responsible as he and Bert, the assignee, share privity of estate. The original lease was by deed, hence legal, and the assignment is by deed. For all intents and purposes, therefore, Arnold and Bert are as landlord and tenant. This makes Arnold's position much stronger under pre-1996 law for it means that, under the rule in *Spencer's Case* (1583), Bert will be subject to the burden of all covenants that touch and concern the land. In this case, there are four covenants in all and each must either be justified by previous authority as 'touching and concerning' or must pass the general test put forward by Lord Oliver in *Swift Investments v Combined English Stores* (1989) – namely: whether the covenant is capable of benefiting any estate owner as opposed to the particular original covenantee; whether the covenant affects the nature, quality, mode of use or value of the land; and whether the covenant is expressed to be personal.

In this problem, the covenant to repair is of no difficulty (*Parker v Webb* (1693)), and the same is true of the covenant against residential occupancy: both clearly 'touch and concern'. There might, however, be thought to be some difficulty with the remaining two covenants and, certainly, the covenant to provide a new television set is clearly personal to Tim in his capacity as an importer of electrical goods. It is not related to use of the land as such. Although not strictly relevant, it is worth noting that the position would have been different had the lease been granted on or after 1 January 1996. In such leases, all covenants run unless they are expressed to be personal, which this is not (**ss 2 and 3** of the **LTCA 1995**). With respect to the covenant against the employment of Orlando, at first blush, this too seems to be personal. However, in *Lewin v American and Colonial Distributors* (1945), a covenant not to allow a named individual to be connected with any business carried on upon the land was held to touch and concern as it was intended to affect the mode of use and value of the land. The covenant in our case is not quite of this kind and could be distinguished from that in the *Lewin* case. It will be a matter for argument because this covenant prevents the covenantor from employing Orlando in any capacity and does not seem to be restricted to an activity taking place on the land. This covenant might be too wide and unconnected with the land for it to touch and concern.[33]

As it is, this is a pre-1996 lease and it seems that Tim, the original tenant, is liable in respect of the television as a matter of contract law (original tenant liability) and probably not liable in respect of the employment of Orlando: after all, Tim has not

---

33 The discussion here shows that the writer is aware of the relevant case law but is then also able to apply the principles derived from those cases in factual situations directly covered by that law.

employed him and the covenant probably does not run to Bert, being personal. Bert, however, is subject to the repairing obligation and the restriction against residential occupancy. Obviously, it is these last two covenants that Arnold will be most concerned with and he has several remedies available – for example, damages, injunction. More than likely, however, he may well seek to forfeit the lease under his right of re-entry.

There is no doubt that, in principle, Bert is subject to forfeiture as the right of re-entry is enforceable against him. Being attached to a legal estate, it is itself a legal right and binding on Bert. However, the right of forfeiture for covenants other than to pay rent – and, here, we are dealing with breach of a covenant against residential occupation (see below for the repairing covenant) is controlled by statute, irrespective of whether forfeiture is by action in the courts or by physical re-entry. Under **s 146** of the **Law of Property Act 1925**, the landlord must serve a '**s 146** notice' specifying the breach that is complained of, requiring compensation and requiring the tenant to remedy the breach if it is capable of remedy. Any attempted forfeiture without following this procedure is void (*Re Riggs* (1901)). It is crucial, therefore, for Arnold to serve such a notice. Furthermore, when the notice is served, Arnold cannot go on to forfeit by action or physical re-entry without giving the tenant a reasonable chance to remedy the covenant, if it is capable of remedy. It is crucial to know, for this reason, whether the covenant is indeed capable of remedy. The appropriate test for this purpose was discussed in *Expert Clothing Service and Sales v Hillgate House Ltd* (1986) and boils down to whether the harm to the landlord could be remedied. In the case of 'negative covenants', for example, as here, with the ban on residential occupancy, this is difficult as, once the action is done, the covenant is broken (*Scala House v Forbes* (1974)). If the breach of a negative covenant is 'continuing', it will be regarded as sufficient to stop the offending action and thereby avoid forfeiture. Similarly, in *Savva v Hossein* (1997), the court held that there was no requirement that negative covenants always should be regarded as irremediable and that the *Expert Clothing* test should be applied individually to the facts of each case. This may result in a less rigid attitude to negative covenants even if the breach is not 'continuing'. Of course, under *Expert Clothing*, a positive covenant (such as to repair) can more easily be remedied by carrying out the required repairs.

Having served a **s 146** notice and given a reasonable time for remedy (if appropriate), Arnold may be able to forfeit by physical re-entry, as this is not a residential property (cf **s 2** of the Protection from **Eviction Act 1977**). However, after *Billson v Residential Apartments* (1992), also a case in which work was done to property without consent,[34] it is clear that even physical re-entry does not destroy the tenant's right to relief from forfeiture under **s 146(2)** of the **LPA**. Such relief can be granted even if a covenant is technically irremediable as the law leans against forfeitures. It is a matter for the courts'

---

34 Drawing parallels in fact situations like this is a good way to show off knowledge of the case law without spending too much time describing, rather than analysing, the relevant principles.

discretion in the circumstances of the case (*Shiloh Spinners v Harding* (1973)). Arnold would be wise, therefore, to seek forfeiture by action in the courts if Bert does not desist from the conversion work and pay compensation. The effect of a successful forfeiture would be to bring the lease to an end. Finally, it may be that due to the redevelopment work, the warehouse is not kept in good repair. If this is the case, Arnold might be better advised to sue for damages for breach of the repairing covenant as the procedure for forfeiture for breach of repairing obligations is complicated by the requirements of the Leasehold Property (Repairs) Act 1938. This gives the tenant added protection under s 146 of the LPA and a longer time to fulfill repairing obligations. Forfeiture for lack of repair will not be necessary if forfeiture for the non-observance of the domestic occupancy covenant is successful.

(B) THE OFFICES

The position here is similar to that above, with the exception that the breach of one covenant has been caused by the action of a sub-tenant. The obvious point is, of course, that Diana is bound by all the covenants as a matter of contract (being the original covenantor) and, if it is true that her lease also contains a covenant to provide a television set, she must do so. This would not be subject to the s 17 of the LTCA notice procedure, as the liability is not in respect of a 'fixed' charge. It is in damages for an unliquidated sum. On the other hand, it is also clear that there is no privity of estate between Arnold and Evelyn. Evelyn is a sub-tenant and is in privity of estate only with her own landlord, Diana. Thus, the burden of the covenants do not run to Evelyn under *Spencer's Case*.

However, this does not mean that Arnold is left without a remedy apart from the contractual action against Diana. In the first place, Arnold can enforce any negative covenants that touch and concern the land (as with the covenant restrictive of user) by injunction under the rule in *Tulk v Moxhay* provided that Evelyn has notice of them (as is most likely: *Gosling v Woolfe* (1893)). Second, however, Arnold can proceed to forfeit the headlease for breach of covenant, although if forfeiting for breach of the covenant not to sub-let, the procedure outlined above has clearly not been followed. There has been no 's 146 notice'. Even if there had been, *Billson* makes it clear that relief from forfeiture can still be granted even where the landlord has forfeited by physical re-entry of the premises (changing the locks) instead of by action in the courts. Furthermore, under s 146 of the LPA a sub-tenant may apply for such relief in an action by the reversioner against the head tenant. Thus, although breach of the covenant not to sub-let may not be capable of remedy (it is a once-and-for-all breach of a negative covenant – *Scala House*), Arnold has not followed the correct procedure of s 146, which was designed to give the tenant or sub-tenant the chance to claim relief.

Alternatively, Arnold could choose to forfeit for non-payment of rent, although again certain procedural limitations exist. For example, it is clear that unless expressly excluded by the lease, a landlord must issue a formal demand for rent if less than six months' rent is owing. We do not know if Arnold has done this. Moreover, Diana has a right to have the proceedings stayed on payment of all arrears and costs and, even after physical re-entry, the court has a discretion to grant relief from forfeiture (*Howard v Fanshawe* (1895)). In general, the court looks very carefully at attempted forfeiture for non-payment of rent as immediate payment plus costs will always remedy the situation. In this respect, threatened forfeiture is a costly way of recovering rent and Arnold would be well advised to use the normal action for rent recovery.

Don't be tempted to

Billson v Residential Apartments must be thoroughly understood before tackling this question, as must the operation of s146 of the LPA and any changes to it under the operation of relevant sections of the Commonhold and Leasehold Reform Act 2002.

Do not forget that some parts of the LTCA 1995 apply to pre-1996 leases.

QUESTION 25

Lyus is the registered proprietor of a dockside warehouse. In 1995, he subdivides the warehouse into two distinct units. The same year, he lets Plot A on a 30-year lease by deed to Tom, an importer of car-tuning kits. Tom covenants not to use the premises for any manufacturing process and to provide Lyus with three free kits each Christmas. Lyus promises 'to maintain in good repair the Premises comprised within Plot A'. In 1996, Tom assigns his lease to Ophelia and she begins to make motorcycle exhaust systems. She continues to store some tuning kits, having purchased Tom's excess stock. In 1997, Ophelia allows her son Jordan, to take over the premises, acknowledging his assumption of the tenancy in a written agreement. Jordan disposes of all the tuning kits and begins large-scale manufacture of motor-cycle exhaust systems. The same year, Lyus assigns his reversion to Ali.

Plot B is let for ten years in 2000 to Charlie, an importer of motorcycle frames. Charlie covenants not to use the premises for any manufacturing process and to supply Lyus with four frames each Christmas. Lyus agrees an identical repairing covenant relating to Plot B to that agreed with Tom concerning Plot A. In January 2001, Charlie is made an offer for his business and assigns his lease to Zoom Ltd. Zoom Ltd use Jordan's exhaust systems in the assembly of motorcycles and no longer import completed machines. In February 2001, Lyus assigns his reversion to Nigel.

Jordan now complains to Ali that the guttering around the building is defective. Zoom Ltd also complains. Ali and Nigel come to you for advice about their leasehold obligations and rights.

How to Answer this Question

❖ Pre-1996 leases and the enforceability of covenants – privity of estate; touching and concerning ss 141 and 142 of the LPA 1925.

❖ Legal and equitable pre-1996 leases.
❖ Leases falling within the **LTCA** – automatic passing of benefit and burdens, personal covenants, no distinction between legal and equitable lease.

Answer Structure

This diagram demonstrates how to apply the pre- and post-**Landlord and Tenant (Covenants) Act 1995** rules to plots A and B.

ANSWER

This problem concerns the enforceability of leasehold covenants between landlords and tenants, and their successors in title, of two separate properties. Importantly, one lease (that of Plot A) is granted before 1 January 1996 and so the covenants are governed by a mix of statute and common law. The second lease, that of Plot B, is granted in 2000 after the coming into force of the **Landlord and Tenant (Covenants) Act 1995** and so falls to be dealt with under this statutory regime.[35]

(A) PLOT A

Being a lease governed by pre-**LTCA** principles, the enforceability of covenants is determined by common law principles overlaid by some statutory modifications. The 30-year lease granted by Lyus (L) to Tom (T) is executed by deed. It is therefore a legal lease, which we can assume is registered under the **Land Registration Act 2002** with its own title number. If it were not so registered, it would take effect only as an equitable lease (see *Brown and Root v Sun Alliance* (1996)), but this is unlikely given that the existence of a deed implies that the parties used a solicitor, who would have registered the lease as a matter of course.[36]

The lease contains three covenants. Two of them – the tenant's covenant prohibiting manufacturing and the landlord's repairing covenant – are clearly proprietary – that is, they 'touch and concern' the land or 'have reference to the subject matter of the lease' within the test laid down by Lord Oliver in *Swift Investments v Combined English Stores* (1989). Consequently, they have the potential to run with the land in appropriate circumstances. The third covenant – T's covenant to provide L with tuning kits – is certainly personal in nature. So, for pre-1996 leases, it is impossible for the burden of this covenant to run to any assignee of the tenant: *Spencer's Case* (1583). Consequently, although Ali (the assignee of the reversion from L) may have been given the benefit of this personal covenant by contract when he purchased the reversion (because the benefit of contracts/covenants can be personally assigned), only T (the original tenant) is liable on it. No liability runs to either Ophelia or Jordan. It is unlikely that Ali will wish to pursue a remedy on this covenant against Tom.

The remaining two covenants present a different picture. It is possible for the benefit and burden of these two proprietary covenants to pass to assignees of the reversion and the lease in appropriate circumstances. Taking Ali first, we are not told whether the assignment of the reversion to him is by deed or merely in writing. However, although the 'legal' status of his reversion can be maintained only if the assignment is made by deed (*Julian v Crago* (1992)) and he is subsequently registered as proprietor, this does not matter as far as the running of the covenants is concerned. By virtue of **ss 141** and **142** of the **LPA 1925**, the benefit and burden respectively of proprietary leasehold covenants pass to an assignee of the landlord. Thus, we know that Ali may enforce the covenant against

---

35 As with an earlier problem in this chapter, this question shows the crucial importance of dates to problem questions.
36 This discussion demonstrates good attention to detail since it recognises that the facts are not clear on the question of registration, but it deals with the matter swiftly.

manufacture and is potentially liable on the repairing covenant. But whom may he sue, and who may sue him?[37]

Clearly, the original tenant (T) remains liable throughout the entire term of the lease. So, Ali may well wish to sue Tom in damages for breach of the manufacturing covenant if no other remedy is available. Ali does not have to comply with the 'problem notice' procedure of the LTCA 1995 (which applies even to pre-1996 leases) because such an action would not be an action for a fixed charge, but for unliquidated damages. Obviously, however, Ali would prefer a remedy against the person committing the breach and we should note here that both Ophelia and Jordan's leases are binding on Ali as overriding interests (if not registered as titles) under s 70(1)(k) of the LRA 1925 if legal and s 70(1)(g) if equitable, and this state of affairs will still appertain even now that the LRA 2002 has come into force (Sched 3 to the LRA 2002). In respect of Ophelia, we are not told whether Tom's assignment to her was by deed. This is critical as the burden of this covenant can run to Ophelia only if she was in privity of estate with Ali and privity of estate depends on the existence of a legal lease (and, hence, an assignment by deed and registration if applicable): Spencer's Case; Julian v Crago; Brown and Root.[38] If such privity existed, Ophelia can be held liable in damages to Ali for the period for which she was in possession under the lease. If the lease is equitable (that is, the assignment was in writing only), no such claim arises and Ophelia cannot be liable (Purchase v Lichfield Brewery (1915)). Again, however, damages may not be adequate for Ali, who may want the manufacturing process halted. This is difficult as it is clear that Jordan is in possession of the property under an assignment from Ophelia that is merely equitable, being made in writing. This means no burden passes to Jordan under leasehold covenant law. Fortunately, however, Ali may be able to rely on a related doctrine. Under Tulk v Moxhay (1848), a proprietary restrictive covenant (as here) can be enforced against any person in possession of the land (for example, an equitable tenant, or sub-tenant or squatter) if that person has 'notice' of the covenant. In registered land, which this is, the bindingness of the restrictive covenant on these occupiers is assured by virtue of s 23 of the LRA 1925 and s 33 of the LRA 2002. So, it is possible for Ali to obtain an injunction against Jordan preventing the manufacture of exhaust systems (Hall v Ewin (1887)).

Finally, we must determine whether any person has the right to sue Ali on the repairing covenant – assuming that the facts disclose a breach. In principle, Tom could have maintained a remedy provided that he has not assigned the benefit of the covenant when he assigned the lease, but not only is it implausible that Tom would wish to sue, he almost certainly has assigned the benefit. Consequently, Ophelia would have enjoyed the benefit of the repairing covenant while she was in occupation either because the lease was legal and privity of estate existed (Spencer's Case) or because of an assignment of the

---

37 This hypothetical question is a good way to set up the structure of the ensuing discussion.
38 The listing of cases here is a quick way to gain marks in showing knowledge of the case law.

contractual benefit by Tom. Again, however, Ophelia cannot obtain anything other than damages for the loss suffered by her while she was in possession and these are likely to be nominal. That leaves Jordan. As we know, Jordan is an equitable tenant and cannot rely on the 'privity' rules. Again, however, if Ophelia has assigned the benefit of the covenant to Jordan expressly, Jordan may sue Ali. Had this been a simple case of assignment of a lease – albeit in writing – we could have readily implied such a personal transfer of the benefit. In our case, however, the matter is doubtful as we are told that Ophelia 'acknowledges' Jordan's assumption of the tenancy. All then turns on whether this acknowledgement expressly or impliedly passes the benefit of the repairing covenant. If it does, we must advise Ali that his attempt to obtain an injunction in respect of the manufacturing process may be met with a counter-plea for damages for lack of repair.

(B) PLOT B

The enforceability of the three leasehold covenants in respect of Plot B raises similar issues to those considered above, save that being contained in a lease granted on or after 1 January 1996, the **Landlord and Tenant (Covenants) Act 1995** is applicable. Consequently, some points of importance can be made. First, it matters not whether the leases are legal or equitable. Under the Act, the enforceability of leasehold covenants does not depend on the quality of the lease in which they are contained. So, whether the original lease and subsequent assignments are legal or equitable does not affect the enforceability of the leasehold covenants (s 28(1) of the **LTCA 1995**). Second, the Act makes no distinction between personal and proprietary covenants. Consequently, all leasehold covenants will run to assignees of the reversion and the lease irrespective of whether they 'touch and concern' or 'have reference to the subject matter of the lease' provided that they are not expressed to be personal (ss 2 and 3 of the **LTCA**). In our case, therefore, the original tenant's covenants against manufacture and the covenant to supply motorcycle frames may well run to assignees as neither are actually expressed to be personal, even though the latter is 'personal' under the pre-1996 Swift test.[39] Third, by force of statute, the benefits and burdens of the leasehold covenants pass to assignees. There is no need to prove privity of estate or to plead ss 141 and 142 of the **LPA**. Both of these rules are irrelevant for **LTCA** leases (s 3 of the **LTCA**). Fourth, the original tenant is released from liability on assignment, subject only to the possibility of being required to guarantee their assignee under an authorised guarantee agreement (ss 5 and 16 of the **LTCA**). The original landlord is not released automatically, although can request the court to grant such release if the tenant objects on receiving a notice to that effect (ss 6 and 8 of the **LTCA** and *BHP Petroleum v Chesterfield Properties* (2002)), and (although not in this case) there could be an *Avonridge* clause limiting liability of the landlord to the period of possession of the reversion.

---

39 This shows that the writer is aware of the changes in the law and the practical implications of those changes following the **1995 Act**.

So, with these general principles in mind, who is liable to whom and for what under the covenants for Plot B? Clearly, Charlie, the original tenant, is not liable under any of the covenants. He has assigned to Zoom Ltd and there is no suggestion that Lyus extracted an AGA prior to such assignment. Charlie is statutorily released from liability although he cannot enforce any covenants, having gone out of possession (s5 of the LTCA). However, as Zoom is an assignee of the tenant, and as no covenant is expressed to be personal, it is clear that Zoom is subject to the burden of both covenants (not to manufacture, to provide frames) and enjoys the benefit of the repairing covenant. This is the effect of the LTCA irrespective of whether the lease is legal or equitable: the benefits and burdens have passed automatically (ss 3 and 28 of the LTCA). Consequently, we now need to know whom Zoom can sue, and who can sue Zoom.

In principle, Lyus has not escaped liability under the repairing covenant merely by assigning to Nigel. For landlords, the LTCA does not provide for automatic release (s6) and we have no suggestion here that Lyus has served a notice requesting such release (s8). However, unless Nigel (L's assignee) is in some way unable to perform the repairing covenant or cannot pay damages, there is no reason for Zoom to sue Lyus. This is simply because Nigel, as assignee, is liable on the repairing covenant under LTCA. The burden has passed to him automatically (s3). Similarly, Nigel may also rely on the LTCA to pass to him the benefit of both the 'no manufacture' covenant and the covenant to provide frames (s3). Nigel may seek an injunction against Zoom in respect of the former (assuming 'assembling' counts as 'manufacture') and may seek damages or maybe even specific performance for breach of the latter.

Don't be tempted to

Do not attempt this unless you know both sets of rules – pre 1996 and LTCA 1995. Examiners do not give extra credit for a great answer on one part of the question and no answer on the next part

Ensure that you relate the answer to the specific facts of the problem. Do not write generally, but deal with the facts as given.

Do not ignore your statute book. An Examiner will not look kindly on mis-quoting the LTCA if you have a copy in front of you.

Licences and Proprietary Estoppel

INTRODUCTION

There is no necessary reason why the law of licences and the law of proprietary estoppel should be considered together. 'Licences' are one way in which a person may enjoy some right or privilege over the land of another person and much of the dispute in this area concerns the theoretical and practical distinction between 'licences' and other types of right over land, such as leases and easements. 'Proprietary estoppel', on the other hand, is a method for the creation of rights over land. Viewed in this way, proprietary estoppel is a mechanism that may give rise to licences, easements, leases or any other kind of right connected with the use and enjoyment of land and should be considered as a doctrine in its own right. However, that said, it is true that many of the cases and most of the textbooks consider licences and proprietary estoppel together. This is because many occasions for the application of proprietary estoppel arise out of situations in which the claimant previously had merely a licence over the defendant's land, although there are of course many examples of proprietary estoppel in which the parties previously stood in no prior relationship at all. For ease of exposition, and consistency with other texts, this chapter will follow the conventional pattern and consider first the law of licences, and then the scope and purpose of the doctrine of proprietary estoppel.

Licences then, involve a permission from the owner of land, given to another, to use that land for some purpose. This can be to do anything from attending a cinema, parking a car or occupying premises to erecting an advertising hoarding. The range of activities that can be covered by a licence are, indeed, virtually limitless and we have already explored this issue in one respect in considering the distinction between leases and licences. Crucially, however, the orthodox view of licences is that they are not proprietary in nature: in other words, they are not interests in land, but rather personal rights over land. As a consequence, the right conferred by a licence can be enforced only against the person who created it. It does not run with the land and, unlike easements and restrictive covenants, cannot be enforced against a purchaser of the land over which the licence exists. The licence is a matter of contract, not property law. In the 1970s, this fundamental theoretical distinction was attacked (although it has been reaffirmed a number of times: *Lloyd v Dugdale* (2002)) and many examination questions now ask students to analyse whether the status of licences has changed over the years as the use of land has changed.

In dealing with both problem and essay questions on licences, students will need to have a firm grasp of what it means to say that something is an interest in land, as well as an understanding of the law of easements and general principles of equity concerning constructive trusts. Case law is particularly important.

Proprietary estoppel is the name given to a doctrine or set of principles whereby an owner of land may be held to have conferred some right or privilege connected with the land on another person. Typically, the right or privilege conferred will arise out of the conduct of the parties, usually because of some assurance made, which is relied upon by the person claiming the right. In other words, proprietary estoppel is a mechanism whereby rights in or over land may be created *informally* in the absence of a deed or signed writing. In this respect, it is close to the doctrine of constructive trusts considered in Chapter 3 and many cases use these doctrines interchangeably. This is not necessarily accurate (see *Stack v Dowden* (2007)), although the precise ambit and differences between the two doctrines have not yet been worked out. In the law of proprietary estoppel, cases are vital (see especially *Yeoman's Row Management v Cobbe* (2008) and *Thorner v Majors* (2009)) as this is a judge-made doctrine, so typical of a court of equity. There are parallels with promissory estoppel in the law of contract, although proprietary estoppel is a much more powerful doctrine. The former is a defence to an action on a contract, the latter is a means of acquiring rights over land belonging to another. It is a sword as well as a shield.

QUESTION 26

Are contractual licences interests in land? Why is the issue important?

How to Answer this Question

- ❖ Define an interest in land – Lord Wilberforce in *National Provincial Bank v Ainsworth* (1965).
- ❖ Define a licence – *Thomas v Sorrell* (1673).
- ❖ Identify types of licence and the roles that licences can play in the use of land.
- ❖ What is the relevance of third parties?
- ❖ Judicial developments – *Errington v Errington* (1952); *Binions v Evans* (1972); *Re Sharpe* (1980); *Midland Bank v Farm Pride Hatcheries* (1981); *Ashburn Anstalt v Arnold* (1989).
  Kewal Investments v Arthur Maiden (1990); *Lloyd v Dugdale* (2002).
- ❖ A brief discussion of some theoretical issues.

Applying the Law

This diagram demonstrates the personal nature of a contractual licence and the relevant case law.

ANSWER

A licence is classically defined in *Thomas v Sorrell* (1673) as a permission to use land belonging to another that, without such permission, would amount to a trespass. It is the consent of the estate owner to the use of their land by another. Importantly, as Vaughan CJ makes clear in *Sorrell*, the orthodox view of a licence is that it 'properly passeth no interest nor alters or transfers property in any thing'; in other words, licences are not proprietary in nature but personal to the parties that created them.[1] In effect, that they are not interests in land and therefore not within the scope of the 1925 and 2002 property legislation and are incapable of binding third parties when the licensor (the grantor of the licence) passes the affected land on to a third party.

However, such an orthodox view has been subject to attack and various cases and theories have sought to explain why licences are, or should be, regarded as interests in land in the full sense. The aim is often to ensure that subsequent transferees of the burdened land are bound by the licence. Not least, this is due to the multitude of purposes that licences can serve. The law reports are replete with cases covering such

1   In an essay like this where the main argument is very clear, it can be useful to spell it out in the introduction and use the rest of the essay to 'prove' your case.

matters as entry by ticket to a cinema (*Hurst v Picture Theatres Ltd* (1915)), permission to use local facilities for a conference (*Verrall v Great Yarmouth BC* (1981)), permission to erect an advertising hoarding (*Kewal Investments v Arthur Maiden* (1990)) and even permission to occupy premises for residential accommodation (*Ogwr BC v Dykes* (1989); *Gray v Taylor* (1998)).[2] Indeed, it is in respect of this last category – so-called occupation licences (but see Chapter 5) – that much of the debate has taken place, for, if it is possible to give licences to occupy property as a residence, it is in the interests of the licensee to claim that the licence can in fact bind any transferee from the licensor.

The various uses of licences are reflected in their traditional categorisation. All categories are noted here, although it must be borne in mind that it is really in respect of the last two that the debate about the proprietary nature of licences has taken place. First, there are 'bare licences', being the most simple form of permission to use land given voluntarily by the owner of property. Typically, such licences allow the 'licensee' to carry on some limited activity on the 'licensor's' land, as where permission is given for children to play. It is intrinsic to this type of licence that the permission may be withdrawn at any time and, because given voluntarily without consideration, does not give the licensee any claim to damages or other legal remedy. Second, there are those licences grouped together because they are 'coupled with an interest in the land'. In essence, these licences comprise the implied permission that a person obtains and which enables them to enjoy some right previously granted over the land, as where a person is granted the right to fish, cut turf or gather wood, as in *James Jones & Son v Earl of Tankerville* (1909). To some extent, however, the label 'licence' is misleading, for the licence is merely incidental and ancillary to the right that has actually been granted over the land: see, for example, the licence to park given to a tenant in *Donington Park Leisure Ltd v Wheatcroft & Son Ltd* (2006). So, the licence will last for as long as the proprietary right is granted and will be enforceable against whomsoever the proprietary right is enforceable against, being merely an ingredient in the greater right.

As noted above, it is with the third and fourth categories of licence that the question of whether they amount to an interest in land has been most commonly posed: those of contractual licences and licences arising by estoppel. Contractual licences are, in principle, little different in nature from bare licences, save that contractual licences are granted to the licensee in return for valuable consideration moving to the licensor; the purchase of a cinema ticket is a good example. Crucially, of course, such contractual licences are governed by the ordinary rules relating to remedies for breach of contract and it is now clear that either an injunction will be granted preventing the licensor from revoking the licence before its contractual date of expiry (*Wintergarden Theatres v Millennium*

---

2   This section makes good use of the case law and demonstrates a lot of knowledge without spending too long describing the different kinds of licences.

Productions Ltd (1948)) or even a decree of specific performance requiring the licensor to permit the activity authorised by the licence to take place (*Verrall v Great Yarmouth*). It is obvious that the effect of the availability of these remedies may, in appropriate circumstances (depending on the contract and the conduct of the parties), make the licence de facto irrevocable throughout the contractual time period (for example, the theatre performance). Of course, this is in reality only an issue between the original licensor and licensee, but the fact that such licences could be irrevocable during their contractual period *and* that they related to land did raise the inevitable question of their effect on third parties. Put simply, the question is asked whether, given that a contractual licence is irrevocable between the licensor and licensee throughout its contractual period, the licensor can nevertheless defeat the licence by conveying the property to a third party during that period?[3] In such cases, the licensee may well have a good claim in contract against the licensor, but that is not the same as allowing the licensee's rights to use the land to continue against the third party for the remainder of the period.

In the event, under the influence of Lord Denning's Court of Appeal, two strands of thought developed that sought to explain why a licence could bind a third party and, perhaps, why it should be regarded as a new species of interest in land. On the one hand, in *Errington v Errington* (1952), Lord Denning regarded a contractual licence as binding on a third party who received the property, which was subject to the licence by a will, her husband being the original licensor. In this case, the reasoning was explicit that since the licensee could restrain revocation of the licence for its period against the licensor, there was no reason why the licence could not continue against a third party who was not a bona fide purchaser of a legal estate for value in the property. This assumes that licences are *capable* of binding third parties in the first place! The reasoning for the decision is unclear, although it seems that the contractual licence was supported by 'an equity' that transformed it into a proprietary right. Unfortunately, this ignores the previous decision of the House of Lords'[4] in *King v David Allen & Sons, Billposting* (1916), which had decided expressly that contractual licences could not bind third parties.

The second line of attack on the traditional view came with the Court of Appeal in *Binions v Evans* (1972). In that case, a purchaser of land subject to what looked like a contractual licence, expressly agreed to take the land subject to that licence. The purchaser later sought to evict the licensee. Two judges in the Court of Appeal actually decided that no licence was involved at all; rather, the occupier had a life interest under a settlement that was protected under the **Settled Land Act 1925**. Lord Denning, however, took a different view and decided that the purchaser was bound to give effect to the licence because he

3   This explanation of what it would mean for a licence to take on a 'proprietary' effect shows that the writer understands the distinction between personal and property rights.

4   The noting of the court here shows the importance and strength of this authority.

had purchased the property subject to it and that such licence was protected by the imposition of a constructive trust on the purchaser. In the case itself, it is not clear whether Denning MR regards these as separate or complementary grounds for the decision, but subsequent decisions (for example, *Bannister v Bannister* (1948); *Re Sharpe* (1980)) have tended to rely on the constructive trust argument as a means of protecting the licence against a third party. However, as we shall see, this does not necessarily mean that the contractual licence has become an interest in land.

This seemed to represent the law until the decision of the Court of Appeal in *Ashburn Anstalt v Arnold* (1989). In that case, Fox LJ[5] relied on the House of Lords' decision in *King* and *National Provincial Bank v Ainsworth* (1965) and reaffirmed the orthodox view that licences were not interests in land. In his view, *Errington* was *per incuriam*, because of the existence of the binding authority of *King*. In any event, *Errington* could have been decided on at least three other grounds (the existence of an estate contract binding a non-purchaser, a *Rosset*-type equitable right of ownership, or estoppel). Indeed, Fox LJ's judgment makes it clear that *as a matter of principle*, licences are not interests in land. This has now been reaffirmed by the Court of Appeal in *Lloyd v Dugdale* (2002) and effectively settles the matter. However, turning to the *Binions v Evans* argument, Fox LJ in *Ashburn* accepted that in appropriate cases a contractual licence may *take effect* against a purchaser behind a constructive trust, if the purchaser has so conducted himself that it would be inequitable for the licence to be denied. Such a trust does not exist merely because the purchaser bought the land 'subject to' the licence, but only if there was unconscionable conduct on the part of the purchaser (for example, paying a lower price as a result of the promise to respect the licence). In any event, the licence is only protected behind a *personal* constructive trust binding on this particular purchaser because of their particular conduct; it has not thereby assumed the status of an interest in land. Again, this has been confirmed by *Dugdale*, in which the court makes it clear that the imposition of a constructive trust on a purchaser can be justified only in exceptional circumstances in which it is clear that the purchaser has, by his conduct, accepted the obligation imposed by the licence.

This position in *Ashburn* and *Dugdale* is, without doubt, a thoroughly orthodox approach to the problem and it serves to highlight the fundamental distinction between interests in land and purely personal interests that just happen to relate to property. It represents the law today. No licences are proprietary interests in land. In fact, now that the House of Lords has asserted in *Street v Mountford* (1985) that residential occupation usually gives rise to a lease and not a licence, there is a symmetry to the picture. To be entirely fair to Lord Denning and the other judges following his lead, their attempt to confer proprietary status on mainly occupation licences came at a time when landowners were able to avoid granting leases. In this respect, attempts to protect occupation licences could be seen as

5   Citing a specific judge shows good knowledge of the case law.

an attempt to protect what were really leases and, after *Street*, would be regarded as such. Indeed, if one takes Lord Wilberforce's definition of an interest in land in *Ainsworth* ('before a right or interest can be admitted into the category of property, or of a right affecting property it must be definable, identifiable by third parties, capable in its nature of assumption by third parties and have some degree of permanence or stability'), it is obvious that there is some circularity in the whole issue. What these cases show us is that the distinction between licences and interests in land is a real and immovable one, but what amounts to either a 'licence' or an 'interest in land' in any given case depends ultimately on the facts of that case.

Don't be tempted to

This is a standard examination question, although it *cannot* be completed successfully without knowledge of case law. The distinction between the ability of a proprietary right to bind a third party because of its inherent nature and the personal way in which a licence may bind someone because of a purely personal constructive trust is most important. Try to avoid merely repeating that there are four types of licence and then describing them. The question is about 'third parties', it does *not* say 'describe four types of licence'.

QUESTION 27

In 2011, Zoe acquired registered title to a small cottage on Dartmoor, formerly part of a large farm and quite close to the old farmhouse. Being fond of animals, she acquires several horses and asks Farmer Roger whether she can keep them on his land. He agrees, but only if he may use the horses to hire to tourists who stay on his farm. Farmer Roger also provides riding holidays for tourists, using his own horses, and Zoe agreed that, if there were insufficient space in the farmhouse, she would accommodate any extra tourists and provide them with breakfast and an evening meal if desired. Zoe also pays Farmer Roger £100 per month to park her car in an old barn on the farm. She also regularly collects firewood from Farmer Roger's land, as her only source of heating is an old wood-burning stove. In 2012, Farmer Roger proposes marriage to Zoe but she refuses. Farmer Roger takes great offence and immediately threatens to turn Zoe's horses out, although he does continue to use them for his riding business. In anger, Zoe refuses to accommodate any of Farmer Roger's tourists and asks those currently staying there to leave. The tourists subsequently sue Roger for a ruined holiday. Roger's response is to sell the barn and fields to Fenland Holidays plc, which immediately refuses Zoe the right to park her car or gather wood.

Zoe comes to you for advice as her car has broken down due to standing in the cold and she cannot live in the cottage without her source of fuel. She hopes to be able to sell the cottage to her friend, Beverley, who would also like to keep horses. It also emerges that Fenland Holidays plc knew of Zoe's activities and paid Farmer Roger a much-reduced price for the land it has purchased. You discover subsequently that Farmer Roger is the major shareholder in Fenland Holidays plc.

How to Answer this Question

❖   Identify the nature of the claimant's rights over the land – are they licences or proprietary interests?

❖   What is the effect of licences between the original parties – remedies?

❖   What is the effect of licences on third parties?

❖   Is there a role for a constructive trust and the personal protection of licences? (*Binions v Evans*; *Chaudhary v Yavuz*)

❖   Are any new licences created?

Applying the Law

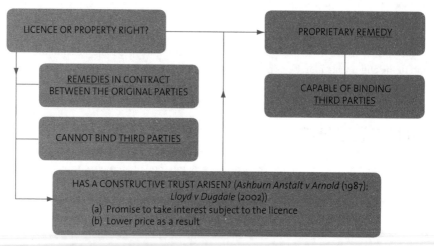

This diagram demonstrates the difference between licences, property rights, and constructive trusts.

ANSWER

This problem concerns the creation of rights over land, the identification of the nature of those rights and the consequences that flow from subsequent dealings with the land over which those rights exist. In essence, as we are asked to advise Zoe, it is necessary to determine: (a) whether she has any right to insist that her horses be accommodated and whether this right can be enforced against Farmer Roger and whether the benefit of the right can subsequently be passed on to Beverley; (b) whether Zoe is under any liability in respect of the displaced tourists and the refusal to house further tourists; (c) whether Zoe has any rights to park her car and collect wood and whether these are binding on

Fenland; and (d) whether Fenland's conduct and the involvement of Farmer Roger suggest any other remedy for Zoe.[6]

(A) THE HORSES

There seems little doubt that Zoe and Farmer Roger have entered into a contract whereby Zoe agrees to allow the horses to be used for Roger's business in return for which Roger allows Zoe to keep the horses on his land. However, the nature of the rights created by this contract are the crucial factor, for that may determine their enforceability and status in respect of third parties.

The contract is purely oral and, if it is to be argued that this contract confers some sort of proprietary interest on Zoe, there are going to be difficulties in fulfilling the formality requirements of **s 2** of the **Law of Property (Miscellaneous Provisions) Act 1989**. In fact, the only possibility of a proprietary right is that Zoe has some lease of the land (cf *University of Reading v Johnson-Houghton* (1985)) in the form of a periodic tenancy, which would be binding on Roger according to its terms and could be assigned to Beverley in the normal way by deed (*Julian v Crago* (1992)). However, the nature of Zoe's right to keep horses, and the circumstances in which it was created, militate against the granting of any proprietary interest. Indeed, it is likely that her right is in the nature of a contractual licence over Farmer Roger's land. Presumptively, a contractual licence is revocable during its term by the licensor, although the licensee (Zoe) would have a claim in damages. On the other hand, however, it is clear from *Wintergarden Theatres v Millennium Productions* (1948) that if, on construction of the contract, a contractual licence was intended to be irrevocable during its period of operation, equity will intervene to restrain breach of that contract by the licensor by way of injunction or specific performance as appropriate. Whether the remedy is available to Zoe will depend on many factors, not least her own conduct. Her willingness to continue to allow her horses to be used (that is, that she kept her side of the contract) will be important, although her apparent refusal to cater for the very tourists who would ride will count against. As far as Beverley is concerned, it has always been true that the benefit of a contract can be expressly assigned and there is no reason why Zoe cannot transfer to Beverley such rights as she has against Roger under the contractual licence for the accommodation of her horses. We might also note that, although not in issue in this problem, the benefit of the contract could have been conferred on Beverley at the time of the contract under the **Contracts (Rights of Third Parties) Act 1999**.[7]

(B) THE TOURISTS

The precise nature of Zoe's liabilities here will depend on the exact terms of the contract she made with Farmer Roger. It may well be that she is in breach of contract in evicting

....

6   The lettering in the introduction here matches the sub-headings in the body of the answer giving a clear structure to the response.

7   This shows knowledge of contractual principles going beyond those normally looked at in relation to land law specifically and would therefore receive extra credit.

the tourists before the end of their holiday and in refusing to accommodate future arrivals. In such a case, Farmer Roger will have a right to sue Zoe in contract and recover the loss caused by the action against him by his disgruntled clients. What is quite clear, however, is that the tourists have no short-term lease over their rooms in Zoe's cottage. Under *Street v Mountford* (1985), there is no doubt that these occupiers are lodgers and, therefore, not tenants. There is the provision of board and services within *Markou v Da Silvaesa* (1986). The tourists may, of course, have a contractual licence to occupy the cottage (see *Royal Bank of Scotland v Mehta* (1999)), although it is difficult to see on the facts how they could be in direct contract with Zoe. If they were, and were occupying on a contractual licence from Zoe, *Tanner v Tanner* (1975) suggests that an injunction could be obtained to prevent eviction for the duration of the licence. However, not only is this the least likely remedy sought by the transient tourists, the *Tanner* case is fundamentally different in that it concerned a long-term occupier who was denied continued occupation by the licensor in very inequitable circumstances.

(C) CAR PARKING AND COLLECTING WOOD

The issue of the car parking and the collection of wood raises issues as to the nature of the rights granted and the impact on the third party who purchased the land over which the rights existed.

As to the car parking, it is clear from *Newman v Jones* (1982) and *Moncrieff v Jamieson* (2008) that it is perfectly possible to have an easement giving a right to park on a neighbour's land.[8] However, it is unclear whether an easement can exist where the right to park is in a defined space as opposed to park generally within a larger area – that is, if it gives exclusive possession or excessive control over the servient land (see *Moncrieff v Jamieson*). In any event, even assuming that this could be an easement, the formality necessary to create a legal or equitable right have not been met and there is little possibility of an estoppel. All in all, this looks as if Zoe has been granted a contractual licence to park her car, which, of course, is enforceable against Roger as the licensor. However, it is now clear from *Ashburn Anstalt v Arnold* (1989) and *Lloyd v Dugdale* (2002) that licences as such are not interests in land and cannot therefore bind a subsequent purchaser of the land. So, subject to what will be said below, at first sight it looks as if Zoe's right to park her car cannot be enforced against Fenland.[9]

The right to collect wood poses different problems. There is no doubt that it is possible for a person to be granted a profit *à prendre* to collect wood for the purpose of fuel,

---

8   Although this is clearly a question about licences in land, it is important to recognise that other topics may come into the answer.

9   This sentence is good because it draws a mini-conclusion in relation to the nature of the car-parking right but shows that this is not the end of the matter.

otherwise known as a profit of estovers (*AG v Reynolds* (1911)). Profits are proprietary rights and any licences attached to the profit to enter onto another's land for the purpose of exercising the profit take the character of the superior right's proprietary status (*James Jones v Earl of Tankerville* (1909), *Polo Woods v Shelton-Agar* (2009)). However, it is also clear that in order for the profit to exist – and, hence, be capable of binding a third party such as Fenland – it must be created in due form. In this case, there is no deed of grant to support a legal profit and no written contract to support an equitable profit. Zoe's only hope is, perhaps, to plead the creation of a profit by estoppel, similar to the creation of an easement by estoppel in *Celsteel v Alton* (1985). However, even if that were the case, Zoe would have to register her interest by means of a notice in order for it to be effective against a purchaser – **s 29** of the **Land Registration Act 2002** – for an equitable easement or profit can no longer override under the **LRA 2002** (it is not within **Sched 3** to the Act and use of the easement or profit does not amount to 'actual occupation' of the burdened land – *Chaudhary v Yavuz* (2012)[10]). There is no evidence that she has so registered. If, on the other hand, no estoppel profit can arise, Zoe's only hope is to prove that it was never the intention of the parties to grant her a profit but, rather, that she has a mere licence to collect wood. Obviously, a mere licence cannot bind Fenland as such – not being an interest in land – but she may gain some comfort from the principle of constructive trusts considered below.

(D) FENLAND AND FARMER ROGER

Although it is clear that the licence to park the car (and to collect wood if established as a licence) cannot bind Fenland as a matter of property law, there is the possibility that a purchaser of land will be bound by a personal constructive trust, imposed to give effect to such licences as exist, because of the purchaser's inequitable conduct. That even a licence can gain protection in this way is accepted in *Ashburn Anstalt v Arnold* and *Lloyd v Dugdale*, for its essence is that equity imposes an obligation on the conscience of a particular purchaser. The nature of the right is not crucial, but *Chaudhary v Yavuz* (2012) makes it clear that this is a very exceptional rule and not easily established. So, it is not enough that the purchaser simply promised to give effect to the licences (*Ashburn, Yavuz*, criticising *Binions v Evans* (1972)). In our case, the fact that the purchaser paid a lower price because it knew of the existence of the licences may well be important (*Dugdale*), although as we know from *Midland Bank v Green* (1981) (in another context), undervalue and knowledge that rights will be defeated do not necessarily amount to inequitable conduct (and see *Melbury v Kriedl* (1999)). It will in essence be a matter for the court. If a constructive trust is imposed, it will ensure that Fenland permits the continuance of the rights of Zoe. It is a difficult plea to make out.

....
10   This shows good knowledge of very recent case law.

Finally, two further points should be noted. First, as with (a) above, Zoe may transfer the benefit of any contract to Beverley irrespective of the nature of the rights created by the contract. That is a matter of contract law. It is not clear, however, whether the transfer of the benefit of the contractual rights to a third party will affect the court's decision to impose a constructive trust on the purchaser of the land over which those rights exists. Second, it may be possible to argue that there is no third-party purchaser at all on the grounds that Fenland is just Farmer Roger in another guise. If that were the case, because Roger is the majority shareholder, no question of the enforcement of licences against third parties arise. It is more likely, however, given the separate legal personality of companies and their owners, that Roger's majority shareholding will be relevant to the question of the imposition of the constructive trust on the 'third party' rather than in deciding that there was no third party at all (see *Jones v Lipman* (1962)).

Don't be tempted to

Do not forget the connection between easements and licences. Although it is possible to answer this question entirely from the perspective of 'licences', a better answer will consider whether any of the alleged rights might also be easements. Land law cannot safely be 'compartmentalised' like some other subjects.

QUESTION 28 --

'The law relating to proprietary estoppel is flexible and may change over time. It is not possible to identify with certainty when a claim of estoppel might be successful, although it is possible to identify the general principles of the doctrine.'

▶ **Do you agree?**

How to Answer this Question

❖   Identification of the general nature of proprietary estoppel and its relationship to rules regulating the acquisition of estates and interests in land.

❖   Briefly, the five probanda for proprietary estoppel (*Willmott v Barber* (1880)).

❖   The modern definition of proprietary estoppel (*Taylor Fashions v Liverpool Victoria Trustees* (1982); *Mathura v Mathura* (1994)).

❖   The role of unconscionability – *Taylor v Dickens* (1998); *Gillett v Holt* (2001); *Kinane v Conteh* (2005); *Yeoman's Row Management v Cobbe* (2008); *Thorner v Majors* (2009).

Applying the Law

This diagram represents the general principles of proprietary estoppel.

ANSWER

Section 2 of the **Law of Property (Miscellaneous Provisions) Act 1989** establishes the minimum level of formality necessary for the valid creation, acquisition or transfer of estates and interests in land. Since **s 2** came into force, purely oral contracts are not in general capable of giving rise to an enforceable right in land. Moreover, **s 2** stipulates a *minimum* level of formality, because compliance with its provisions without more usually results in the creation of an equitable right only. Legal estates and interests on the whole require the additional formality of a deed and (for registered land) registration in the relevant section of the land register (see **ss 25** and **27** of and **Sched 2** to the **Land Registration Act 2002**). It is in such a context, where statute requires a considerable degree of formality for the creation of rights in land, that the doctrine of proprietary estoppel should be examined.[11]

The exact purpose or role of proprietary estoppel is a matter of some debate. On the one hand, proprietary estoppel can provide a defence to an action by a landowner who seeks to enforce his strict rights against someone who has been promised some right or liberty over the land: see for example *Mathura v Mathura* (1994). However, the role of proprietary estoppel is not limited to providing a person with a defence to an action by the paper owner of land because a successful plea of proprietary estoppel can operate positively, in the sense that it can generate new property interests in favour of a claimant (e.g. *Kinane v Conteh* (2005)). As is typically stated, proprietary estoppel is both a shield and a sword

---

11 This introduction explains why the doctrine of proprietary estoppel is so important from the perspective of formalities, and therefore gives the overall angle that the response is taking in addressing the set question.

(*Crabb v Arun DC* (1976)). Moreover, it is the second aspect of proprietary estoppel that relates so closely to the formality requirements discussed above because proprietary estoppel can result in the creation of proprietary rights without a deed, without any writing and without the existence of even an oral or formal contract. It is the creation of rights arising from the action of equity on an individual's conscience.

The doctrine of proprietary estoppel is not a creation of the modern law, although it certainly has come to the fore in recent times. In *Willmott v Barber* (1880), Fry LJ laid down what was to be regarded for many years as the five 'probanda' of proprietary estoppel, being the five conditions that needed to be established before a claimant could be awarded a right to another's land arising informally. These were: first, that the claimant should have made some mistake as to their legal rights; second, that the claimant must have expended some money or done some act on the faith of the mistaken belief; third, that the true landowner must know of the existence of their own right and that it is inconsistent with the right claimed by the claimant; fourth, the landowner must know of the claimant's mistaken belief as to their legal rights; and fifth, that the landowner should have encouraged the expenditure by the claimant, either directly, or by abstaining from enforcing their legal right.

It is obvious that these five conditions are fairly strict and they undoubtedly established a clear framework for ascertaining the likelihood of a successful plea of proprietary estoppel. However, as the doctrine developed, it became clear that courts were prepared to accept a plea of proprietary estoppel when one or more of Fry LJ's probanda were missing (for example, *Berg Homes v Grey* (1980)). Largely this was because the emphasis of proprietary estoppel had shifted from situations in which the purpose was to prevent the true owner from relying on their strict legal rights over land, to a doctrine that asked whether the claimant had any positive right to that land. In short, the focus shifted from the landowner to the claimant, wherein the latter's actions and perceptions became much more central to the issue. Essentially, the modern position is that put forward in *Taylor Fashions v Liverpool Victoria Trustees* (1982). In that case, Oliver J made it clear that proprietary estoppel is not limited to cases in which the landowner knows of their rights, or their extent, but is indeed a flexible doctrine, springing from equity, which should not be unduly restricted by rigid rules.[12]

The position after *Taylor Fashions* (1982) is that a person may be entitled to claim rights in or over land that belongs formally to another where it would be unconscionable to deny those rights. Effectively, this means that the claimant must prove an assurance – express or implied – by the landowner as to the claimant's position in relation to the land, reliance on that assurance by the claimant, and detriment by the claimant as a result of relying on the assurance, although these criteria may well overlap and should not be regarded as

12 This question in asking about the flexibility of estoppel over time is looking not only for a description of historical developments in the law, but also in terms of its current (and potential future) flexibility.

completely distinct requirements. The overall aim is to prevent unconscionability (*Gillett v Holt* (2001)), but the claimant must prove the factual basis for the estoppel – it being 'unfair' to deny the claimant is not sufficient – *Thorner v Majors* (2009). It is true, however, that these criteria are flexible and in some cases little has been required to prove the estoppel. In *Greasley v Cooke* (1980), for example, the Court of Appeal held that if it is clear that assurances have been made, and detriment suffered, it is permissible to assume that reliance has occurred. Likewise, in *JT Developments v Quinn* (1991), it became clear that an estoppel could arise even though there was no intention to create binding obligations, as where the parties had attempted to negotiate a contract in respect of land but failed. Numerous examples now exist of successful claims of proprietary estoppel and cases such as *Re Basham* (1986), *Gillett v Holt, Suggitt v Suggitt* (2012) and *Thorner v Majors* (2009)[13] illustrate that it is an all-purpose remedy resorted to as much by claimants seeking to avoid the formality requirements otherwise imposed for the creation of property rights as by judges seeking to achieve a 'just' result in the case before them.

However, it is also clear that estoppel is not to be regarded as a panacea for all problems. There are some circumstances – illustrated by *Yeoman's Row Management v Cobbe* (2008) – where it is not unconscionable for one party to rely on lack of formality as a means of avoiding an oral agreement, especially if both parties were fully aware of the need for formality as a general rule (see also *Herbert v Doyle* (2010)) Thus, while there are some cases (e.g. *Lim Teng Huan v Ang Swee Chuan* (1992), *Flowermix v Site Developments* (2000)) in which estoppel has been used to 'enforce' a contract that it not otherwise valid – e.g. because of the absence of writing or uncertainty with the failed contract being regarded as the assurance – it is likely that *Yeoman's Row* has made this less likely by emphasising that estoppel should not be used as a device to cure failed contracts, especially in a commercial context. This must be correct, for it is not unconscionable to insist on compliance with *statutory* formalities for the creation of interests in land. Estoppel works outside of these formalities, but only where unconscionability exists – *Thorner v Majors* (2009).

It appears, then, that proprietary estoppel is now the embodiment of the equitable jurisdiction: it allows for the creation of property rights without needing to fulfill the strict requirements of statute, in cases in which it would be 'unconscionable' to do otherwise. The flexibility this permits is apparent in the way that a court may 'satisfy' the estoppel or, in other words, the flexibility a court has to grant the most appropriate remedy to the claimant. For example, if the claimant successfully establishes an assurance supported by detrimental reliance, the estoppel thereby generated may be satisfied by awarding the fee simple to the claimant (*Dillwyn v Llewellyn* (1862); *Pascoe v Turner* (1979)), the grant of an

---

13   This essay calls for discussion of the relevant case law, and listing cases in this way is a good way to show off knowledge whilst managing time effectively.

easement (*Celsteel v Alton* (1985)), a life interest (one view of *Bannister v Bannister* (1948)), a right of occupation until expenditure is repaid (*Dodsworth v Dodsworth* (1973)), a complete readjustment of the parties' rights over the property (*Voyce v Voyce* (1991)), a readjustment of testamentary dispositions (*Re Basham* (1986)), a mortgage (*Kinane* (2005)), a licence to use the property (one view of *Inwards v Baker* (1965)), a cash sum (*Campbell v Griffin* (2001)) or, simply, dismissal of the paper owner's claim for possession (*Mathura* (1994)).[14] In fact, the range of remedies is open-ended and, importantly, does not necessarily have to result in the creation or transfer of a proprietary interest at all. In some cases, it will be the 'expectation loss' of the claimant (that is, that which they were promised). In others, it will be their 'reliance loss', being the repayment of any detriment incurred. In fact, it could be a combination of the two (*Jennings v Rice* (2003)), provided that it is at least the minimum necessary to do justice between the parties.

All in all, the conditions required for establishing an estoppel, and the court's wide discretion in satisfying a successful plea, demonstrate the highly flexible nature of this doctrine. Of course, accompanying such flexibility is a large measure of uncertainty, both for any claimant and their legal advisers.[15] It is not surprising, therefore, that proprietary estoppel has been regarded as a panacea for all ills. Moreover, in so far as it allows the creation of rights over property by entirely informal means, it provides an easy escape route for the claimant who has failed to observe the statutory requirements for the creation of proprietary rights, as in *Lim, Flowermix* and *Joyce v Rigolli* (2004). That said, the existence of a doctrine that enables a court to resolve matters according to the conscience of the parties involved, rather than according to the strict forms of a statute, is a necessary adjunct to any legal system that stipulates formalities as a means to certainty. The key is, however, not to go too far. In this respect, the House of Lords in *Yeomans v Cobbe* (2008) refuses to allow estoppel to save commercial partners from the consequences of their own failure to do things properly, while although a claim was successful in *Thorner v Majors* (2009), the House of Lords emphasised the need to prove the factual basis of estoppel rather than doing what was 'fair' in all the circumstances. There is merit in certainty, especially in relation to transactions concerning land, and policy considerations should not be forgotten when considering the informal and flexible doctrine of proprietary estoppel. This will be all the more important when electronic conveyancing introduces even stricter formality requirements for the creation or transfer of proprietary rights in registered land.

Don't be tempted to

Do not avoid the apparent differences between *Yeomans Row v Cobbe* (2008) and *Thorner v Majors* (2009). Is everything explained because one is 'commercial' and the other 'family', or is there a different underlying tension about the nature and role of estoppel?

....

14   It is important to recognise that flexibility may exist at different levels of application of a particular rule.

15   This conclusion is good because it goes beyond summarising what has been established in the course of the essay and examines instead the merits of the flexibility of the rules.

How specific does an assurance need to be? How much certainty is needed in relation to identifying the land that is subject to the estoppel?

QUESTION 29

'The law of proprietary estoppel has altered fundamentally the distinction between licences and proprietary interests in land. To all intents and purposes, to make such distinctions is no longer practically necessary or theoretically justified.'

▶ **Discuss.**

How to Answer this Question

- ❖ The nature of proprietary estoppel.
- ❖ Its relation to estoppel licences.
- ❖ Estoppels and third parties: land registration.
- ❖ The need for theoretical clarity.

Applying the Law

This diagram shows the relationship between licences and proprietary estoppel.

ANSWER

In recent years, the courts' resort to proprietary estoppel as a means of resolving disputes over property has increased dramatically. Of course, this in itself is worthy of note, but it is not truly startling: the fact that the courts are prepared to intervene more readily where they perceive unconscionability shows that 'equity' remains a developing body of law able to meet in part the demands of a modern law of property for the twenty-first century. Indeed, since *Taylor Fashions v Liverpool Victoria Trustees* (1982) deconstructed the law of proprietary estoppel, by making the conditions for a successful claim less rigid, the doctrine has moved into new fields, as both *Voyce v Voyce* (1991) and *JT Developments v Quinn* (1991) illustrate. It may be that proprietary estoppel emerges as the main counterweight to the formality requirements contained in **s 2** of the **Law of Property (Miscellaneous Provisions) Act 1989** (but only where it would be truly unconscionable to waive those requirements: see, for example, *Cobbe v Yeoman's* 2008 and *Thorner v Majors* (2009)) and the proposed forms for electronic conveyancing found in the **Land Registration Act 2002** However, the development of this doctrine supposes not only that there are clear (or relatively clear) principles that can separate the legitimate from the spurious claim, but also that the consequences of a successful invocation of proprietary estoppel are clearly understood.[16]

It is clear from *Taylor Fashions* that an estoppel will arise in favour of a claimant if they can prove an assurance, relied upon to their detriment. It is also clear from *Crabb v Arun DC* (1976) that, once the court has decided that the equity is established, it may seek to 'satisfy' it in a way appropriate to the case before it, in essence, using its discretion. The cases of *Voyce v Voyce, Mathura v Mathura* (1994) and *Yaxley v Gotts* (2000) in which the court unscrambled the complicated property dealings of the parties and imposed a solution apparently outside of the parties' intention, show that the court's power is wide and unfettered by the actual expectations of the parties. The Court of Appeal has now confirmed this in very clear terms in *Jennings v Rice* (2003). However, none of this settles the question of the nature of proprietary estoppel per se; all it does is tell us that the court may use the doctrine to achieve such results as it thinks fair and reasonable in the circumstances. In particular, the question has arisen in the context of licences that, on the now confirmed orthodox view (*Lloyd v Dugdale* (2002)), are not interests in land. In simple terms, if the result of the courts' deliberations are that one of the parties has a licence over the other's land, generated or protected by estoppel, does this amount to an 'interest in land'? Or, to put it another way, is the estoppel itself an interest in land that can bind third parties in the normal way appropriate to proprietary interests in registered or unregistered land, such that it

---

16 In order to explain and understand the role of licences in relation to estoppel it is necessary here to examine the role of estoppel in modern property law.

can confer such a status on what would otherwise be a purely personal licence to use the land?[17]

At one time, the answer to this question was uncertain, for there was little specific guidance in the case law. This was not surprising given that courts are more concerned with reaching practical solutions to practical problems without delving into the theoretical niceties of the nature of proprietary estoppel (for example, *Bibby v Stirling* (1998)). In general, however, two distinct trends could be distinguished. First, there was some support for the view that licences generated by estoppel, or protected by estoppel, were themselves interests in land. This seems to be another way of saying that an estoppel per se has a proprietary character. Support for this view may have derived from *Ives v High* (1967) and from *Inwards v Baker* (1965), in which dicta suggested that estoppel, once arisen, would bind a third party. A similar hint is given in *Habermann v Koeller* (1996) and, more recently, is inherent in the decision in *Lloyd v Dugdale*, in which the claimant benefitted from an estoppel, but it did not bind because Dugdale was not in 'actual occupation' under (the then applicable) **s 70(1)(g)** of the **LRA 1925** – thus implying that the estoppel *itself* was proprietary and would have bound if Dugdale had been in actual occupation. In unregistered land, this would be through the mechanism of notice (*Ives v High*) and, as noted in *Dugdale*, in registered land, through occupation giving rise to an overriding interest (now) under **Sched 3, para 2** to the **LRA 2002**. Certainly, under this view estoppel has been elevated to an interest in land per se and, now this is without doubt the effect of **s 116** of the **LRA 2002**. However, in respect of licences at least, there are difficulties. First, a distinction should be made between estoppel that creates a right between A and B and estoppel that protects a pre-existing right (created by A and B) against C. It is only the first of these scenarios that gives rise to the problems we are considering. For example, in *Ives v High*, one explanation of the case is that A and B had by their action created an easement binding on A's land and, when the land was sold to C, C so acted as to be estopped from denying the right. In effect, this has nothing to do with the transfer of existing rights to a third party because the third party is bound by estoppel because of their own actions. In other words, C is bound by their own estoppel, not that which existed between A and B. (The same could be said of *Bibby v Stirling*, in which an estoppel *appears* to bind a third party without argument.) Second, there is only fragile evidence that an estoppel licence has ever been held binding against a third party. The acid test would be whether an estoppel-generated licence has ever had this effect, because, given that we know that pure licences cannot bind third parties, any such effect must be due to the estoppel itself. The evidence is equivocal, despite *Lloyd v Dugdale*. It is true that, in *Inwards v Baker*, the court indicated that the claimant should be awarded a licence to occupy that could bind third parties and the same solution was adopted in *Greasley v Cooke* (1980). Likewise, in *Re Sharpe* (1980), the court accepts that the estoppel (the 'equity') can bind a trustee in bankruptcy and there is implied support in *Locabail UK v Bayfield* (1999). However, it is also

....

17 Where an essay asks about the interaction between two issues, it is important to outline in the essay what you think the relevant questions about this interaction are in order to build a clear argument.

true that both *Inwards* and *Cooke* can be justified on other grounds (that the claimant should have had a life interest under a settlement; see *Dodsworth v Dodsworth* (1973)) and, in *Williams v Staite* (1979) the matter was assumed rather than argued. The same assumption was made in *Bibby v Stirling*, although not of course in *Dugdale*.[18]

Indeed, after the decision in *Dugdale*, it may be that a dual approach should be preferred. Thus, while *licences* are not interests in land, 'estoppels' are because of **s 116** of the **LRA 2002**. However, if the court chooses to satisfy the equity by the award of a licence to the claimant, perhaps it will not then be *enforced* against a third party, at least if the equity is crystallised *before* the third party becomes involved, because at that point it is no longer an 'equity by estoppel' within **s 116** but is then a 'licence'. Conversely, if the estoppel is satisfied as a proprietary right *before* a third party becomes involved, then there is no doubt that a third person buying the land over which the right takes effect will be bound by it: they are bound in the same way that any lease, freehold or easement would bind. Of course, if the third party becomes involved before the estoppel is crystallised, this will be regarded as proprietary (**s 116** of the **LRA 2002**), irrespective of the way the court chooses then to crystallise it.[19]

In conclusion, then, whether proprietary estoppel has altered the fundamental distinction between personal rights and proprietary rights depends on the view one takes of the doctrine. Is an estoppel in itself a right, or is it merely a method whereby rights are created, some of which will be proprietary, some of which will be personal? The **LRA 2002** confirms that estoppel gives rise to an interest in land from the moment the equity arises (that is, when the assurance is acted on to detriment) and not the later date on which it is crystallised by the court. This will bring certainty, but will it also restrict courts in that their ability to grant rights arising by estoppel that are not (and should not) bind third parties?[20]

Don't be tempted to

This is a difficult question as it raises an issue to which the courts have not yet given a final answer: namely, the nature of proprietary estoppel. Do not avoid this difficulty and make the answer simple. Help can be obtained from academic comment; see, in particular, Battersby [1991] Conv 36 and (1995) 58 MLR 637. **Section 116** of the **LRA 2002** appears to have has settled the matter for registered land, and see *Henry v Henry* (2010).

Try to avoid simply talking about assurance, reliance and detriment. There is more to estoppel than this.

---

18 This section shows a sophisticated analysis not only of the results of the case law, but of the reasoning employed by the courts in those cases.
19 This is a clear explanation of the potential effects of estoppel in relation to third parties and would be given much credit for explaining a difficult area so succinctly.
20 Finishing this essay with a question highlights the unsettled nature of this area and shows that the writer is aware that there are still issues to be resolved.

QUESTION 30

In 2009, Andrew, Edward and Charles live in Nos 1, 2 and 3 Abdication Street respectively, an area of registered land. Each house has a large garden, although Andrew has concreted over his and uses it to store spare parts connected with his car repair business. Last year, Andrew asked Edward (in No 2) whether he would mind if he (Andrew) constructed a small shed to store some more valuable equipment, even though this meant siting some foundations in Edward's garden. Edward readily agreed and helped Andrew construct the shed. A little later, before the shed was complete, Andrew promised that Edward could store some of his (Edward's) own goods in the shed. Edward also asked if Andrew would mind if his wife's mother, Camilla, parked her cycle in the shed.

Andrew readily agreed, not realising that Camilla drove a very large motorcycle that would occupy considerable space. Meanwhile, Charles has been negotiating with Edward over the purchase of some land owned by Edward at the back of Abdication Street. Edward is unwilling to sell, but permits Charles to occupy the land pending the negotiation of a long lease. Edward asks Charles to pay him £600 per month as 'a down payment' for the lease, but, when Charles comes to pay, Edward tells him to keep his money as he (Edward) has decided to sell and will give him a full price later. Charles subsequently seeks planning permission from the local council to build a pizza parlour on his new land and gets Andrew and Edward's guarantee that they will not oppose planning permission. However, just as he is about to instruct a local builder, Edward informs him that he has sold the property to Pizzatown Inc.

Andrew is distraught at the prospect of a large takeaway restaurant behind his house and manages to sell to Harry. Harry has just discovered Camilla's motorcycle in the shed and has removed it, along with Edward's property. In retaliation, Edward is about to knock down that part of the shed that stands on his land. Charles wants to know whether he has any rights that can be enforced against Pizzatown Inc.

▶ Discuss.

How to Answer this Question

❖ What rights, if any, are created by the actions of the parties – proprietary estoppel?

❖ What are the nature of those rights – how is the equity satisfied?

❖ How, if at all, do those rights affect subsequent purchasers of the land?

Answer Structure

This diagram shows how to apply the rules relating to proprietary estoppel to A, E, C & H.

ANSWER

This problem essentially revolves around two central issues, although their application to the particular facts of the individual circumstances of Andrew, Edward and Charles may vary. First, it is necessary to determine the nature and extent of any interests created by the actions of the brothers in favour of each other. Second, and depending on the answer to the first question, it is necessary to establish whether any or all of those interests are rights binding on the subsequent purchasers of the plots, Harry and Pizzatown Inc.

(A) ANDREW AND THE SHED; EDWARD AND THE STORAGE; CAMILLA AND HER MOTORCYCLE

As a preliminary matter, it is apparent from the facts of the problem that none of the arrangements of the parties have been recorded in writing. This immediately raises the problem that unless the activities fall within one of the recognised exceptions to the formality requirements found in s 2 of the **Law of Property (Miscellaneous Provisions)**

Act 1989, then such interests as may have arisen will be void. Further, although it is not absolutely certain (see *Street v Mountford* (1985)), there is little evidence that any of these arrangements – particularly those relating to storage in Andrew's shed – were intended to, or do, amount to a lease. If that were the case, if the lease were three years or less, the absence of writing would be immaterial (s 54(2) of the Law of Property Act 1925) and it would be binding on Harry according to its terms as a legal lease and an overriding interest under Sched 3, para 1 to the Land Registration Act 2002.

The absence of writing means that Andrew, Edward and Camilla may all have to rely on proprietary estoppel if they are to claim property rights. It is then another matter whether these rights will be binding on subsequent third parties. Alternatively, these rights could arise from contract and be in the nature of contractual licences and, so, not presumptively binding on any third party (*Ashburn Anstalt v Arnold* (1989); *Lloyd v Dugdale* (2002)).

(I) THE SHED
Clearly, Edward, the owner of the land over which the shed will protrude, has agreed that Andrew can build that shed in the full knowledge that use of his own land will thereby be diminished. In such circumstances, Andrew will have a reasonable chance of establishing that Edward is bound by proprietary estoppel from demolishing the shed. In the language of *Taylor Fashions v Liverpool Victoria Trustees* (1982), Edward made an assurance to Andrew (albeit in response to Andrew's request – see *Thorner v Majors* (2009) for the flexible nature of the assurance) that the shed could be built, which was relied upon by Andrew to his detriment. The fact that Edward assisted in the building can only reinforce this presumption. In such circumstances, following cases such as *Crabb v Arun DC* (1976) and *Ives v High* (1967) (and subject to what will be said below in respect of Edward's claim of storage), it is unlikely that Edward will be able to renege on his promise and destroy the shed. Equity will intervene by way of an injunction.

What is not clear, however, is what will happen if either or both of the properties are sold. There is authority that the *benefit* of the estoppel cannot be transferred to a successor in title (*Fryer v Brook* (1984)) because it is merely personal to the promisee, although this appears to have been contradicted by Lord Denning in *Ives v High* and indeed, it is difficult to see why the alleged personal nature of an estoppel (even *if* this were true) should stop the *benefit* passing to another (and see, also, the analysis in *Bibby v Stirling* (1998)). In our case, then, it is unclear whether the estoppel that exists in favour of Andrew can be passed on to Harry when he purchases the land.[21] However, Harry might argue that the benefit of the right has been expressly assigned to him under the contract of sale (that is, as a personal transfer of a personal right). Likewise, if Edward were to sell his house

---

21 It is perfectly acceptable to argue that a rule is unclear or unsettled.

(although there is no evidence here), it is unclear whether the estoppel binding on him could be made to bind a subsequent purchaser.

The matter is considered in more detail below.

(II) THE STORAGE OF EDWARD'S GOODS

The position here is somewhat complicated. On one view of the facts, Andrew has simply agreed that Edward can store his goods in his shed. This may have been done as a personal favour – in which case Edward has a bare licence – or it may have been done as a counterpart to Edward's promise and assistance with the shed – in which case it may be a contractual licence. If it is a bare licence, it seems that it is revocable at will by Andrew (*Thomas v Sorrell* (1673)), although, if it is contractual, it may be irrevocable by Andrew according to its terms (*Wintergarden Theatres v Millennium Productions Ltd* (1948)). However, in either case, it is clear that a contractual licence as such cannot be binding on a third party (Harry) (*Ashburn Anstalt v Arnold; Lloyd v Dugdale*).

An alternative view is, however, that there has been some form of estoppel generated in Edward's favour by Andrew's conduct in relation to the storage. It would be necessary to establish that there was an assurance, reliance and detriment (*Taylor Fashions*), although it might well be difficult on the facts of the case as there appears to be little in the way of detriment suffered by Edward in reliance on the promise (and such detriment is crucial: *Gillett v Holt* (2001)). However, if the estoppel is made out, Edward could go on to argue, first, that the estoppel should be satisfied by the granting of an easement of storage in his favour. However, this would need to be protected by an entry on the register (a notice) in order to be binding on Harry: **s 29** of the **LRA 2002**.[22] We know, however, from the law of easements, that a right to storage may be incapable of being an easement because it amounts to exclusive possession of the servient tenement (*Copeland v Greenhalf* (1952); *Grigsby v Melville* (1974); cf *Moncrieff v Jamieson* (2008)). Alternatively, therefore, Edward could argue that the estoppel itself is capable of binding a third party, irrespective of whether it generates an easement or a licence (*Lloyd v Dugdale*; **s 116** of the **LRA 2002**). If this is the case – that an estoppel is an interest in land – it might be binding on the purchaser Harry as an overriding interest, possibly under the catch-all **Sched 3, para 2** to the **LRA 2002** on the basis of discoverable actual occupation – *Henry v Henry* (2010).

(III) THE SHED AND THE STORAGE

In the above analysis, we have assumed that the shed building and the storage were separate events. It might be possible to argue that they are so interconnected that, at least for Andrew and Edward, they must be taken together. Hence, by analogy with *Ives v High*, it could be argued that, if Andrew wants the benefit of the shed, he must be subject to the burden of the storage of Edward's goods, although *Thamesmead Town v Allotey*

---

22 Never forget about registration requirements!

(1998) suggests that this type of reciprocal benefit/burden is not truly *mutual* benefit and burden. This would, of course, prevent either of the original parties from reneging on their agreement. Whether the 'burden' of Andrew's obligations could be passed to Harry is another matter. There is no evidence that Harry purchased Andrew's land with express knowledge of Edward's rights (or in an inequitable manner), so as to subject him to a personal constructive trust within *Ashburn Anstalt v Arnold, Lloyd v Dugdale* and *Chaudhary v Yavuz*. Alternatively, however, if Harry seeks to make use of the shed, it is just possible that the court would stipulate that if he wished to take the benefit, then he must be subject to the burden. The problem with this is, however, that we could apply it to every subsequent purchaser of the two plots with the effect that purely personal rights could evolve into proprietary obligations. This is not an attractive solution.[23]

(IV) THE MOTORCYCLE

The position over Camilla's motorcycle is very similar to the position above in respect of Edward's goods and it may well be difficult for Edward to establish anything other than a bare or contractual licence to support the parking/storage. Moreover, if we were to approach this issue on a benefit/burden analysis, it may well prove decisive that the 'benefit' is to be conferred on someone other than the person who is subject to the burden of the shed: viz, the benefit is Camilla's, but the burden of submitting to the shed falls on Edward. This makes it highly unlikely that Harry would be bound by this obligation when he purchases Andrew's land (*Allotey*). The right is essentially personal and the analogy with benefit and burden is not appropriate.

(B) CHARLES AND THE PLOT OF LAND AND PIZZATOWN INC

The first matter is to determine the nature of Charles's interest, if any, in the plot of land that Edward has sold, and then to see whether this interest is binding on the purchaser, Pizzatown Inc.

Clearly, Charles and Edward start off by negotiating the terms of a lease, as that is the clear intention of the parties following Edward's initial refusal to sell the land. Equally clearly, there is no doubt that Charles and Edward fail to reach agreement on the terms of the long lease. On the other hand, Charles is let into occupation by Edward on the grounds that he can occupy pending successful conclusion of negotiations and provided that he pays £600. At first sight, this may appear to raise the possibility of a periodic tenancy. If this could be established then Charles would have an overriding interest against the purchaser Pizzatown (**Sched 3, para 1** to the **LRA 2002**), who would be bound by the terms of the lease. Unfortunately for Charles, however, it appears from *Javad v Aqil* (1991) that occupation and payment of rent (and there was none here, merely offered) will

---

23 Even in problem questions it is important to analyse the merits of any solution as well as applying the law to the facts.

not give rise to a periodic tenancy if the occupation can be attributed to negotiations pending the grant of a 'real' lease. This is Charles's position and he will be a tenant at will, which, even if it is binding on Pizzatown Inc, can be terminated. Circumstances then take a different turn. Edward makes it clear that he will now sell to Charles and Charles, acting in reliance on this, begins to make plans for his small restaurant. Edward even re-enforces this by promising not to oppose a planning application (see a related factual matrix in *Cobbe v Yeoman's* (2008)). This may, then, raise a proprietary estoppel in Charles's favour, provided that he can establish assurance, reliance and detriment in the normal way. On the facts, Edward will argue that he simply made an offer to sell that he has now withdrawn (see, for example, *Ravenocean v Gardner* (2001)), whereas Charles will argue that he has relied on the promise to such an extent as to raise an estoppel in his favour, as in *Thorner v Majors* (2009). The answer is one of judgment, but, certainly, Charles does not appear to have suffered the same degree of detriment as the promisees in other cases such as *Re Basham* (1986), *Pascoe v Turner* (1979) and *Inwards v Baker* (1965) and, although the cases of *Lim Teng Huan v Chuan* (1992), *Flowermix v Site Development* (2000) and *Kinane v Conteh* (2005) offer some support, it may be that the estoppel cannot be made out as the promise is legitimately withdrawn (*Canty v Broad*; *Taylor v Dickens* (1998) and *Yeoman's Row v Cobbe* (2008)).[24] However, were it to be accepted that Charles had an estoppel in his favour, there is every chance that this could be binding against Pizzatown. Either: the court will satisfy the equity with the award of a proprietary right (for example, the freehold: *Pascoe*), which could be binding on the purchaser as an overriding interest under Sched 3, para 2 to the LRA 2002, Charles being in discoverable actual occupation; or, the estoppel itself can be regarded as an interest in land (s 116 of the LRA 2002), which will bind Pizzatown in the same way; or, in the most extreme case, the court could nullify the sale to Pizzatown and order a sale to Charles.

Don't be tempted to

Do not write a general essay on estoppel. This question is about specific facts and specific claimants. Always relate your law to the facts you are given – not to those you would like to be there. Examiners give marks for applying law to facts.

---

24 This section demonstrates that the writer has very good knowledge of the case law and would receive a lot of credit in the exam.

Easements

INTRODUCTION

Easements comprise those rights that one landowner may exercise over the land of their neighbour. Common examples are the right of way, the right of light and the right of support. It is essential to the understanding of the law of easements that the student appreciates that every easement has two aspects: one landowner will enjoy the benefit of an easement and another will be subject to its burden. This is just another way of saying that easements exist over a servient tenement for the benefit of a dominant tenement. It is important to remember the dual nature of an easement as this will make problems concerning the transmission of easements to third parties easier to understand. It is often said that easements can either be 'positive' or 'negative' in character. The former are those that allow the dominant tenement owner (the person who has the benefit) to do something on the servient land, such as enjoy a right of way, while the latter prevent the servient tenement owner (the person subject to the burden) from doing something on their own land, such as building new premises. However, it is obvious that most easements have a positive and negative aspect, depending on how you look at it, and the distinction is not of great practical use. Its one advantage is that it illustrates that many so-called negative easements are similar to restrictive covenants and perhaps their subject matter would be more appropriate to the legal regime of the latter rather than the former.

Checklist ✔

Questions on the law of easements can come in either problem or essay form and the student should be aware of the following issues:

- the nature of easements;
- the creation of easements;
- the distinction between legal and equitable easements;
- the transmissibility of easements to third parties, both benefit and burden;
- the 'conveyancing dimension;
- reform of the law of easements.

QUESTION 31 --

'The law of easements is constrained by the innately conservative principle that the categories of admissible easement must not dramatically overstep the boundaries of the kinds of easements already recognised.'

(Gray and Gray, *Elements of Land Law* (5th edn, 2009) Oxford: Oxford University Press, p. 617)

▶ How far is the above statement accurate, and is there any consistent policy evident in the rights that the courts have recognised as easements?

How to Answer this Question

The answer should discuss the following areas:

❖ *Re Ellenborough Park* (1956);
❖ positive and negative easements;
❖ relationship to restrictive covenants;
❖ public policy.

Applying the Law

This question shows the requirements of valid easements.

ANSWER

An easement is essentially a right of property that is enjoyed or exercised over land belonging to another. In one sense, the law of easements can be regarded as the private law equivalent to public planning law as where an easement prevents the owner of land from doing something on their own property. For example, if land is subject to an easement of light, this effectively prevents the owner of that land from building so as to obstruct that light. However, easements are not only negative in nature. Many easements authorise a neighbour to use the land subject to the easement in a way that would otherwise be a trespass. Thus, a right of way enables the owner of the easement to walk across their neighbour's land. Indeed, this distinction between 'negative' and 'positive' easements is often said to be one of the most important factors in the law of easements, since case law establishes that the law should be wary of accepting new negative easements, as in *Phipps v Pears* (1965), in which it was alleged (and rejected) that the servient owner was under a negative easement preventing him from demolishing his premises. In fact, it is inherent in the nature of all easements that they comprise both a positive and a negative aspect, for what the dominant owner is allowed to do, the servient owner must suffer. In this sense, irrespective of whether the easement is positive or negative, all easements comprise a benefit and a burden. The land subject to the easement (the servient tenement) bears the burden of that easement whilst the owner of the land entitled to enjoy the easement (the dominant tenement) has the benefit of it. It is important to remember this duality when considering questions of the transmissibility of the benefits and burdens of easements to subsequent purchasers of the dominant or servient land.

The traditional starting point for a discussion about the essential characteristics of an easement is the judgment in *Re Ellenborough Park* (1956). This gives us a four-fold test. First, there must be a dominant and a servient tenement. Second, an easement must accommodate (that is, benefit) the dominant tenement. Third, the dominant and servient tenement owners must be owned or occupied by different persons and, fourth, the easement must be capable of being the subject matter of a grant. If the alleged right satisfies these conditions, it is most likely to be recognised as an easement irrespective of the name given to it by the parties that created it. The only small caveat to this is that occasionally certain rights that fulfill these criteria are not accepted as easements on grounds of public policy. It is rare, however, for an alleged easement to be disallowed on this ground explicitly and it is more likely that a judge will prefer to base his decision of lack of fulfilment of one of the flexible *Re Ellenborough* criteria.

The essential duality of an easement is evident from the first condition. It is crucial that if an easement is to exist, there must be a dominant and servient tenement. The easement must burden land, but it must also benefit land, and in technical terms the easement cannot exist in gross (*Hawkins v Rutter* (1892)). The easement runs with the land, both the benefit and the burden.

The second condition established by *Ellenborough* is that the easement, or rather the alleged easement, must confer a benefit on the dominant tenement: it must accommodate it. Easements are proprietary rights and therefore confer benefits on land, not persons (*Manson v Shrewsbury Railway* (1871)). Rather like covenants that touch and concern the land, easements must benefit the user of land, the value of land or the mode of occupation of land. This particular requirement can be manifested in several ways. Thus, the servient tenement must be sufficiently proximate to the dominant tenement to be able to confer the benefit on it (*Bailey v Stevens* (1862)). However, the most widely cited example of an alleged easement that was disallowed as not conferring a benefit on the dominant tenement was the personal advantage in *Hill v Tupper* (1863), in which the owner of a canal granted the plaintiff the right to put pleasure boats on the canal. This was deemed not to be sufficiently connected with the land as to amount to an easement. It is not, however, authority for the proposition that mere commercial advantages cannot be easements. *Moody v Steggles* (1879) makes it clear that an easement that benefits a trade or occupation carried on on the land, such as a public house, as where a pub sign is hung on adjacent property is permitted. Similarly, in *Platt v Crouch* (2003), the right to moor boats at a riverbank was capable of subsisting as an easement for the benefit of a hotel on the dominant land. Of course, the distinction here is sometimes difficult to draw, and with such flexible criteria, consistency cannot be guaranteed. On the other hand, this criterion does give judges a certain amount of hidden discretion to exclude those rights that, for matters of policy, should not fall within the ambit of easements.[1] In *Hill*, for example, it may well have been against the public interest for a particular individual to have exclusive rights to a waterway. The same cannot be said for the easement in *Moody*.

As indicated above, an easement has a dual aspect. It confers both a benefit and a burden. It is essentially a right in another's land. For that reason, the third *Ellenborough* condition is that the dominant and servient tenements must not be both owned and occupied by the same person (*Roe v Siddons* (1888)). Indeed, should the dominant and servient tenements come into the ownership and possession of the same person, any easement over the servient land will thereby be extinguished. In effect, this means that a person cannot have an easement against themselves, although due to the operation of the rule in *Wheeldon v Burrows* (1879) an easement may be created in such a situation when part of the merged land is sold off. The rule is, however, that the dominant and servient tenement must not be both owned and occupied by the same person and so there is nothing to stop a tenant having an easement against their landlord, as in *Wright v Macadam* (1949) (and vice versa).

Finally, no right may amount to an easement unless it is capable of forming the subject matter of a grant or, in other words, an easement must be capable of being expressly

---

1   It is good to point out the potential downsides of a flexible jurisdiction like this.

conveyed by deed. This appears to be an all-engrossing condition, itself having several different manifestations.[2] First, there is the obvious point that an easement cannot exist unless there is a capable grantor – that is, somebody legally competent to create an easement – and a capable grantee. So, for example, no easement can exist where purportedly granted or received by a limited company having no power to grant or receive easements under its articles of association. Second, it is clear that all rights that are capable of forming the subject matter of a grant must be sufficiently definite. In the case of an easement, therefore, the right must be capable of clear description and precise definition. So, for example, in *Re Aldred* (1610), a right to a good view could not exist as an easement. Similarly, there is no easement of privacy (*Browne v Flower* (1911)) and no easement to receive light generally, as opposed to a right to receive light through a defined window. It is, however, with the final element of this condition that consistency gives way to flexibility and, to some extent, judicial discretion. Only those interests actually lie in grant that are capable of lying in grant or, in other words, the right must be within the general nature of rights recognised as easements or be rights by close analogy thereto. This does not mean, of course, that new easements for new times cannot exist. Thus, there has been an easement to use a letterbox in *Goldberg v Edwards* (1950), an easement to use an airfield in *Re Bolton Paul* (1976) and an easement facilitating use of a supermarket in *London and Blenheim Estates v Ladbroke* (1994).

In essence, this last condition means that the courts will strike down alleged easements that do not appear to the particular judge to be within the class of rights that should be recognised as such.[3] Of course, some general principles have developed and it is often said that no new easement will be recognised that requires the servient owner to spend money (*Phipps v Pears*). Again, according to *Phipps*, the law will look unfavourably on claims to an easement that gives the dominant tenement owner the right to prevent the servient tenement owner from doing something on his land. These so-called 'negative easements' are more properly to be regarded as within the sphere of restrictive covenants. It is also said that no right will be recognised as an easement that gives the dominant tenement owner the right to use exclusively the servient tenement. So, in *Copeland v Greenhalf* (1952), no easement could exist to store tools of the trade on the servient land and, in *Grigsby v Melville* (1974), a right of storage in a cellar could not be accepted. In *Hanina v Morland* (2000), use of a neighbour's flat roof was too extensive to be an easement. And in *Mulvaney v Gough* (2002), while a cottage owner could make use of a communal garden at the rear of her cottage, the planting of a flower bed in a specific location would amount to exclusive use. Similarly, the right

....

2 Being explicit that this is really more than one rule is both clearer, and analytically more convincing, than attempting to discuss all aspects of this rule simultaneously.

3 Splitting up the paragraphs like this gives each section a definite focus and shows that the answer is a clear response to the question.

to park in a defined space in a car park cannot be an easement (nor if it amounts to storage of cars: *Batchelor v Marlow* (2003); *Central Midlands Estates v Leicester Dyers* (2003)), although as *Newman v Jones* (1982) and *London and Blenheim Estates v Ladbroke* make clear, there can be an easement to park generally on a piece of land.[4] The position here is, however, somewhat policy-orientated, for, as *Macadam* shows, the particular facts of a case may require the granting of an easement so as to facilitate commodious living. In that case, the tenant successfully claimed an easement of storage of coal in a small part of the landlord's coal shed. There is no real distinction that can be sensibly drawn between this and *Copeland* and *Melville*, other than to say that the court in *Macadam* believed that the tenant deserved the right claimed. Such flexibility is inherent in the *Ellenborough* conditions and it would be unfortunate if the development of the law of easements were hindered by too exacting and rigorously applied conditions.

At present, the *Re Ellenborough* rules provide an outline outside of which a judge usually will not go, but inside of which he may recognise an easement or not according to the circumstances of the case, the needs of the property and, indeed, the behaviour of the parties. In this sense, of course, the law is uncertain as it becomes difficult to predict whether a new right will be regarded as an easement. However, to some extent, many issues that formerly would have fallen within the range of easements are now dealt with under the law of restrictive covenants and local planning regulations. Of course, the easement has one great advantage. Not only is it proprietary like the restrictive covenant (so, therefore, capable of binding third parties), it may, unlike the restrictive covenant, be legal and bind those third parties automatically in unregistered land. The same is true – at least so far as those created before 2003 are concerned – in registered land, where they will be overriding interests, although, in line with the policy of the **Land Registration Act 2002** to reduce the number of overriding interests, legal easements expressly created after the Act came into force are registrable dispositions and must be completed by registration if they are to have legal effect; if created by implication or prescription, they will, unless the person entitled has exercised them during the year before a disposition of the servient tenement takes place, only be overriding interests if the disponee had actual knowledge of them or if they would have been obvious on a reasonably careful inspection. Even with this arguably more limited position in registered land, the powerful effects of easements on servient lands and on successors in title to those lands means that care has to be taken when considering any proposed reform in the definition of these rights.

---

4   There has been a lot of academic commentary on this line of cases which could be brought in here.

NOTES

This has to be one of the most textbook-based questions any examiner can ask. It is straightforward and easy to score a 'safe' mark. Any attempt at criticism will be rewarded, as most students repeat verbatim the same answer, as above. It is difficult not to.

> **Aim Higher** ★
>
> Introduce analysis into that part of your answer dealing with 'must be capable of forming the subject matter of a grant'. Issues such as the right to park have been the subject of numerous recent decisions.

QUESTION 32

Apart from easements established by long user, by what methods can easements be created?

How to Answer this Question

The answer needs to include a discussion of the following:

* ❖ distinction between 'grant' and 'reservation';
* ❖ express creation;
* ❖ implied creation; necessity; the rule in *Wheeldon v Burrows* (1879); s 62 of the LPA 1925 (*Long v Gowlett* (1923); *P&S Platt v Crouch* (2003)); common intention (*Stafford v Lee* (1992); *Peckham v Ellison* (2000));
* ❖ legal and equitable easements.

Applying the Law

This diagram demonstrates the different methods of creating easements.

ANSWER

Easements are, essentially, a species of right that one landowner enjoys over the land of another. They are proprietary in the sense that they attach to the land rather than to the owners of the land. Moreover, like restrictive covenants, easements have a dual aspect. They both confer a benefit on one piece of land to be enjoyed by the owners for the time being thereof and they impose a burden on land that must be accepted by the owners for the time being of the servient land. It is intrinsic in this duality that the benefit and the burden of an easement can be transmitted independently. Thus, it is quite possible for the benefit of an easement to be passed on to several owners of the dominant tenement even though ownership of the servient tenement remains in the hands of the person who granted the easement. Likewise, it may be only the servient land that is transferred, or both. Indeed, the ability of easements to bind third parties is one reason, perhaps the most important, why it is necessary to have clear rules governing both the creation of easements and the conditions that must be fulfilled before an easement can be regarded as legal or equitable.

All easements are either created expressly, impliedly or by long user under the law of prescription.

Generally speaking, and putting prescription on one side, the creation of easements is either by express or implied grant or express or implied reservation. A grant is where the owner of the servient tenement grants an easement to the owner of what will become the dominant tenement. A reservation is the opposite. It is where the transferor of land reserves to themselves an easement over the land they are transferring. In very broad terms, it is easier to grant easements to somebody else than it is to reserve easements to oneself because of the rule that a person cannot generally derogate from his grant.

Turning first to reservation.[5] If A sells land to B, A may expressly reserve to himself an easement over the land sold. The easement will be legal if it is reserved in a deed and it will be equitable if it is reserved in a written document. Likewise, however, it is clear that an easement of necessity and arising by common intention can be impliedly reserved by the vendor. Thus, if A sells land to B, but the only access to the land retained by A is over the land sold to B, an implied reserved easement of necessity will exist in A's favour, as in *Pinnington v Galland* (1853) (see *Peckham v Ellison* (2000) for a reserved easement by common intention). However, in order for an easement of necessity to be reserved in this fashion, it must be true that the land retained by the vendor would be unusable without the easement claimed and no easement will be allowed where it is merely inconvenient to use another route, as in *Re Dodd* (1843). It should be noted that impliedly reserved easements may also be legal or equitable. The easement is implied into a sale by A to B in

....

5   The distinction between reservation and grant is crucial with regard to implied easements and should always be at the front of your mind.

favour of A. If, therefore, the sale is by deed, the easement is implied into a deed and is legal. If the sale is by written document for valuable consideration, the easement is implied into that document and will be equitable. In other words, the easement carries the character of the document into which it is implied.[6]

Turning now to easements by grant, as where one landowner (A) expressly grants an easement to his neighbour B, either by deed or in writing, or where A sells some land to B and as part of that sale grants B an easement over the land retained by themselves. In the first case, of course, the easement is expressly granted and will be legal or equitable according to the form it takes. In the second case, the easement may well be expressly granted, as part of the sale. However, it is this second scenario, the sale of land by A to B, that most often gives rise to implied grant. In fact, implied grant can take one of four forms, although, in all cases, the principle is the same: that an easement is implied into the grant of land by A to B so that the land sold becomes the dominant tenement and the land retained becomes the servient tenement. As with reservation, if the easement is implied into a deed, the easement will be legal and, if it is implied into a written transfer, it will be equitable. First, it is clear that easements may be impliedly granted by way of necessity. So, if the land granted cannot be used except by, say, access over the land retained by the vendor, an easement of necessity will exist. As in *Wong v Beaumont* (1965), an easement of ventilation by necessity was held to exist when the land granted was intended to be used as a restaurant, but could not be so used without a ventilation shaft over the land retained by the vendor. Generally speaking, it is easier to claim an implied grant of an easement of necessity than it is an implied reservation but, as *Re MRA Engineering* (1987) shows, a real necessity must exist, not merely a more convenient use of the land.

Second, easements may be impliedly granted under the rule in *Wheeldon v Burrows* (1879). As we know, no easement can exist where the dominant and the servient tenement are owned and occupied by the same person. However, it often happens that a landowner will use one part of their land for the benefit of another, as where a landowner walks across a field to get to their house. These are sometimes known as 'quasi-easements' because they would be easements had the land been in separate ownership or possession. So, if it should happen that the owner of the entire plot of land should sell the quasi-dominant part of his land, in the previous example, the house, or, in other words, the land benefited by the right, the rule in *Wheeldon v Burrows* stipulates that the vendor will have impliedly granted that right to a purchaser. This rule, which is based upon the idea that a person cannot derogate from their grant, can be expressly excluded and, of course, they cannot grant as easements any rights that are incapable of being easements. Furthermore, it appears from *Wheeldon* itself that the rights that are

---

6   This is an important idea to get to grips with and it is useful to state it explicitly in an easements answer so that the examiner is aware of your understanding of this point.

impliedly granted must have been used by the vendor at the time of the grant for the benefit of the part sold (for example, the path must be being used), and the easement must be continuous and apparent and/or necessary for the reasonable enjoyment of the part granted. (It is most likely that the second and third conditions are alternatives and they were so treated in *Wheeldon*.[7]) Provided, however, that these conditions are fulfilled, the purchaser of that part of the common owner's land which is the dominant part will acquire those easements impliedly granted in the conveyance of the land. Again, the right may be legal if the conveyance of the land was by deed or equitable as in *Borman v Griffith* (1930), in which the grant of the land was under an equitable lease. Furthermore, if the common landowner grants the dominant part to X and, at the same time, grants the servient part to Y, it is clear that the rule in *Wheeldon* operates to give X an easement over Y's land, as in *Swansborough v Coventry* (1832). Although the rule in *Wheeldon* does not apply to reservations of easements (confirmed in *Ellison*), it is obvious that any owner of land who intends to sell that land in parts may well find their own land bound by easements they have impliedly granted. It is, in fact, a very powerful means of creating easements.

Third, easements may be impliedly granted under s 62 of the LPA 1925. At the outset, however, it should be noted that s 62 only applies to conveyances that are defined in the LPA as transfers by deed. Thus, s 62 can operate only to create legal easements because it only operates when there has been a transfer of land by deed or its registered land equivalent, the registered disposition. Section 62 is a very wide-ranging statutory provision and it has many purposes beyond the creation of easements. Moreover, it is clear that it is not limited to rights that are continuous or apparent or reasonably necessary as in *Wheeldon*. The only requirement is that the right is capable of being an easement. The factual situation of s 62 is, however, quite different from *Wheeldon*. If a landowner has two or more plots of land and, then, conveys by deed one of those plots to a purchaser, the purchaser will be granted by s 62 all of those rights that were previously enjoyed with the land. This is straightforward enough, but s 62 will convert into easements all of those rights enjoyed for the use of the land sold, even though prior to sale they were merely precarious, in the sense of being exercised by permission only. According to *Sovmots Investments v Secretary of State for the Environment* (1979) (following *Long v Gowlett* (1923)), it is essential for the operation of s 62 that the land owned by the vendor was in prior diversity of occupation before the sale. Practically, this means that, before the land is sold to the person acquiring the easement, it must have been used by either a tenant or a licensee of the vendor who enjoyed rights over that land. If, then, the land is conveyed to that person (or possibly any other person) by deed, that person will be impliedly granted the rights previously enjoyed. So, in *Goldberg v Edwards* (1950), a licensee enjoyed a right over her landlord's land and when a new

---

7   It is difficult to bring your own analysis into a 'textbook' question like this, but any inconsistencies or discrepancies in the case law are a good place to start.

tenancy by deed was granted to her, that licence was transformed into an easement (see, also, *Wright v Macadam* (1949); *Hillman v Rogers* (1998); *Hair v Gillman* (2000)). This has potentially devastating consequences for the landowner, although **s 62** can be avoided by an express contrary stipulation. The requirement of prior diversity of occupation does of course limit the effects of its operation, so it is particularly interesting to note that, in *Platt v Crouch* (2003), the Court of Appeal decided that the section could still operate even in the absence of 'prior diversity' if the right claimed was continuous and apparent.[8] If this interpretation is correct – and it does appear to contradict a significant body of precedent – it means that **s 62** significantly overlaps *Wheeldon v Burrows*, but may have a wider operation than is traditionally thought. In any event, a landowner must be careful. Of all of the cases of implied grant, it is the most far removed from the intention of the parties.

Finally, the fourth method by which easements may be impliedly granted again arises in situations in which the owner of land sells or leases part of it to another and is taken to have impliedly conveyed with that sale or lease an easement for the benefit of the part conveyed, to the detriment of the part retained. In this case, however, the easement is said to arise from the 'common intention' of the parties to the transaction. An example is provided by *Stafford v Lee* (1992), in which the plaintiff claimed an easement of right of way over the defendant's land for the purpose of transporting materials for the construction of a house on the plaintiff's land. Both parcels of land had once been in the possession of the defendant's predecessor in title and the plaintiff had purchased his plot from the predecessor with the clear purpose of building a house upon it. The Court of Appeal held that an easement of common intention could be implied into the original sale by deed of the land to the plaintiff, which, being legal, now bound the defendant. Importantly, an easement by necessity could not be implied for there were other routes to the plaintiff's property, albeit inconvenient and unsuitable for the carrying of construction materials. This case makes it clear that easements arising through common intention are quite distinct from easements of necessity, for, in this case, the only requirements are that there was in fact a common intention to use land in a certain way and that an easement is required to give effect to that purpose. Of course, the plaintiff in such cases bears a heavy burden of proof, having to explain why, if there was such a clear common intention, the easement was not expressly inserted into the conveyance in the first place.[9] Consequently, the creation of easements by this method will be relatively rare, although they may be both impliedly granted (*Stafford*) and reserved (*Peckham*) although 'reservation' will be very difficult to establish (*Chaffe v Kinsgley* (2000)).

....

8   As a highly controversial case, the interaction between *Platt v Crouch* and the previous case law is interesting, and has attracted much academic comment which could be brought into the answer here.

9   Thinking about what a person claiming an implied easement would actually need to argue had taken place in the run up to the acquisition of the estate in land is a useful way of approaching problem questions as well as essays and helps to point you in the right direction.

NOTES

Although a long question, it is relatively simple. Most textbooks deal with this issue thoroughly. It is essential to grasp the distinction between a 'grant' and a 'reservation' of an easement. Note also that in due course, the formalities for the creation of an easement will change under s 93 of the LRA 2002, after the entry into force of which, an easement may not exist unless it is entered on the register.

Students may also wish to consider making reference to the Law Commission Consultation Paper No 186: *Easements, Covenants and Profits à Prendre*. A report and draft Bill setting out final recommendations for reform of this area of law is expected in Spring 2011. A summary may be found at **http://www.lawcom.gov.uk/easements.htm**

> ### Aim Higher   ★
> Include an evaluation of the exact effect of the decision in *PS Platt v Crouch*, considering how far it overlaps with the Rule in *Wheeldon v Burrows*.

QUESTION 33

In 1993, Gerald, the owner of three adjacent terraced houses, title to which was registered, decided to realise some capital and resolved to sell two of his properties whilst remaining in the third. In the conveyance of No 20 to Frank, Gerald promised to allow Frank to park his 20-foot horsebox in his (Gerald's) garden, in return for which Frank allowed Gerald to site a satellite dish on his (Frank's) roof. Gerald also agreed orally that Frank could hang a small sign advertising his horsebox building business (which was based on an industrial estate some five miles away) on his end wall. When negotiating a sale of No 22 to Ivor, the latter insisted that he be given the right to temporarily store some roofing materials in Gerald's garden (next to the horsebox), should he run out of space in his yard opposite. This was agreed in the conveyance.

Gerald has just sold his house (No 21) to Ben, who is unhappy with the elaborate sign that Frank had erected and with the horsebox taking up most of his garden. Frank, however, has just retired and sold his business, the horsebox and house to Christine, who is threatening to remove the satellite dish unless the horsebox and the sign are allowed to stay. Meanwhile, Ivor has been storing materials on a permanent basis in the garden of No 21, and Ben decides to remove them.

▶ Discuss.

How to Answer this Question

The following areas need to be included:

- ❖ the nature of easements;
- ❖ creation of easements;
- ❖ legal and equitable easements and third parties.

Answer Structure

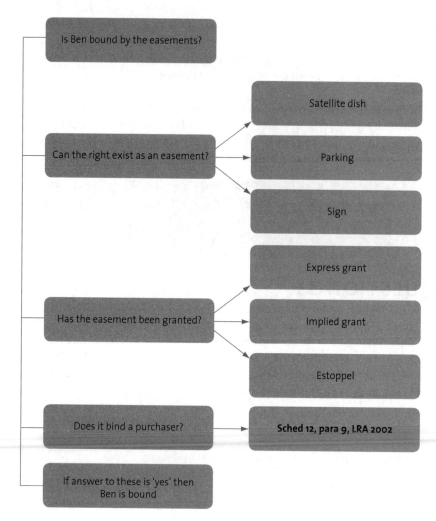

Is Ben bound by the easements?

Can the right exist as an easement?

Satellite dish

Parking

Sign

Has the easement been granted?

Express grant

Implied grant

Estoppel

Does it bind a purchaser?

Sched 12, para 9, LRA 2002

If answer to these is 'yes' then Ben is bound

This diagram shows how to establish whether in this problem Ben is bound by the various easements.

ANSWER

This problem concerns the acquisition of easements and their effects on persons who subsequently come into possession of the servient and dominant land. In essence, there are two separate problems here, as the relationship of Gerald's property to each of the premises he has sold should be considered independently. Of course, in all cases, it is first necessary to determine whether the alleged right is capable of existing as an easement, then whether any easement that does exist is legal or equitable and then, finally, its effect on a purchaser of the dominant or servient tenement, as the case may be.[10]

(A) GERALD AND FRANK, AND THE SUBSEQUENT SALES OF BOTH HOUSES

In this situation, there are three rights that it is alleged may amount to easements: the erection of the satellite dish in favour of Gerald's property, and the parking of the caravan and erection of the sign on Gerald's property in favour of Frank's property. Can these interests amount to easements? If they cannot, they amount only to personal licences between the original parties, which cannot bind on successors in title (*Ashburn Anstalt v Arnold* (1989); *Lloyd v Dugdale* (2002)). Clearly, in respect of all rights, there is a capable grantor and grantee, there are two properties that could be the dominant and servient tenements, and both tenements are not owned or occupied by the same person. Thus far, there is no difficulty with the requirements for a valid easement laid down in *Re Ellenborough Park* (1956). However, some difficulty may exist in the need to show that the alleged rights benefit the dominant tenement *qua* tenement, and whether they fall within the general nature of rights capable of being created as easements. This issue, and the nature of any right satisfying the *Ellenborough* formula, will be considered in respect of each right.[11]

(I) THE ERECTION OF THE SATELLITE DISH IS PERHAPS THE LEAST CONTENTIOUS

There seems little doubt that such a right is of benefit to the dominant tenement in much the same way as the easement to run telephone lines over neighbouring land was accepted in *Lancashire and Cheshire Telephone Exchange Co v Manchester Overseers* (1885).[12] It is clear that there is no necessary reason to deny the existence of new easements, provided that they do not contradict the *Ellenborough* principles. There is no expenditure required of the servient owner and no exclusive occupation of his premises and the right is sufficiently definite. It would seem to be able to qualify as an easement.

Assuming that to be correct, the facts of this problem make it quite clear that the right was expressly reserved by Gerald when he sold the house to Frank. There is, then, no difficulty over its creation and, because it is expressly reserved in a conveyance (that is, a transfer by deed), this is a legal easement. What happens when the servient land is sold to Christine? Being registered land, the easement would have been registered against Frank's title when he became registered proprietor. If it were not, as an expressly created legal easement it would have been an overriding interest under s 70(1)(a) of the LRA 1925

---

10 Highlighting your approach to the structure of the problem question in the introduction makes your answer easy to follow and clear for the examiner.

11 Where certain aspects of the problem are straightforward, do not spend too much time on them, as that is not where the high marks are to be found.

12 Easements is one topic where facts of other cases can be very useful for drawing parallels, as here, and good answers will analyse why certain facts are relevantly similar.

and such rights are 'preserved' as interests which override under the **Land Registration Act 2002**, thus binding the servient land automatically (**Sched 12, para 9** to the **LRA 2002**). In either case, therefore, Christine is bound to give effect to the easement allowing erection of the satellite dish. It should be noted finally that, when Gerald conveys the dominant tenement to Ben, the benefit of the easement is transferred to Ben under the general rule that a benefit of an easement becomes annexed to each and every part of the legal estate and passes with it.

(II) CAN FRANK (AND THEN CHRISTINE) CLAIM AN EASEMENT OF PARKING OF THE HORSEBOX?

This particular claim raises difficulties for the owners of the alleged dominant tenement. There is no doubt that an easement of parking does exist (*London and Blenheim Estates v Ladbroke* (1994); *Moncrieff v Jamieson* (2008)). However, it is also clear that easements in general must not amount to exclusive use of the servient land (*Copeland v Greenhalf* (1952)) and, for this reason, it is highly unlikely that a right to park in a defined space can be an easement (see the uncertainty in *Saeed v Plustrade* (2002)).[13] Certainly, a right to store many cars cannot: *Batchelor v Marlowe* (2003). The easement of parking in *Newman v Jones* (1982) was in respect of a general area of land and not a regular spot. Likewise, in *Grigsby v Melville* (1974), a right of storage in a cellar was thought to connote exclusive use such as to oust an easement and the case in which storage was permitted (*Wright v Macadam* (1949)) should be seen in the context of a dispute between a powerful landlord and a badly treated tenant. Unfortunately, therefore, it seems that this right amounts only to a personal permission between Frank and Gerald: in other words, a contractual licence. So, even if the benefit of this contract has passed to Christine, the burden of it is incapable of binding a successor in title of the alleged servient tenement (*Ashburn Anstalt v Arnold; Lloyd v Dugdale*, despite the contrary view in *Plustrade*). Ben will not be bound.

(III) THE SIGN

Once again, this presents certain problems. There is no doubt that erecting a sign on a neighbour's property can amount to an easement, as in *Moody v Steggles* (1879). It matters not that this is to advertise some commercial activity on the land, so long as the activity is intimately connected with the land and not a 'pure' commercial venture, as in *Hill v Tupper* (1863). Moreover, there is, it would seem, no objection in principle to a grant of an easement to a landowner on the occasion of a conveyance of property X (the house), where the easement is to benefit property Y (the horsebox factory). After all, easements can be created by deed between landowners irrespective of any sale, as where a freeholder grants a right of way to their neighbour.

However, every easement must accommodate the dominant tenement and, in this case, when the land was sold to Frank, the business was carried on on property some five miles

---

13   It might be useful to bring some academic commentary in here.

away. It is well known that, while the dominant and servient tenement need not be adjacent, there must be proximity between them (*Pugh v Savage* (1970)). This will be a question of fact in each case. Yet, even if the right is capable of existing as an easement, there is a further problem. How has it been created? This is not a case of implied grant (there is no necessity, scant evidence of common intention, no claim under **s 62** and no quasi-easement within *Wheeldon v Burrows* (1879)) and, in any event, the aim seems to have been to create the easement expressly. Also, we are told that the intended right is not expressly included in the conveyance to Frank and it cannot, therefore, be legal: not being by deed (more accurately, not by registered disposition, as this is registered land). Of course, easements can be expressly granted by other means, but then they will be only equitable and, once more, there are formality problems. In order to be equitable, it is clear that the easement would have to have been granted by a valid contract, which, if specifically enforceable, equity would treat as an equitable easement (*Walsh v Lonsdale* (1882)). The 'contract' in this case is not in writing as required by **s 2** of the **Law of Property (Miscellaneous Provisions) Act 1989** and there is no possibility of an equitable easement by this route. The only hope is that Frank can claim an easement by proprietary estoppel, in similar circumstances to those in *Ives v High* (1967) and *Bibby v Stirling* (1998). Clearly, there seems to have been a promise made and we are told that Frank erects an elaborate (and hence expensive?) sign. This may be detrimental reliance. Further, it is no objection to the existence of an estoppel that it did indeed arise out of a failed explicit bargain (*Voyce v Voyce* (1991) and *Flowermix v Site Developments* (2000), although *Canty v Broad* is critical of this, as is *Thorner v Major* (2009), at least where the parties are experienced commercial parties). If an estoppel is established, the court may crystallize this estoppel into an equitable easement. In such circumstances, Christine will have obtained the benefit of the easement under the normal rule that it is annexed to the land, Ben, the purchaser of the servient tenement, may well have been bound by the estoppel easement because of the decision in *Celsteel v Alton* (1985) (followed in *Thatcher v Douglas* (1995)). Albeit subject to much criticism, this case tells us that an equitable easement arising out of an estoppel may have amounted to an overriding interest under **s 70(1)(a)** of the **Land Registration Act 1925** and, of course, such rights are expressly preserved **under s116 LRA 2002**. As such, it binds the purchaser, Ben, automatically. (For the sake of completeness we can note that, if created after 13 October 2003, equitable easements cannot now be interests which override and must be protected by notice on the register.)[14]

(B) GERALD, IVOR, THE ROOFING MATERIALS AND BEN

Once again, the initial question to be answered is whether the right to store is capable of being an easement. As noted above, it is an essential characteristic of an easement that it

14 Estoppel gives rise, at first, to an equity by estoppel which is itself a property right capable of protection against third parties. In order to crystallise this right, the parties will need to go to court and the court will determine how to 'satisfy the estoppel'. The outcome may result in an easement, and often will do, but it could also result in a money payment, or a licence.

does not amount to exclusive use of the servient tenement (*Hanina v Morland* (2000)). Thus, in *Copeland v Greenhalf*, *Grigsby v Melville* and *Batchelor v Marlowe*, a right of storage was not admitted into the category of easements. However, we are told here that the right expressly granted was a right to store temporarily when the need should arise. This may be completely different as there are many easements (for example, a right to use a lavatory: *Miller v Emcer Products* (1956)) that, when being exercised by the dominant tenement owner on the servient land, exclude any other use by the servient owner. One view is that the right of temporary storage is analogous to the right to park generally on a piece of land and, in any event, a right to store trade produce has been accepted as an easement in *AG of Southern Nigeria v John Holt and Co* (1915). Thus, it is a matter for argument whether this can exist as an easement. Of course, if it does, it seems that Ivor is going beyond its explicit terms and, of course, this can be restrained by injunction. Finally, if the easement does exist, it is clear that it has been expressly created by the conveyance (that is, by deed/registered disposition) and is legal. As with the legal easements considered above, this will bind Ben, the purchaser of the servient tenement, whether as being registered against his title or as an overriding interest under s 70(1)(a) of the LRA 1925 given continuing validity by the transitional provisions of the LRA 2002.

QUESTION 34

Elizabeth is the owner of a large farm in Huntshire, title to which is unregistered. Last year, she built a small bungalow on her lower field for her retirement and asked her daughter, Anne, to look after it in the meantime. Anne moved in with her boyfriend, Mark. The only access to the bungalow is along a dirt track over the farm proper or by boat along the River Garter, which flows through the property. Three months ago, Anne and Mark had a serious row and Anne moved out. Elizabeth, who was never fond of her daughter's boyfriend, agreed with Mark in writing that he could occupy the premises for five years at £800 per month and an initial sum of £2,000. However, before any rent was paid, Mark met another woman and moved in with her. Fortunately, soon after, Elizabeth was able to sell the bungalow to John by registered disposition for a large profit. A month later, she decided to retire to Jamaica and sold the rest of the farm to Norman.

John has just resurfaced the dirt road in order to obtain access for his car. Norman, seeing the chance for a small profit, has asked John for £1,000 to use the new road. John seeks your advice as to whether he should pay.

How to Answer this Question

The following areas need to be discussed:

❖ the creation of easements by implied grant – s 62 of the LPA 1925; *Hillman v Rogers* (1998); *Hair v Gillman* (2000);

❖ equitable or legal?

❖ effect on third parties of new easement.

Answer Structure

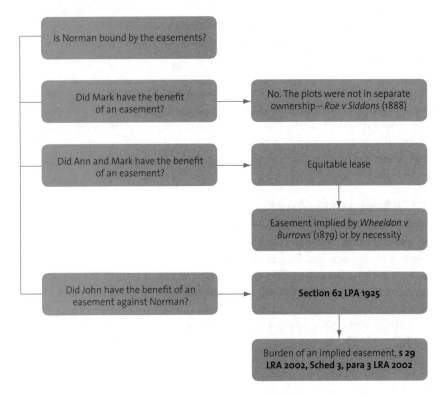

This diagram shows how to apply the rules relating to the transmissibility of the benefits and burdens of easements in the situation involving Norman.

ANSWER   --

This question involves complicated issues about the creation of easements and their effect on third parties. In general, the position is simple enough. Legal easements must be created by deed, prescription or statute and equitable easements by written document under s2 of the **Law of Property (Miscellaneous Provisions) Act 1989** or by the law of proprietary estoppel (*Ives v High* (1967)). It is, of course, essential to determine whether any easement is legal or equitable, for this may determine its ability to bind a purchaser of the servient land. However, in this problem, there is the further complication that there appears to be no express grant of the alleged easement. Such sales of the land as there are make no mention of any rights of way. Thus, we are thrown back on the creation of easements by implied grant: either by necessity, common intention under s62 of the **Law of Property Act 1925** or the rule in *Wheeldon v Burrows* (1879). However, whatever method, if any, is appropriate to this case, one important feature needs to be kept in mind. Under implied grant, the easement is said to be implied into a sale of the dominant tenement – that is, it is as if the grantor (who usually retains the servient tenement) did include the easement in the transfer document. Thus, it necessarily follows that, if an easement is impliedly granted, it takes its legal or equitable character from the grant into which it is implied. So, implied grant can give rise to legal and equitable easements depending on the quality of the transfer to the owner of what becomes the dominant land.

Clearly, then, John, the purchaser of the bungalow, will wish to assert an easement of way over the road that passes over the farm of which it was formerly a part. The only way to determine whether the easement exists is to consider the position of the three occupants in turn: Anne and Mark, Mark, and then John. Moreover, if such an easement exists, it falls to be determined whether the easement binds Norman, the purchaser of the allegedly servient land and, even if it does, what the precise scope of the easement is.[15]

(A) ANNE AND MARK

When Anne and Mark occupy the bungalow, it is clear that they do so at the invitation of the owner, Elizabeth. There is no express grant of an easement to them. Moreover, it appears from the facts that they do not occupy the premises by virtue of a grant of any estate. There is no sale of it to them and there is no lease of it to them. They appear to be licensees occupying with the consent of the owner under a family arrangement wherein there is no intention to create legal relations (*Street v Mountford* (1985) and *Heslop v Burns* (1974)). There is, therefore, no grant into which an easement can be implied. In any event, in order to create an easement where none already exists, there must exist a dominant tenement that is itself proprietary in nature. A licence is not proprietary and no easement can be created on the occasion of a grant of a licence to occupy rather than a lease (*Ashburn Anstalt v Arnold* (1989); *Lloyd v Dugdale* (2002)).

(B) MARK

When Anne leaves the property, the status of the remaining occupant, Mark, would appear to change. As we are told, Elizabeth, the owner, agrees by writing that Mark can occupy the premises. This is clearly an attempt to create a lease in Mark's favour, although the lease is not legal, not having been created by deed. Neither can it qualify as a legal periodic tenancy because no rent has been paid and, in any event, a premium (or 'fine') has been taken (s 52(2) of the LPA). This is, in effect, an equitable lease under a specifically enforceable contract within *Walsh v Lonsdale* (1882). This has one immediate consequence in that s 62 of the LPA cannot be used to establish the implied grant of an easement. Section 62 applies to 'conveyances', which, under s 205(1)(ii) of the LPA, do not include a contract to grant an estate (*Hillman v Rogers* (1998)). So, there is no scope for the implied creation of an easement by this method. This leaves us with two viable alternatives: creation by *Wheeldon v Burrows* (which can apply to contracts: *Borman v Griffith* (1930)) or by virtue of necessity. There is nothing exceptional to suggest use of common intention (*Peckham v Ellison* (2000)).

....

15   This is good because it shows that a systematic approach is being taken to a difficult question.

As to the rule in *Wheeldon*, this applies where an owner grants part of their land and, because of the rule that a person cannot derogate from their grant, is taken to impliedly grant easements necessary for the proper enjoyment of that land. In the normal case, these impliedly granted easements were rights that the owner themselves exercised for the benefit of the plot sold, being a burden on the plot retained. In our case, this would be if Elizabeth had used the path to get to the bungalow and then granted an estate to Mark. In our case, however, the vendor was not exercising such quasi-easements before partition: it is a case in which the person to whom the land was sold was exercising those rights. It is doubtful whether *Wheeldon* can apply in these circumstances because the rule appears to be that, as well as the easements being necessary for the reasonable enjoyment of the property (and/or continuous and apparent), they must 'have been and are at the time of the grant used by the owner of the entirety for the benefit of the part granted'. This does seem to rule out implied grant by *Wheeldon* unless we can say that, prior to the sale, Mark was exercising the alleged easement on behalf of the owner of the entirety. Perhaps this is possible on the facts given that Mark seems to have been a 'housesitter'. If it is, then an impliedly granted equitable easement will result and this will be binding on Norman, the purchaser of the servient tenement, only if it is registered as a Class D(iii) land charge. There is no evidence that it has been so registered and so would be void against Norman (*Midland Bank v Green* (1981)).

Assuming then that there is no new novel application of *Wheeldon* so as to support an easement, has one arisen by necessity? There is no doubt that an easement of way can arise though necessity, as in *Pinnington v Galland* (1853), but, as *MRA Engineering Ltd v Trimster Co Ltd* (1987) confirms, an easement of way can be implied only where the land cannot be used at all, and not simply where it would be convenient to imply an easement. Moreover, in the Privy Council decision of *Manjang v Drammah* (1990),[16] Lord Oliver relied on the Scottish decision in *Menzies v Breadalbane* (1828) as authority for the proposition that if access to land was available by water, this could negate an easement of way over terra firma. There is some doubt, then, over whether an easement of way by necessity could exist. Even if it did, it is impliedly granted to Mark in an equitable lease and is itself equitable. It would be void against Norman for lack of registration as a Class D(iii) land charge.

(C) JOHN

If John is to claim an easement, it seems that, once again, it will be by virtue of an implied grant. In his case, he has been sold the bungalow by registered disposition and so has acquired legal title in the normal way. Being a conveyance of the legal estate, John can claim the benefit of s 62 of the LPA 1925.

Under s 62, a purchaser of a legal estate in the land will be impliedly granted, as easements, all those rights previously enjoyed with the property that are capable of being

---

16 Highlighting the court which decided the case is a good technique to show that you are aware of the strength of the authority that you are relying on.

easements, provided that there is no express provision in the conveyance to the contrary and provided that there was diversity of occupation between the alleged dominant and alleged servient tenement prior to the grant (*Sovmots Investments Ltd v Secretary of State for the Environment* (1979), but see *Platt v Crouch* (2003)).[17] In this case, there clearly was diversity of occupation (Elizabeth and Mark) and there is no contrary intention. Of course, this case is somewhat different from the usual situation in which the person to whom the land is granted was the very person enjoying the right prior to that grant. However, the words of s 62 seem wide enough to cover the situation as here in which the grantee (John) acquires land, but the right that is translated into an easement was in fact exercised by somebody else (Anne and Mark) and this is now supported by the decision in *Hillman v Rogers*, applying s 62 in just such circumstances.[18] The point of s 62 is, indeed, that rights benefiting the granted land are not personal but proprietary. If, then, an easement is impliedly granted under s 62, the easement will necessarily be legal (*Hair v Gillman* (2000)). Consequently, since it was created not only after the LRA 2002 came into force, but after October 2006, as a legal easement created by implication it will only enjoy overriding status – and so be binding on Norman – if its existence would have been obvious on a reasonably careful inspection of the land, or Norman, as the purchaser of the servient land, had actual knowledge of it (Sched 3, para 3(i)).

QUESTION 35

In 2005, John became the registered leasehold proprietor of no. 35 Main Street. Title to this property included the alleyway between no. 35 and no. 37. Alan was the registered leasehold proprietor of no. 37 and he accessed the upper floor of no. 37 by a staircase that he had installed in the alleyway following a written agreement with John. In 2008 John sold no. 35 to Bob. In 2009, Alan granted a lease of the first floor of no. 37 to Claire and Claire was duly registered proprietor of the leasehold estate. Bob does not wish Claire to use the staircase.

In addition, Claire decided to set up a beauty salon on the first floor of no. 37. Before transferring the lease of the first floor Alan had run a ventilation system from the first floor to the ground floor. Claire wishes to use this system as she needs to keep her salon at just the right temperature. Alan had also been using the hot tub on the roof of Claire's flat. The lease to Claire included the roof space. Alan has now sold the lease of the ground floor to David who wants to block off the ventilation shaft although he was aware of Claire's use of the ventilation shaft at the time of sale. Claire is refusing to let David use the hot tub whilst the dispute goes on, but David insists that he is entitled to use the hot tub.

▶   Advise Claire.

....

17   If struggling for analysis, once again the decision in **Platt v Crouch** provides a good springboard for bringing in the sorts of ideas that will really make your answer stand out.

18   This kind of detail is the sort of information that will really get credit with the examiners as it shows that you are really thinking about the application of the rules to the specific problem, rather than re-hashing a prepared answer.

How to Answer this Question

The answer needs to include a discussion of the following:

- ❖ Leasehold estates and easements
- ❖ creation of easements
- ❖ easements and purchasers
- ❖ inequitable conduct and constructive trusts – *Lloyd v Dugdale* (2002).

Answer Structure

This diagram demonstrates how to determine whether the easements in this problem are binding on the purchasers.

ANSWER

In this problem, Claire wishes to continue to use the stairway and the ventilation system. David would like to use the hot tub on the roof of Claire's flat and Claire wishes to prevent him from so doing. In order to determine Claire's position it is necessary to look at these three issues independently to ascertain whether an easement has arisen, and what its current effects are. This involves analysis of the types of rights that can constitute easements, as well as the methods of creation of such rights, and the effects of these rights on third parties.

The first thing to note here is that relevant estates are leasehold estates, and Alan is Claire's landlord since he carved a sub-lease out of his own estate. This does not affect the operation of the easements and as long as there is a dominant and servient tenement in separate ownership, it does not matter than Alan is Claire's landlord.[19]

(A) THE STAIRWAY

Whether or not Claire has a right to use the stairway, will depend, firstly, on whether this right is capable of being an easement, secondly on whether an easement arose between the original parties, John and Alan, and then finally whether the current parties have the benefit of and are burdened by that easement.[20]

The use of a stairway to access property is capable of being an easement (*Liverpool CC v Irwin* (1976), *Chaudhary v Yavuz* (2011)). It is, in essence, a right of way. It is thus capable of lying in grant as it fits within the category of recognised easements (*Re Ellenborough Park* (1956)). Clearly also there is a dominant and a servient tenenment and these are in separate ownership. It does not matter for this that the properties may (or may not) have the same freeholder. Furthermore, the use of the staircase can be precisely defined and does not remove all reasonable uses of the passageway (*Montcrieff v Jamieson* (2007), *Batchelor v Marlow* (2001)). It clearly benefits the dominant land allowing easy access to the upper floor. This right is capable of being an easement in these circumstances.

The next question then is whether such an easement arose as between the original parties, Alan and John. John had agreed with Alan in writing that Alan could use the stairway. In order to be a legal easement, a deed and entry as a notice on the register would have been required (**Section 52, LPA 1925, Sched 2, Para 7 LRA 2002**) and so this easement is an equitable easement by virtue of the doctrine in *Walsh v Lonsdale* (1882). The fact of its being an unregistered equitable easement means that although there is a valid easement between Alan and John's leasehold estates, there may be some difficulty in showing that John's successor, Bob, is bound by that easement. As successor in title to Alan, Claire is

---

19 Dealing with this primary issue here saves time later on.

20 Although you may feel as though you are repeating yourself when outlining the structure of your answer overall, and then of each section, it is likely to lead to a better quality answer.

entitled to the benefit of any property rights which ran with the land. Easements would fall into this category. Thus if Bob is bound, Claire is able to enforce the easement.

Whether or not he is so bound will depend on the rules relating to priority in the LRA 2002. We know that Bob provided valuable consideration for the transfer of the leasehold estate such that **Section 29** determines the relative priorities of the interests (*Halifax v Popeck* (2008) outlines what is meant by 'priority' here). The easement, not being the subject of a notice, can only bind Bob if it operates as an overriding interest under **Sched 3**. As an equitable easement, it does not fall under **Sched 3, Para 3** which applies to implied legal easements. As a result Bob will only be bound by this easement if it is protected by actual occupation under **Sched 3, Para 2**.

It is far from straightforward to see how an owner of an estate in the dominant tenement could purely by virtue of his easement be in actual occupation of the servient land. The logical possibility of this was accepted in *Saeed v Plustrade* (2002) following a concession by counsel, but there the situation involved a parking space and was factually very different to Claire's situation. The possibility of protecting an easement under **Sched 3, Para 2** by the building of a staircase was discussed in *Chaudhary v Yavuz*. The court concluded that simply having placed the staircase in the alleyway did not constitute actual occupation of the land over which the easement ran. In fact, the staircase which was used only for passing and re-passing (as here) was said not to be occupied by anyone. This seems to be a correct evaluation of the situation.[21] As a result, this easement would not bind Bob as purchaser of no. 35. Claire cannot therefore continue to use the staircase to access the property. It is also important to note here that there is no mechanism whereby the court will 'imply' an easement here under the rule of easements of necessity. There needs to be a conveyance into which such an easement can be implied, and so this conveyance must be between the potential grantor and grantee of that easement, which is not the case here. Easements of right of way cannot be created simply to avoid land being landlocked as a matter of public policy (*Nickerson v Barraclough* (1979)).

(B) THE VENTILATION SYSTEM

The first thing to note here is that the passage of air through a defined channel, such as a ventilation shaft, is a recognised easement (*Wong v Beaumont Properties* (1964)).

Claire wishes to continue to use the ventilation system. In order to achieve this she must first demonstrate that an easement has arisen in her favour, and then secondly she must show that it binds the subsequent purchaser of the land. There is no expressly granted easement here, and so we must see whether one of the four methods of implying easements will assist Claire. These are: easements of necessity; common intention; the

---

21   The facts of this case are so similar to the facts of the problem that it can be relied on to a large extent in addressing the issue of actual occupation.

rule in *Wheeldon v Burrows* (1879) and the operation of **Section 62 LPA 1925**. The rules on easements of necessity will not assist Claire here, as they only really come into play where land may be left landlocked following the division of a plot of land (*MRA Engineering v Trimster* (1987), *Manjang v Drammah* (1999)). We must however look at the other three methods in turn.

Firstly, the rules relating to common intention may be relevant here (*Pwllbach Colliery Co Ltd v Woodman* (1915)). Alan was aware that Claire wanted to use the top flat as a beauty salon. The test for intention in common intention cases is strict (*Stafford v Lee* (1993), *Chaffe v Kingsley* (2000)) and most importantly the intention must be one shared between the parties. The most plausible explanation of the Alan's intention here is that although he knew Claire wanted to set up a beauty salon, he did not mind whether this succeeded or not as long as she could pay him for the leasehold interest. There was nothing in the nature of a joint enterprise here, suggesting that the rules on common intention would not assist Claire here (see *Wong v Beaumont Properties*).

The other two methods, the rule in *Wheeldon v Burrows* and the operation of **Section 62 LPA 1925** are based on the principle of non-derogation from grants and can be used to impliedly grant easements only (*Peckham v Ellison* (1998)). The rule in *Wheeldon v Burrows* operates so as to imply an easement into a deed of grant of an estate in land where the grantor had previously used the land in such a way as to amount to a quasi-easement. Here, since Alan had been using the ventilation shaft himself for the passage of air. This usage could be said to amount to a quasi-easment. Furthermore, the operation of the rule in *Wheeldon* requires that the use of the quasi-easement be continuous or (possibly and, see *Hillman v Rogers* (1998) and *Millman v Ellis* (1996)) apparent at the time of transfer. The passage of air through the system is likely to be continous and the existence of the ventilation shaft it likely also to have been obvious. Finally, in order that the easement be implied under the rule in *Wheeldon* it must also be necessary for the reasonable enjoyment of the land. This is difficult to define precisely, and it is is entirely context dependent, but we can say that it is certainly reasonably necessary for use of the land as a beauty salon.

Thus an argument based on *Wheeldon v Burrows* has a reasonable chance of success, but Claire may also wish to use **Section 62 LPA 1925** which will imply easements into conveyances of a legal estate where the conditions for its application are met. *Sovmots Investments v Secretary of State for the Environment* (1979) stipulated that in order to transform a mere permission into an easement, there must have been prior diversity of occupation of that land. That was not the case here, and so this requirement would appear to be fatal to Claire's chances of using **Section 62**. The highly controversial decision in *Platt v Crouch* (2003) however suggests that as long as the usage was continual and apparent (as here) there is no need for prior diversity of occupation. If this is so, it is difficult to see what role remains for the rule in *Wheeldon v Burrows*, and certainly it appears that the comments in *Platt* form part of the *ratio* of that decision.

They do however conflict with previous authority, and there is much scepticism as to whether this decision would be followed.[22]

As a result it seems likely that Alan would have been subject to an easement of passage of air through a defined channel as a result of the rule in *Wheeldon v Burrows*, but this does not tell us whether David must respect this easement. Once again we must rely on the rules contained in the LRA 2002. As an implied legal easement, this easement will fall under Sched 3, Para 3 LRA 2002. Such easements can be unregistered interests which override where known to the purchaser at the time of the disposition, or where obvious on a reasonably careful inspection of the land. It is likely that a court would conclude that both would apply here in fact, but even if they did not, since the ventilation shaft had been used in the previous year, David would be bound by this easement. Thus Claire will be able to continue to use the ventilation shaft, and will be able to prevent David from blocking it off.

(C) THE HOT TUB

The final issue here then concerns the hot tub and whether Claire must permit David to use the hot tub on the roof. The most difficult issue here is whether or not the use of a hot tub can constitute an easement. According to *Re Ellenborough Park*, a right that is purely recreational is not capable of being an easement. This is despite the fact that the right in that case, the right to use a pleasure garden, was considered capable of being an easement even though it too seems purely recreational. The possibility of the use of a swimming pool being a valid easement was discussed in the Court of British Columbia in *Grant v MacDonald* (1992).[23] In that case it was concluded that the use of a swimming pool was capable of constituting an easement. It is suggested however that even if that decision was correct (see Baker), the use of a hob tub goes even further than the use of a swimming pool. The swimming pool could be said to constitute access to a large area of recreational space, akin as such to a pleasure garden. The hot tub is more easily characterised as a mere permission to use a facility on another's land. It is therefore likely to be a mere licence and it is unlikely that a court would consider that this right could be an easement. As a result, being a licence, it would not be capable of binding a third party (*Ashburn Anstalt v Arnold* (1989), *Lloyd v Dugdale* (2002)). There is no reason to believe that a constructive trust would have arisen in David's favour either (see *Ashburn Anstalt*).

Even assuming that this right was capable of being an easement however, it is still very unlikely that David would be able to use the hot tub. There is no express grant of an easement to use the hot tub – no agreement that this permission would continue was

---

22 There is always a fine line to be drawn when discussing controversial cases between pointing out the weakness in their authority, and in recognising that they may still be binding on a lower court.

23 This case would not be binding in an English or Welsh Court, but overseas cases provide some useful discussion of the very issues you are looking at and certainly credit will be given for considering them, as long as they are not relied on too heavily.

made – and so there was no legal or equitable easement granted to Alan. At most there was an oral permission to Alan that he could continue to use the hot tub and given the nature of the activity, it is likely that the court would not view this as even an attempted grant of an easement such that an estoppel might arise (*Flowermix v Site Developments* (2000), *Kinane v Mackie-Conteh* (2005), *Crabb v Arun DC* (1976)), but as a precarious and personal permission. Alan therefore did not have the benefit of any easement to pass on to David. Thus, David cannot use the hot tub on the roof.

As a result, although Claire is able to use the ventilation shaft, she will not be able to make use of the stairway. It is also very unlikely that David would be able to make use of the hot tub.

Common Pitfalls

Take care to adopt a structured approach. Ensure that, for each right claimed, you have considered both whether it can be an easement – that is, has it the necessary characteristics? – and also by what method it can be acquired.

Freehold Covenants

INTRODUCTION

In Chapter 5 on leases, we examined the law surrounding the operation of leasehold covenants. However, it is not only landlord and tenant who may wish to enter into promises affecting the mode of use of their property. Freeholders may also wish to control the use that neighbours may make of their land, as where owners of residential property may wish to preserve the non-business character of their area, or the owners of an industrial estate may wish to limit the type of activity carried on there. Obviously, freeholders do not stand in a relationship of landlord and tenant with each other and the rules of leasehold covenants are inapplicable. Consequently, a set of principles have developed – mainly in connection with restrictive covenants – that govern the running of covenants between freeholders. Like leasehold covenants (and easements), each freehold covenant comprises a 'benefit' and a 'burden'. It is always necessary, when considering problems in this particular area, to remember that before a claimant can sue a defendant on a particular covenant, the benefit must have passed to the claimant and the burden must have passed to the defendant. Indeed, it can quite easily happen that the benefit of a covenant has passed, but the burden has not, or vice versa. So it is imperative when dealing with these issues to consider the issue of the benefit of a covenant separately from questions relating to the burden.

Aim higher ★

Be very clear about the rules for passing the benefit and burden of covenants. They are different.

Understand the avoidance techniques currently employed.

Be aware of the Law Commission's proposals for the reform of the law of covenants – Report No. 327, *Making Land Work: Easements, Covenants and Profits à Prendre* (2011).

In problem questions, often it is wiser to tackle the issue of passing the burden first, and then move to the benefit. First, identify your defendant and why they are liable, and this will define who can be the claimant.

QUESTION 36

'The case of *Crest Nicholson Residential (South) Ltd v Mc Allister* [2004] EWCA Civ 410 is an important milestone in the lengthy development through the case law of the law of restrictive covenants. When these are read collectively judicial decisions in the area provide one of the richest areas of fantasy in written English. *Crest Nicholson*, though tediously lengthy as is the way with contemporary judgments, blows a breath of fresh air into the gloom created by the mysterious judgment in *Federated Homes Ltd v Mill Lodge Properties*.'

(P Kenny [2005] *The Conveyancer and Property Lawyer* 2)

In the light of the above statement, consider whether the rules relating to the running of freehold covenants adequately ensure that successors in title can enforce the benefits obtained by an original covenantee.

How to Answer this Question

- ❖ The meaning of 'benefit' and the original covenantee – s 56 of the LPA.
- ❖ 'Successors in title' – s 78 of the LPA.
- ❖ Benefit at common law – s 78 of the LPA.
- ❖ Benefit in equity – annexation: *Federated Homes v Mill Lodge* (1980); *Whitgift Homes v Stocks* (2001); *Crest Nicholson Residential (South) Ltd v McAllister* (2004).
- ❖ Assignment.
- ❖ Building schemes.

Applying the Law

This diagram shows the rules relating to the transmissibility of the benefit of a freehold covenant.

ANSWER

Nowhere is it more true than in the law of real property that no man is an island. The use by one person of his or her land can seriously affect the quality of enjoyment, the mode of use, or the occupation of their neighbour. This is obvious and it should come as no surprise that the law of real property has developed rules and principles that allow one landowner to control the use to which their neighbour may put their own land. This can be achieved through the law of easements or through the law of covenants in leases. It can, however, also be achieved where the neighbouring landowners are freeholders. The law relating to freehold covenants applies in all of those circumstances in which no privity of estate exists between the parties – that is, where the claimant and defendant do not stand in the relationship of landlord and tenant. However, like covenants in leases, covenants between freeholders also have a dual aspect. Thus, each covenant will confer a benefit and a corresponding burden. Indeed, it is a curiosity of the law of real property that rules relating to the transmission of the benefit of a freehold covenant – that is, to somebody who buys the land from the original covenantee (the person to whom the covenant was made) – are entirely independent from the rules relating to the transmission of the burdens of the covenant – that is, to a person who buys land from the original covenantor (the person who made the promise). It is quite possible, therefore, for the benefit of a covenant to run to a successor in title of the original covenantee, but for the burden of that covenant to have been destroyed or to bind only the original covenantor, and vice versa.[1]

This particular question raises issues concerning the transmission of the benefit of freehold covenants or, more accurately, whether a successor in title to land of the original covenantee gains the right to enforce covenants made for the benefit of land when he acquires that land. In very general terms, and putting aside for the moment situations in which there has been an express assignment of contractual rights (see below), the benefit of a covenant will pass provided that the covenant 'touches and concerns' the land of the original covenantee when it was made. This is simply another way of saying that property law is concerned with the transmission of proprietary rights, not personal advantages. It also ensures that title to land is not cluttered up by obligations that are merely transient, uncertain or personal in nature. So, as with covenants in pre-1996 leases, it is essential to determine whether the covenant 'touches and concerns' according to the flexible guidelines put forward by Lord Oliver in *Swift Investments v Combined English Stores* (1989). Assuming, however, that the freehold covenant does 'touch and concern' the land, then it is possible that the right to sue on the covenant may pass either 'at law' or 'in equity' to a successor to the original covenantee. As we shall see, the methods by which this benefit may actually pass in law or in equity are very similar, the requirements of equity being slightly less demanding. If a claimant had the choice of suing on the benefit of the covenant at law or in equity (which occurs frequently), much would depend on which remedy the claimant required.[2] A suit at law usually would result in the award of damages, whereas in equity the discretionary remedies of injunction to prevent breach of a restrictive covenant or order of specific performance to compel performance of a positive covenant would be available. Bearing this in mind, the position at law will be considered initially and consideration of the position in equity will follow. Ultimately, once the 'touching and concerning' requirement has been met, it seems that three further conditions must be satisfied if the benefit is to run to the successor in law.

First, the persons seeking to enforce the covenant must own some legal estate in the land. Prior to the enactment of s 78 of the **Law of Property Act 1925**, the person seeking to enforce the covenant at law had to own the same legal estate as the original covenantee.

---

1   This introduction puts the discussion as to the running of the benefit of a restrictive covenant into context.
2   It is important in a question like this to be aware of the practical consequences of the benefit running in law as opposed to equity and vice-versa, not just the different rules governing the passing of the benefit.

So, if the original covenantee was a freeholder, the successor had to be a freeholder. Section 78 has, however, made it clear that the successor need only have some legal estate, such as where the original covenantee being a freeholder lets the land to a successor on a lease by deed. This has clearly made the transmission of the benefit at law slightly simpler. Second, it is clear that the covenant must benefit the land of the original covenantee. In most cases, it will be enough that the covenant touches and concerns the land because, from this, the fact of benefit will be presumed (*Whitgift Homes v Stocks* (2001)). However, in theory, it is open to somebody disputing the fact that the benefit has run at law to claim that the land of the original covenantee never could have benefited from the particular covenant made and therefore cannot pass to a successor in title: see *Wrotham Park Estate v Parkside Homes* (1974). Third, and most importantly of all, the covenant must have been annexed to the land in order for the benefit to run with the land.[3] In this respect, the decision in *Federated Homes v Mill Lodge Properties Ltd* (1980) has made the position much simpler. According to the Court of Appeal decision in that case, now fully confirmed in *Whitgift Homes v Stocks* and *Crest Nicholson v McAllister* (2004), the benefit of every covenant whether positive or negative and whether in law or in equity will be annexed to the land and, indeed, to every part of it, provided that the land is identified in the covenant or can be identified by extrinsic evidence (*Whitgift*). It is true, however, that later cases (*Roake v Chadha* (1984); *Crest Nicholson*) have made it clear that this statutory annexation can be excluded by clear contrary intention. Nevertheless, the decision in *Federated Homes* has clearly provided successors in title to original covenantees with a safe and certain method of claiming that they are entitled to the benefit of a covenant. We should note, however, that the decision in *Federated Homes* has been subject to criticism. For example, it has been correctly pointed out that s 78 does not precisely say what the Court of Appeal alleges and that it is a decision favouring certainty at the expense of individuality. Nevertheless, as noted above, it has been confirmed by a strong Court of Appeal in *Whitgift Homes v Stocks* and, unless overruled by the House of Lords (which seems most unlikely), this decision will govern the running of the benefit of covenants both at law and in equity.[4]

Indeed, if we now turn to the position in equity, we will see that *Federated Homes* has had an impact here also. Once again, assuming that the covenant touches and concerns the land, the person seeking to enforce the covenant must have some estate or interest in the land, although of course this may now only be equitable. If that is established, it seems that there are three methods by which the benefit may transfer in equity. The first of these is under the rule of statutory annexation that we have just considered in relation to covenants at law. As noted then, *Federated Homes* applies with equal vigour to the

---

3   This paragraph does a good job of providing a clear and coherent structure to the rules being discussed. It is important to be systematic in this way.

4   This sort of analysis of the continuing strength of an authority and its acceptance in the courts is a good approach to take to controversial decisions.

annexation of covenants in equity, so a covenant will be statutorily annexed to each and every part of the land provided that it is clear what land is intended to be benefited. Indeed, the efficacy of the *Federated Homes* principle is such that the other two methods of transferring the benefit in equity may now be largely redundant, except perhaps in the limited circumstances of express contrary intention (*Roake*) or when the advantages of a building scheme are required.

The building scheme is the second method by which the benefit may be transferred. This is a rule based upon common intention and practicality. It allows a common vendor (such as a property developer) to transfer the benefit of the covenants received by them from every purchaser of a plot of land to every other purchaser of a plot of land. It is an attempt to create mutually enforceable obligations. Of course, there is nothing unique in this because under the normal rules, the benefits of the covenants made by early purchasers will be automatically transmitted to later purchasers who buy part of the retained land. However, the advantage of a building scheme is that it allows the benefit of later purchasers' covenants to be given to earlier purchasers even though the time of later purchases is out of synchronisation. The requirements for a valid building scheme were laid down in *Elliston v Reacher* (1908). There must be a common vendor, the land must be laid out in definable plots, the benefits must be intended to be mutually enforceable, and these must be the conditions upon which all purchasers buy. These are, however, not inflexible and later cases such as *Re Dolphins Conveyance* (1970) and *Baxter v Four Oaks* (1965) illustrate that the benefit will run under a building scheme even though all of the requirements have not been met.[5] Importantly, however, no building scheme can exist unless it is clear what land is subject to the scheme (*Whitgift Homes v Stocks*). It is essential to such a scheme that the owners of land know the full reach of the mutuality of their obligations. It should be noted also that a building scheme does not affect the running of the burden of covenants and if the obligations are to be truly mutually enforceable, the normal steps for transmitting the burden of restrictive covenants must be followed. Usually, this will mean registration of the covenants against the title of all purchasers.

Finally, the third method of transmitting the benefit of covenants is the assignment. It is trite law that the benefit of a contract (that is, a covenant) may be expressly assigned. So, for example, if a purchaser of the covenantee's land is expressly assigned the benefit of that covenant, they will be able to enforce it. However, this method does have some disadvantages. It seems that this is a method of transferring the benefit personally. So, following *Re Pinewood* (1958), where there has been an assignment of the covenant to the first successor of the original covenantee, a chain of assignments is required if the benefit

---

5   This paragraph makes good use of case law to show the flexibility of the rules relating to building schemes.

is to be assigned to subsequent assignees. Assignment is a personal not a proprietary method of transfer. Of course, after *Federated Homes*, such a method is largely redundant and, in all cases of the transmission of the benefit in equity, the claimant (that is, the successor in title) is at the mercy of the court when seeking a remedy. Equitable remedies are discretionary and it is quite possible that a person who is in principle entitled to enforce covenants may not gain the remedy of injunction or specific performance if they do not come to the court with 'clean hands'. It should be apparent from the above that it is relatively straightforward to transmit the benefit of a covenant both at law and in equity. The decision in *Federated Homes* has made this even more likely and the only real limit (except possibly for personal assignment) seems to be that the covenant must touch and concern the land. Of course, having the benefit of a covenant is useless unless there is somebody who is subject to the burden. In this respect, the rule that the burden of restrictive covenants only may run, and then only in equity, is a real limitation on the practical enforcement of covenants. It means that in all cases in which the original covenantor has parted with their land, only restrictive covenants will be relevant and then only that the rules of equity will be in play. As we have seen, these give rise to only a discretionary remedy and the successor in title to the original covenantee will have to establish a bona fide claim if they are to succeed.

Don't be tempted to

Do not ignore the differences between enforcement at law and in equity.

Remember that case law might not be consistent: *Federated Homes* has been qualified by *Crest Nicholson*.

QUESTION 37

In what circumstances may the burden of a freehold covenant pass to a successor in title of the original covenantor?

How to Answer this Question

❖   Identify the original covenantor;

❖   the rules concerning successors in title and s 79 of the LPA;

❖   requirements of registration.

Applying the Law

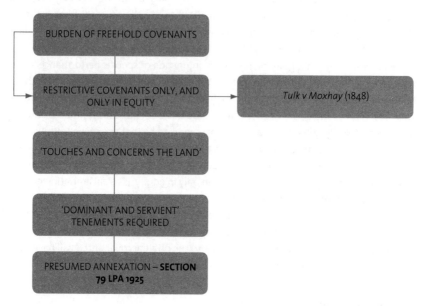

This diagram shows the options for the running of the burden of a freehold covenant.

ANSWER

It is a general principle of English law that, while the benefit of a contract can be assigned to a third party, the burden of a contract cannot. In the law of real property, this can cause serious difficulties, for it means that when an owner of land makes a promise by covenant to do or not to do something on their land (in other words, imposing a burden on that land), then any successor in title to that original covenantor may well be able to acquire the land free of the burden placed upon it. Obviously, this is of great advantage to the successor to the original covenantor, but it is of no use to those persons who enjoy the benefit of the covenant, for they may see the benefits that they so carefully extracted destroyed on the first sale of the burdened land. Fortunately, the law of real property has mitigated the harshness of the contractual rule by providing that, in some circumstances, burdens attached to land by way of covenant may assume a proprietary nature and may be passed on to any person who subsequently acquires that land.

As is well known, the position is relatively straightforward if the covenantee and their successors and the covenantor and their successors stand in the relationship of landlord and tenant. Then, for pre-1996 leases, the matter is governed by *Spencer's Case* (1583) and the doctrine of privity of estate and, for leases granted on or after 1 January 1996, the **Landlord and Tenant (Covenants) Act 1995** has imposed a statutory scheme. If, however, the covenant was made between freeholders or concerns persons not otherwise in privity of estate under a pre-1996 lease, such as a landlord and a sub-tenant (including a sub-tenant under a lease granted on or after 1 January 1996), the rules commonly known as the rules of freehold covenants come into play. Not surprisingly, the rules allowing the transmission of burdens in non-leasehold cases are quite strict, as it is a general policy requirement that title to land should not be unduly cluttered.

In essence, the starting point for a discussion of the transmission of the burden of freehold covenants must be the decision in *Tulk v Moxhay* (1848). In that case, concerning a restrictive covenant not to build in Leicester Square, it was decided that if a covenant touched and concerned the land, it could, as a matter of conscience and equity, be binding on any purchaser of the land burdened by the covenant who had notice of its existence. Although the principles have developed considerably since *Tulk*, the limits put on the doctrine by that case still exist. Thus, it is clear that burdens of covenants may only run in equity and, as an equitable doctrine, there are all of the attendant problems associated with equitable rights, including the fact that remedies are discretionary. Moreover, despite some attempts to argue the contrary, it is clear that only the burden of restrictive or negative covenants may run in equity (*Rhone v Stephens* (1994)).

The conditions for the transmission of the burden of a covenant are as follows. First, the covenant must touch and concern the land and therefore pass the test in *Swift Investments v Combined English Stores* (1989). Second, the covenant must be negative in nature and this is a question of substance not a question of form, normally resolved by asking whether the owner of the burdened land is required to expend money. Third, the doctrine takes effect in equity only thus opening up the possibility that the equitable interests (that is, the negative covenants) may be defeated by a sale to a purchaser of a legal estate for value. Of course, in many cases, these hurdles are not formidable and, in most cases, the restrictive covenant will satisfy these initial tests. If it does, there are further matters that must be satisfied before a burden will run to a successor in title. First, and most importantly of all, the covenant must have been made for the benefit of land owned by the covenantee. In other words, the burden cannot run unless it is a burden that benefits the land of the covenantee. Like easements, there must be a dominant and servient tenement. In effect, this means that not only must the original covenantee have owned land at the time the covenant was created but also that the particular covenant must have been capable of benefiting that land (*Whitgift Homes v Stocks* (2001)). This is a question of fact, although the onus is on the person seeking to deny the covenant to prove that the land of the covenantee was not in fact benefited (*Wrotham Park Estates v Parkside Homes* (1974)) and may often be presumed from the fact that the covenant touches and concerns (*Whitgift*).[6] The meaning of benefit is crucial in

---

6   This description of the burden of proof here shows that the writer is aware of the detail of the rule and its operation in practice.

these circumstances and, according to *Re Gadd's Transfer* (1966), it has several components: for example, does it affect the value or mode of use of the land? Next, it is necessary to establish that the burden of the covenant is annexed to the land. Express words of annexation can, of course, be used. So, for example, a covenant expressed to be for X and their heirs and successors in title would effectively annex the covenant to the land. However, such long-windedness is no longer needed because of s 79 of the LPA. This provision effectively incorporates words of annexation into every deed of covenant. The net effect is that the burden of restrictive covenants will be automatically annexed to the land unless the deed of covenant expressly contains a provision to the contrary. The position is effectively the same as that achieved for the benefit of the covenant under s 78 of the LPA, as interpreted in *Federated Homes v Mill Lodge* (1980).[7]

Assuming these conditions are established, the covenant now has a proprietary nature. This means that the burden of the covenant can, in principle, bind successors in title to the original covenantor's land. However, as we have noted above, these restrictive covenants take effect in equity and, like all equitable rights, they are capable of being defeated by a sale to a purchaser of a legal estate for value. Before 1925, as *Tulk* itself makes clear, a purchaser of the covenantor's land would only be bound by restrictive covenants, even if they had passed the above tests, if they purchased that land with notice of the covenants. Now, of course, notice has been replaced by registration, both in registered and unregistered land. Thus, in order for a proprietary restrictive covenant to bind a purchaser, it must be registered in the relevant way. In registered land, the covenant will, under the **Land Registration Act 2002**, be an interest protected by registration and must be protected by placing a notice (usually agreed but also on occasion unilateral) on the register. In unregistered land, the restrictive covenant is classified as a Class D(ii) land charge and must be registered accordingly. It should be noted, however, that the requirement of registration is needed only to bind purchasers of the legal estate. Thus, because these covenants are already proprietary, if the covenantor's land comes into the possession of somebody who is not a purchaser of a legal estate (such as a squatter or an equitable tenant or a person receiving the property by way of gift), then a restrictive covenant will be binding, whether registered or not.

These, then, are the conditions upon which the burden of a restrictive covenant may be binding. As is obvious, the rules are quite strict, applying only to restrictive covenants and only operating in equity, thereby making covenants subject to a requirement of registration. Obviously, the burden of positive covenants cannot run and of course this can cause hardship. For this reason, there are a number of avoidance devices that may be used. None of these are entirely satisfactory[8] and, in particular, the concept of 'mutual

---

7   This comparison with the rules relating to burden adds an extra dimension of analysis to the discussion.
8   This section takes the essay beyond the main focus of the passing of the burden of negative covenants giving an extra dimension to the answer.

benefit and burden' has been restricted by case law (*Thamesmead Town v Allotey* (1998)). Consequently, it is only if the Law Commission's 2011 proposals for reform are adopted (and this seems unlikely at present) that the situation will change substantially. Those proposals would introduce the concept of a 'land obligation' which could be either positive or negative in substance, and whose benefit and burden would be registered against the title of the covenantee's and covenantor's titles respectively.[9] If so registered, the land obligation would be enforceable by successors in title to the covenantee's land against successors in title to the covenantor's land, irrespective of whether it was positive or negative. Clearly, this would solve some of the present problems in the law and make the avoidance devices unnecessary.

Don't be tempted to

Be very clear that, here, you are being asked to write about the person who gave the covenant – that is, the covenantor – and who will subsequently be bound by that covenant. You are not being asked to discuss the right to sue on or enforce that same covenant. Do not confuse benefit and burden.

QUESTION 38

Wordsworth was the freehold owner, registered with absolute title, of five shops in Parnassus Road Redbridge. No 5 sold bread and cakes, No 6 general hardware, No 7 was a chemist and Nos 8 and 9 were empty. Two years ago, Wordsworth sold No 8 to Virginia, who covenanted that she would not carry on any trade other than a hair salon at No 8. Just after, Wordsworth sold No 9 to Marlowe who covenanted 'with Wordsworth and the owners for the time being of the shops in Parnassus Road' that he would use No 9 for no other purpose than the breeding and wholesale of pet chinchilla rabbits and would erect and maintain a fence to protect his neighbours in the event of an escape.

Last week, Wordsworth let No 5 on a four-year lease in writing to Chaucer, who immediately sub-let to Betjeman. At the same time, Wordsworth sold No 6 by registered disposition to Wordsworth, who turned the premises into a garden centre. Wordsworth has since discovered that his original tenant of No 7, the chemists, left the property some months ago and it is now occupied by Trevelyan, a squatter, who is selling second-hand electrical goods.

In the course of her hairdressing, Virginia has invented a new miracle shampoo and has begun a small-scale manufacturing and retail outlet from her premises. Meanwhile, Marlowe found that chinchilla breeding was not profitable and has turned to breeding parrots and budgerigars. Unfortunately, this has got out of hand and Parnassus Road is overrun with birds escaping from No 9. Wordsworth's entire stock is threatened.

9   It is always good to show that you are aware of reform proposals, especially where they are recent, and that you know some of the specifics of those proposals.

Advise the occupants of Parnassus Road as to their respective rights and obligations.

How to Answer this Question

❖ What is the position of the original covenantors and covenantees;

❖ Analyse the running of the benefit at law and in equity;

❖ Consider s 78 of the **LPA** and *Federated Homes* (1980); *Whitgift Homes v Stocks* (2001); *Crest Nicholson v McAllister* (2004);

❖ Consider s 56 of the **LPA** – *Amsprop Trading v Harris* (1997);

❖ Note the position of squatters.

Applying the Law

This diagram shows the options for the running of the benefit of a freehold covenant.

ANSWER

This question concerns the operation of covenants in situations in which there is no leasehold estate between claimant and defendant and their respective successors in title. The problem concerns the law of freehold covenants. However, as is made clear from the facts of this problem, there is no issue here of the running of the burden of the covenant: both the original covenantors (Virginia and Marlowe) are still in occupation of the burdened land and it is against them that an action for breach of the covenants will be directed.[10] Turning first to the nature of these covenants, the covenant by Virginia is clearly restrictive in nature and without doubt touches and concerns the land. Likewise, Marlowe's covenant to keep only chinchilla rabbits is restrictive and, because it affects the mode of use of the land (*Swift Investments v Combined English Stores* (1989)), it also touches and concerns. Marlowe's second covenant – to erect and maintain a fence – does touch and concern, but it is positive in nature, requiring expenditure by the owner of the burdened land. However, the fact that one covenant is positive is not crucial in this case, as it is only successors in title that cannot be made liable on the burden of positive covenants. Here, the defendants are the original covenantors and there is nothing to prevent the benefit of a positive covenant passing to successors of the original covenantee.

First, we need to determine who the original parties to the covenants are, for they will be able to sue on the benefit of the covenant against Virginia and Marlowe (the original covenantors), irrespective of any question of the passing of the benefit under land law rules. This would be simply a matter of contract. Clearly, Wordsworth, the original freeholder (and now the landlord of No 5 and owner of No 7), has the benefit of all covenants by both Virginia and Marlowe, being an original covenantee: he can sue on all the covenants at law and on those covenants in equity where he is still in possession of the land (*Chambers v Randall* (1923)). Of course, the remedy at law will be damages and they will be nominal if Wordsworth does not possess the land at the time of any breach of covenant. In practice, he will wish to obtain an injunction for breach of both restrictive covenants and a decree of specific performance in respect of the positive covenant to build a fence.[11] This will require him to sue in equity and, therefore, he should sue as freeholder of No 7. It is clear also, however, that Virginia, the purchaser of No 8 (and an original covenantor to Wordsworth), is actually an original covenantee of the covenants made by Marlowe. As we are told, Marlowe's covenants are made with his vendor (Wordsworth) but also the 'owners for the time being of the shops in Parnassus Road'.[12] This description includes Virginia who, by then, is an owner of a shop in Parnassus Road, and so under s 56 of the **Law of Property Act 1925**, Virginia is deemed to be a party to the deed of covenant. That section allows a person 'to take the benefit' of any covenant as an original party to it so long as they are in existence at the date of the covenant and the covenant is intended to benefit them as a party (*Amsprop Trading v Harris* (1997)). Thus, Virginia may enforce both the positive and negative covenants against Marlowe in law or in equity, being an original covenantee. Of course, the reverse is not true, as the benefit of Virginia's covenant has never been passed to Marlowe, either by deliberate assignment or under the rules to be discussed below.

....

10 The introduction to a problem question is a good place to close off 'blind alleys' and to show that you are aware of the precise issues arising in the problem.

11 It is important to show the practical remedial consequences of the continuing distinction between law and equity in relation to freehold covenants.

12 Where a problem question gives you the precise wording of an agreement, as here, it is likely that the wording itself is going to be relevant to the answer, and so it is worth analysing that wording closely.

We can now turn to the position of successors in title to the original covenantees (Wordsworth). It is trite law that the benefit of a covenant may be transmitted to a successor either at law or in equity, provided that the covenant touches and concerns the land (except possibly in cases of contractual assignment). Each successor needs to be considered in turn and the nature of the covenants has been discussed above.[13]

(A) THE SUCCESSORS TO SHOP NO 5: CHAUCER AND BETJEMAN

It is clear that Chaucer and Betjeman will be able to claim the benefit of these covenants only in equity. Chaucer's estate in the land is under a four-year lease in writing – not by deed – and so it must amount to an equitable lease (*Walsh v Lonsdale* (1882)). Chaucer has only an equitable estate and thus his tenant Betjeman can be in no better position. So, both have equitable interests and we need to consider whether the benefit of the covenant has passed in equity (*Mellon v Sinclair* (1996)).

Clearly, all covenants touch and concern the land, and both Chaucer and Betjeman have some interest in the land, entitling them to sue. We may note here that neither of them need have the same interest in the land as the original covenantee (Wordsworth), so long as they have some interest within s 78 of the LPA 1925. Moreover, the covenants will be presumed to benefit the land (*Whitgift Homes v Stocks* (2001)) and, in any event, seem to be within the meaning of benefit put forward in *Re Gadd* (1966). However, has the benefit passed under one of the three ways recognised by equity: assignment, a building scheme or annexation? There is no evidence of the first, and the second is clearly inappropriate on the facts. However, after *Federated Homes v Mill Lodge Properties* (1980), it is established that the effect of s 78 of the LPA 1925 is to attach the benefit of a covenant automatically to the land, provided that the land is readily identifiable (*Whitgift Homes v Stocks*; *Crest Nicholson v McAllister* (2004)), unless this is explicitly precluded, as in *Roake v Chadha* (1984).[14] There is no such exclusion in this case. Moreover, it is immaterial that the present claimants have an interest in only part of the land originally benefited by these covenants. Under *Federated Homes*, a covenant is attached to each and every part of the land, so long as each and every part is capable of benefiting from it. That is clearly the case here. It should also be noted that *Federated Homes* applies to positive covenants in exactly the same way as negative covenants and so no distinction can be drawn between the covenants made by Virginia and those made by Marlowe. Thus, the benefit of all three covenants has run in principle to Chaucer and Betjeman and they can take action to restrain unlawful use of No 8 and No 9 as well as force Marlowe to build a secure fence, subject to the court's right to refuse the discretionary remedies in equity (*Gafford v Graham* (1998)). Of course, the action will be commenced by Betjeman, the present occupant of No 5 and, indeed, Chaucer will be permitted to sue in respect of his reversionary interest only if Betjeman does not take action.

....

13   The answer here is made much easier to follow by the use of sub-headings.
14   This section demonstrates a wide knowledge of the case law.

(B) THE SUCCESSOR TO SHOP NO 6: WORDSWORTH

The position with Wordsworth is much the same as above, except that Wordsworth has a legal estate in the land. He may sue, therefore, either at law or in equity depending on whether he wishes damages or an injunction and specific performance. To recap: there is no doubt that Wordsworth has an estate in the land, that the covenants touch and concern the land and that the benefit has been annexed to his part of the land under *Federated Homes*.[15] He may enforce all three covenants against Virginia and Marlowe respectively.

(C) THE SUCCESSOR/OCCUPIER TO SHOP NO 7: WORDSWORTH AND THE SQUATTER

We have already noted above that Wordsworth is an original covenantee and may sue on all three covenants as a matter of contract. Moreover, he is still in possession of No 7 so may sue for a legal or equitable remedy at his choosing. Yet, what of the squatter, Trevelyan (the person actually in occupation), for he may wish to enforce the covenants if his occupation and use of the property is being disrupted? Once again, the covenants touch and concern the land and, under *Federated Homes*, they are annexed to each and every part of it. However, it does appear that Trevelyan has no interest in the land that could entitle him to sue. This is not fatal. If we examine **s 78** of the **LPA 1925** closely, it declares that successors in title may obtain the benefit of covenants and then says that 'in connection with covenants restrictive of the use of land successors in title shall be deemed to include owners and occupiers for the time being of the land'. Clearly, this means that even a squatter, being an occupier, can obtain the benefit of a restrictive covenant if all of the other conditions are met. Thus, Trevelyan can sue on the covenants restricting the use of premises and so can prevent Virginia from manufacturing shampoo and Marlowe from breeding parrots and budgerigars.

Don't be tempted to

Do not confuse the law of freehold and leasehold covenants. A leasehold covenant must be *in* a lease, *not* simply that one of the parties is a tenant or sub-tenant.

QUESTION 39

In 2003, Hubert, a businessman from the town of Casterbridge, decided to purchase a country house in the nearby village of Melchester. Finding a farm cottage with a paddock in a small private road, he offered to buy it from Bertram Belcher, the owner of the farm of which it was part. The sale was completed by deed and contained covenants by Hubert, to contribute to the cost of the upkeep of the road, to maintain the paddock as an open space, to use the premises for residential occupation only and not to alter the external appearance of the cottage. These covenants are expressed to be made with 'the vendor and the owners for the time being of No 2 and No 3 Hazel Lane, being similar properties'.

---

15 This shows how to summarise the relevant law quickly to justify the conclusion reached without wasting time going over material already covered in the answer.

Five years later, Hubert's business has suffered a number of setbacks and he finds he can no longer afford the cottage in Melchester. He sells the property to Durbeyfield, a builder, who announces that he is going to subdivide the cottage into a flat and a workshop, adding a small studio at the back. He has no use for the field and Tess a squatter, starts to build herself a small wooden cabin. Farmer Belcher has already lost several sheep due to holes in the fence and the residents of Hazel Lane wish to resurface the road.

▶ **Discuss.**

How to Answer this Question

❖   Consider the original covenantees; **s 56** of the **LPA**; *Amsprop Trading v Harris* (1997).

❖   Identify the nature of the covenants.

❖   Consider the running of the burden in equity.

❖   What are the requirements of registration?

❖   Note mutual benefit and burden; *Thamesmead Town v Allotey* (1998).

Applying the Law

This diagram shows the rules relating to the transfer of the burden of restrictive freehold covenants.

ANSWER

In this problem, a landowner has entered into various covenants in respect of his land for the benefit of adjoining properties. Unfortunately, when the land subject to those covenants was sold to a third person – that is, someone not a party to the covenants – it appears that the covenants were broken. Consequently, the owners of the adjoining land, who have the benefit of those covenants, will wish to enforce them against the successor in title to the original covenantor. The issue thus revolves around the transmission of the burden of covenants in cases in which there is no leasehold estate.

Before we can deal with the substance of the matter in more detail, two preliminary points must be addressed. First, irrespective of all other matters, only the burden of those covenants that touch and concern the land are capable of being transmitted to purchasers from the original covenantor (*Rogers v Hosegood* (1900)). In our case, there are five covenants and it would seem that all satisfy Lord Oliver's test for 'touching and concerning' put forward in *Swift Investments v Combined English Stores* (1989).[16] The only doubt may be over the covenant to pay for the upkeep of the private road, as this seems to be related to property other than land owned by the surrounding occupants. However, in itself this is not fatal, for the benefit is in the use of this road for surrounding properties, rather than the facility of a well-made road for its own sake. For that reason, this covenant also 'touches and concerns' (see also *Thamesmead Town v Allotey* (1998)). Second, it is trite law (*Austerberry v Corp of Oldham* (1885); *Rhone v Stephens* (1994)[17]) that it is only the burden of restrictive covenants that may run, and then only in equity. It is necessary, therefore, to determine which covenants are restrictive, and this is done by examining their substance, rather than the form in which they are expressed (*Tulk v Moxhay* (1848)). In substance (and one test is whether the covenantor is required to spend money: *Hayward v Brunswick Permanent Benefit Building Society* (1881)), the covenant to contribute to the cost of the road is positive in nature. So, subject to what will be said below about avoidance devices, this covenant cannot be enforced against the purchaser Durbeyfield or the squatter Tess. All the other covenants are restrictive.

In essence, whether the burden of a restrictive covenant will run against a successor in title to the original covenantor will depend on two further factors, as supplemented by the requirements of the **Land Registration Act 2002** or **Land Charges Act 1972** as appropriate. First, at the date of the covenant, the covenantee must have had land capable of benefiting from the covenant. In other words, the burden will run only if the covenant was made for the benefit of other land and that other land is in fact benefited (*London and South Western Railway v Gomm* (1882)). In our problem, there was in existence at the time of the covenant land owned by the covenantee – Farmer Belcher – and it is a question of

---

16 Where an issue is relatively straightforward in a problem, it is good to deal with it quickly to leave time in the exam for covering the complicated issues in more detail.

17 Citing both cases here shows the strength of this rule.

fact whether that land is benefited by these covenants, with the onus on the defendant to prove that it does not (*Whitgift Homes v Stocks* (2001); *Crest Nicholson v McAllister* (2004)). In any event, even if it was thought that these covenants do not benefit land retained by Farmer Eves because they are 'residence' oriented (which is highly unlikely), it is clear that the covenants are also made with the owners of No 2 and No 3 Hazel Lane. Although not parties to the deed, these owners are intended to be benefited by the covenants as parties and, under s56 of the LPA, they are therefore deemed to be in the position of original covenantees (*Amsprop Trading v Harris* (1997)). Their properties are also benefited. Thus, the first criterion is satisfied.

Second, the burden of the restrictive covenant must be annexed to the land of the original covenantor. Fortunately, this condition is easily satisfied, as s79 of the LPA effectively annexes the burden of all restrictive covenants unless a contrary intention is expressed in the deed of creation. There is no contrary intention here and so all four restrictive covenants are annexed.[18]

Presumably, then, the burden of these covenants is capable of running with the land. However, it is inherent in the *Tulk* rules that such covenants – being equitable – in practice will bind only a purchaser of a legal estate who has notice of them. Notice has, of course, been replaced by registration.[19] Thus, if this is registered land, these covenants will be interests that need to be protected by the placing of a notice on the register to bind Durbeyfield, as he is a purchaser of a legal estate. If they are not, they are void against him and all future successors. Likewise, in (the admittedly now rare) case of unregistered land, the covenants must be registered as Class D(ii) land charges to bind a purchaser of a legal estate. In short, only if this requirement is satisfied is Durbeyfield bound in practice by these restrictive covenants. The squatter, Tess, is however in a different position. A squatter is not a purchaser of a legal estate in the land and, therefore, it is immaterial whether the covenants are registered or not (*Re Nisbet and Potts Contract* (1905)). So long as the restrictive covenants fulfill all other requirements, they become proprietary in nature and will bind. The squatter cannot plead lack of registration, because she is not a purchaser and she at least will not be able to build on the paddock.

Finally, we should note that there is one way in which Durbeyfield might be forced to pay for the upkeep of the road, even though this is a positive covenant entered into by his predecessor in title. Under *Halsall v Brizell* (1957), if a person wishes to take the benefit of certain rights, they can be compelled to honour his obligation to contribute to the cost of their provision. This is the principle of mutual benefit and burden: for example, he who

---

18 'Mini-conclusions' like this throughout the answer help to show the reader where the answer has got to and what the position is so far.

19 The discussion of the relevance of notice here shows the origins of the rules whilst recognising the change in approach represented by land registration.

takes the benefit of a private road must take the burden of the obligation to pay for its upkeep. The validity of this principle has been affirmed in *Thamesmead Town v Allotey*, in which it was held that an obligation to contribute to the upkeep of certain common facilities (the burden) was enforceable as the counterpart of enjoying those facilities (the benefit), provided that the person liable actually chose to take advantage of the benefit in practice. So, if Durbeyfield wishes to use the road, he can be made liable for a share of the cost of its maintenance.[20]

Don't be tempted to

Do not look for difficulties where there are none: this question demonstrates that the passing of the 'burden' of a restrictive covenant is reasonably easily achieved although the requirements of registration are vital.

Do not confuse the different positions regarding the running of the burden at common law and in equity.

QUESTION 40

The Boxfield Housing Company has just completed the redevelopment of a large inner city estate in Westhampton. It is Boxfield's intention to ensure that the entire estate should be for residential occupation only and it proposes to impose restrictive covenants on all purchasers to ensure this. It also wishes to impose an obligation on all purchasers to keep the properties in good repair, so as to preserve the character of the neighbourhood. Advise Boxfield of the various methods by which this can be achieved, if at all.

How to Answer this Question

- ❖ Identify the original covenantees and original covenantors.
- ❖ Consider the passing the benefit under s 56 of the LPA and *Federated Homes* (1980); *Crest Nicholson v McAllister* (2004).
- ❖ Consider passing the benefit under a building scheme; *Whitgift Homes v Stocks* (2001).
- ❖ Passing the burden – negative covenants and requirements of registration.
- ❖ Mechanisms to pass positive burdens and their effectiveness.

---

20 It would be easy in the exam to forget about the road covenant once it had been established as being a positive covenant but it is important to consider all aspects of the problem in full.

Applying the Law

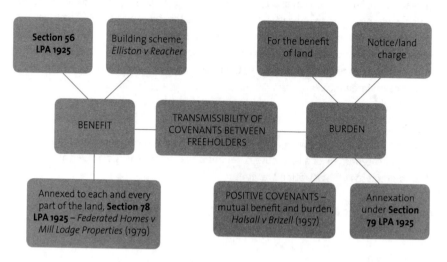

This diagram shows the structure of the rules relating to the transmissibility of covenants between freeholders.

ANSWER

This question invites consideration of the law relating to the transmissibility of covenants between freeholders. Of course, if the Boxfield Housing Company had wished to retain the freehold of this large estate and lease out the properties to tenants on long leases, then the objectives of ensuring only residential occupation and ensuring full repair of the properties could have been achieved with relative ease under the law of leasehold covenants. In those circumstances, the **Landlord and Tenant (Covenants) Act 1995** would have enabled both positive and negative covenants to flow to, and be binding on, successors in title. Of course, it would have meant that Boxfield became responsible for enforcement of the covenants, but at least the objectives could have been achieved.

Clearly, it is the wish of the development company to ensure two things: first, that each purchaser from it is placed under the burden of a covenant against non-residential use and the burden of a positive obligation to repair; and, second, that each purchaser obtains the right to enforce every other purchaser's covenant. There is, in other words, a need to ensure mutuality of obligation between all the purchasers of properties on the estate. In considering these questions, however, it is wise to deal separately with the benefit of the covenants and then the burden.

(A) THE BENEFIT

In this problem, there is both a positive and a negative covenant, although, as regards transmission of the benefit to successors in title from the original covenantee, there is little distinction between the two types of covenant. However, since it is the stated objective to ensure that there is mutuality of obligation amongst the prospective purchasers of the properties, it is clear that we are really concerned with transmission of the benefit in equity. The reason is, quite simply, that the burdens of covenants (at least restrictive ones) can be transmitted in equity only.[21]

Clearly, there is no difficulty with the requirement that the covenants must touch and concern the land (*Rogers v Hosegood* (1900)) or that the covenants do in fact benefit the land (*Re Earl of Leicester* (1863)). Likewise, each intending purchaser will have an estate in the land benefited and the original covenantee will have land capable of benefiting at the time the covenant was made (although note the problem of the last sale, considered below). The difficulty is, however, with the remaining requirement – namely, that the benefit must be transmitted by one of the methods recognised by equity. The position is not straightforward for one simple reason. The developer owns all the land prior to any sale. On sale to the first purchaser, that purchaser will make the required covenants for the benefit of the land retained by the developer. In fact, under the *Federated Homes v Mill Lodge Properties* (1980) interpretation of **s 78** of the **LPA**, as confirmed in *Whitgift Homes v Stocks* (2001), and *Crest Nicholson v McAllister* (2004), the benefit of the covenant will be annexed to each and every part of the retained land. So, when the second purchaser comes along, and buys a piece of the retained land, they will clearly obtain the benefit of the first purchaser's covenants. Their own covenants will, of course, then go to benefit the retained land in the same way as those of the first purchaser. The difficulty is, however, that on this analysis, it is impossible for the first purchaser to gain the benefit of the second purchaser's covenants and, indeed, for the second purchaser to gain the benefit of the third's and so on. In fact, although later purchasers always get the benefit of earlier purchaser's covenants, previous purchasers never get the benefit of those who buy later because, when the subsequent purchasers actually buy the land, the previous purchasers have already bought their plots, which are, consequently, no longer part of the developer's retained land. This problem, which is essentially one of timing, can be solved in two ways.[22]

First, when subsequent purchasers purchase their property, they can expressly include all previous purchasers as original covenantees. This will put those previous purchasers in the same position as the developer. Moreover, it is not necessary to list all such persons, or even make them parties to the deed. **Section 56** of the **LPA 1925** allows the benefit of a covenant to be passed to a third party as an original covenantee provided that they were intended to benefit as a party and were in existence and the time the covenant was made (*Amsprop Trading v Harris* (1997)). There may be some difficulty with the last purchaser from the

---

21 This is an unusual problem question in that it is asking advice on how to achieve a certain end, rather than in establishing what the position of the parties is following certain facts, and it is important to recognise the angle from which you are being asked to discuss the problem.

22 The identification of this practical problem is the key to this question.

developer, as after that purchase the original covenantee (the developer) will have no interest in the land and this is required for transfer of the benefit in equity. However, this problem can be avoided by ensuring that one of the previous purchasers who does have land capable of benefiting is actually made a party to the deed. Of course, this is a cumbersome method of achieving the desired effect, but it would ensure that the benefit of every purchaser's covenant – negative and positive – was transmitted to every other purchaser.

A much simpler way to achieve the same effect is to ensure that the transfer of benefit takes place under a building scheme. This is a rule of limited effect that allows a common vendor (for example, Boxfield) to achieve the mutuality of benefit desired without having to worry about timing, or lack of land for the final sale or even the use of s 56 of the LPA 1925. Under *Elliston v Reacher* (1908), if there is a common vendor, an allotted plan for the building site wherein the land is laid out in lots, a well-defined area (see *Whitgift*) and an intention that each purchaser shall be under the same obligation, then the benefit of all covenants can be given to all purchasers without more and irrespective of the time they purchase their own individual plot. Indeed, as later cases show, it may even be possible to omit some of the *Elliston* conditions, as where there is no allotted plan (*Baxter v Four Oaks Properties* (1965)) and where, as in *Re Dolphin's Conveyance* (1970), there is no common vendor. The advice to Boxfield is, then, to follow this reliable and accepted method of ensuring mutuality of benefit and, in this connection, to ensure that the land that is to be subject to a building scheme is clearly identified so that all purchasers know the extent of their mutual rights (*Whitgift*).

(B) THE BURDEN

This is not inherently difficult; rather, it is that the present state of the law allows the burden to flow in only limited circumstances. Thus, it is only the burden of restrictive covenants that can pass to successors in title of the original covenantor (*Austerberry v Corporation of Oldham* (1885); *Rhone v Stephens* (1994)). To ensure this, the covenant must touch and concern the land, the covenantees must at the time of the covenant have had land capable of benefiting from the covenant and the burden must be attached to the land. The first two requirements are clearly satisfied, as each purchaser will make a covenant with the developer as they purchase the land. (On sale of the last plot, the developer is treated as having land because of the special rules relating to a building scheme.) Moreover, annexation of the covenant will occur automatically under s 79 of the LPA and there will be no problem of this effect being deliberately excluded. Of course, if the covenants are to bind successors in title from the original purchasers/covenantors, they must be either protected by a notice on the register in registered land or Class D(ii) land charges in unregistered land. The developer must ensure this takes place as otherwise the covenants will be unenforceable after the first sale of each burdened plot.

As to the positive covenant to repair, there is little the developer can do. Of course, as suggested at the outset, it could decide to let the property as a leasehold development and rely on the rules relating to leasehold covenants. In fact, even if the purchasers were later to enfranchise their leaseholds, the covenants would still be binding. However, this is not usually the object of a developer who does not wish to become a managing landlord.[23] Neither is there any scope for the doctrine of mutual benefit and burden under *Halsall v Brizell* (1957) and *Thamesmead Town v Allotey* (1998). That principle applies only in cases in which there is some shared utility or service, such as a road or sewer. It would be possible for each original covenantor/purchaser (who, of course, is under the obligation to repair as matter of contract) to extract a covenant to repair from any purchaser from them, thus creating a chain of covenants. Of course, this 'chain of indemnity' is only as strong as its weakest link and depends on the ability and desire of the original covenantor to impose such an obligation on a successor.[24] A final chance – at least if this were registered land – would be for each purchaser of a plot to permit the entry of a restriction against their title, requiring any future purchaser from them to enter a direct covenant with the remaining owners to pay for the upkeep of the property. Such a covenant would then be a condition of purchasing the land. This would work, but it is cumbersome and might well deter prospective purchasers from buying from Boxfield in the first place.

In essence then, it is reasonably straightforward for Boxfield to achieve the desired effect of giving each purchaser a right to sue on these covenants. The burden is, however, more problematical and it is only the burden of the restrictive covenants that could be guaranteed to run, a rule that has been confirmed in *Rhone v Stephens*.

QUESTION 41

Tastee Ltd, a frozen food manufacturer, owns large premises on an industrial estate just outside Grandtown. Title is unregistered. In 1995, it decides to sell off parts of its property in order to meet mounting company debts. Unit 1 is sold to Michael, who covenants not to carry on any trade or business in food manufacture on the site and to require his staff to use the catering facilities established by Tastee Ltd on the estate. Later that year, Tastee Ltd sells Unit 2 to Neil on a seven-year lease in writing. Neil makes identical covenants as to those made by Michael and immediately sub-lets the property to Otto by a lease in writing on the same terms. Otto has since inherited a fortune and makes a gift of the premises to his nephew Henry, a major confectionary manufacturer. Subsequently, Michael sells his property to Priscilla who begins to make birthday cakes and opens a small cafeteria for her staff. Meanwhile, Tastee Ltd has sold its remaining property to Titanic Foods Inc, which immediately contemplates litigation. Unfortunately, Neil has disappeared and it transpires that none of these covenants were registered.

▶ Advise how would your advice differ if the covenants had been registered?

23 The analysis of this alternative solution shows creativity which will be given credit in the exam.
24 Recognising the practical limitations of a valid 'legal' solution shows that you are analysing the law throughout, rather than simply describing it.

How to Answer this Question

❖   Do the covenants that touch and concern the land?

❖   Is it possible that burden and/or the benefit may run with the land?

❖   Note the lack of privity of estate in a *pre-1996 lease*.

❖   Consider the requirements of registration and effect – purchasers and others.

Answer Structure

This diagram shows how to apply the rules relating to restrictive covenants to the food manufacture and cafeteria covenants.

ANSWER

It is clear that in this problem there are difficulties concerning both the transfer of the benefit and the transfer of the burden to successors in title of the original parties in respect of covenants affecting freehold land. In order to consider this problem in detail, it is first necessary to determine the nature of these two covenants – the covenant not to carry on any food manufacture and the covenant to ensure that staff working on the burdened land eat at the covenantee's cafeteria. The first point is whether these covenants touch and concern the land. There is no difficulty with the covenant restrictive of use, as this is a type of covenant often employed to control the use of land (*Re Gadd* (1966)). On the other hand, there is a serious doubt whether the covenant to use the cafeteria of the covenantee does touch and concern the land. It is doubtful whether it affects the value or mode of use of the land (*Swift Investments v Combined English Stores* (1989)) and appears to be only personal in nature. If this is the case, then this particular covenant can bind only the original parties, being Michael and Neil. It is a matter of contract. In addition, if, as a matter of construction, Otto's covenant with Neil in the sub-lease was intended to be made with Tastee Ltd (the head landlord) under s 56 of the Law of Property Act 1925, Otto will be bound in contract with Tastee as well as Neil (s 56 applies even to covenants that do not touch and concern). That apart, this covenant binds no successor in title, being personal in nature. So, Priscilla cannot be sued on this covenant even if it were negative and fulfilled all the other conditions relating to the transmission of the burden of freehold covenants (or leasehold covenants in a pre-1996 lease). Likewise, its benefit cannot be transferred automatically to Titanic Foods under property law principles when it buys the original covenantee's land. Of course, the benefit of it can be expressly assigned as a matter of contract, under the rule that contractual benefits can be assigned personally.[25]

That leaves us, then, with the restrictive covenant against certain types of user. First, does the benefit of this run in equity to Titanic Foods? (Note the position at law is not relevant as the burden of the covenant can only be transmitted in equity and thus the claimant must sue in equity.[26]) For the benefit to run in equity, the claimant must have some estate in the land within s 78 of the LPA 1925 and the covenant must have benefited land of the original covenantee. The fact of benefit will be presumed (*Whitgift Homes v Stocks* (2001); *Crest Nicholson v McAllister* (2004)) unless the contrary is shown. In any event, there is clear benefit within the definition of *Re Gadd* because the covenant affects the mode of use of the land. There is no difficulty with either of these conditions. In addition, however, the benefit of the covenant must have been transmitted in a method accepted by equity. In this case, there is clearly no building scheme and no evidence of an express assignment of the benefit. We must, therefore, rely on annexation. Clearly, there has been no express annexation but this is much less important after the decision of *Federated Homes v Mill Lodge Properties* (1980), which makes it clear that this covenant will be statutorily annexed under s 78 of the LPA unless the covenant contains a contrary intention, which this does not. In fact, the covenant is attached to each and every part of the land, so it is not only Titanic Foods that can enforce the covenant, but also Neil and Henry, the first of whom purchased an estate in part of the benefited land before Michael's covenant and the second is an occupier of that land entitled to the benefit of a restrictive covenant within s 78 of the LPA 1925. However, it is likely that only Titanic Foods will wish to enforce this covenant and Neil (if he could be found) will be prevented from doing so unless Henry refuses to act.

....

25 The personal nature of this covenant makes the solution here quite straightforward – it is important not to look for 'more' in a question than is really there.

26 This demonstrates to the examiner that the writer is aware of these rules without wasting time going through them when they cannot help in the instant case.

Second, what of the burden of this covenant, for it appears that it has been broken in respect of both Unit 1 and Unit 2? Turning first to Unit 1,[27] can this restrictive covenant bind Priscilla? It seems clear that the conditions required to give the burden of this covenant a proprietary nature have been satisfied. On the one hand, at the time of the covenant, there was land owned by the covenantee (Tastee Ltd) that was capable of benefiting from the covenant, as required by *London and South Western Railway v Gomm* (1882). Similarly, the burden of the covenant appears to have been annexed to the land under s 79 of the LPA 1925 there is no contrary intention expressed. So, the covenant is proprietary within the rules of *Tulk v Moxhay* (1848). However, this means only that the covenant is *capable* of binding a successor in title to the original covenantor, not that it actually does so. In order for it to bind a purchaser of a *legal* estate in the land – which presumably Priscilla is – it must be registered as a Class D(ii) land charge in unregistered land. We are told that it is not and so even this covenant is not binding on her, nor can it be binding on any subsequent purchasers having been statutorily voided by the Land Charges Act 1972 Obviously, if the covenant had been registered, the position would have been the reverse.

Third, what of the successors in title to Unit 2, being Neil and now Henry (via a gift of Otto's lease)? The position concerning whether the covenant is proprietary is, not surprisingly, the same as with Unit 1: the covenant was made for the benefit of land of the covenantee and it is annexed to that land. However, it also is unregistered. Yet, in this case it is not necessarily the case that the covenant is void for lack of registration. Under s 4 of the LCA 1972 a Class D(ii) land charge is void for lack of registration against a purchaser for money or money's worth of a legal estate in the land. When Neil acquires the land, he acquires it by virtue of a lease in writing – not by deed – so he purchases only an equitable estate.[28] Moreover, Henry does not even purchase the land, for he obtains the land by gift. Consequently, both Neil and Henry are bound by the covenant even though it may not be registered. Of course, had registration occurred, this would make the covenant safe against any future purchaser of a legal estate, but it is not necessary on these facts.

Finally, for the sake of completeness, it should be noted that Neil could enforce all covenants against Otto, his tenant, under privity of contract. Likewise, Tastee Ltd, and then Titanic Foods, can proceed to forfeit Neil's lease for breach of covenant if the lease contained a right of re-entry. Subject to the normal safeguards surrounding forfeiture,

---

27 If you are clear and precise about exactly what you are considering and when, it makes the answer easier to follow for the examiner, and also makes it more likely that you will not miss an issue.

28 Sometimes where a problem question focuses on a particular topic, here, freehold covenants, it is easy to forget about formality and registration rules. It is a good habit to check whether these have been complied with at each and every stage in all problem questions.

this would terminate Henry's occupation also and would result in de facto enforcement of the covenant against user (*Pennell v Payne* (1995)).

Don't be tempted to

Do not consider the burden and the benefit together. Deal with them separately. The claimant can sue if they have the benefit, and the defendant is liable if they have the burden (and there has been a breach). However, both these need to be true in order for there to be an action on the covenant.

The Law of Mortgages

INTRODUCTION

There is no doubt that, for the ordinary person, the purchase of a house is their most direct contact with the law of real property. For this event most people require a mortgage, and the subsequent repayment of the mortgage becomes one of their most pressing economic concerns. However, the use of the mortgage as a device to *acquire* property is a relatively modern development. In fact, for so long as people have been capable of owning land (or more precisely, an interest in it), the mortgage has been a way of converting a fixed economic asset (the land) into a flexible economic asset (its monetary value). The mortgage is, in essence, a way of realising and releasing the capital value of the land. Fundamentally, therefore, a mortgage is a security for a loan. This rather bland statement hides a multitude of consequences, not least the idea that a mortgage – being a proprietary right – is subject to controls not otherwise found in 'ordinary' loan contracts. Indeed, one of the most frequent examination questions asks the student to assess the extent to which a mortgage really is a right in property or just another species of contract.

Checklist ✔

In order to deal with mortgage issues, three reasonably distinct areas have to be addressed. First, how are mortgages created, both legal and equitable, and are there any specific reasons for choosing a particular method? Second, what are the rights of a mortgagor (the borrower) under a mortgage and in particular what is the nature and extent of the 'equity of redemption'? Third, what are the rights of the mortgagee (the lender) under a mortgage and what remedies may be suitably employed in the event of a defaulting mortgagor? These questions largely depend on the application of traditional equitable principles, as supplemented by statute where appropriate. A good knowledge of case law is invaluable.

QUESTION 42

Analyse the methods by which legal and equitable mortgages might be created since 1925. What was the purpose of the 1925 reforms?

How to Answer this Question

The following areas need to be discussed:

- ❖ definition of a mortgage – *Santley v Wilde* (1899);
- ❖ the use of the charge;
- ❖ ss 85 and 86 of the LPA 1925; s 23 of the LRA 2002;
- ❖ s 53(1)(c) of the LPA 1925;
- ❖ *Walsh v Lonsdale* (1882); s 2 of the Law of Property (Miscellaneous Provisions) Act 1989;
- ❖ proprietary estoppel;
- ❖ purposes of reform – protection of the borrower; the mortgage as a charge;
- ❖ ease of creation.

Applying the Law

This diagram shows the different methods of creating mortgages.

ANSWER

All land has an economic value, and a mortgage is one of the most effective ways by which an owner may realise it. Although today the mortgage is most commonly employed to enable the purchase of land in the first place, the true nature of a mortgage is that it is a lender's security for money lent to the borrower. Of course, the mortgage is much more than a simple contract of loan, for the mortgagee will acquire an interest in the land over which the mortgage operates. In technical terms, a mortgage is regarded as a conveyance of an estate in the land to the mortgagee, with a provision that the mortgagee's interest shall lapse upon repayment of the loan plus interest and costs, although this is no longer the way in which mortgages are actually created. It is one of the most important aspects of the mortgage that the lender obtains not only a right to have the money repaid but also a proprietary interest in the land charged as security for that loan. However, as well as being a powerful form of security for a lender, a mortgage also has advantages for the borrower or mortgagor. It is a general principle of the law of property that 'once a mortgage always a mortgage', which effectively means that the borrower has a right of full access to his property once the loan secured on it has been repaid. In other words, the proprietary nature of the mortgage lasts only for so long as the debt remains outstanding. Thus, the mortgagee's remedies (which can be proprietary or contractual in nature) only endure so long as the borrower owes money.

Before 1925, if an owner of a legal or equitable interest in land sought to raise money on security of that land, the borrower's interest in the property was usually conveyed in full to the lender. If a fee simple was mortgaged, a fee simple was transferred, and so on. In his turn, the mortgagee promised to re-convey the estate on repayment of principal, interest and costs. Moreover, originally, not only did the mortgagee have the actual estate of the borrower vested in them, the contract also made provision for the lender to retain that interest if the borrower failed to repay the loan on the date stipulated in the contract. This date, known as the 'legal date of redemption', became crucial, and the consequences for the borrower of missing payment on that date were severe: the borrower lost their estate entirely. Fortunately, equity was soon to intervene. Adopting the policy position of 'once a mortgage always a mortgage', equity developed the 'equity of redemption' and its counterpart, the 'equitable right to redeem'. Essentially, this meant that the borrower was entitled to a re-conveyance of their property should they pay the full charges due under the mortgage, even though the legal date for payment had passed. In fact, this was equity's way of ensuring that a mortgage really was security over the land, and not an easy method by which a creditor could obtain the property of someone in debt. Likewise, equity took the view that if a mortgagee went into possession of the property in pursuance of the right they had been granted (which, of course, they were perfectly entitled to do), they should be called to account strictly for any rent and profits that could have been earned by the land. These rents and profits were held for the borrower and could then reduce the mortgage debt. This effectively meant the end of possession as a remedy, except in cases of last resort. This then was the background to the changes made by the Law of Property Act (LPA) 1925 to the methods by which mortgages could be created.[1]

The general principle underlying the 1925 property reforms is that, as far as possible, the owner of land should retain the fullest interest possible in their own property even when seeking a mortgage of it. Hence, since 1926, freeholds can no longer be mortgaged by a conveyance of the fee simple to the mortgagee and the mortgagee is limited to receiving some lesser right in the land. With obvious and necessary modifications, this principle also applies to mortgages of leaseholds.

The position of legal mortgages of freeholds is now as follows. In respect of *unregistered land only*,[2] under s 85(1) of the LPA 1925, there are two methods only of creating a legal mortgage of a freehold. First, the borrower may demise a term of years absolute to the lender and no mortgage may take effect by absolute conveyance of the legal estate (s 85(2)). In effect, this is the granting of a long lease to the mortgagee with a provision for cesser on redemption (that is, that the term of years shall cease when the loan is repaid). In the typical case, the term granted is usually long, such as 3,000 years. The demised term will also fix a contractual date for redemption, being the legal right to redeem, and that is usually six months after the date of the mortgage or later if the mortgage is payable by instalment. However, as was the case before 1926, the mortgagor has an equitable right to redeem on the payment of the loan at any time after this legal date has passed. The clear effect of these provisions is that the mortgagor retains their legal fee simple and the mortgage is more clearly regarded as the security for a loan, although all of the pre-1926 rights of the mortgagee are preserved and, of course, the mortgagee still has *some* proprietary interest in the land by virtue of their term of years.[3] Moreover, this approach has one major practical advantage. Since 1925, it has been possible for the mortgagor to create further legal mortgages of their land, in order to raise further sums. So, because the mortgagor retains the legal fee simple, it is perfectly possible to grant another mortgage for another term to a second lender, as where the first mortgage was for a relatively small sum. The second term granted will necessarily be longer than the first, so as to give the second mortgagee a notional legal interest in the property distinct from that of the first mortgagee. The net effect of these provisions is that the mortgagor always retains final legal title to their property, irrespective of the number of mortgages created and, of course, that every mortgagee gains some legal estate in the land. This has enhanced the basic principle of 'once a mortgage always a mortgage'.

....

1   In a question like this, it is always useful to give background to the reforms being discussed to put your discussion into some context.
2   Always be clear about the scope of the rules that you are discussing.
3   Although this question does not specifically ask whether the reforms meet their purpose, approaching your analysis from this angle is a good way to integrate both aspects of the question into the answer.

The second method of creating a mortgage of a legal freehold of unregistered land since 1925 is the charge by deed expressed to be by way of legal mortgage. This is an invention of s 87 of the LPA 1925: the legal charge is simply a statutory form of mortgage that is easier and less expensive to execute than a formal demise of a term of years. In fact, the legal charge is the main method of mortgaging legal estates currently in use. Under s 87, this charge must be made by deed and it must be expressed to be by way of legal mortgage but, that done, it is clear that a legal chargee (a lender) gets exactly the same protection, powers and remedies as if they had been given a term of 3,000 years in the normal way (s 87 of the LPA; *Regent Oil Company v Gregory* (1996)). For all practical purposes, therefore, the legal charge is as effective as a mortgage by way of demise of term of years. It is, however, cheaper, shorter and more efficient. Consequently, in respect of registered land – which, of course, now comprises the majority of titles – the **Land Registration Act 2002** provides that the charge is the only way of mortgaging a legal estate in registered land (s 23 of the LRA 2002) and that it must be registered to complete the legal formalities (**Sched 2** to the **LRA 1925**). In reality, the mandatory use of the charge for registered land merely reflects the practical position before the **2002 Act**.

As far as leaseholds are concerned, the position is substantially similar. Before 1925, the leaseholder (the tenant) would assign their lease to the mortgagee just as the freeholder would transfer their fee simple. Now, however, by virtue of s 86 of the LPA 1925, a legal mortgage of a leasehold of *unregistered title* can be created by two methods only. The first is the charge by deed expressed to be by way of legal mortgage. This is effectively the same as in the case of freeholds. The second is by a sub-lease for a term of years to the mortgagee. This sub-lease will necessarily be shorter than the term of years that the leaseholder actually has and, in practice, the mortgagee's term will be ten days shorter than the original leaseholder's. This is to ensure that the leaseholder can grant subsequent legal mortgages of their leasehold by creating a term longer than the first mortgagee's but shorter than their own. Once again, any attempt to avoid these provisions by assigning a lease will operate only as a sub-lease for a term shorter than that of the tenant (*Grangeside Securities v Collingwood Securities Ltd* (1964)). Of course, as far as registered leasehold titles are concerned, the charge method is now compulsory (s 23 of the LRA 2002).

Turning now to equitable mortgages, these can be split conveniently into two categories. First, it may well be that the borrower only has an equitable interest and it necessarily follows that any mortgage of that equitable interest will itself be equitable. The LPA 1925 and the LRA 2002 have not affected this matter to any great extent[4] and mortgages of equitable interests (such as a beneficiary's rights under a trust) are still carried into effect by a conveyance of the whole equitable interest to the mortgagee. This will, of course, be

---

4   As well as showing what the reforms of 1925 onwards did achieve, it is important to outline what they did not do, in order to demonstrate the breadth of any changes.

accompanied by a provision for re-transfer when the loan is repaid (*William Brandt v Dunlop Rubber* (1905)). As far as formality requirements are concerned, there is no need to use a deed, but because this mortgage will amount to a disposition of a subsisting equitable interest (that is, that of the mortgagor), it must comply with s 53(1)(c) of the LPA. This requires the mortgage of the equitable interest to be in writing, on penalty of voidness, unless saved by estoppel (*Kinane v Conteh* (2005)).[5]

The second issue is the creation of the informal mortgage or, in other words, a mortgage that does not comply with the formality requirements necessary for the creation of a legal mortgage. As with many other equitable interests in land, an informal mortgage commences life as a contract to create a legal mortgage that, if capable of specific performance, will be treated as an equitable mortgage along the same lines as equitable leases in *Walsh v Lonsdale* (1882). It is vital, however, for this informal mortgage that the contract be in writing under s 2 of the LPA 1989 (*United Bank of Kuwait v Sahib* (1997)).[6] It must also, of course, be capable of specific performance, although that requirement is usually met in the case of contracts concerning land. If the requirements of a written contract and specific performance are met, the contract to grant the mortgage will be treated in itself as an equitable mortgage – *Parker v Housefield* (1834) – although usually the money will have to have been advanced before equity will intervene. Prior to the 1989 Act, it was also possible to create an equitable mortgage by deposit of title deeds with the lender. The deposit of the borrower's deeds was treated as both evidence of the contract and performance of that contract under the then s 40 of the LPA (*Re Wallis* (1974)). This was a very informal but relatively efficient way of creating a mortgage. After 1989, contracts need to be in writing and this cannot be presumed from the deposit of title deeds (*Sahib*). As such, it is clear that this method of creating equitable mortgages by deposit is now defunct. However, it may well be possible to treat the deposit of title deeds as a form of proprietary estoppel. As we know from *Taylor Fashions v Liverpool Victoria Trustees* (1982), if one person promises an interest in land to another and that is relied upon to their detriment, equity will enforce the promise and give effect to the claim of the promisee. Thus, if a lender has actually advanced money on the basis of a promise (represented by the deposit of title deeds), it is possible that the mortgage will be enforced under estoppel despite the absence of any formality, provided that there is evidence of unconscionability. This was the result in *Kinane v Conteh*, the first clear example of an estoppel mortgage. Of course, equitable mortgages do suffer from the vulnerability of all equitable rights in land, viz, the prospect of being lost if the land is sold to a purchaser of a legal estate: s 29 of the LRA 2002. Finally, mention must also be made of the equitable charge, a completely informal way of securing a loan over property. This requires no special form of words, only an intention to charge property with a debt

---

5   'Side points' like this show that you understand the inevitable limitations of formality requirements.

6   You need to be aware that it is not just the 1925 reforms, and the 2002 Act that have had profound effects on the law in this area.

(*National Provincial and Union Bank of England v Charnley* (1924)). Such a method is extremely precarious and is rarely used in either commercial or residential mortgages.

It is apparent, then, that the 1925 legislation introduced a significant change in the way that mortgages could be created and this has been taken further by the LRA 2002. Relying on the principle of 'once a mortgage always a mortgage', legal estates could be mortgaged only by giving the lender some subsidiary right in the land, not a transfer of the borrower's entire interest, and this is now largely achieved through the device of the charge by deed. Not only does this simplify the process of mortgage creation, but it also emphasises the nature of mortgage as a security. In addition, it allows the borrower to create successive legal mortgages in a way that gives protection and security to those successive mortgagees as well as bringing certainty for the mortgagor.

NOTES

This is as straightforward a question as it is possible to get on mortgages. Good use of case law will reinforce knowledge of the statutory provisions. Be clear that a mortgage over registered land will not actually exist as a legal charge until it is entered on the register, as with all dispositions of a registered estate: ss 25 and 27 of and Sched 2 to the LRA 2002.

> **Aim Higher   ★**
> Include an explanation of why since the **LRA 2002** the only form of legal mortgage is the charge by deed method.

QUESTION 43

To what extent do the rights of a mortgagor under a legal mortgage provide sufficient protection for the borrower?

How to Answer this Question

The following areas need to be discussed:

❖ the nature of the mortgagor's rights – the legal right to redeem; the equitable right to redeem and the equity of redemption;

❖ the doctrine of clogs and fetters – options; collateral advantages; oppressive terms; unconscionable conduct; *Jones v Morgan* (2002).

Applying the Law

This diagram shows the rights of the mortgagor under a legal mortgage.

ANSWER

The mortgage is one of the most versatile and unique of property law concepts. It is, on the one hand, a simple contract of loan between lender and borrower and, on the other, it creates a valuable and powerful proprietary right in land. It is a concept governed by contract law and property law and the different philosophies of each can sometimes cause confusion and difficulties. However, since 1925, the very way in which mortgages can be created is designed to reinforce the essential nature of a mortgage as a security charged on land for a loan.

In the normal course of events, a legal mortgage of a registered estate will be created by the execution of a legal charge by way of mortgage: s 23 of the Land Registration Act 2002 This is deemed to be the creation of a proprietary interest under s 87 of the Law of Property Act 1925 and has the same effect as if the mortgage was created by the old method of demise. This means that the mortgagor retains their interest in the land subject, of course, to the rights of the mortgagee. At the same time, as the mortgage is also a contract of loan, there are stipulations relating to the repayment of the loan and certain remedies that the mortgagee may pursue in the event of default on the loan. However, the mortgage remains at all times a loan and this means that the mortgagor does have a considerable degree of protection, both of their interest in the land and in respect of their position under the loan contract.

As a matter of contract, the mortgagor has a contractual right to redeem on the date specified in the contract. Traditionally, this was six months from the date of the mortgage, but may be at any date specified by the parties and will often be later in instalment mortgages. At one time, if the mortgagor did not redeem on this date, they lost their security even though redemption could have been made at a later date. However, equity soon developed the maxim that 'once a mortgage always a mortgage' and allowed redemption of the mortgage after this date, on payment of principal, interests and costs (*Thornborough v Baker* (1675)). This became known as the 'equitable right to redeem' and, without doubt, is a valuable part of the mortgagor's protection under a mortgage. In fact, the equitable right to redeem is just part of the wider rights that the mortgagor has under the mortgage. In equity, the mortgagor is protected by the equity of redemption.[7] This equity of redemption represents the sum total of the mortgagor's rights in the property: in essence, the residual rights of ownership that the mortgagor has, both in virtue of his paramount legal estate in the land and the protection that equity affords them (*Re Sir Thomas Spencer Wells* (1933)). The equity of redemption is valuable in itself for it represents the mortgagor's right to the property (or its monetary equivalent) when the mortgage is discharged or the property sold. In fact, on subsequent mortgages, the second and third lenders are able and willing to grant further loans precisely because the mortgagor has this valuable right. The equity of redemption is a proprietary right in itself and may be dealt with by the mortgagor as such.

The inherent quality of the equity of redemption is demonstrated by the fact that equity will intervene to protect the mortgagor and their equity of redemption against encroachment by the mortgagee: *Jones v Morgan* (2002). As noted above, equity regards the mortgage as a loan, which can be redeemed, and not as an opportunity for the lender to acquire the mortgagor's property. This protection manifests itself in various ways.[8]

First, it is a general principle that a mortgage cannot be made irredeemable: it is a security, not a conveyance, and the right to redeem cannot be limited *pro tanto* to certain

---

7   It is important to explain clearly the difference between the equity of redemption and the equitable right to redeem.

8   Using sentences like this helps the examiner to follow your structure and allows a clear presentation of the arguments.

people or certain periods of time (*Re Wells*). However, a provision postponing the date of redemption may be valid where the mortgage is not otherwise harsh and unconscionable, so long as the right to redeem is not made illusory (*Knightsbridge Estates v Byrne* (1939); *Fairclough v Swan Brewery* (1912)). Again, a provision in a mortgage that provides that the property shall become the mortgagee's or which gives the mortgagee an option to purchase the property is void (*Samuel v Jarrah Timber* (1904); *Jones v Morgan*). The rationale is, of course, that the mortgagor needs protection when negotiating for a loan, often being in a vulnerable position. Thus, an option to purchase given to the mortgagee in a separate and independent transaction can be valid, as not forming part of the mortgage itself (*Reeve v Lisle* (1902)).

Second, as a matter of principle, the mortgagor should be able to redeem the mortgage and have the mortgagee's rights extinguished free from any ancillary conditions in the mortgage other than the payment of principal, interests and costs. The basic principle is, again, the mortgage as a security that ends when its reason – the money – is repaid. Thus, on several occasions the courts have struck down 'collateral advantages' made in favour of a mortgagee, as where the mortgage contract stipulates that the mortgagor should fulfill some other obligation as a condition of the mortgage. An example is where the mortgagor promises to buy all their beer or supplies from the mortgagee. At one point, such collateral advantages were uniformly struck down, as being a clog on the equity of redemption (cf *Bradley v Carritt* (1903)). However, it is now clear that there is no objection to a collateral advantage that ceases when the mortgage is redeemed (*Santley v Wilde* (1899)). This is a matter of contract between the parties and, provided that the terms are not unconscionable or do not in fact restrict the right to redeem, they will be valid (*Biggs v Hoddinot* (1898)). Indeed, at least with commercial mortgages made between equal parties at arm's length, *Kreglinger v New Patagonia Meat and Cold Storage Company* (1914) suggests that a collateral advantage that does continue after redemption (for example, a continuing obligation to take supplies from the mortgagee) may be acceptable so long as the mortgagor's property returns to the mortgagor in the same form that it was mortgaged. Clearly, this is a flexible principle that can be used to invalidate harsh, unreasonable terms as the situation demands. On the other hand, courts are aware that the parties' business dealings should be upheld as far as possible in the absence of unconscionable conduct. (Such an approach can be seen in the recent case of *Brighton & Hove City Council v Audus* (2009).)[9]

Third, the court has the power to strike down any term that, in effect, destroys the equity of redemption. Thus, a high interest rate might render the mortgagor's equity of redemption valueless (*Cityland and Property (Holdings) v Dabrah* (1968)) or the terms of the mortgage might be so oppressive as to make it harsh and unconscionable, although it

---

9   Putting in extra information like this shows that you are aware of the context of recent case law.

must be more than merely unreasonable or unfair (*Multiservice Bookbinding v Marden* (1979); *Jones v Morgan*).

Fourth, the mortgage may be struck down in whole or in part on the ground that the mortgagor's consent was obtained by undue influence.[10] It is rare for the mortgagee themselves to have exerted the undue influence, but the mortgagee can be tainted with the undue influence of the person who persuaded the mortgagor to sign (such as a co-mortgagor, a husband or lover). This will occur if the person exercising the undue influence can be said to be the agent of the mortgagee (rare) or if the mortgagee has notice of the undue influence (*Barclays Bank v O'Brien* (1994); *Royal Bank of Scotland v Etridge* (2002)). A mortgagee tainted by 'actual' undue influence (that is, the undue influence is proven on the facts) is, without more, unable to enforce the mortgage (or such provisions as are tainted), whereas in cases of 'presumed undue influence' (in which the undue influence arises by presumption because of the relationship between the parties), the mortgagee will not be prevented from enforcing the mortgage unless the mortgage was to the 'manifest disadvantage' of the claimant (*National Westminster Bank v Morgan* (1985); *Royal Bank of Scotland v Etridge*). In recent years, 'undue influence' has been a favourite defence for a mortgagor resisting the possession claims of the mortgagee and recent case law (especially *Etridge* in the House of Lords) has sought to confine the plea to manageable and defensible limits.

Finally, it is also clear that mortgages, being contracts, are subject to normal contractual rules governing credit relationships and related matters. The vast majority of first mortgages on residential property offered by banks, building societies, local authorities and other similar lenders will be regulated by the Financial Services and Markets Act 2000.[11] Even if the mortgage is not covered by that Act – for example because it is a second mortgage or mortgage of business premises – if the borrower is an individual, he or she might still gain protection from s 140A–C of the Consumer Credit Act 2006 if the court is satisfied that there is an unfair credit relationship between the borrower and the lender. A mortgage transaction may also set aside as being in restraint of trade (*Esso Petroleum v Harper's Garage* (1968)).

All in all then, the mortgagor does benefit from a considerable amount of protection, both by virtue of equity protecting the equity of redemption and by statute and general common law principles applicable to contracts per se. In addition to these, when the mortgagee seeks to exercise their remedies under the mortgage, statute intervenes to

....

10 Strictly speaking, this can be seen as a matter of contract, but it interacts uniquely with the position of mortgagor as both contracting party, and institutional lender.

11 Although a problem question, or indeed an essay, may not ask you to go into detail regarding the consumer protection legislation, it is worth being familiar with the requirements.

restrain, exclude or modify those remedies, particularly in the case of mortgagees seeking to obtain possession by court order of a dwelling house (s 36 of the Administration of Justice Act 1970). The mortgage is, after all, only security for a loan.

NOTES

This is a good question to answer if you know the doctrine of clogs and fetters. A good answer also considers the nature of a mortgage as a contract as well as a security and this is where knowledge of the law of undue influence is vital. The Court of Appeal decisions such as that in *Jones v Morgan* (2001) may signal wider use of the unconscionability rule.

Common Pitfalls

Much of the law in this area is case-based. Answers that do not exhibit sufficient knowledge and use of these suffer for that lack.

QUESTION 44

How extensive are the remedies available to a legal mortgagee?

How to Answer this Question

The remedies of a legal mortgagee need to be discussed:

- ❖ action on the contract for debt, possibly leading to bankruptcy;
- ❖ appointment of a receiver;
- ❖ sale;
- ❖ possession;
- ❖ foreclosure;
- ❖ degree of protection for the mortgagor varies according to the type of mortgage and the circumstances of default.

Applying the Law

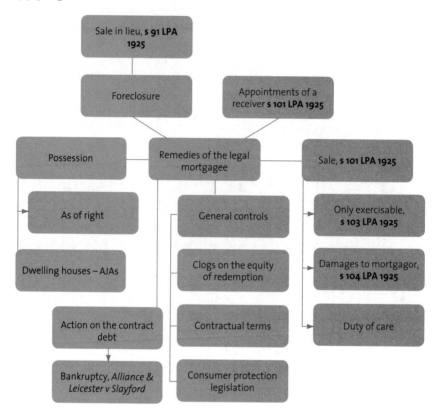

This diagram shows the remedies of the legal mortgagee.

ANSWER

It is trite law that a mortgage is properly to be regarded as security for a loan so that, on repayment of the principal, interest and costs, the property mortgaged returns in full to the mortgagor. However, it is equally apparent that a mortgagee should have some means by which it can protect and/or enforce its security in the case of a breach of any of the terms of the mortgage by the mortgagor. In the usual case, this breach arises from non-payment of sums due under the mortgage, but the mortgagee will also be concerned to protect itself from other breaches, as where a mortgagor in possession sub-lets the property in violation of a stipulation in the mortgage. Fortunately for the mortgagee, the fact that a mortgage is both a contract of loan and springs from the grant of a proprietary right means that the mortgagee enjoys a range of remedies should the mortgagor breach the terms of the mortgage. The particular remedy or remedies employed by the mortgagee (for they are cumulative and not mutually exclusive: *Cheltenham and Gloucester BS v Grant* (1994); *Alliance & Leicester v Slayford* (2001)) will depend on the precise nature of the default of the mortgagor and the requirements of the mortgagee. As explained below, some are more suitable for recovery of unpaid interest, while others are more suitable for recovery of the entire loan and the ending of the charge, either because of non-payment of sums due or for some other default.

The first and most straightforward of the mortgagee's remedies against a defaulting mortgagor arises because the mortgage is a contract of loan between the parties. The mortgagee has an action on the express covenant given by the mortgagor for repayment of the sum due on a certain date plus interest. As soon as this date has passed, the mortgagee may sue for the sum owed and is normally entitled to a payment order for the full amount. Of course, this remedy may be of little practical use if the mortgagor has no funds other than those tied up in the secured property, but it is often an adjunct to possession proceedings against them. It may, however, lead to the mortgagor becoming bankrupt and this, in turn, can lead to a sale of the property at the request of the trustee in bankruptcy (*Alliance & Leicester v Slayford*). This is a useful weapon of last resort if the mortgagee is unable to secure a sale in their own right (for example, because of a *Boland*-type overriding interest).

A second way of recovering the whole sum due and ending the mortgage occurs if the mortgagee should seek to exercise his power of sale. In most cases a mortgage will contain an express power of sale, although by virtue of s 101(1)(i) of the **Law of Property Act 1925** a power of sale is implied into every mortgage made by deed unless a contrary intention appears. This power arises as soon as the legal (contractual) date for redemption has passed or, in the case of instalment mortgages, when one instalment is in arrears (*Twentieth Century Banking v Wilkinson* (1977)). However, under s 103 of the **LPA** the power only becomes exercisable when either: (a) notice requiring payment of the mortgage money has been served and the mortgagor is three months in arrears since the notice; or (b) interest under the mortgage is two months in arrears and unpaid; or (c) the mortgagor has breached some covenant in the mortgage (other than the covenant to pay) or some provision of the **LPA**. These provisions in effect give the mortgagee a power of sale of the property should the mortgagor be in serious default and the result is that the mortgagee receives such money as he is owed if sale proceeds permit. In fact, the sale conveys the land to the purchaser free from the mortgagee's mortgage, all subsequent mortgages (which are paid off in order, before the mortgagor) and the equity of redemption (ss 88 and 113 of the **LPA**) and subject only to any previous mortgages. Obviously, a sale of the mortgaged property is calamitous for the mortgagor, with often only a small percentage of the sale proceeds reaching them after all outstanding liabilities have been settled. Consequently, it is not surprising that equity steps in to mitigate the harshness of this procedure.[12] Thus, the selling mortgagee is under a duty of care to the mortgagor to obtain the best price reasonably obtainable (*Standard Chartered*

---

12   Thus limiting the practical scope of the mortgagees' powers.

Bank v Walker (1982), and see *Medforth v Blake* (2000)), although an open sale by auction, even when prices are low, satisfies this rule (*Cuckmere Brick Co v Mutual Finance* (1971)).[13] If the mortgagee is negligent and thereby obtains a lower price than it would otherwise have obtained, it is liable to the mortgagor (*Cuckmere*) and the mortgagee cannot sell to himself or his agent (*Williams v Wellingborough Council* (1975)). However, this duty is owed to the mortgagor only and not to a person having merely an equitable interest in the property (*Parker-Tweedale v Dunbar* (1990)). Likewise, the mortgagee is not trustee of the power of sale and its motives in choosing to exercise the power of sale are irrelevant.

Usually, of course, the mortgagee will wish to sell the property in order to realise its security and to do this effectively,[14] the property must be sold with vacant possession. In practice, therefore, before sale, a mortgagee may wish to exercise its third remedy: the right of possession. Indeed, taking possession of the mortgaged property can also be used as a method of securing recovery of any outstanding interest on the loan, as where a mortgagee in possession sub-lets or runs the business over which the mortgage exists. Possession then does not necessarily mean the end of the mortgage. At the outset, however, we must be clear that the mortgagee's right to possession is exactly that. By virtue of the way in which mortgages are created, the mortgagee will have an estate in the land and an immediate right to possession of the property the moment the ink is dry on the mortgage, irrespective of any fault on the part of the mortgagor (*Four-Maids v Dudley Marshall* (1957); *Ropaigeleach v Barclays Bank* (1999)), although in the normal course of events the mortgagee will not exercise its right of possession and might even promise not to seek possession unless the mortgagor defaults on the interest repayments or breaches some other term of the mortgage. In fact, there is a positive disincentive for a mortgagee to take possession, as a mortgagee in possession will be called strictly to account for any income generated by its possession (*White v City of London Brewery* (1889)). This means that the mortgagee will be taken to have received not only any actual income generated – which can go towards interest payments – but also any income that it should have received had the property been managed to the high standard expected. Any shortfall will then have to be made up by the mortgagee, who may find that it actually owes money to the mortgagor. This is why most commercial mortgagees desist from seeking possession. This 'protection' for the borrower has been somewhat undermined by the decision of the High Court in *Horsham Properties Group v Clark* (2009).[15]

In the residential context possession is still an option for the mortgagee, often as a prelude to sale. Here, however, the mortgagor is protected from a zealous mortgagee. Under **s 36** of the **Administration of Justice Act (AJA) 1970** (as amended by **s 8** of the

---

13   Although simply relying on a reputable estate agent may not be enough.
14   In practice, possession is not a legal prerequisite to sale.
15   Which highlighted that public interest justifies strong remedies, amongst much else.

AJA 1973), a mortgagee's application for possession of a dwelling house may be suspended, adjourned or postponed by the court, in its discretion, if it appears that the mortgagor would be able to pay within a reasonable period any sums due under the mortgage. Due to s 8 of the AJA 1973 (reversing *Halifax BS v Clark* (1973)),[16] 'any sums due' may be treated only as those instalments missed and not, as most mortgages provide, the whole sum once one mortgage payment is missed. Likewise, the relief is available for endowment mortgages, despite the elliptical wording of the Act (*Bank of Scotland v Grimes* (1985)), although there is some doubt whether the statutory discretion is available if the mortgagor is not actually in default under the mortgage (*Western Bank v Schindler* (1977)) and, certainly, there can be no relief if the possession warrant has been executed (*Bristol and West plc v Dace*). Neither is the power available if the mortgagee takes possession under its common law right without a court order, albeit that this is rare and dangerous for a mortgagee (*Ropaigeleach v Barclays Bank*). In addition, while it is clear that the 'reasonable period' that the mortgagor is given to repay his arrears might actually be the rest of the mortgage – so as to spread the debt evenly (*Middlesbrough Mortgage Corp v Cunningham* (1974); *Cheltenham and Gloucester BS v Norgan* (1996)) – there is no discretion if there is no prospect of the mortgagor making a reasonable attempt to actually repay the accumulated debt, let alone meet future repayments (*First National Bank v Syed* (1991); *Ashley Guarantee v Zacaria* (1993)). However, the courts do show considerable sympathy to mortgagors pleading s 36 of the AJA, and *Cheltenham and Gloucester BS v Norgan* suggests that the court will postpone possession if it appears that the mortgagor will be able to repay at some future time and not within an arbitrary period chosen by the court. Clearly, this is a generous interpretation[17] of s 36 and, while it is understandable given the social utility of protecting residential occupiers, it does compromise significantly the undoubted right of the mortgagee to seek such possession (see also *Quennell v Maltby* (1979)).

The fourth of the mortgagee's remedies may also be used to recover the interest owed rather than ending the mortgage. The mortgagee's right to appoint a receiver is often expressly included in a mortgage but, in any event, such a power will be implied into every mortgage by deed (s 101 of the LPA). Any express power is exercisable according to its terms, although the statutory power becomes exercisable only in those circumstances in which the statutory power of sale becomes exercisable and is often an alternative to that remedy. The great advantage of the appointment of a receiver as opposed to the mortgagee taking possession of the property is that the receiver is deemed to be the agent of the mortgagor, not the mortgagee (*Chatsworth Properties v Effiom* (1971)), with the consequence that any negligence on the part of the receiver is not attributable to the latter.

---

16   The use of this case in this way shows the examiner a good depth of knowledge of the relevant case law.
17   It is always good to express clearly your own view on the case law.

Finally, the mortgagee has a powerful remedy in the event of major default by the mortgagor. The remedy of foreclosure, if successful, will extinguish the equity of redemption and cause the transfer of the property to the mortgagee, entirely free of any rights of the mortgagor. It is one of the peculiarities of a mortgage that this most final of remedies actually becomes exercisable as soon as the legal date for redemption set by the mortgage has passed, although once again it is common practice for mortgagees to covenant not to foreclose without notice and only in respect of specified breaches of the mortgage terms. Essentially, should the need arise, the mortgagee will begin an action in court asking for foreclosure of the mortgage unless the mortgagor repays the sums owed (principal, interest and costs) within a specified time. If the mortgagor fails to do so, the mortgagee will be given an order 'foreclosure nisi', which in effect gives the mortgagor a further period (usually six months) in which to raise the money to pay off the loan. Failing that, the foreclosure nisi will be made absolute and the mortgagor's interest in the property will be extinguished. This is the end of the matter save that, in exceptional circumstances, the court may open a foreclosure absolute and allow the mortgagor to redeem the mortgage at a later date (*Campbell v Holyland* (1877)), although this is very unlikely if the mortgagee has since sold the property to a purchaser with no notice of any previous mortgage. In view of the powerful nature of foreclosure, the court has power under s 91(2) of the LPA to order sale in lieu of a foreclosure (and in other circumstances: *Palk v Mortgage Services Funding* (1993)) and this means that any surplus funds after redemption of the mortgage will be paid to the mortgagor. Obviously, such a solution is desirable where the mortgage debt is far less than the value of the property. As noted above, the effect of a foreclosure is to vest the mortgagor's estate in the mortgagee and to extinguish the mortgage and its terms. Any mortgages made prior to the mortgage foreclosed remain unaffected as they are still binding on the land, although subsequent mortgages will be destroyed. In practice, this means that subsequent mortgagees are given an opportunity to redeem any previous mortgages if foreclosure is likely.

Clearly, then, the mortgagee has a wide range of remedies, albeit that statute provides some relief to the mortgagor. Likewise, we must not forget that a mortgagee is subject to the general rule that there must be no clog on the equity of redemption and credit controls (in the form of s 140A–C of the Consumer Credit Act 2006) if the court is satisfied that there is an unfair credit relationship between the borrower and the lender. Moreover, common law principles of undue influence and restraint of trade are applicable to mortgages as to other loan contracts. Yet, even with these limitations, the bona fide mortgagee who takes security over land for a loan has a considerable array of remedies in the face of a defaulting mortgagor.[18]

---

18 Remember always in a 'how wide' question to give an overall assessment like this.

Aim Higher ★

Emphasise that, here, you are talking about rights, which are not dependent on any default, and remedies, which are normally only exercisable after a default.

Give clear explanations of issues such as the interpretation of the **AJAs**.

QUESTION 45

In 2004 Angus and Coleen combined their life savings of £80,000 in order to purchase No. 1 High Street with the assistance of a mortgage advance of £250,000 provided by the Scotsdale Bank. Title to the house was registered in the name of Coleen subject to a registered charge in favour of the Bank. Angus had agreed to the mortgage and had met with the Bank to discuss this with his own solicitor. The agreement meant that the interest rate was variable at the discretion of the Bank, and in 2007, the Bank quadrupled its interest rate for all customers with red hair, including Coleen.

Angus and Coleen (who had both been contributing to the mortgage) could not make these payments and went on holiday. While they were away, the Scotsdale Bank sent a letter addressed to No. 1 High Street to Coleen, informing her that the Bank proposed to take possession of the house and offer it for sale at auction in three days' time.

A month later Angus returned to discover that the Bank had sold the house for £305,000 to a bidder who turned out to be the brother-in-law of the manager of the local branch of the Bank. Coleen, by this time, had run off with a waiter she met on holiday, and wished to sell keep the proceeds of the sale once the bank had been paid all for herself in order to buy a new property on the Costa Brava.

▶ Advise Angus and Coleen.

How to Answer this Question

❖ Establishment of a common intention constructive trust;
❖ priority;
❖ interest rates – unconscionability, implied term, clog on the equity of redemption;
❖ Process of possession and sale.

Answer Structure

Does Angus have an interest in the property? → Implied trust, *Stack v Dowden* (2008), *Jones v Kernott* (2011)

Does Angus' interest have priority? → Implied waiver, *Paddington BS v Mendelsohn* (1985)

Was Angus' consent brought about through undue influence? → *RBS v Etridge No. 2* (2001)

Is Coleen bound by the mortgage agreement? → Unconscionability

→ Implied term

→ Clog in the equity of redemption

The process of going into possession → As of right, *Four-Maids v Dudley Marshall* (1957)

The sale transaction → Price and duty of care

→ Sale at auction

→ Identity of purchaser

This diagram shows how to apply the rules relating to trusts and mortgages in the situation involving Angus and Coleen.

ANSWER

Angus (A) wishes to establish an interest in the property which takes priority over the Bank's interest. Coleen (C) will wish to maximise the proceeds of sale by challenging the interest rate rise, as well as seeking damages for loss suffered.

ANGUS' INTEREST IN THE PROPERTY

As a preliminary issue, as a result of the registration of Coleen (C) as sole registered owner, A, under the approach outlined in *Stack v Dowden* (2007) and *Jones v Kernott* (2012)

is presumed to have no interest in the property unless an express or implied common intention to the effect that he is to have such an interest can be demonstrated. Although this is a sole names case, and the extent to which *Kernott* etc covers this case is therefore uncertain,[19] we can be fairly sure that A would be entitled to an equitable interest in this property as a result of his contribution to the purchase price and mortgage.

Once it is established that A does have an interest, it is necessary to determine the size of his equitable share, as outlined by Baroness Hale in *Stack*. If no express intention as to the size of the share is demonstrable, then such an intention can be either implied or imputed (*Kernott*). In this case, without information as to the proportions contributed by each to the deposit, or the mortgage, we cannot be certain as to quantity, but given the mutually communal nature of this relationship (see Gardner, and Gardner and Davidson[20]), somewhere in the region of a 50% share seems reasonable.

PRIORITY OVER ANGUS' SHARE

We can conclude therefore that C holds on trust for herself and A. This means that B will have to demonstrate that its charge takes priority over A's interest. From the facts it is not clear that A waived his priority over the bank (it is likely that his interest would otherwise be protected by his actual occupation of the house under **Sch 3, Para 2 LRA 2002**), but such a waiver can be implied (*Paddington BS v Mendelsohn* (1985)). Certainly, A knew of the mortgage and agreed to it and it is likely that such consent would be sufficient to mean that B's charge takes priority over A's interest.

The only potential caveat to this is if A's consent to the mortgage was obtained as a result of C bringing pressure to bear on A such that he was put at a manifest disadvantage to bring the rules of undue influence into play (*RBS v Etridge No. 2* (2001)). It seems unlikely that there was undue influence here given that A had taken independent advice from a solicitor. Even if there was pressure as between A and C however, the steps apparently taken by the Bank in this case mean that they would not be 'tainted' by any undue influence that may have existed. As a result, it seems that B's interest would have priority over A's interest in the property, as a result of his implied waiver.

---

19 Where, as here, it is relatively straightforward to demonstrate that A is likely to have a share in the property, you need to make a judgment as to how much detail to provide in relation to co-ownership issues and the relevant case law, including the uncertainties in that case law.

20 Mentioning academic commentators in an answer like this not only avoids the risk of plagiarising others' ideas, it also shows that you have read around the topic and are aware of the on-going academic debates in the field.

THE INTEREST RATE RISE

The Bank quadrupled their interest rates for all customers with red hair, including C. C herself may wish to challenge this increase on the grounds that it is unconscionable; is in breach of an implied term; is a fetter on the equity of redemption; and/or is regulated by the consumer protection legislation so as to increase her sale proceeds.

(A) UNCONSCIONABILITY

The general principle is that the parties are free to decide whatever mortgage terms they wish. The possible imbalance in bargaining power between borrower and lender has however led both the courts and the legislature to intervene to prevent abuse of this imbalance. Whether *ad hoc* judicial intervention is to be welcomed is another issue entirely.[21]

The first mechanism which is used to achieve such control is found in the power of the court to strike down any term of the mortgage which, combined with conduct in relation to that term, 'shocks the conscience of the court' (*Multiservice Bookbinding v Marden* (1977), *Jones v Morgan* (2001)). The difficulty that C will have in relying on this is that the application of this principle has been strict. *Alec Lobb* (1984) (referred to positively in *Jones v Morgan*) requires that (a) one party was at a serious disadvantage to the other (poverty, ignorance, lack of advice etc); (b) that this weakness was exploited in a morally reprehensible manner; and (c) that the resulting agreement was oppressive. Given that the circumstances in *Jones v Morgan* did not give rise to a sufficient degree of unconscionability to allow the court to intervene, it is highly unlikely that the facts of this case would allow the court to do so either. C appears to have been aware of the nature of a mortgage and there is nothing unconscionable in a term allowing variation of the interest rate *per se*. This term does not itself take advantage of any particular weakness on the part of C. It is the use of this term that appears unconscionable here, but the rule in *Mulitservice* and *Jones v Morgan* seems to require that both the term itself, and the use of it, are morally reprehensible.

As a result, an argument based on general unconscionability which is so severe as to be morally reprehensible does not appear to be one with a high prospect of success.

(B) IMPLIED TERM

The second route that C may wish to take here relates to the controversial rule outlined in *Nash v Paragon Finance* (2001). The mortgage agreement in that case also contained a term allowing unfettered interest rate adjustments on the part of the mortgagee. Here it

---

21 Although this is a problem question, there is no reason not to question the merits of the rules being applied, as long as you leave enough time to cover all the relevant issues.

was held that '*the discretion to vary interest rates should not be exercised dishonestly, for an improper purpose, capriciously or arbitrarily*' (paragraph 32). By way of example, Dyson LJ suggests that, '*An example of a capricious reason would be where the lender decided to raise the rate of interest because its manager did not like the colour of the borrower's hair*' (paragraph 31).[22]

It is unnecessary here to consider the issue of Wednesbury unreasonableness in the context of interest rates rises since B's conduct goes beyond unreasonableness into the realm of capricious behaviour.

Even if breach is established, it is far from clear how the court would remedy this breach, and what affect this would have on the C's current position. In *Paragon Finance* it was concluded that there was no breach of the implied term so no assistance can be derived from that case, nor from *Paragon Finance v Pender* (2005). From the general principles relating to breach of contract however we can conclude that C would be entitled to an award for damages to compensate her for any loss suffered as a result of the breach of the implied term. Given that she does not appear to have paid B any of the increased interest, she has suffered no loss in that respect. Any loss which she has suffered is as a result of receiving less of the surplus money after sale (see **Section 105 LPA 1925**) as a result of calculating the interest owed on the basis of the higher rate. If £250,000 was insufficient to cover the money owed plus interest, then it can be concluded that C's debt outstanding after sale would be reduced to account for the breach.

It may be possible for C to recover any consequential loss suffered from not being able to pay the mortgage instalments as a result of the interest rate rise. She would need to demonstrate on the balance of probabilities that but for the interest rate rise she would not have fallen into arrears and therefore the bank's power of sale under **Section 101 LPA 1925** would not have arisen (see below). If she could demonstrate this, then she may be able to recover damages for the difference in value between the value of the house, and the sale price.

(C) CLOG ON THE EQUITY OF REDEMPTION

The first thing to note about the clog on the equity of redemption doctrine is that the judiciary does not appear fond of this rule – *Samuel v Jarrah Timber* (1904), and Lord Mersey in *New Patagonia Meat Company v Kregliner* (1913). In fact, as Thompson suggests, the courts seem more willing to look at unconscionable terms on the basis either of implied term or on the general doctrine of unconscionability in *Multiservice Bookbinding*. *Jones v Morgan* is a rare modern example where an argument based on clogs has

---

22 Where possible the use of quotations, or paragraph numbers, shows that you have revised the detail of cases, as well as the general principles, but an effort to learn quotations should not detract from your overall revision.

succeeded. In that case however the clog was to be found in the ability of the mortgagee to obtain title to the mortgaged property, which is an option not open to B here. The circumstances are very different to that in *Jones*. It seems unlikely that a court would take this route here.

Thus, C's best option, it appears, is to argue that the interest rate rise is so capricious that it breaches an implied term of the mortgage agreement such that they are entitled to damages.

THE PROCESS OF B GOING INTO POSSESSION AND SALE

'As soon as the ink is dry' on a mortgage agreement, the mortgagee has interest in possession. They can therefore go into possession of the mortgaged property at any time (unless otherwise specified in the mortgage agreement) subject to the need to obtain a court order for possession to avoid committing a criminal offence, *Four-Maids v Dudley Marshall* (1957), *Ropaigealach v Barclays Bank* (1998). It was therefore entirely within the Bank's right to go into possession when the A and C were away. Furthermore, as *Ropaigealach* highlights, **Section 36 AJA 1970** as amended does not provide protection to the mortgagor if the bank does not seek a court order for possession. It is therefore of no relevance here. Furthermore, *Horsham Properties v Clark & Beech* (2008) highlights that B would not need to go into possession in order to sell.

As far as the power of sale is concerned, **Section 101 LPA 1925** outlines when the power of sale has arisen such that the mortgagee is able to transfer good title to a purchaser (**Section 104 LPA 1925**). The power of sale will arise as soon as the contractual date for redemption has passed, or when an instalment mortgage is in arrears (*Twentieth Century Banking v Wilkinson* (1976)). The power of sale has therefore arisen here. This means that unless knowledge of impropriety on the part of the purchaser can be shown, the sale transaction cannot be set aside (see below).

Section 103 outlines when the power of sale can be exercised, i.e. when one of the three conditions are met. These are (i) notice requiring payment of the entire sum has been given and three months have passed since the notice and no such payment has been forthcoming; (ii) some interest owed under the mortgage is two months in arrears; or (iii) there has been a breach of some other term of the mortgage agreement. In this case it seems likely, although it is not certain, that the interest under the mortgage is more than two months in arrears. As a result, the power of sale is exercisable. If the power of sale was not exercisable at this point, then C would be entitled to an award of damages under **Section 104 LPA 1925**. The measure of such an award were it available is discussed below.

As a result, it seems likely that C has no recourse in relation to the means by which B took possession. It also seems likely that the power of sale has arisen and become exercisable.

THE SALE

When a mortgagee sells the mortgaged property he is under a duty of care in relation to that sale to obtain to the best price reasonably available at the time (*Standard Chartered Bank v Walker* (1982), *Cuckmere Brick v Mutual Finance* (1970)). This duty does not however require that the mortgagee go beyond selling in an appropriate manner, *Silven Properties* (2003), *Bishop v Blake* (2006). In fact, as *Bishop v Blake* and *Michael v Miller* (2004) highlight, the crucial issue is not the price actually achieved but the steps taken to achieving that price.

In this scenario there are three issues to consider. The sale took place one month after B went into possession which seems to suggest sufficient advertising of the relevant auction. Secondly, the price, although lower that A and C paid for the property, seems within the realm of possibility given that the sale took place at auction and the drop in house prices since 2007. The price is not so low as to raise a question mark over whether B has discharged its duty as seller, when compared with the purchase price in 1996. Finally, the house was purchased by a relative of an employee of the local branch of B. Each of these factors causes a question mark to be raised over whether W has discharged its duty, although none is decisive in itself.

Furthermore, the process of sale at auction appears to be an appropriate mode of sale as can be seen in the Court of Appeal decision in *Michael v Miller*. Although *Glatt v Sinclair* (2011) casts some doubt on this, it is suggested that the approach in *Michael v Miller* is still good law such that the use of auction seems to have been acceptable. Certainly it appears that the starting point at least is that the mortgagee can determine himself the process of sale. The fact that the property was sold at auction then does seem to weigh in C's favour.

Finally, however, the fact that the sale was to a connected person must be considered. Although there is a strict duty on a bank not to purchase the property itself (*Williams v Wellingborough Council* (1975)) it is possible for an associate of an employee of the bank to purchase the property (*Halifax v Corbett* (2002)), if there was no impropriety in their so-doing. If the sale was improper, and P was aware of this, then the sale can be set aside. As can be seen in *Halifax v Corbett* however, there must be bad faith on the part of the purchaser *vis-à-vis* the mortgagor which results in the low price obtained. That does not appear to have been the case here.

It seems then that C's only potential remedy lies in damages. Whether this is because of the breach of the implied term, or (less likely) because of a breach of B's duty of care during the sale, the damages can only reflect what C has actually lost. This will mean, at most, that she is entitled to the difference between the true value of the property minus the money owed at the lower interest rate, and what she has actually received by way of surplus after sale. The sale proceeds would then be divided according to the percentage equitable share. It is highly unlikely that A would be able to set aside the sale given that the bank's interest had priority over his but he would be entitled to some of the proceeds of the sale.

NOTES

This problem puts into practice the law discussed in the previous two answers, although it does concentrate more on the rights and protection of the mortgagor. An even fuller answer would have gone on to consider undue influence in more detail and s 140A–C of the Consumer Credit Act 2006.

QUESTION 46

To what extent have recent decisions of the House of Lords clarified[23] the circumstances in which a person may plead 'undue influence' as a defence to a mortgagee seeking to exercise its remedies under the mortgage?

How to Answer this Question

The following areas are relevant:

- ❖ the consequences of undue influence if established;
- ❖ establishing undue influence – actual, presumed and the meaning/purpose of manifest disadvantage;
- ❖ fixing a mortgagee with undue influence – agency, notice;
- ❖ how does a mortgagee protect itself?
- ❖ *Barclays Bank v O'Brien* (1994); *CIBC v Pitt* (1994); *National Westminster Bank v Morgan* (1985); *Royal Bank of Scotland v Etridge* (2002); *National Westminster Bank v Amin* (2002).

---

23 'Clarified' suggests confusion, so your answer should show the 'path' to the current position for top marks.

Applying the Law

This diagram demonstrates the operation of the rules relating to undue influence and mortgages.

ANSWER

The law of undue influence may be called in aid by a mortgagor seeking to avoid the consequences of a mortgagee's exercise of one of its remedies. Often, it is pleaded as a defence to a possession action and, if successful, may prevent the mortgagee realising their security (but contrast *Alliance & Leicester v Slayford* (2001)). Obviously, the defence of undue influence may be raised in a variety of circumstances, although two particular situations are relevant here. First, a mortgagor may claim that the mortgagee (such as a bank) has exercised undue influence over them directly, with the effect that the mortgage is set aside. Such cases are now relatively rare given the regularised lending practices of most institutional mortgagees and the industry's codes of conduct. Second, a mortgagor (often a husband or male partner) may have sought a mortgage from an institutional lender over property that is jointly owned with another person (for example, a wife or sexual partner). Should this be the case, the other joint owner must consent to the mortgage if the lender is to have adequate security (see *William & Glyn's Bank v Boland* (1981) for the consequences of failing to secure consent). Of course, it lies in the power of the joint owner to refuse such consent, but their emotional ties to the person seeking the mortgage might well persuade them to agree, especially if it is to secure finance for their partner's business. If, then, at a later date, difficulties arise such as to give the mortgagee cause to seek possession or sale of the property, the consenting owner may well claim that their consent to the mortgage was procured by the undue influence of their partner. In other words, that there was no real consent to the mortgage at all and that it should be set aside either in its entirety or in so far as it binds them (*TSB v Camfield* (1995)). In reality, then, undue influence is a plea that the mortgage should be set aside because of either the action of the mortgagee directly or more likely because of the action of the other mortgagor that in some way affects the mortgagee. It is this second aspect that has caused much controversy and which is examined below.

The rationale for the doctrine of undue influence is clear. However, it must be remembered that a vibrant mortgage market[24] – with adequate protection for lenders – is just as important as providing protection for the homes of persons who may have been 'persuaded' to enter a mortgage that they did not really want. A balance must be struck. At one time, the law of undue influence was regarded as a panacea available to most mortgagors at the slightest hint of unfairness in the mortgage transaction. Thus, it was perfectly possible for a mortgagor to avoid the consequences of default by pleading simply that the mortgagee was in a dominant position when the mortgage was made. However, this rather liberal approach was rejected in *National Westminster Bank v Morgan* (1985). In that case, the House of Lords made it clear that two major requirements had to be met before undue influence could be established. First, the mortgagor had to show some victimisation, pressure or unfair advantage by the mortgagee or by a person whose conduct could taint the mortgagee. The equitable defence was not available simply because the bargain was unfair or unreasonable (*Banco Exterior Internacional v Thomas* (1997)). Second, and more controversially, the House of Lords indicated that even if the fact of undue influence could be established, a mortgage would not be set aside unless it could also be shown to be 'to the manifest disadvantage' of the mortgagor. It was not enough, in their Lordships' view, that undue influence existed, for that in itself was no reason to set aside a transaction. This is clearly a limitation on the undue influence defence, although after the full judgments of the House of Lords in *Royal Bank of Scotland v Etridge* (2002), it is clear that the concept of manifest disadvantage does fulfil a vital function (see below).

As first explained by the House of Lords in *Barclays Bank v O'Brien* (1994) and *CIBC v Pitt* (1994), there are three steps to establishing the defence of undue influence. First,

---

24 Where the 'social' consequences of the rule are important, as in relation to mortgages, it is always good to flag this up to the examiner to highlight that you understand the wider policy framework.

establish the undue influence. Second, ask whether the mortgagee is tainted by it. Third, assess whether the mortgagee has taken steps to prevent its mortgage being voided by the undue influence. As to the first step, these two cases established that undue influence could either be 'actual' or 'presumed'. Actual undue influence arose where the facts established positively the existence of undue influence by the wrongdoer over the 'victim'. In contrast, presumed undue influence arose either where the relationship between the persons was of such a nature that the presumption of undue influence arose automatically (for example, doctor/patient, solicitor/client and parent/child: so-called 'Class 2A cases'[25]) or where the substance of the relationship was that one person placed so much confidence in the other that the presence of undue influence should arise (so-called 'Class 2B cases': for example, husband/wife or lover/lover). In addition, manifest disadvantage was required for all presumed cases, but not in actual cases.

The second step was that the mortgagee had to be tainted with the wrongdoer's actions. This would occur if the wrongdoer was the agent of the mortgagee or the mortgagee had 'notice' of the undue influence. Agency will, of course, be very rare as lenders do not usually appoint one borrower to act for it in securing the other owner's consent. However, cases of notice were much more likely as such notice would exist where there was a substantial risk that some form of pressure may have been exerted and the mortgagee was aware of facts that gave rise to that risk. In fact, it soon became clear that such a risk was present in very many cases and lenders soon concentrated on the third hurdle: that is, identifying those steps that a mortgagee should take to protect itself in the event that it was on notice of the risk of undue influence. In general terms, these steps boiled down to the fact that the lender should advise the potential victim to seek independent advice and that, if the giving of advice was confirmed (for example, by a solicitor in a letter to the bank), the lender could assume that its mortgage was safe.

All this seemed clear enough after *O'Brien*, but in reality there was too little clarity. In particular, assuming the mortgagee was put on notice, precisely what steps must it take to avoid being tainted by any undue influence? What constituted 'independent advice'? Could a mortgagee rely on the confirmation of a reputable solicitor that such advice had been given, even when the advice was defective (*Massey v Massey*) or not given wholly independently of the other mortgagor (*Banco Exterior Internacional v Mann* (1995)), provided that it was in fact given (*TSB Bank v Camfield* – no independent advice at all)? Did the mortgagee have to force the co-mortgagor to take advice? How could it do this? Also, what was meant by 'manifest disadvantage' and was a lender really always at risk that a transaction was procured by undue influence? These uncertainties soon led to much litigation, several appeals to the Court of Appeal and, eventually, an eight-case

25 Using recognised labels like this is a good way to avoid unnecessary lengthy repetition.

consolidated appeal to the House of Lords. The result was a 'bright-line' judgment in *Royal Bank of Scotland v Etridge*. Once again, the issue can be broken down into three questions.

First, prove undue influence by the 'wrongdoer' over the claimant. If the evidence adduced by the claimant established actual undue influence, then this hurdle was surmounted. 'Actual' in this sense means evidence that shows, on a balance of probabilities, that the wrongdoer so acted as to render the claimant's consent to the mortgage no real consent at all. Where actual undue influence is established, there is no need to prove that the impugned transaction was to the claimant's 'manifest disadvantage', as such disadvantage only helps to prove undue influence (see below) and so by definition is not needed in 'actual' cases. If the case is not one of actual undue influence, undue influence may be presumed. However, this is an evidentiary presumption that merely shifts the burden of proof from the claimant to the wrongdoer. Successful reliance on the presumption of undue influence does not mean that undue influence exists, but rather that the burden of explaining why the impugned transaction was not caused by undue influence passes to the alleged wrongdoer. The alleged wrongdoer may still dispel any whiff of undue influence by producing evidence as to the propriety of the transaction. Consequently, when viewed in this light, there is no real merit in adopting the *O'Brien* categories of 'Class 2A' presumed undue influence cases and 'Class 2B' cases. There are some relationships, such as parent/child and doctor/patient (the old 'Class 2A' cases), which necessarily and irrebuttably establish a relationship of trust and confidence and, if the transaction called for an explanation (was 'manifestly disadvantageous'), this shifts the burden of proof to the alleged wrongdoer to explain the transaction. Failure to do so necessarily leads to a finding of undue influence. There are other cases in which the claimant can demonstrate on the evidence that a relationship was one of trust and confidence (the old 'Class 2B' cases) and, if the transaction called for an explanation (was 'manifestly disadvantageous'), this then shifts the burden of proof to the alleged wrongdoer to explain the transaction. Consequently, two things are now clear. First, that the 'presumption' of undue influence is no more than a tool to explain the shift of the evidentiary burden from the claimant and so 'manifest disadvantage' is necessary as it explains why the burden should shift. Second, the difference between the now defunct Class 2A and Class 2B cases is simply that, in the former, the fact of trust and confidence could not be disputed by the wrongdoer, whereas in the second, it could.

The second issue is whether the lender is put on inquiry (that is, does the lender have notice as to the risk of undue influence?). The House of Lords in *Etridge* adopted a robust and blunt approach to this question. Recognising that there are difficulties, that its answer is broad brush rather than precisely analytical, the solution provided by the House of Lords is that a lender will always be put on inquiry (have notice) if a person is standing as a surety for another's debts, provided that such surety is not offered as a commercial service (that is, the guarantor is not charging for the service, as would a bank or other institution). Although this is an extension of the law, it has the great merit[26] of ensuring that lenders do not have to probe the relationship of the parties in order to assess whether they are on inquiry. They are if it is a non-commercial surety. Thus, it is not the relationship between the parties that triggers the 'notice', but rather the very nature of the transaction irrespective of the relationship. The principle therefore applies outside the wife/husband situation. If, however, the loan is made to the parties jointly for their joint purposes (that is, the claimant is not merely guaranteeing the wrongdoer's borrowing), the lender is not put on inquiry unless it is aware (or ought to have been aware) that in reality the money was for the wrongdoer's purposes alone.

Third, if on inquiry, what steps should the lender take to avoid being tainted by the undue influence and risk losing its security? At first sight, it appears that the judgment in *Etridge* is not principally concerned with preventing the occurrence of undue influence over a claimant at all, but rather identifying what a lender must do to avoid being tainted by it if such influence occurs. Fortunately (although it is not accidental), the steps that a lender must now take are such that the chances of undue influence occurring will be much reduced, but it is important to appreciate that the primary purpose of these steps is to protect the lender, not to stop the undue influence. For past cases – that is, mortgages executed prior to the *Etridge* decision – the lender must take steps to ensure that the wife understands the risk she is running and should advise her to seek independent advice. For future cases – that is, mortgages executed post-*Etridge* – the lender must insist that the wife attend a private meeting with the lender at which she is told of the extent of her liability, warned of the risk she is running and urged to take independent legal advice. How this will operate in practice for past cases will still be attended with some doubt, although it seems that it is not the lender's responsibility to see that no undue influence has been exercised, nor necessary that it seeks confirmation from a solicitor that no such influence exists (as opposed to confirmation that advice has been given). This is because the solicitor will be acting for the claimant and the lender can expect the solicitor to act properly for their client. Consequently, if a solicitor gives inadequate advice, the lender is not affected, provided that the lender does not know (or ought to have known) that no advice was received or that it was inadequate (as may have been the case in *National Westminster Bank v Amin* (2002), a post-*Etridge* case but considering a pre-*Etridge* mortgage). After all, the claimant can sue the solicitor. In reality, then, the past practice of relying on solicitor's certificates will suffice, unless the lender knows or ought to have known that the claimant was not thereby properly warned of the nature of the transaction or of the risks it posed. In this sense, *National Westminster Bank v Breeds* (2001) is rightly decided, as the lender should have known that the advice given to the claimant was defective despite receiving a certificate from the advising solicitor (see also *Amin*: lender knew that the client could not speak English and that the solicitor could not speak Urdu).

---

26 It is always good to integrate your own analysis of the rules into your explanation of them as it shows that you are thinking independently about the topic under consideration.

For future transactions, the House lays down what will almost certainly become a code of conduct for lenders. First, the lender should check directly with the claimant for the name of the solicitor who is acting for them, advising that it will seek written confirmation that advice about the proposed transaction has been given. The claimant should be told that this is because the lender does not intend that the claimant should be able to dispute the mortgage later. The claimant should also be told that they may (but not must) use a different solicitor from that which their partner uses. The lender must await a response from the claimant before it proceeds. Second, the lender should provide the advising solicitor with all the necessary financial information required for the solicitor to give proper advice: for example, level of total indebtedness of the husband, copy of the application form, etc. This usually will require the consent of the other party. Third, the lender must inform the solicitor of any concerns it has over the genuineness of the claimant's consent or understanding. Fourth, the lender should obtain written confirmation that all these steps have been complied with and that appropriate advice has been given. If such steps are taken, the lender will be protected, as may well be the claimant, subject only to any defects in the role of the solicitor that the lender knew of, or ought to have known of.

It now seems as if *Etridge* has resolved the uncertainties left by *O'Brien*. It even appears to have forced a change in lending practices, but this has been absorbed into the administrative practices of the competent lending institutions. As for the law, we now know or have had confirmed that the 'presumption' of undue influence is really a presumption that reverses the burden of proof and is not a presumption that such influence really exists. Hence, it can be met with an explanation of why the transaction is undue influence-free: that 'manifest disadvantage' in the weak sense of a transaction that on its face needs explaining is still an element in 'presumed' cases because it (merely) helps to prove the presumption to reverse the burden of proof; that the Class 2A and 2B dichotomy is not helpful; that a lender will always be on inquiry ('have notice') in non-commercial surety cases; that in other cases, the lender will be on inquiry only in exceptional cases because it is entitled to assume that a person knows what they are doing when the loan is for their own benefit; that, for past cases, reliance on a solicitor's certificate will normally protect a lender; that, for future cases, the steps a lender must take are greater than before, but not onerous and may both protect the lender and prevent any undue influence from arising in the first place; and finally, that a lender can never be protected when it knows, or ought to know, that the claimant has not received the guidance and counsel they needed to judge the appropriateness of the transaction.[27]

---

27 This is a very detailed answer, and in the exam you may not have enough time to deal in such depth. It is therefore important to work out strategies for conveying this information in a shorter space if time requires it.

QUESTION 47

To what extent is freedom of contract inconsistent with the traditional view of a mortgage as being the grant of a proprietary interest in land merely as a security, albeit one that deserves special protection from a court of equity?

How to Answer this Question

The answer needs to include the following areas:

- ❖ the nature of a mortgage, but founded in contract;
- ❖ the ability of the mortgagee to impose contractual terms versus the equity of redemption;
- ❖ the mortgagee's contractual remedies modified by statute;
- ❖ mortgages as loan contracts under the Consumer Credit Acts.

Answer Structure

This diagram demonstrates many of the main issues when looking at the question of whether mortgage law prioritises freedom of contract or looks more at the proprietary nature of a mortgage interest.

ANSWER

In one very important sense, this question is misleading.[28] A mortgage is both an interest in land and a contract. It partakes of the attributes of both and in the great majority of situations the dictates of contract and property law are complementary, not mutually exclusive. In other words, just because a contract is at the heart of the dealings between mortgagor and mortgagee does not mean that the mortgage cannot also operate as a proprietary right. Thus, the mortgagee has remedies on the contract (for example, to sue for money due), as well as remedies arising because of their proprietary interest in the land (for example, the right to possession). Likewise, the mortgagor has obligations under the contract (for example, to repay the loan and observe other covenants) as well as rights founded in their equity of redemption, a proprietary right. However, that said, it is true that, in some situations, the nature of a mortgage as a security over land, regulated by equity, can come into conflict with the contract negotiated between the parties.[29]

The most obvious example of this potential conflict arises because of the general rule that equity will safeguard the equity of redemption, sometimes in contradiction of the express terms of the bargain agreed between mortgagor and mortgagee. Thus, an option to purchase granted to the mortgagee in the mortgage deed will be void (*Samuel v Jarrah Timber* (1904); *Jones v Morgan* (2002)) and terms that make the mortgage irredeemable will be struck out (*Fairclough v Swan Brewery* (1912)), even if agreed by the parties. Of course, the court is astute to give effect to the bargain made between commercial parties who are deemed to be able to take care of themselves, especially if they are financing a commercial enterprise (*Knightsbridge Estates v Byrne* (1939)), but that does not allow them to change the essential nature of a mortgage. It is still a security for a loan under which the proprietary interest conveyed to the mortgagee can be recovered on the payment of interest, principal and costs (*Re Sir Thomas Spencer Wells* (1933)). In particular, this emphasis on the equity of redemption has led the court to examine any 'collateral advantages' that are stipulated in the mortgage, being benefits extracted by the mortgagee in consideration for the loan. Originally, such advantages were frowned upon, as constituting a clog on the equity of redemption, but, in recent times, a collateral advantage that is neither harsh or unconscionable nor destructive *in fact* of the equity of redemption will be permitted (*Santley v Wilde* (1899)). Indeed, if the advantage represents the true commercial bargain between the parties and is not void on the above grounds, it will be permitted as an exercise of freedom of contract, even where it continues after the mortgage has been redeemed (as in *Kreglinger v New Patagonia Meat and Cold Storage Co* (1914)).

---

28 Analysis of this sort which questions the 'sense' of the question demonstrates a sophisticated approach to an essay.

29 This is good as it outlines the faultlines of the conflict, giving the examiner a clear understanding of how you are approaching your response.

In addition, it is not only a court of equity that will protect a mortgagor. General contractual principles may also be called in aid.[30] Thus, the general common law doctrine of undue influence may allow a mortgagor to avoid a mortgage contract in much the same way as a party may avoid any other contract (*Barclays Bank v O'Brien* (1994); *Royal Bank of Scotland v Etridge* (2002)). Again, the **Consumer Credit Act** applies to mortgages as with other loan contracts as does the doctrine of restraint of trade (*Esso v Harper's Garage* (1968)). All of these, and the **Unfair Contract Terms in Consumer Contracts Regulations 1999** (*Falco Finance v Gough* (1999)), support the court's intervention when seeking to protect the mortgagor's proprietary right in the equity of redemption.

From the mortgagor's point of view, then, both the contractual and proprietary nature of the mortgage can give protection against a mortgagee. When we look at the mortgagee, however, it seems that both statute and general equitable principles do intervene substantially to control (that is, limit) the exercise of remedies under the mortgage contract. In this sense, the contractual nature of the mortgage does take a back seat to its essential nature as a security. Thus, although the mortgagor has a contractual (and proprietary) right to take possession of the mortgagor's property, both statute and equity restrict the full exercise of this right. In the former case, s 36 of the **Administration of Justice Act 1970** (as amended by s 8 of the **AJA 1973**) gives the court power to set aside the claim for possession in respect of a dwelling house (but note *Ropaigeleach v Barclays Bank* (1999)), although only if the mortgagor is likely to be able to meet their commitments under the mortgage and pay off any sums due within a reasonable time (*Bank of Scotland v Grimes* (1985); *Cheltenham and Gloucester v Norgan* (1996); *First National Bank v Syed* (1991)). This is supported by s 91 of the **Law of Property Act 1925** (see *Palk v Mortgage Services Funding* (1993)). In the second case, the equitable rule that a mortgagee in possession must account strictly for any income that is derived or could have been derived from the property during his period of possession (*White v City of London Brewery* (1889)) means that most mortgagees of commercial premises will not seek this remedy, although they may rely on the appointment of a receiver instead. Clearly, the court's ability to restrict the right of possession is a firm indication that the nature of a mortgage as a security takes priority over the claims of the mortgagee based on his contract and the proprietary right thereby obtained.

Likewise, the power of sale available to most mortgagees is restricted by the intervention of equity, even though statute (**LPA 1925**) clearly contemplates this as one of the major remedies of the mortgagee. The duty of care owed to the mortgagee to obtain the best price reasonably obtainable (*Standard Chartered Bank v Walker* (1982)) and the trust imposed on any surplus from the sale (after payment of the mortgage) do act as a brake

------

30 The idea that contract rules themselves limit freedom of contract is separate to the freedom of contract vs. property conflict, but a good answer will tease out the ambiguities and contradictions in this 'conflict'.

on an eager mortgagee, although, in so far as they prevent fraud on the part of a mortgagee, these principles cannot be criticised. The same is generally true of the mortgagee's power of foreclosure (see s 91 of the LPA 1925), although this right – itself stemming from the nature of a mortgage as a proprietary right – is often a weapon of last resort. Technically, such a right arises as soon as the legal date specified in the contract has passed, but in reality the mortgagee often contracts not to exercise the right until some specified breach of covenant has occurred, such as non-payment of interest. This is an example of contract modifying the proprietary nature of a mortgage.[31]

To conclude, one must reiterate that which was stated at the start of this answer. The mortgage that springs from contract is effected by means of the creation of a proprietary right in the mortgagee, and partakes of the rules and principles of both contract and property law. It should not be thought that there is a great deal of tension between the two philosophies and even where the equity of redemption is concerned – the most well guarded of the mortgagor's rights – the commercial nature of the mortgage and its role in releasing the economic value of real property has been recognised in the law relating to the mortgagee's remedies.[32] The same is true in such matters as undue influence (*Royal Bank of Scotland v Etridge* (2002)) and is illustrated by the fact that the court is only willing to interfere with mortgages on the basis of s 140A–C of the Consumer Credit Act 2006 if it is satisfied that there is an unfair credit relationship between the borrower and the lender.

NOTES

This is perhaps one of the most interesting questions that can be asked on the law of mortgages. The interaction between property and contract law does cause problems in practice, especially in commercial transactions. The question also requires some knowledge of how mortgages are created and therefore provides a good test of a student's understanding.

Aim Higher ★

The law of mortgage, including the role of the equity of redemption, represents a coming together of a number of sources of law: contract; equity; land law; and consumer statutes. Making this link will improve your answer.

---

31 Introducing the 'mirror image' in this way shows you have considered both sides of the question and demonstrates an imaginative approach to the answer.

32 This is a clear but balanced conclusion and shows what can be done where the question itself is ambiguous or oversimplified.

Miscellaneous Problems

INTRODUCTION

The issues considered in this chapter bear no obvious relation to each other and no attempt shall be made to find one. However, they do share one important practical characteristic: they are issues that feature occasionally in examinations in land law, rather than being habitual favourites of examiners. Of course, that makes them no less important, for a well-answered question on say, adverse possession, is worth just as much as a well-answered question on co-ownership. That said, this chapter deals with issues such as adverse possession and fixtures and chattels with no particular attempt to treat them as intrinsically connected.

Adverse possession – or squatting – is a doctrine that truly reflects the feudal origins of English land law and the common law systems based upon it. Behind the ability of a trespasser to actually acquire 'ownership' of land that on paper belongs to somebody else is the concept that, in fact, owners only own 'estates' or titles in the land, not the land itself. Thus, it is perfectly possible for some other person to gain a better title without any formal transfer of 'ownership'. The very idea of adverse possession is based upon relativity of title, not absolute ownership of land. It is now trite law that in England there is no equivalent of the civil law concept of *dominium* and, in practice, this means that one person's title to land is only as good as the absence of a person with a better title. This traditional justification for adverse possession is, however, rapidly becoming an anachronism. Not only were doubts raised on human rights grounds (*Beaulane Properties v Palmer* (2005)) – although in *Ofulue v Bossert* (2008) the Court of Appeal subsequently confirmed that principles of adverse possession were, as a matter of principle, compliant with human rights law – but also, most noticeably, with the coming into force of the **Land Registration Act 2002** the philosophy of a guarantee of title has superseded the justifications behind the rules on limitations. Under this Act, registration as a proprietor is, even with the continued ability to seek rectification of the register, closer to an absolute guarantee of title than has formerly been known in the law of England and Wales. As a consequence, under the registered title scheme, while adverse possession is not impossible to establish, it is, nevertheless, often exceedingly difficult.

Checklist ✔

Today, adverse possession is a mixture of common law rules overlain by statute. The student therefore needs to have an understanding of the doctrine of estates in English land law, a working knowledge of the **Limitation Act 1980** and a feeling for the purpose behind the principle of limitation of actions. Likewise, recent decisions such as *Buckinghamshire County Council v Moran* (1990), *Colchester Borough Council v Smith* (1992), *Hounslow LBC v Minchinton* (1997), *Central London Commercial Estates v Kato Kagaku* (1998), *Pye v Graham* (2003), *Beaulane Properties v Palmer* (2005), *Clowes Developments v Walters* (2005), *R (Wayne Smith) v Land Registry & Cambs CC* (2010), and *Zarb v Parry* (2012) give considerable guidance on the practical application of these rules. It is also vital that there is a clear understanding of the reforms to adverse possession as it applies to registered land affected by the **Land Registration Act 2002** and the way in which these have operated (*Baxter v Mannion* (2010)).

The rules concerning fixtures and chattels are often more important to practising conveyancers than students of land law. Essentially, the question is what, apart from the house/land itself, does a purchaser of property buy on completion of the contract of sale? Does the greenhouse also pass with the title? How about the garden statues and the wall coverings? The answers to these and related questions are to be found mainly in judicial pronouncements, which, while developing a general set of principles, can vary considerably in the confused circumstances of a real case. As with adverse possession, there is no better way to understand the law of fixtures and chattels than a thorough knowledge of case law.

QUESTION 48

To what extent is it possible to define the circumstances in which an occupier of land may make a successful claim of adverse possession against the title holder?

How to Answer this Question

The following areas need to be discussed:

* ❖ the general purpose and role of adverse possession;
* ❖ the concept of limitation – the limitation period;
* ❖ the mechanics of establishing adverse possession;
* ❖ special circumstances – licences, future intentions;
* ❖ stopping the clock;
* ❖ the compromise of disputes.

Applying the Law

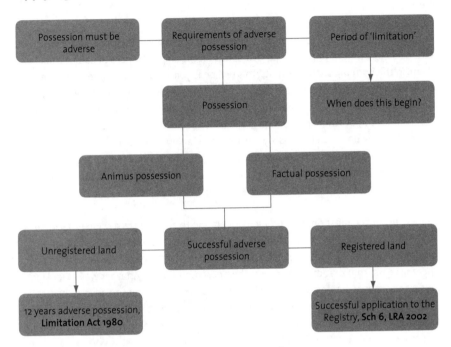

This diagram shows the requirements of adverse possession.

ANSWER

Adverse possession – squatting or limitation of actions – embodies one of the most fundamental principles of English land law: that a person may only own an estate in the land, not the land itself. It follows from this that any person with a superior estate (better title) may assert that title so as to claim seisin of the land. However, if an estate owner sleeps on their rights, a court will not enforce them against the person actually in possession of the land. In this sense, adverse possession operates negatively: it does not vest a title in any other person (see, however, the application to register title by the successful squatter of registered land) but, by virtue of the doctrine of relativity of title, the person in actual possession may have the best claim to the land and thereby become effective 'owner' of it.

Adverse possession involves three basic issues: first, after what period of time does a paper owner of land lose their right to sue to recover possession of it for unregistered land? In registered land the question becomes how long must a possessor be in possession before he can make an application to be registered. Second, when does that period start to run and how can it be brought to an end? Third, what is the effect of expiry of this period, both for the paper owner and the adverse possessor? What must be determined here is the extent to which each of these issues can be defined with precision.[1]

As far as the first issue is concerned – the period of limitation – the period after which no action can be brought to recover land depends on the circumstances of each particular claim. In the normal course of events, this will be 12 years from the moment of adverse possession by the squatter (s 15 of the **Limitation Act (LA) 1980**). There are certain special cases in which the period is different, as where Crown lands are involved (30 years: Sched 1 to the **LA 1980**) or where possession is alleged to be adverse to a remainderman, when generally speaking the period is six years from the falling in of the remainder or 12 years from the adverse possession against the life tenant, whichever is the longer (s 15 of the LA 1980). For registered land, the rules regarding which are, as highlighted above, not based on the concept of limitation, the period is 10 years,

Second, by far the most difficult problem in relation to adverse possession is deciding when this period begins. In other words, at what moment in time does the actual occupation of land by another person become adverse to the paper owner so as to give them 12 years from that date to enforce their paramount title? Another way of looking at this is to ask what actions of a person in actual possession amount to adverse possession so as to give rise to the possibility that, after the limitation period has expired, the paper owner's title will be extinguished. The particular rules concerning this vital question are not to be found in statute. The **LA 1980** does not tell us how to assess whether adverse possession has occurred, only how it works and what its consequences are, and the same can be said of the **LRA 2002**. The rules are entirely judge-made and thus flexible, open-ended and subject to a variety of applications as the circumstances of each case permits.

Following a number of cases that illustrated the uncertainties in the law, the House of Lords in *Pye v Graham* (2003) sought to codify, and clarify, the principles of adverse possession and this case, together with the earlier decision of the Court of Appeal in *Buckinghamshire CC v Moran* (1990), may be regarded as the definitive statements of the modern law.[2] In *Moran*, there was a claim of adverse possession by a squatter against the council.[3] In deciding in favour of the squatter, the court enunciated the basic principles behind establishing adverse possession. First, the adverse possessor should have an intention to possess the land to the exclusion of the whole world, including the paper

---

1   The use of the words 'extent' and 'defined' here reflects the wording of the question and shows that you are clearly addressing the question set.

2   Extra 'credit' can often be found by mentioning the court in which the case you are mentioning was decided, since this shows that you are aware of the strength of the authority of that case.

3   Remember, you do not need to spend a long time in your response discussing the facts of cases where they do not advance your argument. A brief explanation of the facts can however sometimes be useful to put the decision into a context.

owner (*Pye v Graham*). It was stressed that this was an intention to possess adversely, so that any belief that the possession was with the permission of the paper owner necessarily vitiated this requirement (see *Clowes Developments v Waters* (2005)). Likewise, a belief that possession might become authorised by the paper owner can mean that the adverse possessor fails to demonstrate a *sufficient* immediate intention to possess to the exclusion of all (*Pye*). However, it seems clear from *Moran* that the same act that amounts to the second part of a successful claim (actual adverse possession) may also be enough to establish an intention to possess to the exclusion of the whole world, as where the squatter fixes a padlock to a gate on a fence surrounding the paper owner's land with the object of excluding everybody (see also *Hounslow LBC v Minchinton* (1997)).

Second, as indicated, the squatter must actually take adverse possession of the land as a matter of fact, either in consequence of the dispossession of the paper owner or following discontinuance by him. Dispossession occurs where the paper owner is effectively driven out by another (*Rains v Buxton* (1880)) and discontinuance where the paper owner abandons the land (*Smith v Lloyd* (1854)). In either case, the loss of possession by the paper owner must be followed by actual adverse possession by the squatter. This will be a question of fact in each case, although it is clear that the degree of physical possession required will vary with the type of land involved (for example, *Lambeth v Blackburn* (2001) – making a flat secure was sufficient – as was clearing a derelict shed, erecting a new roof and fitting a makeshift door fixed by a chain: *Purbrick v Hackney* (2003)). It may well be easier to establish adverse possession over land that is not susceptible to developed use (*Red House Farms v Catchpole* (1977)) and there are some indications that adverse possession is easier to prove in cases of discontinuance as opposed to cases of dispossession (*Red House Farms*). Yet, as noted, it is a question of fact in each case (*Powell v McFarlane* (1970)) and there is no requirement that the adverse possession must actually inconvenience the paper owner (*Treloar v Nute* (1976)). Certainly, it seems that possession will not be taken from acts equivocal in nature or temporary in purpose, such as growing vegetables or clearing land so as to enable one's children to play (*Wallis's Cayton Holiday Camp v Shell-Mex and BP* (1975); *Techbild v Chamberlain* (1969)), but motive is irrelevant if the acts of the squatter effectively exclude the paper owner (*Minchinton*; *Lambeth v Blackburn*). In this regard, however, we must also note the comments of Lord Browne-Wilkinson in *Pye* that over-conceptualisation of the difference between discontinuance and dispossession could add to complication. The question was better put as the single, simple one: was the squatter in possession of the land without the permission of the landowner?

Moreover, it is clear that the possession must be adverse to the paper owner: it must not be with their consent or permission as that amounts to a licence to occupy and will not start the period of limitation. Prior to the decision in *Moran*, this particular requirement could easily defeat a claim for adverse possession as it was held in a number of cases (*Leigh v Jack* (1879); *Shell-Mex*) that, if the squatter's use of the land was not inconsistent with the paper owner's future intended use of the land, an implied licence would be presumed in the squatter's favour authorising their use of the land and so ensuring that the possession was not adverse. This seemed to be the case whether or not the squatter knew of this future intention. Clearly, such a rule was extremely favourable to the paper owner and was subject to much criticism on the ground that it could be used in nearly every circumstance to defeat a squatter's claim. Now, however, *Moran* and *Pye* have made it clear that there is no presumption of a licence in favour of a squatter where possession is not inconsistent with the paper owner's planned use of the land. That is not to say, of course, that a licence cannot be implied from the actual facts of the case – as where a squatter is aware of the future plans and *agrees* to occupy pending the instigation of those plans – but it does mean that a claim to adverse possession cannot be defeated merely by the existence of some future plan in the breast of the paper owner. Nevertheless, if possession was once with permission, but then such permission ceased, it may be difficult to prove the relevant intention *if* the adverse possessor's activities on the land remained consistent with the permission, as in *Pye* (no adverse possession) but not in *Blackburn* (successful claim).

Assuming, then, that adverse possession is running against the paper owner, the law of limitation means that they have 12 years from the start date to bring an action to recover possession of the land. Of course, a successful action will stop the adverse possession and any future claim will have to begin afresh. The same is true of other acts that show an intention on the part of the adverse possessor to acknowledge the paper owner's title, as where the squatter pays rent or by written acknowledgement of title before time has expired (**ss 29** and **30** of the **LA**). However, apart from actually initiating proceedings, it is not clear what other actions by the paper owner will be sufficient to 'stop the clock'.[4] In *Moran*, a letter asserting title was not sufficient, although a letter evincing a definite intention to sue may well be (*Shell-Mex*). Recent guidance on this issue has however been provided by the Court of Appeal in *Zarb v Parry* (2012). Here the registered owner of the land had attempted to end the adverse possessor's possession by starting to put up a fence. They did not finish the construction of the fence however, and so the court concluded that although they had started the process that would have brought the adverse possessor's possession to an end, they had not completed it. Once again, this makes clear that whether or not adverse possession has been brought to an end will be a matter of construction of the relevant circumstances. Over this matter, we therefore have relative certainty only that it is difficult to predict the outcome in borderline cases.

What does seem reasonably clear is that once the limitation period has expired, both the paper owner's right to sue and their title are extinguished by operation of statute (**s 17** of the **LA**). After this date, the conventional wisdom is that no acknowledgement, written or otherwise, and no payment, can revive the paper owner's title (*Nicholson v England*

---

4   The use of the word 'clear' again here ties back to the question, and shows that you have in mind always the specific task set by the examiner.

(1962)). This should be uncontroversial as it is simply the consequence of the existence of the limitation doctrine. However, the Court of Appeal has held in *Colchester Borough Council v Smith* (1992) that, in some circumstances, a written acknowledgement of the paper owner's title, even after the period has ended, can be enough to prevent the squatter relying on adverse possession in the face of a possession suit by that owner. This remarkable decision[5] is now unlikely to be reversed and it seems to rest on the principle that a bona fide compromise of a dispute between two persons (that is, paper owner and squatter), both of whom had legal advice, should be upheld on public policy grounds, even if the 12-year period has run. In other words, a person will be bound by his contract. Unfortunately, this seemingly unobjectionable principle does not, in the context of adverse possession, recognise that it is also a policy consideration – recognised and effected by Act of Parliament no less – that sleeping on one's rights deprives a person of those rights, which cannot later be revived by threatening protracted litigation with the adverse possessor. In short, the judgment in *Smith* fails to explain why 'act of the parties' can override the express provisions of an Act of Parliament and so we are left here, once again, with a need for further clarification.

More recently, adverse possession has been challenged, but also clarified, from two directions. The first direction is characterised by the decision in *Beaulane Properties v Palmer* (2005) and the question (already raised previously in the Court of Appeal hearing of *Pye*) of whether adverse possession, particularly in relation to unregistered land and registered land operating under the **Land Registration Act 1925**, is contrary to human rights principles as stated in the **Human Rights Act 1998**. In 2007, this issue was finally resolved when, in *JA Pye (Oxford) Ltd v United Kingdom* (2007), the Grand Chamber of the European Court of Human Rights held that this legislation was human rights-compliant. Confirmation in the courts of England and Wales that principles of adverse possession are, in general, not at odds with human rights law can be seen in *Ofulue v Bossert* (2008), in which the Court of Appeal followed *Pye* and ignored *Beaulane*. We can therefore now say with relative certainty that a claim in adverse possession will not fail on human rights grounds.

The second direction that we must be aware of, however, is that the **LRA 2002** effects radical changes in the case of registered title, not in the operation of the established rules for proving adverse possession, but in that the registered title owner can no longer be said to 'lose' his title and the time period is effectively reduced to ten years. Under **Sched 6** to the Act, after he has been in adverse possession for ten years, the squatter can apply to the Land Registry to be registered as proprietor of the estate. Notice of this application is then given to the registered proprietor and to a number of other people with interests in the property, for example, a legal mortgagee. If the recipients do not

---

5   For higher marks, this can be tied to academic commentary on the case, e.g. Dixon, (1992) 51 Cambridge Law Journal 420.

oppose the application or simply do not respond to it, then the applicant may be registered as proprietor of the estate. If the proprietor or another recipient does oppose the application, then unless the adverse possessor falls within one of three special cases – which may be summarised as estoppel, some other right to the land or a reasonable mistake as to boundaries – it will be rejected. In such a case the registered proprietor now has an opportunity to recover the property. If, however, he does not do so, then if the applicant remains in adverse possession for another two years, he can then make another application and must be registered as proprietor. The operation of these procedural rules has been considered in *Baxter v Mannion* and it can be said that we are approaching clarity over the procedure that goes into obtaining title to registered land by adverse possession, even if there is less certainty over the substantive requirements in relation to both unregistered and registered land.

Thus, although in recent years the law of adverse possession has taken on more clarity and certainty, mainly due to the clear exposition in *Moran* and the application in cases like *Minchinton* and *Pye*, there are still areas of uncertainty. Of course, each case will depend on its facts, but at least there is clarity in what those facts are supposed to prove. Indeed, unlike *Smith*, *Moran* and *Pye* were cases favourable to the adverse possessor, both in result and in the substance of the rules it established. Those cases represent a welcome restatement of the fundamental feudal principle of relativity of title and remind us of the transient nature of 'ownership' in the law of real property in England and Wales.

NOTES

This is a general question on the law of adverse possession, although a good answer will rely heavily on *Moran*, *Pye* and *Blackburn*, being the most recent thorough expositions of the subject. Consideration should also be made of the human rights issues. Further matters that could be considered are the social purpose of a doctrine of limitation and the differences between adverse possession and prescription. As can be seen, the LRA 2002 emasculates adverse possession as it applies to registered titles and the effect of the Act needed discussion

Aim Higher ★

A good answer should deal in detail with at least three issues:

❖ the actual, substantive rules and what they are;
❖ the human rights issues and how they have been resolved;
❖ the effect of the **LRA 2002** (see *Baxter v Mannion* (2010)).

Read a detailed comment on these issues such as Tee [2000] Conv. 113.

QUESTION 49

In 1990, Ratty purchased an island in the middle of the River Flyte and built a bridge from his adjoining land on the shore. He intended to use the island as a country retreat and throughout 1990–1994 made regular fishing trips. He even built himself a cabin, cultivated a small vegetable garden and laid the foundations for a more substantial house in the future. Unfortunately, in 1994, Ratty became ill and had to leave for the clean air of Austria. Eventually, the vegetable garden became overgrown, the cabin ran to ruin and finally the bridge fell down, leaving the island as isolated as it was before. However, in anticipation of his departure, Ratty had managed to sell the land on the shore to his neighbour Mole, who was enthusiastic about the prospects of establishing a salmon fishery, but had no use for the island. Mole soon set about making enquiries of the local authority for planning permission for his fishery buildings and sought finance from several merchant banks. Again, however, things went awry and Mole could not raise the necessary capital. He resolved to wait until his resources grew and was content to use the land for walking and the occasional spell of private fishing. In 1998, Weasel, the local poacher, decided that the land bordering the river and the island were going to waste and he decided to move in and use the land for his own purposes. Shortly, he was rowing regularly to the island where he re-established the garden, rebuilt the cabin and began charging tourists for day fishing permits for fishing from the island's shore. This became so successful that he purchased a luxury caravan and parked it on Mole's land, where he began to live. There he also planted a vegetable garden, cleared the land to make way for a dirt road and began keeping horses, also to hire to tourists. Eventually, he had to build a fence to keep the horses from straying. In 2007, Mole became concerned about the extent of Weasel's activities on his land, and although he had tolerated them up to then, having no immediate hope of establishing his fishery, registered his title to the land believing that this would help him in trying to get rid of Weasel. He turned up at Weasel's caravan and began to erect a fence trying to stop Weasel from reaching the caravan. Mole did not finish the fence before he was called away on business. However, in 2010, on hearing (falsely, as it turned out) that Mole had raised the money, Weasel extended the fence and placed a locked gate across the dirt road. In 2012, Mole eventually raised enough money for his project and sought possession of the land. Weasel resisted and when Mole told him that Ratty would also issue possession proceedings, he asserted title to the island as well.

▶ Discuss the position of Weasel.

How to Answer this Question

The answer needs to deal with the following areas:

❖ intention to possess;
❖ discontinuance, dispossession and adverse factual possession;
❖ acts of possession – equivocal acts;
❖ implied or actual licences to use;
❖ acts of possession – unequivocal acts.
❖ The difference between registered and unregistered land for the purposes of adverse possession.

Answer Structure

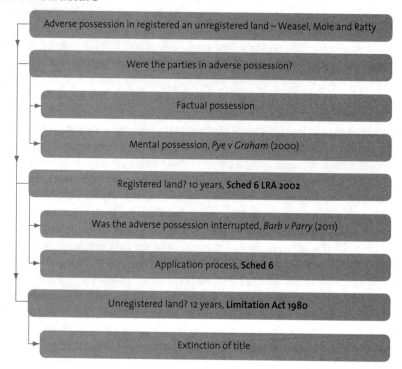

This diagram shows how to apply the rules of adverse possession in registered land to the problem of Weasel, Mole and Ratty.

ANSWER

This question requires discussion of the law of adverse possession, for this is at the root of any case that Weasel may have to resist the claims of possession of both Ratty and Mole. In order to establish adverse possession, it is clear from *Buckinghamshire CC v Moran* (1990) and *Pye v Graham* (2003) that Weasel must establish a number of matters: first, that he had an intention to possess the land; second, that he possessed the land following a discontinuance or dispossession of the paper owner; third, that that possession was adverse to the paper owner. In addition to proving adverse possession, Weasel must also show that this adverse possession has been sufficient to entitle him to resist possession proceedings. In relation to unregistered land then, he must have been in possession for the 12-year period of limitation specified by s 15 of the **Limitation Act (LA) 1980**. For registered land, he would have to show 10 years of adverse possession as well as that the procedural steps in **LRA 2002, Schedule 6**, had been taken.[6]

---

6   Where there are many different issues to be discussed in a problem, it is good to use the introduction to give the answer shape. Here, the most important thing to notice is that the two plots of land must be dealt with very differently, since one is registered, the other not.

(A) THE ISLAND

The position in respect of the island seems relatively straightforward. There is no doubt that from 1990–1994, Ratty was in possession of the island and his activities there clearly demonstrated his ownership, backed as it was by paper title. However, in 1994, Ratty was forced to leave the country and the following events tend towards the conclusion that he abandoned or discontinued ownership. This is supported by the implication that Ratty wished to sell all his property but, except for the land on the shore, was unable to find a buyer. He appears to have no future plans for the island such as would indicate continued interest. Indeed, there seems to be positive proof of abandonment in that the bridge falls down and is not rebuilt, as in *Red House Farms v Catchpole* (1977). Of course, Ratty may argue that he was unable – as opposed to unwilling – to continue possession of the land as his emigration was forced through ill health. However, this is unlikely to rebut the presumption of abandonment so clearly indicated by the facts we are given. In such circumstances, it seems that even very slight acts by a trespasser will be sufficient to constitute adverse possession of the property (*Wuta-Ofei v Danquah* (1961); *Red House Farms*).

Second, does Weasel make use of the land as if he were owner, combined with an intention to assert ownership? Remembering that this is a case of discontinuance, the re-establishing of the vegetable garden and the rebuilding of the cabin may well suffice but, even if these are regarded as equivocal (*Powell v McFarlane* (1970)), the fact that he charges tourists for fishing rights clearly manifests both an intention to possess and sufficient acts of possession. He is, in fact, treating the land as if it were his own (*Hounslow LBC v Minchinton* (1997)). In such circumstances, assuming that Ratty has done nothing in the intervening period to stop time running, the paper owner's title will be extinguished some 12 years later, around 2010 (**s 17** of the **LA 1980**). Thus, he obtains a *de jure* title by statutory conveyance (*Central London Commercial Estates v Kato Kagku* (1998)).[7]

(B) THE RIVERSIDE PROPERTY

The position in respect of the property owned by Mole is not so easily determined. Firstly, it must be noted that as a result of Mole's actions, title to this land is registered and since Weasel was not in possession for 12 years prior to the coming into force of the **LRA 2002**, this issue will be dealt with under **Schedule 6**. Clearly, on the facts of the case, Mole has not abandoned the property. He has a clear, future use for the property and is actively seeking the money to finance it. There is no discontinuance. It is necessary, therefore, for Weasel to establish that he has dispossessed the paper owner and followed this by his own adverse possession, uninterrupted, for 10 years, and that the procedures outlined in **Schedule 6** have been followed.

....

7   It is a good idea to outline the consequences of the law you are applying in one sentence at the end of a section – this makes your conclusion easier at the end as it will save time when you are looking back over your answer to summarise your findings.

(I) THE POSITION UP TO 2007

It is clear that, originally, Mole had a clear, future intention to use the land and that, as a matter of fact, the acts of the trespasser were not inconsistent with this intention. In other words, up to 2007, Weasel's acts on the land did not preclude the later establishment of a fishery by the paper owner. Formerly (for example, *Leigh v Jack* (1879)), these facts would have justified the implication of a licence in favour of Weasel issuing from Mole. The effect of this licence – or permission – would have been to remove any possibility that the possession of the occupier was adverse to the paper owner. However, following *Moran* (and confirmed in *Pye*), it is clear that the existence of future intentions cannot, of itself and without more, justify the court in implying a licence in the actual possessor's favour.[8] So far, then, as a result of *Moran*, Weasel's claim is not defeated. However, it is still necessary for him to establish his own possession of the land following dispossession of the paper owner. In this respect, the acts of Weasel may be too equivocal to count. Thus, the planting of the vegetable garden (*Powell*) and the keeping of animals (*Techbild v Chamberlain* (1969)) may not be sufficient. Likewise, the building of the fence seems designed as much to keep the animals in as to keep the world at large out. This is also equivocal (*George Wimpey v Sohn* (1967)). On the other hand, the clearing of land for the driveway may amount to an act of ownership (*Williams v Usherwood* (1981)), although in *Williams* the road was paved and not left as a dirt track. The establishment of the caravan is also important, but again it does not necessarily evince an intention to exclude the world, merely to occupy the land. It is therefore likely that Weasel has not been in adverse possession, but it is possible that the clearing of the land may provide the necessary factual possession.

(II) THE EVENTS OF 2007

If Weasel has indeed been in adverse possession, since Weasel had been in adverse possession for only 9 years to 2007, the outcome of the events of 2007 are crucial for any potential adverse possession claim. The key events were (a) Mole's decision to register his title to the land; (b) the attempted erection of the fence on the shore land. Both of these events will potentially have significant consequences for Weasel's claim in adverse possession.

Firstly, in relation to the registration of title, the effect of this is to mean that although Weasel's possession commenced whilst the land was unregistered, registration at any point before the required period of possession is up, will result in the issue being dealt with as a matter of registered land (Schedule 6, Para1(4), LRA 2002). The effect of this will be discussed below. Secondly, as far as the erection of the fence is concerned, the question is whether the erection of an incomplete fence in this way can bring Weasel's possession to an end. It seems likely that it would not have had this effect, as a result of the decision in *Zarb v Parry* (2012) where an incomplete fence was considered to not have

---

8   Referring to the older case law rules in this way is a good technique for showing off your knowledge of the topic without going too far off track in a problem question answer.

brought adverse possession to an end. The reasoning of the court was based on the idea that a paper title holder may well take steps to bring the possession to an end, but these steps must actually result in the adverse possessor no longer being in possession, which is not the case here as the quality and nature of Weasel's possession of the land was not altered by the existence of the ineffective fence, as evinced by his actions in 2010. Thus we can conclude that the fence did not 'stop the clock' and so the question will now turn on the application of Sched 6, LRA 2002.

(III) SCHED 6, LRA 2002

Sched 6 determines when an adverse possessor of registered land will be successful in obtaining title to that land by virtue of his possession. It outlines, that where the adverse possessor has been in possession for 10 years, as Weasel has, he must make an application to become registered proprietor (Para 1(1)). Since Mole has not abandoned his land, it is likely that if his contact details are up-to-date, he will object to this application, (Para 3(1)). The result of this is that the application will be dealt with under Para 5 and Weasel will only be able to be registered proprietor if one of the exceptions in this paragraph applies. The only potentially relevant exception is the boundary exception, but crucially, it is clear that Weasel does not reasonably believe that the land belonged to him, and so this exception will not assist him. As a result, Weasel will not be registered as proprietor, even if he were to apply before Mole brought his possession proceedings.

Thus, although Weasel is likely to be able to resist Ratty's claim for adverse possession, he is probably unable to do so in relation to the shore land. This conclusion fits in fact with the justifications for adverse possession since although Ratty has abandoned his land, putting it to no economic use, Mole has active plans for his land. As a result, if adverse possession is seen as a way of ensuring that land is put to good use, then the way the rules apply in this scenario seem to suggest that a good balance is being struck.[9]

NOTES

This question asks the student to apply the general principles of limitation and of adverse possession of registered land and most questions of this type give facts similar to those situations found in previous cases, as does this one. The decision in *Smith* does not feature in this question, but being controversial, it is likely to play a part in some problem questions.

Common Pitfalls ✗
Beware of failing to deal logically with the various events that happen and their effect or otherwise on a claim for adverse possession.

9   In a question where there is little analysis to be found as the answer to the problem is going along, one way to bring analysis in, is to question at the end whether the rules as applying in the problem meet with the aims behind those rules.

QUESTION 50

Some years ago, when Hannibal arrived back in the country from a long stay overseas, he sought your help in finding a quiet secluded property for his family as well as an office in town from which to run his optician's business. Unfortunately, the first house that he purchased proved too small for his needs and after several years he wished to move to a larger house. Hannibal experienced great difficulty and delay in selling his previous house but, finally, last month he went to view Roman Villas, an old property on the edge of town. After some doubt, he has just completed the purchase of Roman Villas from Vesuvius. Unlike the situation with his house, Hannibal had not, however, had any difficulty in finding suitable office accommodation and had agreed with Pontius, the freeholder, for a seven-year lease of suitable premises in a good location. He soon installed his equipment in the premises, fixing lights to the ceiling and a suitable chair to the floor and, in order to make the place more welcoming for his customers, he refitted one room with oak panelling and a large wall-mounted fish tank. Four years ago, on the expiry of the lease, he and Pontius had agreed a further four-year term. Now, on the purchase of Roman Villas, Hannibal has decided to work from home and has removed all the equipment, including the lights and chair as well as the oak panelling and fish tank. He moves them to Roman Villas, only to find that Vesuvius has removed the greenhouse, the rose bushes, the garden ornaments, the television aerial and some antique bannisters, all of which Hannibal greatly admired when being shown around the property before contracts were exchanged.

Hannibal comes to you for advice as to whether he should sue Vesuvius for the return of items, only to find that you have been instructed by Pontius to sue him (Hannibal) for the recovery of the equipment removed from the office in town, as it seems that Pontius had arranged to let the premises to a new optician.

▶ Discuss.

How to Answer this Question

The following areas need to be discussed:

- ❖ fixtures and chattels;
- ❖ the relevance of the distinction – s 62 of the LPA;
- ❖ the way to make the distinction – *Holland v Hodgson* (1872); *Elitestone Ltd v Morris* (1997); *Botham v TSB Bank* (1997); *TSB v Botham* (1996); *Chelsea Yacht and Boat Club Ltd v Pope* (2000);
- ❖ tenant's fixtures.

Applying the Law

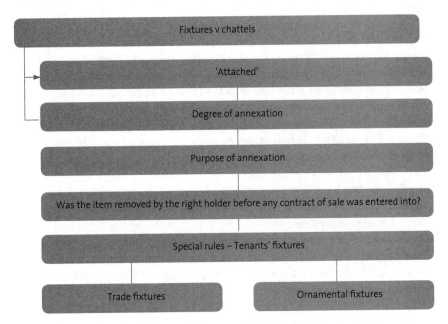

This diagram shows the how to determine whether an item is a fixture or a fitting.

ANSWER

It is a general principle of land law that what becomes attached to the land becomes part of the land (*Minshall v Lloyd* (1837); *Elitestone v Morris* (1997)). Thus, any articles attached to the land in such a way as to indicate that they have merged with it are treated as the land itself: they are fixtures. In practice, this has important consequences. First, it means that when one person conveys land to another, they will also convey all fixtures, save those that have been expressly excluded from the conveyance or can be removed by the vendor by virtue of some exceptional right (see s 62 of the Law of Property Act 1925).[10] Second, it means that should one person affix articles to land owned by another, those articles fall into the ownership of the landowner, as where a tenant affixes articles to the land they are leasing so that at the end of the lease they fall into the ownership of the landlord. In our problem, although there are two separate factual situations to consider, the essential points at issue are the same: first, whether the articles that are removed from the land by Hannibal and Vesuvius are fixtures so as to make them

10 Even when making general statements, it is always good practice to back up your statement with statute or case law.

presumptively liable for such removal; second, if they are fixtures, whether removal could be justified by exceptional circumstances.[11]

(A) ROMAN VILLAS

The general rule in relation to the Roman Villas is clear enough. All articles that, at the date of the contract, can be regarded as fixtures will belong to the new purchaser (Hannibal) on completion of the contract (s 62 of the LPA; *Phillips v Lamdin* (1949)). If Vesuvius, the vendor, is to have good title to any of the articles he has in fact removed, he must show either: (a) that he removed them before the contract was signed; or (b) they are not fixtures at all but chattels personally owned by him; or (c) that, if they are fixtures, his removal was by virtue of some exceptional right.

First, it is clear that a freehold owner may, at any time before they contract to sell, remove any item from their land as this is part of their normal rights of ownership (*Re Whaley* (1908)). However, in our case there is nothing to suggest that Vesuvius removed the items before the contract was signed and, indeed, we are told that all such items were present when Hannibal was shown around the property prior to signing the contract. In the absence of any other evidence, one can conclude that all the articles were present when the contract was signed.

Second, are the items fixtures or chattels? It is only if they are fixtures that any problem arises. Chattels are personal goods, not forming part of the land and, therefore, not conveyed as such to a purchaser of it. The general test as to whether an item can be regarded as a fixture was summarised by Blackburn J in *Holland v Hodgson* (1872), while the most detailed recent discussion of what could be fixtures in the context of ordinary household goods is found in *Botham v TSB Bank plc* (1997). Consideration must be given to the *degree* of annexation to the land and the *purpose* of annexation to the land. It is clear, however, that the primary test is the degree of annexation and presumptively any item that rests upon its own weight is only a chattel (*Mather v Fraser* (1856)); a fixture needs to be attached to the land in some substantial way, even though it could be removed quite easily (*Culling v Tufnal* (1694)). Yet, there is also no doubt that the answer supplied by this simple practical test can be overridden (or indeed supported) by the *purpose* of annexation. Thus, where affixing is necessary for the proper use of the article and implies nothing about its relation to the land, the item may remain a chattel (*Leigh v Taylor* (1902)). This was the case in *Chelsea Yacht and Boat Club Ltd v Pope* (2000) (cf *Cinderella Rockerfellas Ltd v Rudd* (2003)). Conversely, items intended to enhance the value of the property may be fixtures even though resting on their own weight (*D'Eyncourt v Gregory* (1866)). All in all, whether an article is a fixture or a chattel can only be decided on

----

11 In problem questions, use your introduction to help outline your structure. This will help in the exam as it shows the examiner what to expect from your answer, but also keeps you disciplined to ensure that you address all the relevant issues required in the time allotted.

the facts of each case, bearing in mind the nature of the property, the use of the articles and the physical relation of them to the land itself.

Turning then to the articles removed in this case.

(I) THE GREENHOUSE

If the greenhouse is fixed to the land, it will be a fixture, as with the temporary sheds in *Webb v Frank Bevis* (1940). However, there is clear authority that a free-standing greenhouse is to be regarded as a chattel (*HE Dibble Ltd v Moore* (1970)) and a 'Dutch barn' was still a chattel even though it was founded in sockets in the land to give it more support (*Culling v Tufnal*).[12] It is, then, reasonably clear that Vesuvius was entitled to remove the greenhouse as a chattel provided that it was not actually affixed to the land in a permanent way or was not part of an ornamental garden designed for the betterment of the land as a whole (see below).

(II) GARDEN ORNAMENTS

Prima facie, the garden ornaments are chattels as they are, in all probability, free-standing and not attached to the land at all. This was at the root of the decision in *Berkley v Poulett* (1976) when a sundial and statue on plinths were held to be chattels. However, it is clear from *D'Eyncourt v Gregory* that, if garden ornaments are part of a general garden design created to enhance the particular house, they will be regarded as fixtures that pass with the land. This is a clear example of the purpose of annexation overriding the degree of annexation (see also *Hamp v Bygrave* (1983)). Once again, then, presumptively these will be chattels unless the ornaments are integral to the property. They can be removed by Vesuvius.

(III) TELEVISION AERIAL

This is a somewhat difficult article to consider as it is clearly designed to facilitate the use of another article (a television), which is so obviously a chattel. However, it is quite common that television aerials are attached to property (for example, on the chimney) and if this is the case, the presumption will be that it is a fixture. This is reinforced by the fact that the aerial can be detached from the television and is not an integral part of it. *Jordan v May* (1947) could be of assistance here, for there a fixed electric engine was held to be a fixture even though the batteries that powered it were held to be chattels. On the other hand, *Credit Valley Cable v Peel Condominium Corp* (1980) held a television cable to be a chattel, being for the better use of a television and not better use of the land. Perhaps the only solution is to revert to the basic *Holland* test: the degree of annexation. If this decrees that the aerial is a fixture, it is no reply that it thereby confers a personal benefit on the new owners of the land; so do ornamental statues, fixed greenhouses and permanent tapestries.[13]

12 Use similar factual cases to draw parallels.
13 If there is no clear case on point, then you can make your argument from first principles.

(IV) THE BANNISTERS

Once again, this will depend on an application of the *Hodgson* test, although there seems little doubt that these will be affixed to the land in what is intended to be a permanent fashion. If fireplaces can be regarded as fixtures (*Buckland v Butterfield* (1820)), surely so must bannisters. Vesuvius is not entitled to remove them any more than he would be entitled to remove the floorboards.

(V) THE ROSES

Here, the position is clear. Roses, as with other trees, shrubs and flowers growing on the land are part of the legal definition of the land within **s 205** of the **LPA**. Thus, they belong to the estate owner and were conveyed to Hannibal when he purchased the land. Vesuvius is not entitled to remove them.

Thus, as far as Roman Villas is concerned, it is clear that the roses and bannisters and probably the television aerial are fixtures. This means they are conveyed to Hannibal with the conveyance – **s 62** of the **LPA** (assuming no express reservation of Vesuvius' title was made). Moreover, there are no grounds by which Vesuvius can claim an exceptional right to remove these fixtures once the purchase is completed.

(B) THE OFFICE

As noted at the outset, a tenant who brings articles on to the land and then fixes them to it effectively passes title to those articles to the landlord. They cannot, therefore, be removed at the end of the lease unless some special rule so provides. In our case, there are the lights, the chair, the oak panels and the fish tank. However, before we consider whether these are fixtures or merely chattels, one important issue must be considered that may well save time.

There is a general rule that a tenant has a right to remove certain types of fixture from the land at the end of the lease – that is, that even though in law they are fixtures and within the title of the landlord, the tenant may reassert ownership for special reasons. One important category of such fixtures is 'trade fixtures', which may be removed by the tenant during the continuance of the lease or (probably) within a reasonable time after its end (*Poole's case*). Of course, this right is lost if the tenant does not remove trade fixtures during the term (or just after), but it is clear that the tenant does not lose the right to remove fixtures attached during one lease that then ends, if that lease is immediately followed by a new term in continuation of it (*New Zealand Government Property Corp v H and M Ltd* (1982)). This is the case here and it seems certain that the lights and the chair can be removed by Hannibal as trade fixtures when he quits. Of course, if they are not fixtures, he can remove them anyway. Indeed, the same may be true of the oak panelling and the fish tank, for we are told they are added to the property for the benefit of Hannibal's customers. However, they are not necessary for trade as such and probably must be considered outside this rule.

In these circumstances, can it be said that either the oak panelling or the fish tank are fixtures at all or merely personal chattels? This also seems unlikely, at least for the oak panelling, as there is authority that panelling (*Buckland v Butterfield*) and even tapestries (*Re Whaley*, but contrast *Leigh v Taylor*) are fixtures because of the degree of annexation to the property. If this is followed, the oak panelling is a fixture and must remain. The fish tank might be different, as Hannibal could claim that it is fixed to the wall for steadying purposes, not as an attachment per se and, indeed, it is a curious item to regard as part of the land. Some help is given by *Viscount Hill v Bullock* (1897), in which a collection of stuffed animals nailed to the wall were held to be chattels. In any event, however, even if the fish tank is a fixture, Hannibal can claim that he has a right to remove it under another exception – namely, the right of a tenant to remove ornamental fixtures during his lease so long as this can be done without damage to the building (*Martin v Roe* (1857)). Indeed, one case (*Spyer v Phillipson* (1931)) suggests that even panelling (assuming it is a fixture) may be removed under this general heading, although it will be rare that this can be done without damage to the premises.

All in all then, the chair and lights can be removed whether they are fixtures or not (the trade exception), the fish tank may not be a fixture but, if it is, could be removed under the 'ornamental/domestic' exception, and the oak panelling is probably a fixture and could be removed under the 'ornamental/domestic' exception only if there is no damage to the premises.[14]

NOTES

This is a long question, although really quite straightforward. It concentrates on the definition of a fixture and asks in what circumstances even fixtures can be removed from the land. Case law is important here, although *Holland v Hodgson* (supplemented by one or two others) is vital.

Aim Higher ★

Include a short explanation/ analysis of why many decisions appear to be inconsistent. This is due to a shift in emphasis from the degree of annexation to the purpose.

---

14 In problem questions where time allows you should always reach a clear and reasoned conclusion, just like an essay.

Index